PATHS in HEIDEGGE
LATER THOUGHT

PATHS IN HEIDEGGER'S LATER THOUGHT

Edited by Günter Figal, Diego D'Angelo,
Tobias Keiling, and Guang Yang

Indiana University Press

This book is a publication of

Indiana University Press
Office of Scholarly Publishing
Herman B Wells Library 350
1320 East 10th Street
Bloomington, Indiana 47405 USA

iupress.indiana.edu

Manufactured in the United States of America

Library of Congress Cataloging-in-Publication Data

Names: Figal, Günter, [date] editor.
Title: Paths in Heidegger's later thought / edited by Günter Figal, Diego
    D'Angelo, Tobias Keiling, and Guang Yang.
Description: Bloomington : Indiana University Press, 2020. | Series:
    Studies in continental thought | Includes bibliographical references and
    index.
Identifiers: LCCN 2019021137 (print) | LCCN 2019981515 (ebook) | ISBN
    9780253047199 (hardback) | ISBN 9780253047205 (paperback) | ISBN
    9780253047212 (ebook)
Subjects: LCSH: Heidegger, Martin, 1889-1976.
Classification: LCC B3279.H49 P3825 2020 (print) | LCC B3279.H49 (ebook)
    | DDC 193—dc23
LC record available at https://lccn.loc.gov/2019021137
LC ebook record available at https://lccn.loc.gov/2019981515

1 2 3 4 5   25 24 23 22 21 20

Contents

PATHS IN HEIDEGGER'S LATER THOUGHT

Introduction

$W_{EGE, \; NICHT \; WERKE}$ ("Ways, not works"). According to the report of Heidegger's personal assistant, Friedrich-Wilhelm von Herrmann, published in the first volume of the *Gesamtausgabe*, this is the motto Heidegger intended for his collected works. If one takes Heidegger at his word, then, his own philosophy is about pursuing different "paths" of thought rather than defining a single set of truths. Philosophy is a process rather than a result, a process evolving along more than one intellectual direction. How Heidegger's "works" have been received testifies to this idea. There is, indeed, scholarly discussion on specific questions in the interpretation of Heidegger, yet the different ways in which his philosophy is interpreted and transformed may well be more important for understanding, even in its transgression, what is genuine to Heidegger's thinking.

This proves to be the case as the publication of additional material from the *Nachlass* and a growing number of studies on Heidegger's thought successively engage the breadth and complexity of his oeuvre. The recent publication of the "Black Notebooks" makes Heidegger an all-the-more difficult case. If the "Black Notebooks" show how closely Heidegger's philosophy of history is intertwined with his personal and ideological prejudices, this defines, however, an additional task for Heidegger studies—namely, to understand the interaction between his philosophy and these individual prejudices. But Heidegger's philosophy of history, and the history of Being (*Seinsgeschichte*) specifically, does not absorb the entirety of his philosophical work, nor do Heidegger's commitments as a person undercut the possibility of studying his works philosophically. That Heidegger is one of the most important, and surely the most controversial of, figures of twentieth-century continental philosophy is only confirmed by the publication of the "Black Notebooks."

It greatly contributes to the import of Heidegger's philosophy that it is read, translated, interpreted, and continued around the globe, interacting with local intellectual traditions and different academic cultures. As an international group of scholars educated at European universities, we intend, in gathering these essays, to present a range of ways in which Heidegger can be read and a diversity of styles in which his thought can be continued. To any one particular audience, some of these styles of thinking will appear foreign and strange. But restricting the tone and voice of thinking takes away the philosophical richness that Heidegger's thought has achieved and continues to achieve. To explore this richness, however, there is no other starting point than Heidegger's texts; it is a hermeneutical endeavor, beginning with an interpretation of his writings.

Despite the chapters' diversity in approaching Heidegger, this hermeneutic orientation constitutes one of the leitmotifs in this volume: the authors contributing to it are greatly indebted to the European tradition of Heidegger studies and its hermeneutic approach to the history of philosophy. Each author attempts careful and often close readings that avoid the alternative of either blindly imitating Heidegger's style of writing or forcing his thinking into categories alien to it. Over the last decades, research in the later period of Heidegger's thought has been a prominent interest in the European (French, German, and also Italian), Continental tradition of Heidegger scholarship, while Anglo-American research on Heidegger has often focused on *Being and Time* and surrounding texts. This defines the specific aim of our collection: to bring to a broader, international public voices in Heidegger studies that have addressed Heidegger's later philosophy but that are not always prominently represented in the Anglo-American discourse. Rounding up the collection are also a few noted philosophers from the Anglophone tradition who, for different reasons, stand particularly close to the aforementioned hermeneutic reading of Heidegger.

Embracing the diversity of Heidegger studies in the hermeneutic tradition, we decided to concentrate on four topics, defining the arrangement of chapters in the volume: First, an inquiry into language, not so much into the human capacity to speak or to use signs but into language as a manifestation of Being itself. Second, the notion of φύσις emerging prominently in Heidegger's reception of the pre-Socratics. Third, the question of Heidegger's relation to phenomenology in his later thought, a question for which "the thing" (*das Ding*) and its manifestation in what Heidegger calls "the fourfold" (*das Geviert*) is central. Fourth, the discussion of "ground" and "non-ground" (*Grund, Ungrund*), representing a core moment in Heidegger's readings of eighteenth- and nineteenth-century authors such as Leibniz and Schelling. This is hardly an exhaustive account of the different philosophical topics Heidegger addresses, yet these fields cover much of the terrain of Heidegger's later thinking.

Setting up this collection in such a way does not only allow moving away from the question of how many Heideggers succeeded each other in the course of his writing, a question more of historical than of philosophical interest. It also has an implication for how we think Heidegger should and should not be read: Heidegger's ontological discourse, the changing ways of asking the question of Being (asking for "Being," the "meaning of Being," the "truth of Being," or the "place of Being") pervades all of his work. Yet, rather than structuring it in its entirety, we believe it bears witness not only to chronological shifts but also, and more importantly, at least for his later writing, to thematic variations. One finds recurring arguments and descriptions that define different regions within the landscape of his thought and give one possible direction in which an engagement with the later Heidegger can be pursued. As the motto to the *Gesamtausgabe* indicates, Heidegger eventually came to embrace the idea that even the question of Being, rather than giving his philosophy a center, can only be pursued in an irreducible plurality of ways. We propose to consider and explore the topical variations of this questioning rather than to search for a single set of ideas defining *the* later Heidegger.

Nonetheless, there are some general features that, while not necessarily setting the later Heidegger apart from the early, appear in various forms in each of the four areas of Heidegger's work we identify. One fundamental concern, no matter in which direction Heidegger's thought is developed, is to span the ontic and the ontological, the specific and the speculative. Even when Heidegger aims to explore the meaning of Being itself, he orients philosophy toward very specific phenomena: the meaning of home; a poem by Georg Trakl; what we communicate by greeting one another; the manifestation of an earthen jug; the beautiful shining of things; a rare and enigmatic German word. The attempt to bring specific phenomena such as these to bear on abstract philosophical questioning and on Heidegger's ontological project represents the concrete, descriptive, and interpretive side of Heidegger's thinking. If there is an overarching problem that Heidegger may be said to be concerned with, it may be pursuing his ontological or speculative ambitions without losing sight of the ontic and manifest, modifying the understanding of phenomenology in such a way as to allow his method to serve these ambitions. If there needs to be an answer to the question of what propels Heidegger's philosophical work, this is at least one: if *Being and Time* shows one way in which phenomenology and ontology can be joined, Heidegger's later works assume that this jointure was problematic or has proven insufficient. The fact that Heidegger's work after *Being and Time* responds to what he has been led to see as a philosophical failure gives a good reason why Heidegger addresses such diffuse themes and writes in such different styles without forging his ideas into a new systematic unity.

Despite the wish, in the spirit if not the letter of phenomenology, to do justice to the concrete, it is typical for Heidegger's language to also draw from a very different register from that of nuanced description, scholarly comment, or careful interpretation. The register of the enigmatic, speculative, and mystical defines the second feature typical of the later Heidegger, making for the often-recognized difficulty in approaching this period of his writing. Heidegger's magnum opus integrates the discussion of specific phenomena into a systematic framework which, taken as a whole, presents an attempt to understand the meaning of Being. In his later works, by contrast, the descriptive and the speculative ambition of his texts do not so effortlessly converge in a single philosophical project. While some writings, such as the *Bremen Lectures*, show a rhetorical force, argumentative rigor, and conceptual precision similar to that for which Heidegger's early lectures and *Being and Time* are famous, other writings, particularly the numerous manuscripts Heidegger never published, cannot but be called vague or obscure. Often enough, one finds bold statements that, taken out of context, can hardly be said to present a philosophical claim.

Consider, for instance, the famous adage from the "Letter on 'Humanism'": "Language is the house of Being." There is no doubt that this sentence is meant to grasp and relate the function of language to the whole of Being—but how? Or take the notion that a thing should be understood as a "gathering" (*Versammeln*)—gathering what? And why should we adopt this notion? Or consider the idea that a basic ancient Greek word such as φύσις articulates an understanding of Being that defines the epoch of pre-Socratic philosophy and, at the same time, is to be retrieved (and translated) for the future philosophy Heidegger envisages. Only to the extent that Heidegger's language, in these speculative turns, makes manifest the philosophical ideas behind these statements can it be said to succeed. To do justice to Heidegger's writing, the essays of this volume follow Heidegger as he attempts to bridge the speculative and the phenomenological.

* * *

The essays of the first section, "Language, *Logos*, and Rhythm," take their point of departure from ideas in Heidegger's philosophy of language. Although language can arguably be considered a central topic of Heidegger's interest since the earliest writings and seminars, the only explicit reference to language in a seminar title is from the summer 1934 seminar, *Logic as the Question concerning the Essence of Language*. This title announces a deep connection between language and logic that, while crucial for the early Heidegger, will be rejected in later years: if the task of Heidegger's discussion of language in the 1930s lies in referring logic back to language, his later thought will be concerned with the relation of spoken and written language to λόγος, to the very possibility and elemental structure of intelligibility. The essays of the collection *On the Way to Language* in particular, gathering texts written between 1950 and 1959, attempt to address this elemental structure without reducing it to logic. The chapters of the first section discuss how Heidegger describes this elemental structure outside the traditional discourse of logic.

In his contribution, Jeff Malpas links Heidegger's renewed attention to language after the Second World War with a shift from time (obviously crucial for *Being and Time*, among other writings) to space or, more precisely, to τόπος, or "place" (*Ort* or *Ortschaft*). If language is, according to the "Letter on 'Humanism,'" the house of Being and therefore the home in which human being dwells, then clearly—according to Malpas—the relation between dwelling in a certain place and language is crucial to understanding not only language but also Being itself. Against the background of Heidegger's reading of Hölderlin, Malpas shows that Heidegger's reflections on language are inseparably tied to poetry.

In a similar vein, Markus Wild analyzes the relation between language and poetry. His main reference is to the work of Trakl rather than Hölderlin, following a different path in Heidegger's encounter with poetic language. Wild's central aim is to address some problems he sees in the literature on Heidegger's understanding of language. Particularly, Wild accuses current scholarly literature of having been too keen on linking the later to the early Heidegger in order to avoid confrontation with other debates. Secondly, Trakl is often referred to as one poet among others with whom Heidegger confronts his philosophy in the later years. According to Wild, however, Heidegger's reading of Trakl is of pivotal importance. Missing this point has hindered an accurate understanding of Heidegger's texts on Trakl. Thirdly, Heidegger is often seen as just "opposing the tradition," as if he wanted to show the tradition to be simply wrong. But he actually often states the correctness of traditional views, only aiming to show the "deeper significance" of the phenomenon in question—for example, language. Only "clearing the path" of these assumptions will make it possible to reach a comprehensive account of Heidegger's understanding of language and the importance of Trakl's poetry.

The kinship of language and experience emerges with peculiar clarity in engaging with Heidegger's interpretation of Hölderlin in the way Diego D'Angelo proposes. By analyzing the conceptual constellation surrounding the destiny of Being (*Seinsgeschick*) and the thinking of the holy (*das Heilige*), D'Angelo highlights the importance of greeting (*Grüßen*). By characterizing the language of the poet as greeting, Heidegger proposes to understand the different epochs of the history of Being as opened up by the greeting of the gods and transposed into language by the poets. As D'Angelo shows, the centrality of greeting for Heidegger emerges from the idea that greeting describes the joining of the ideal and the real, of past and future in the destiny of Being. Greeting can thus be said to constitute the structural unity of this destiny, defining one of the ways in which Heidegger attempts to grasp the experience of Being.

Yet if even the idea of a greeting of Being yields to a phenomenological interpretation, this may serve as an example overcoming the accusation that Heidegger's later thought is incomprehensible, mysterious, or mystical in this sense. There is no doubt that it needs a certain form of translation, but it is nonetheless susceptible to such a hermeneutic effort. Tristan Moyle lays bare the methodological roots of such an approach, aiming at "naturalizing" Heidegger, not by reducing his philosophy to the language of natural sciences, but by translating his philosophy into a vocabulary rooted in everyday experiences. Moyle does this by introducing concepts, such as the idea of a rhythm of experience, that are alien to Heidegger's own philosophy, prima facie at least. In Moyle's reading, what Heidegger essentially describes is a specifically aesthetic faith.

* * *

The essays in the second section focus on Heidegger's analysis of the notion of φύσις. This notion is central to Heidegger's encounter with early Greek thinking and his attempt at retrieving an originary Greek beginning of thinking. Situated within his general critique of Western metaphysics, the notion of φύσις is to serve as a key to understanding pre-Socratic and classical Greek philosophy and, at the same time, open a new way of thinking. Thus, for Heidegger, the entire history of Western philosophy is gathered in the history and future understanding of the word φύσις.

In her essay, Claudia Baracchi undertakes to analyze this project and Heidegger's attempt to define the historical experience accessible at the end of philosophy by referring back to the beginning of philosophy in pre-Socratic thinking. At this limit, primordial truth is experienced as unconcealment, a position Heidegger exposes in "The End of Philosophy and the Task of Thinking," one of the central lectures in which Heidegger defines his philosophical legacy. Drawing from Greek philosophy and referring to such notions as νοῦς and αἴσθησις, Baracchi argues that such inceptional experience, understood as being open to the self-concealing clearing (*Lichtung*) and accessible by renewing the Greek understanding of φύσις, takes place prior to logical determination and truth in metaphysical sense. The term *experience* here mutates into a kind of attentiveness to the matter (*Sache*) of thinking, which transgresses the dichotomy of theoretical activity and practical engagement.

But what exactly is implied in Heidegger's account of a fundamental experience of φύσις? In addressing this question, Damir Barbarić points to the tension expressed by this notion. φύσις, in the ontological sense Heidegger wishes to give to that notion, entails both emergence, a coming forth, and the simultaneous self-withholding, a form of rest Heidegger calls *standing* (*Stehen*). This tension is indicative of the verbal or processual character of Being; Being is not presence (*Anwesen*) but presencing (*Anwesung*). In Barbarić's reading, φύσις refers to an elusive dimension of depth irreducible to any form of directed movement. Even further, φύσις is the name the Greeks gave to a momentary exposure to Being itself. The fact that entities exist manifests itself in abundance and excess, which Heidegger sees as defining Being's character as φύσις. It is in the face of such experience that the Greeks expressed wonder (θαυμάζειν), which Heidegger marks as the fundamental attunement of early Greek philosophy. However, in the history of Greek thought Heidegger sketches, the originary manifestation of φύσις did not persist; its phenomenal traits were covered over by the idea of substance (οὐσία) as metaphysics took the place of the pre-Socratics' inceptional thinking.

In line with Barbarić's inquiry into the tensional structure defining φύσις, Guang Yang in his essay focuses on the phenomenology of rest or repose in its intimate relation to movement. Yang argues that Heidegger's nuanced analysis of the primordial Greek experience of φύσις cannot be reduced to an ontological movement, to an emerging event of Being that was successively lost in the history of philosophy. Rather, the unique intertwining of movement and rest is an often-overlooked moment in the phenomenology of movement. It is in the phenomenology of movement that Heidegger's ontological and historical speculation gains footing in the manifestation of things. Through an in-depth interpretation of "On the Essence and Concept of *Physis*" and other relevant texts, Yang shows that rest is not to be understood as negation of movement. Instead, rest gathers movement in its highest form, and it is their belonging together that characterizes Heidegger's "Greek" φύσις.

Thomas Buchheim's essay delineates the itinerary of Heidegger's engagement with φύσις. In "On the Essence and Concept of *Physis*" Heidegger identifies a late echo of early Greek φύσις in Aristotle's treatise, the *Physics*. Even though Heidegger's interpretation has often been criticized after publication, he did indeed think much ahead of his time. According to Buchheim, many of Heidegger's interpretative insights are consistent with today's state of the art in scholarly research on Aristotle. Buchheim also points to an important continuity in Heidegger's writing: already in texts from the 1920s, Heidegger conceives the capacity of Dasein to project a world as a response to the primordial withdrawal associated with φύσις.

* * *

In its historical and phenomenological dimensions, Heidegger's discussion of φύσις aims to give a description of the world, the whole of experience, or Being. Yet Heidegger's work is not solely centered on the history of what he takes to be the fundamental concepts of philosophy. There is, along the speculative side of his thinking, evident in the engagement with the pre-Socratics, a parallel concern for a renewal of a descriptive, phenomenological form of philosophy. One of the very late examples of this concern is a recently published set of notes, dating from 1973–75, to which Günter Figal draws attention in the first essay of the third section. These notes present an astonishing merger of Heidegger's interest in pre-Socratic philosophy, specifically Parmenides, and his wish to better understand the manifestation, the showing (*Zeigen*), and the self-showing (*Sichzeigen*) of things. Figal discusses the different ways in which Heidegger interprets the Parmenidean statement that Being and perceiving are the same: τὸ γὰρ αὐτὸ νοεῖν ἐστίν τε καὶ εἶναι. Among Heidegger's different readings of this statement, perhaps the most challenging is the one put forth in the later notes. While Heidegger's interpretations have always taken the notion of "the same" (τὸ αὐτὸ) as key to this statement, the notes situate this idea in the context of

phenomenology. If showing (φαίνεσθαι) is central to the notion of the phenomenon, as Heidegger argued in *Being and Time* (§ 7), the sameness of Being and
perceiving expressed the self-showing of this same, or, with the Greek terminology Heidegger invents, *phenomenóphasis* is *tautóphasis*. Yet as Figal points out,
the form of quasi-phenomenological philosophy Heidegger envisages, what he
calls "tautological thinking" (*tautologisches Denken*) in the Zähringen seminar,
is threatened to become aporetic, for it is unclear how an articulation of "the
same" can do justice to the differences of the appearing world and specific, perhaps even singular, events of manifestation.

This leads to a problem addressed by Jussi Backman in his essay. Heidegger's
adherence to both the phenomenological orientation toward the particular and
the ontological ambition to articulate a unifying meaning in all there is force
him to revisit the relation of identity and difference. Taking his departure from
a reading of Heidegger's entire philosophical project as a deepening form of con-
textualism, Backman describes Heidegger's ontological project as moving from
the inherent temporal structure of Being to the thought that the uniqueness
(*Einzigkeit*) or singularity (*Einmaligkeit*) of each event represents the hallmark
of ontological meaning. Alongside Reiner Schürmann, Backman sees Heidegger
as endorsing the contextual singularity of Being. An expression of this thought is
Heidegger's discussion of the so-called *fourfold* (*Geviert*), which Backman takes
as the attempt not to define a fixed set of ontological categories but to offer a
dynamic matrix for understanding the manifestation of entities, or, as Heidegger
prefers to call them, *things* (*Dinge*).

Andrew Mitchell approaches this notion of a "thing" from another direction. While Heidegger considered his postwar lecture "The Thing" (*das Ding*) the
most immediate articulation of his later thinking, he also emphasizes that the
notion of *das Ding* is meant to correct the problematic "objectification" of things
he takes to be endemic to the history of philosophy. Mitchell reconstructs the
history of the "thing" Heidegger sketches, through Aristotle's natural philosophy
and Eckhart's account of *dinc*, from which Heidegger takes the idea that things
are a gathering (*Versammeln*). Mitchell adds to Heidegger's "history of things" by
considering Husserl's lecture course *Thing and Space* as well as *Being and Time*.
For Mitchell, Heidegger's discovery of "the thing" marks the very initiation of
the later period of Heidegger's later thought, while his magnum opus still participates in and reinforces the neglect of things.

Rather than looking back on the history of thought from Heidegger's writing, Nikola Mirković's essay explores Heidegger's own influence, taking as an
example *All Things Shining* by Hubert Dreyfus and Sean Kelly. While Dreyfus
and Kelly show themselves as deeply influenced by Heidegger's later philosophy,
taking their departure from the idea that the present, secular age is threatened
by nihilism, the way in which they conceive of "shining" is, Mirković shows,

incomplete in relation to Heidegger's understanding. Turning to Heidegger's engagement with Nietzsche in the 1930s and his correspondence with the literary scholar Emil Staiger in the 1950s, Mirković argues that the most relevant context for understanding Heidegger's notion of shining is his philosophy of art. Similar to Plato's understanding of beauty as ἐκφανέστατον, "shining" (*Scheinen*) and "shining-forth" (*Hervorscheinen*) are the hallmark of the manifestation of the beautiful. As the discussion with Staiger reveals, however, Heidegger did not conceive the beauty of art to be lost in the present age. On the contrary, only the continuous shining of artworks, such as the poem by Eduard Mörike that initiated the Staiger correspondence, makes possible the renewal of meaning Dreyfus and Kelly envisage.

* * *

The three essays of the fourth section have their common theme in the notion and philosophical image of a "ground" (*Grund*), one of the central themes in Heidegger's later engagement with ontology. While the first two essays discuss Heidegger's interpretations of Leibniz and Schelling, the most important philosophical interlocutors with respect to the notion of ground, the third essay questions Heidegger's use of ground as a philosophical metaphor. In his contribution, Hans Ruin traces the trajectory of Heidegger's engagement with Leibniz from an early stage in the 1920s, culminating in "On the Essence of Ground," to Heidegger's last lecture course in 1955. Central to this engagement is Leibniz's formulation of the principle of sufficient reason, *der Satz vom Grund*. But what does it mean to say that everything has a reason/ground, and how does the correlation between reason and grounding shape our understanding of rationality and of thinking itself? And why should the principle of sufficient reason hold at all? In the first stage of his reading of Leibniz, Heidegger asks these questions with regard to his own fundamental ontology, answering that the principle of reason and the commitment to the form of rationality it embodies must in turn be "grounded" in the freedom of human Dasein. While that position overcomes the transcendent grounding for the principle of reason Leibniz upheld, it also reiterates the commitment to grounding as ontological relation and the giving of reasons as eminent logical form. By the time of the late lecture course, however, Heidegger came to see the principle of reason as the pinnacle of a problematic form of rationality. Rather than aiming to renew it within fundamental ontology, Heidegger's understanding of Leibniz now takes the subversive form of hearing the principle of reason in a new key: if it is to transgress the alternative between rational and irrational thought, meditative thinking progresses "without why," thereby relinquishing the Leibnizian principle.

Complementing Heidegger's dissatisfaction with the *Satz vom Grund* is his consideration of the non-ground (*Ungrund*) and the abyss (*Abgrund*). As Sylvaine Gourdain shows in her essay, the way in which Heidegger molds these terms into philosophical concepts cannot be understood without considering the influence of Schelling's philosophy. It is Schelling who allows Heidegger to redefine, rather than abandon, the very concept of ground by emphasizing its inherent negativity. From his engagement with Schelling, Heidegger draws the idea that the reason/ground of an entity is not its positive ontological basis but the withdrawing of manifest being, or in Schelling's terminology, the ground is not a condition of the existence of entities (*Existenz*) but that which renders *impossible* any prior condition, because it refuses and eludes incessantly. Whereas Schelling emphasizes the negativity of the ground, Heidegger integrates this meaning into his discussion of *Ungrund* and *Abgrund*. Gourdain shows that the duality between an existing entity and its ground not only lies at the center of Heidegger's reading of Schelling's freedom essay but comes to influence a much larger share of Heidegger's writings. Both the idea of a strife of earth and world in Heidegger's artwork essay and the notion of a "grounding" (*Gründung*) in *Contributions to Philosophy* display a close structural affinity to the dualism first exposed in Schelling's freedom essay. If it is from Leibniz that Heidegger learned to be skeptical regarding the metaphysical suppositions and the implications of a notion of positive grounding, of *ratio*, it is from Schelling that Heidegger draws his account of ground as manifest negativity.

This negative meaning of ground is also at play in the third essay of the section. Tobias Keiling, however, strikes a critical note regarding Heidegger's discussion of ground. Taking his departure from the discussion of projection (*Entwerfen*) in *Being and Time*, Keiling points to the fusion of the image of ground and of projection Heidegger sees in the word *Erklüftung* (typically translated as *sundering*), used in key passages from *Contributions to Philosophy*. While the notion of projection determines the form in which the temporal constitution of human Dasein and Being is revealed, Heidegger also holds that Dasein can be said to be grounding in its own right. But how, in the logic of philosophical images, can something be both a secluding ground and the process in which a specific endeavor is projected into an open future? Does the latter not presuppose an open space, which the former denies? Heidegger's answer refers to the process of *Erklüftung, sundering*, attempting to turn into a philosophical notion an extremely rare and enigmatic German word. For Keiling, the fact that Heidegger quickly discards the notion is indicative of its inherent metaphorological contradiction.

* * *

It is our hope that this volume will help to broaden the discussion of later Heidegger's works, drawing from the enormous historical effect Heidegger's philosophy has come to display around the globe. Rather than advocating an existing or new paradigm, we intend to exhibit the diversity of ways in which his philosophy can be unfolded. The idea for such a collected volume was first conceived during a series of workshops organized at the Albert-Ludwigs-University Freiburg, Germany, in 2012. We thank all those who have since contributed to its realization.

Diego D'Angelo, Günter Figal,
Tobias Keiling, Guang Yang
December 2017

I.
LANGUAGE, *LOGOS*, AND RHYTHM

1   "The House of Being"

Poetry, Language, Place

Jeff Malpas

1.

One of the characteristic features of Heidegger's later thinking is its concern with language. Indeed, one might say that the centrality of this concern is a clear marker of the more strongly hermeneutical character of the later thinking (the thinking of the postwar years especially) compared to the earlier[1]—a character that is present in spite of Heidegger's explicit claim to have abandoned hermeneutics (or, at least, to have abandoned the term) in his later work.[2] The concern with language in the later Heidegger also coincides with a more explicit turn toward the topological—toward *topos*, or place (*Ort/Ortschaft*).[3] This is no coincidence. Not only are the topological and the hermeneutical themselves bound together,[4] but Heidegger's topological "turn" itself (which is really a *return* to something that is present throughout his thinking) develops out of his increasing engagement with both language and poetry, especially as this engagement is mediated through the work of Hölderlin.[5] That poetry, language, and place are indeed tied together in the later Heidegger is especially evident in the 1947 "Letter on 'Humanism.'" There Heidegger famously characterizes language as "the house of being," adding that "in its home human being dwells."[6] The themes of home and dwelling, and the very nature of the language that is invoked here, are connected directly back to Hölderlin[7] in a way that continues from the engagement with the poet that had been under way in Heidegger's thinking for at least the previous fifteen years (from the early Hölderlin lectures beginning in 1934 to the *Ister* lectures of 1943[8]) and that would continue long after (including the 1959 volume *Unterwegs zur Sprache*[9]). Heidegger's discussions of poetry and language, as well as his relation to Hölderlin, have often claimed the attention of commentators, but the way poetry, language, *and place*, and especially the place of language within the topology of being, come together in late Heidegger is seldom remarked upon—perhaps unsurprisingly considering the lack of real attention that is given to place in particular.

Yet it is not only the topological character of language—or even of language *and poetry*—that is brought into view here. When Heidegger talks of language as "the house of being," what is at issue is as much the idea of the *house*, and what it is *to house*, as is the idea of language or, indeed, of being. The house is itself a topological concept: a mode of place and placing—perhaps one of the most basic modes of place and placing. The house is that within which one dwells, that in which one is given a place, afforded shelter, and allowed rest as well as activity; through its delimitation of space, the house grants space, room, and dimension. This remains true regardless of the emphasis on the homelessness of our contemporary condition, regardless even of the critique of home as a site of oppression, subjugation, or violence. What is at issue is not merely the house or home in its contingent instantiations but the house as that which does indeed give place to being. To be the house of being, in Heidegger's formulation, is also to give home to human being. To dwell is to find oneself housed, to be at home. Once again this does not mean that one finds oneself secured against all uncertainty or questionability but rather that one first finds oneself placed in the world and thus one's own being appears as an issue. In this fashion, only the one who is already at home can be "homeless"; only the one who is already housed can be in need of housing. Gaston Bachelard writes that "on whatever theoretical horizon we examine it, the house image would appear to have become the topography of our intimate being."[10] Although this claim plays out in a number of different ways in Bachelard's work, it nevertheless indicates something of the fundamental nature of the house, and so of home, *as topological* and so also *as ontological*.

In claiming language as the house of being, as the structure in which human beings dwell, Heidegger claims this very nature *for language*. Language is thus the structure within which one dwells, which gives place, affords shelter, and allows rest and activity. One may even be led to say that, if language is the house of being, then there must also be a sense in which language itself grants space, room, and dimension precisely through its delimitation of the same. Part of the task before us is to understand both how and why this might be so—*what does it mean for language to have such a nature?*—but in equal significance, the task is to understand the topology that is at work here. How can we speak of the house—and so of place or dimension—as belonging to the character of language or of being? What does it mean to speak of them in this way?

In the "Letter on 'Humanism,'" Heidegger comments that "one day we will, by thinking the essence of being in a way appropriate to its matter, more readily be able to think what 'house' and 'dwelling' are," suggesting that we think less readily in such a way now.[11] The comment comes in the context of a warning against reading the phrase "the house of being" as if it were merely an "adornment of language" or as if it involved "the transfer of the image 'house' onto being."[12] It is at this point that the question of poetry comes directly into view, not only in terms of the way it sheds light on the questions of being or of language but in terms of its own nature and the nature of poetic language, including its own relation to the topological. Moreover, if the poetic and the topological seem to be brought together here, then it is not poetry alone—or even poetry as tied to language—that is at issue. The inquiry into the place of language within the topology of being, with which the question of poetry is implicated, includes within it the question of topology itself. What, we may ask, is the nature of topology, such that language and poetry are so closely bound to it? Or, to put a familiar Heideggerian remark and phrase into an interrogative form: What is the character of the saying of place that is involved in the topology of being, and what is the topology of being, such that it takes the form of "a poetry that thinks?"[13]

2.

A mode of topological inquiry, even if not made explicit, is present in Heidegger's thinking almost from the start. Yet, although this means that Heidegger's thinking can be construed fundamentally as an attempt to contemplate the essentially placed character of being, the nature of the *placedness* (and of place itself) at issue here cannot simply be taken for granted. The famous "question of being" is thus inseparable from the question of place—the response to both questions takes exactly the form of a *topology*—and yet the question of place brings with it further questions about the thinking that place demands and about those concepts with which place is most immediately associated, notably time and space. If the focus of Heidegger's early work often leads in the direction of the thinking of place through the thinking (and rethinking) of time, then much of the later work leads toward a rethinking of space or, perhaps better, of dimensionality, within a more direct and explicit thinking of place itself. Such a rethinking is especially important given the way in which the Western philosophical tradition, increasingly so within modernity, has tended to prioritize space over place, as it has also tended to prioritize the spatial over other concepts. This is why the critique of the "Cartesian ontology of the world," essentially an ontology based on the idea of a homogenous and leveled-out mode of spatiality, is such an important element in the argument of *Being and Time*.[14]

The centrality of the questions of both place and space is brought to particular clarity in the period after *Being and Time* with the increasing focus in Heidegger's work on truth as *aletheia*—unconcealment (*Unverborgenheit*)—and on the associated concepts of the "clearing" (*Lichtung*), the "open" (*Offene*), and the "between" (*Zwischen*), as well as on time-space (*Zeit-Raum*) and directly on place or locality itself (*Ort/Ortschaft*). Although the idea of language as the house of being occurs quite late, a topological conception of language nevertheless seems to be present, even if sometimes equivocally, from relatively early on in Heidegger's thinking—in the way, for instance, in which the character of language, and more fundamentally, of *logos*, is understood as a pointing out of things in their being. Understood thus, language already seems to depend on a certain sort of placing, even as it is itself a form of placing or bringing near. So any sort of speaking opens into a space in which that speaking takes place, even while such speaking itself depends, as a condition of its possibility, on being already placed.

One might argue that all of these concepts—including the topological conception of language, the idea of truth as unconcealment,[15] and even the notion of the "event" that is so central to Heidegger's later thinking[16]—can be seen as aspects of the "there/here" (*Da*) that looms so large in *Being and Time* and remains in the later work, even if its occurrences there are less frequent. One might argue, in fact, that the term *Da* appears less often in the later thinking precisely because of the way that idea is taken up in the various forms of *topos* that appear there. Moreover, Heidegger's emerging concern, particularly under the influence of Hölderlin, with earth (*Boden, Erde*) and later sky (*Himmel*), a concern that reaches its full realization in the idea of the Fourfold (*Das Geviert*), not only powerfully reinforces the topological orientation of Heidegger's thinking in general but also does so in a way that is focused directly on the question of the poetic and, perhaps more immediately, the question of language.

3.

As Heidegger so often emphasizes (and Gadamer frequently reiterates), language is not to be understood as merely something that human beings possess. Human being is linguistic—which is to say that it is pervaded by language, that it is a being *in* language. As human being is tied to language, so language is also intimately tied to the possibility of world: "Language is not merely a tool which man possesses alongside many others; language first grants the possibility of standing in the midst of the openness of beings. Only where there is language, is there world, that is, the constantly changing cycle of decision and work, of action and responsibility, but also of arbitrariness and turmoil, decay and confusion. Only where world holds sway is there history. . . . Language is . . . the primal event [*Ereignis*] which disposes of the highest possibility of man's being."[17]

The openness of beings that is granted through language is not a matter of language creating either an open domain for appearance or what comes to appearance within that domain. In this sense, language is neither something possessed nor something that produces. There is thus no sense in Heidegger of any form of linguistic constructionism (or any form of social constructionism either). Language grants openness, and in so doing, language may also be said to be a form of freeing or clearing that allows beings to come forth *in their being*—that is, as the things they already are.

That language lets beings appear in their being does not mean that beings thereby come to presence in a way that is somehow complete or transparent.

The supposition of such transparent presence would, in fact, be to misunder-
stand the very nature and possibility of what it is for something to come to presence. It would also be to forget Heidegger's constant insistence on the character
of every revealing, every appearing, as belonging within the play of concealing
and unconcealing that is truth as *aletheia*. Thus the appearing of beings is such
that they appear always with a certain cast or look—this is the very nature of
what it is to appear or to come to presence (and it can be understood as tied to the
character of any appearing as always situated or placed). Yet even though beings
come to presence in particular ways, and so in different ways, they nevertheless
come to presence as the beings they are. That we speak of things in different languages does not mean that there must be different things of which each language
speaks. Indeed, the very nature of things is that they can indeed be spoken of
differently—across utterances and across languages. In letting beings appear in
their being, language thus lets beings appear and does so in a way that does not
curtail the inexhaustible possibilities in which the being of beings consists. For
this reason, Heidegger can say of language that it "beckons us [*winkt uns*], at first
and then again at the end, towards a thing's nature [*das Wesen einer Sache zu*]."[18]
It draws us into nearness to beings without determining beings in that nearness.

So long as we remain with a conception of language that takes language as
merely another natural phenomenon that occurs within the world—as part of the
natural history, as it were, of the human species (and so also as a phenomenon
continuous with forms of animal communication)—then we will fail to penetrate
the essence of language that is at issue here. What concerns us is not language as
natural or biological but language *as ontological*. If we often fail to recognize this,
the reason is partly to be found in the nature of language itself. Precisely because
language is so pervasive and so fundamental, it tends to withdraw in the face of
that which it lets come to presence. It is thus easy to overlook the linguisticality
of human being, and instead to see the human as more fundamentally grounded
in what is pre- or nonlinguistic—in the pragmatic engagement with things, for
instance, in the bodily or experiential. In this way, we seem to see through language, not in the sense that it is the means by which we see (for that would be to
treat it as some medium between us and the world, which it assuredly is not), but
in the sense that we do *not* see it, and are indeed given to disregard it or to reduce
it to its ordinary and specific instances, whether as speech or text or as formal-
ized semantic and syntactic structure.

As a letting of beings appear in their being, the granting of the openness of
beings in and through language is a letting of beings into their own, into what
is proper to them. But as such it is also a letting of beings into their proper relation with one another—both as together and apart. The granting of openness is
thus a granting of both difference *and* sameness. This is the real character of the
openness that is at issue here—why it is indeed *a freeing* and *a clearing*—and why

it also implicates things and world, as well as human beings (in their singularity and communality) and things. In the last of the passages quoted above, language is said to be "the primal event [*Ereignis*] which disposes of the highest possibility of man's being." The German term *Ereignis*—the event—carries within it a sense of "what is proper to," or what is often rendered into English as "appropriation" (giving rise to the sometime translation of *Ereignis* as "event of appropriation").[19]

The idea of language as that which lets beings appear in their being, and so in terms of that which is indeed proper to them, in their difference and their sameness, thus already indicates a connection between language and the notion of the event as "appropriative"—that is, as that which lets beings into what is proper to them. Consequently, Heidegger writes of the event: "The event of appropriation is that realm [*Bereich*], vibrating within itself, through which man and being reach each other in their nature. . . . To think of the event as the event of appropriation [*Das Ereignis als Er-eignis denken*] means to shape the structure of the event as this self-vibrating realm. Thinking receives the materials for this self-suspended structure from language. For language is the most delicate and thus the most suspended vibration holding everything within the suspended structure of the appropriation. We dwell in the event inasmuch as our active nature is given over to language."[20]

The topological characterization of the event that is evident in this passage (the event as realm, as that "through which man and being reach") and elsewhere in Heidegger's thinking should not be overlooked. Yet just as important is the way in which the topology at work here also encompasses language. Language and the event are once again seen as belonging together, though in two different ways: not only does language "hold everything within . . . the event," but we are said to "dwell in" (*wohnen . . . im*) the event inasmuch as we are given over to language. Here one might say that it is the event, rather than language, that appears as "that which gives home to human being" (to use the language of the "Letter on 'Humanism'"), except that the very distinction between language, or the essence of language, and the event seems not to be such as to allow one to exclude the other. To use words Heidegger uses elsewhere, language, or the being of language, and the event now appear as "the same."

4.

The same topology, the same connection between dwelling, the event, and language, recurs throughout many of Heidegger's later essays—including, of course, the "Letter on 'Humanism,'" in which it is language that provides a dwelling place for human being, just as language is also the house of being. Within this topology, the possibility of appearing, the possibility that beings can come to presence in their being, is seen as dependent upon or occurring within a certain mode of dimensionality that in Heidegger's earlier thinking is most often referred to as the open or the between, sometimes in terms of nearness (*Nähe*), but in the later thinking it is sometimes also referred to in terms simply of the dimension [*Dimension*] or dimensionality. In the "Letter on 'Humanism,'" Heidegger talks of being itself as this very dimension. He writes that "in the determination of the humanity of the human being as ek-sistence what is essential is not the human being but being—as the dimension of the ek-stasis [*als die Dimension des Ekstatischen der Ek-sistenz*]."[21] The talk of being as dimensionality occurs together with the assertion of language as the house of being. The dimension that appears is not, as Heidegger is at pains to stress here and in similar passages, anything spatial in the usual sense, although it is a dimensionality that frequently appears in contexts in which it might be thought to have spatial connotations in some sense. It is a dimensionality that appears most clearly perhaps in the dimension that is opened up between earth and sky—the dimensionality that belongs, one might say, to world and also to place—which Heidegger elaborates on in "Poetically Man Dwells" (1951):

> The upward glance passes aloft toward the sky, and yet it remains below on the earth. The upward glance spans the between of earth and sky. This between is measured out for the dwelling of man [*dem Wohnen des Menschen zugemessen*]. We now call the span thus meted out the dimension [*die Dimension*]. This dimension does not arise from the fact that earth and sky are turned toward one another. Rather, their facing each other depends on the dimension. Nor is the dimension a stretch of space as ordinarily understood; for everything spatial, as something for which space is made, is already in need of the dimension, that is, into which it is admitted. The nature of the dimension is the meting out—which is lightened and so can be spanned—of the between: the upward to the sky and the downward to the earth. We leave the nature of the dimension without a name.[22]

Significantly, Heidegger once again refers to the dimension that is invoked here as that which allows for *dwelling*. Dwelling depends, Heidegger tells us a few lines later, "on an upward-looking measure-taking of the dimension, in which sky belongs just as much as earth."[23] The "measure-taking" is also a spanning of the dimension between earth and sky, and as such, it depends on a taking of the measure of that dimension into which human being is gathered and in which it belongs (in and to which it is "appropriated").[24]

If Heidegger does not refer directly to language at the same time as he talks of "measure-taking," it is not because language and measure-taking stand apart from one another. The measure-taking on which dwelling depends is *poetry* (poetry is that which *builds* dwelling, and it does so by *taking measure*[25]), and the essence of language is, as we have already seen, to be found in poetry. Consequently, if poetry is a measure-taking, then such measure-taking must also belong to language—or perhaps we should say that the measure-taking in which poetry consists stands in an essential relation to the character of language as precisely that which allows us into the dimension of being, which beckons us toward that dimension.

In a later essay ("The Nature of Language," 1957–58—from *On the Way to Language*), Heidegger is explicit in drawing attention to the being of language: "saying" [*Sagen*] and "nearness" belong together. Such nearness, moreover, is given in the encounter between the regions of world (earth and sky, gods and mortals) that occurs in the Fourfold:

> Anticipating, we defined Saying. To say means to show, to make appear, the lighting-concealing-releasing offer of world. Now, nearness manifests itself as the motion in which the world's regions face each other. There arises the possibility of seeing how Saying, as the being of language, swings back into the presence of nearness. Quiet consideration makes possible an insight into how nearness and Saying, being of the persisting nature of language, are the Same. Language, then, is not a mere human faculty. Its character belongs to the very character of the movement of the face-to-face encounter of the world's four regions. There arises the possibility that we undergo an experience with language, that we enter into something which bowls us over, that is, transmutes our relation to language. How so? Language, Saying of the world's fourfold, is no longer only such that we speaking human beings are related to it in the sense of a nexus existing between man and language. Language is, as world-moving Saying, the relation of all relations. It relates, maintains, proffers, and enriches the face-to-face encounter of the world's regions, holds and keeps them, in that it holds itself-Saying in reserve.[26]

And elsewhere, in "Hebel—Friend of the House" (1957), Heidegger writes: "A word of language sounds and resounds in the voice, is clear and bright in the typeface. Voice and script are indeed sensuous, yet always within them a meaning is told and appears. As sensuous meaning, the word traverses the expanse of the leeway between earth and sky. Language holds open the realm in which man, upon the earth and beneath the sky, inhabits the house of the world."[27]

Here language appears explicitly as that which grants openness, which lets things into their proper relation with one another, but this occurs in relation to the elements of the Fourfold itself, especially in relation to earth and sky, and so "holds open" the realm of human dwelling. Moreover, this relating and opening, which, as we saw earlier, encompasses both sameness and difference, does indeed seem to imply a dimensionality that belongs to relating and opening as such—a dimensionality that is surely the same as that to which Heidegger refers in the "Letter on 'Humanism'" and in "Poetically Man Dwells." It is the role of language as that which grants the openness for such dimensionality, which can be understood as itself a form of dimensionality that grounds the characterization of language as the house of being.

The way Heidegger brings language and dimensionality together in the later works (in these passages and others) is directly connected with the character of language as both opening and relating. Opening is an opening of the dimensional—it is a clearing, a making-room, even, one might say, a *spacing*. Relationality requires such dimensionality, since relationality only arises between what appears together and yet also apart.[28] Dimensionality in turn, however, also requires relationality—there is no opening up into an unlimited, horizonless realm, but always and only into the realm of the between. The dimensional is this very realm—as is the relational also. For this reason, one might say here that the dimensional and the relational are not separate but rather are two sides of the same. Both arise out of the between, or as one might also say, out of the bounded open that is place (as open, it can also be said to be boundless, but as such that boundlessness belongs always and only together with the bounded).[29] It is thus that the language of the house, and the home, recur so often in Heidegger's discussions of these matters—the house provides a delimited realm that, precisely through its delimitation, gives room to things, allows them leeway, and grants them a place. The house provides a dimension within which things come into their own, which also means they come into the world, and this is precisely why language can be said to be the house of being. Language is thus dimensional and relational—and if it is, as Heidegger claims, "the relation of all relations,"[30] then perhaps it should also be said to be the "dimension of all dimensions."

As language belongs together with the event, so what is said of language can be said of the event too. As appropriative, and so as letting things into their proper relation as both different and the same, the event is both relational and dimensional. The connection to the event also shows, however, that neither the relationality nor the dimensionality at issue here can be a matter of the simple standing of one thing over against and apart from another.[31] Heidegger talks of the glance as "spanning" the between, of the regions of world as "turning," of saying as "world-moving," of the word as "traversing" the leeway between earth and sky. The relationality and dimensionality that concerns Heidegger—nearness, the between, the open, the clearing—is thus the relationality and dimensionality that is also tied inextricably to activity and to movement. The event draws together this sense of the active and mobile with the relational and dimensional, hence the description of the event in *Identity and Difference* as the "self-vibrating realm" and of language as "the most delicate and thus the most suspended vibration holding everything within" the realm that is the event. Thus, we can say that the event is the happening of dimensionality and of relationality and that this happening is the happening of language. In the "Letter on 'Humanism,'" Heidegger comments that: "The one thing thinking would like to attain and for the first time tries to articulate in *Being and Time* is something simple. As such, being remains mysterious, the simple nearness of an unobtrusive prevailing. The nearness occurs essentially as language itself."[32]

One might add that language, in its own turn, occurs as this same nearness and it is thus that it is the very house of being, that in whose home human beings dwell. In this way, language appears as itself a *place*, a *topos*, and as that which grants such a place—which is why topology can indeed be understood as a "saying" of the place of being. Moreover, topology here names both *the saying of place that occurs in thought and in poetry* (in "the poetry that thinks") and *the giving of place to being that occurs in and through the belonging together of saying and being as such.*

5.

If language is dimensional, if it is relational, then why is it not also *spatial*? Certainly that seems to be the implicit direction in which much of this discussion leads. As we saw earlier, however, although Heidegger recognizes that a sense of spatiality seems to be invoked in talk, for instance, of the dimension, he also insists that what is at issue is nothing spatial, or at least nothing spatial "as ordinarily understood."[33] In the passage in which this is addressed in the "Letter on 'Humanism,'" Heidegger comments that "the dimension is not something spatial in the familiar sense. Rather, everything spatial and all time-space occur essentially in the dimensionality [*im Dimensionalen*] that being itself is."[34] Dimensionality and spatiality are here distinguished in a way that, on the face of it, seems peculiar—after all, what is dimensionality if it is not spatial? One cannot answer that the dimensionality at issue is temporal rather than spatial, since not only is there an obvious question as to whether this would not simply involve treating the temporal as itself implicitly spatial (the problem, after all, is that dimensionality seems to bring spatiality with it), but it also seems to ignore the fact that what seems to be indicated here, even if not made explicit, is that both the spatial and the temporal occur in the dimension (thus one might say, analogously, that the event character of the event is "not something temporal in the familiar sense"). Moreover, if it is indeed the case that dimension is not to be construed as spatial "in the familiar sense," then surely the same ought to be said of the dimension *as dimensional*, especially since "in its familiar sense" the dimension *is* spatial. Indeed, one might argue that to claim that the dimension is not spatial "in the familiar sense" is thereby also to claim that it is not dimensional "in the familiar sense."

In fact, what almost certainly lies behind Heidegger's refusal of a spatial understanding of the dimension is, first and foremost, the desire to rule out any notion of the dimension that is associated with space "construed physically-technologically"—with the idea of space "that was first determined by Galileo and Newton" and that consists in the idea of a "homogenous separation that is not distinct in any of its possible places, that is equivalent in all direction, but not sensibly perceptible."[35] The passage from the "Letter on 'Humanism,'" however, might be thought to make for complications here, since although Heidegger there refers to the dimension as indeed "not something spatial in the familiar sense," he also says that "everything spatial and all time-space" occur in the dimensionality of being. In a note appended to the phrase "everything spatial," he adds, "Space neither alongside time, nor dissolved into time, nor deduced from time."[36] Moreover, his comments in the "Letter on 'Humanism'" are echoed in the discussion of the dimension in "Poetically Man Dwells": "everything spatial, as something for which space is made, is already in need of the dimension, that is, into which it is admitted."[37] This might be taken to imply that the dimensionality at issue is marked off not only from spatiality "in the familiar sense" but from all and every sense of spatiality.

Whether or not (in the passages in question) it is Heidegger's intention to exclude every sense of spatiality from the dimension, such an attempt to exclude the spatial completely would raise problems in those passages themselves (since the spatial seems at odds with the qualifications "as ordinarily understood" and "in the familiar sense"). But it would also be at odds with the way Heidegger later treats spatiality as amenable to a reading that does indeed seem to be very close to the way he also treats dimensionality. Immediately prior to his assertion in "The Nature of Language" that saying and nearness belong together, Heidegger considers the character of nearness itself and, in so doing, is led directly to consider the nature of space and, with it, time. Heidegger distinguishes between time and space "conceived as parameters" (presumably what underpins the "ordinary" or "familiar" sense of both terms) and the "timing and spacing" that "moves the encounter of the four world regions" and to which the character of language is itself bound.[38] In "Art and Space" (the source for the characterization of space in its Galilean-Newtonian sense quoted above) from 1969,[39] the focus is primarily on space (time does not appear in this discussion except inasmuch as there is an emphasis on activity). But the movement of thought is very similar. Heidegger first identifies what we may think of as the ordinary or familiar sense of space in its "physical-technological" construal, but then he asks whether this must count as "the only true space" and, more importantly, how we can find "what is peculiar to space." In response to the latter question, Heidegger writes: "There is an emergency bridge, one that is narrow and swaying. We attempt to listen to language. Whereof does it speak in the word 'space' [*Raum*]? Clearing-away [*Räumen*] speaks in it. This means: to clear out [*roden*], to make the wilderness open. Clearing-away brings forth what is free, the open for humans' settling and dwelling."[40]

Here, and in the subsequent discussion, Heidegger follows the clues given by language toward a thinking of space that is more fundamental than what is given in space as "physical-technological" and that does indeed seem to converge with his thinking of nearness and of the dimension.

Perhaps significantly, the language of the dimension in particular is absent from "Art and Space," as it is also absent from "The Nature of Language." In the latter, it seems to have been replaced by the talk of nearness and the "face-to-face encounter" of the Fourfold. In the former, it appears to have given way to a rethought conception of the spatial as grounded in clearing-away, which is itself understood in terms of "making-space" [*Einräumen*] and then again as "granting and arranging" [*Einrichtens*]: "On the one hand, making-space admits something. It lets what is open hold sway, which among other things grants the appearance of present things to which human dwelling sees itself consigned. On the other hand, making-space prepares for things the possibility of belonging to their respective whither, and out of this, to each other."[41]

The way in which Heidegger here talks of making-space—which he also goes on to connect directly to place in a way that is highly significant[42]—understood as at the heart of space and the spatial, seems to parallel the way in which he elsewhere talks of language or of saying. Indeed, in thinking of language as the house of being, we are already thinking of language as a making-room in the sense Heidegger employs in "Art and Space." If we understand each, not in terms of what is usual or familiar, but it terms of what is proper to it (in terms of the essential and originary), then language and space appear as belonging closely together. Language, saying, is indeed making-space, *spacing*. But so too, perhaps, must space, making-space, be understood *as saying*. Although the latter idea is not explored in "Art and Space," it nevertheless seems to be a conclusion to which we are inevitably drawn. It is precisely what seems to emerge from Heidegger's previous reflections on language, in which space is already at issue, even if sometimes obscurely so. To think language topologically, then, is not only to allow the relation between language and place to emerge but also to attend to the very spatiality of language itself—a spatiality that is nevertheless always bound to place.

6.

The consideration of space and the spatial illuminates the character of both space and language, as well as their relation to the dimension and to nearness and so also, of course, to place. In addition, however, it brings directly into view the issue of the meaning of the terms that are at work here and so also the nature of the thinking in which Heidegger is engaged. It is commonplace, especially among English-speaking readers, to treat the later Heidegger as having moved away from philosophy toward poetry, and his topological approach to language, as well as the vocabulary and style of that approach, may be thought to confirm this. What is the talk of language as "the house of being" or as "nearness," if it is not poetry or an attempt to engage in a form of poetic expression? Moreover, if such thinking does indeed move in the direction of the poetic, then surely this also means that what is at work here is a mode of thinking that, like poetry itself, operates primarily within the realm of the metaphorical. Many readers of Heidegger's later thinking who see the "poetic" character of that thinking as a barrier to any properly philosophical engagement undoubtedly base their reaction in just such a reading. Thus one can easily conclude, as is so often claimed, that the later Heidegger gives up on philosophy and instead lapses into poetry and mysticism.

Commonplace though this reaction is, it nevertheless represents a serious misreading of the later thought, and indeed of the development of Heidegger's thinking overall. There can be no doubt that Heidegger is critical of traditional philosophy, that he can be said to have abandoned it and so to have proclaimed the end of philosophy. Yet what is abandoned is indeed a traditional mode of philosophizing rather than, necessarily, philosophy as such. It might even be said that, on one possible reading, what Heidegger intends, in his very focus on the end of philosophy as such, is itself a move back toward philosophy—toward that which lies at the origin of philosophy, since the end is also the beginning[43]—rather than a move away from it. The question of philosophy aside, however, it is clear that the poetic shift in Heidegger's thinking is no mere accident, nor is it only stylistic. It instead arises out of the very nature of that thinking and is integral to it. Moreover, it is also not a shift toward a metaphorical mode of expression but rather an attempt to return to a more primordial mode of speaking, one that is attuned to the very place of speaking, of thinking, of being.

In the "Letter on 'Humanism,'" referring back to his early work as well as to ideas in the letter itself, Heidegger writes that "the reference in *Being and Time* (H54) to 'being-in' as 'dwelling' is no mere etymological play. The same reference in the 1936 essay on Hölderlin's word, 'Full of merit, yet poetically, man dwells upon this earth,' is not the adornment of a thinking that rescues itself from science by means of poetry. The talk about the house of being is not the transfer [*Übertragung*] of the image 'house' onto being."[44]

Immediately following this passage, Heidegger adds: "But one day we will, by thinking the essence of being in a way appropriate to its matter, more readily be able to think what 'house' and 'dwelling' are."[45] Heidegger is emphatic that the poetic language at work here is not to be dismissed as mere play or adornment, nor is it to be treated as involving the transfer of an image (as the etymology of the "metaphoric" might be taken to imply). Elsewhere Heidegger explicitly attacks the metaphorical itself. It serves, he says, "as a handy crutch in the interpretation of works of poetry and of artistic production in general . . . [that] . . . exists only within metaphysics," urging us to be wary "that we don't precipitously take the talk of thinking as a listening and a bringing into view to be mere metaphors and thus take them too lightly."[46] Yet although it is quite clear that Heidegger rejects metaphor, it is equally clear that this involves no rejection of poetry. Indeed, Heidegger's rejection of metaphor occurs in just those passages in which the issue of poetic language, and Heidegger's own use of such language, is at the fore. It occurs, one might say, as part of Heidegger's defense of poetry.[47] It would seem that the obvious conclusion to be drawn is that, as Heidegger sees it, poetic language, and so too the language of genuine thinking, is not itself to be construed as based in the metaphoric.[48]

If we take this conclusion seriously, then it has important implications for our reading of the topological in Heidegger.[49] The language of place and of space as well—which means the language of the dimension, nearness, the open, the between, house, dwelling, earth, sky, even of the event—cannot be treated, if it ever was, as mere metaphor (thereby allowing us to effectively set it aside and turn our thinking to something else), whether because the metaphor is seen as philosophically irrelevant (so the metaphor becomes the marker for what we can ignore) or because the metaphor is philosophically essential *as metaphor* (and so in its character as always a carrying across or a pointing beyond). Instead we must attend to place and to space—to dimension, nearness, the open, the between, house, dwelling, earth, sky, the event—as they are in their own character, which is to say, *in their being*. This is the very point that is contained in the remark in the "Letter on 'Humanism'" that "one day we will, by thinking the essence of being in a way appropriate to its matter, more readily be able to think what 'house' and 'dwelling' are."[50] Heidegger's claim here is that it is by thinking *being* that we will come to understand *house* and *dwelling*. This might be thought strange, as if we have to think through being in order to get to the thinking of house and dwelling, except that it simply restates Heidegger's familiar claim that all genuine thinking is a thinking *of being*. This can now be seen to carry with it the refusal of metaphor, since metaphor is construed as something precisely other than this.

Here we see why metaphor and metaphysics are so much bound together—both are forms, perhaps, one might say, the *same* form, of *forgetting*. Not only is metaphor metaphysical, then, but metaphysics is itself metaphorical: it is, in the language of the ontological difference, a crossing over of the ontological difference in which that difference is also effaced; it is a movement away from being toward beings; it is also, in the language of the topological, a movement away from place that is essentially displacing and disorienting. In this latter sense, one might say that in both the metaphor and metaphysics we lose sight of the place in which we nevertheless always remain.

7.

If Heidegger's language, and especially the language of topology, is not to be construed metaphorically and explicitly so, then one might suppose that such language must instead be understood, in some sense, *literally*. The literal is that which is not metaphorical, and what is at issue in, for instance, Heidegger's talk of "house" and "dwelling" is the question of what dwelling and house themselves *are*. This is surely just the question of the literal meaning of the terms at issue here, their first meaning, as it were[51] (though once the notion of the literal is deployed in this manner, the question then arises as to just how the literal itself should be understood—a question that is, however, all too seldom even considered). Such an approach might be taken to involve a significant reversal of the usual understanding of the idea of the poetic: rather than being given over to the metaphoric and the nonliteral, it may well be taken as more properly literal and so more properly "first" than language in any of its other forms (including, for instance, that of the scientific).

Yet it might also be thought that the very notion of the literal is itself problematic in this context (even if it can be applied elsewhere) no less than is the metaphorical. The literal is surely the prosaic, the ordinary, the familiar, and yet the mode of speaking that is at issue here is quite other than prosaic, other than ordinary, other than familiar. The literal is often taken to bring with it a sense of speech as constrained and univocal, as determinate and without ambiguity (which is, one might say, part of what seems to be at issue in the contrast with the metaphoric—the latter being taken as a form of polysemy or equivocity and the former of monosemy or univocity), whereas poetic speaking, the speaking in which Heidegger is engaged, while not lacking in lucidity, surely brings with it an excess that goes beyond any narrow constraint of meaning.[52] Moreover, one might well argue that what is at issue here is a mode of speaking that is the origin for all and any speaking whatsoever, and so comes before any possible distinction between the metaphorical and the literal.[53]

The originary saying of being, which is an event that is given to human beings and to which they are already given over, is indeed neither literal nor metaphorical. Heidegger makes no claims about either metaphoricity or literality in relation to that event. Such speaking is a form of poetic speaking—poetic speaking in its most original form as *poiesis*. But it is the speaking of language, which can be heard in poetry (and indeed in all language) and yet which is not itself spoken by the poet or the thinker. It is the speaking in which language speaks the human, not the language in which the human speaks. Instead, what is at issue in the discussion of metaphor in Heidegger is the manner in which the form of poetic speaking that is indeed undertaken by poet and thinker is itself to be understood. It is the form of speaking exemplified in Hölderlin's poetry, in Heidegger's own thinking, and in any genuine attempt to address the question of being, of language, or of place. It is here, *and only here*, that the issue of metaphoricity arises or even can arise as a question. It cannot be a question for the speaking that belongs to language as such. So, also here, and only here, can any question of literality arise as well.

The distinction between the metaphoric and the literal (and so too the notions themselves) plays no significant role in Heidegger's thinking more broadly. Thus, Heidegger offers no substantive theory of the working of metaphor or of the relation between metaphoricity and literality. This also means that the distinction can be seen as a purely correlative one—what appears as literal in one context may be metaphorical in another (the same is true of the distinction between "dead" and "live" metaphor)—and so concerns two different ways of understanding language, two different interpretative approaches, rather than two substantively different modes of meaning or, indeed, of linguistic being.[54] Moreover, Heidegger's rejection of any metaphorical reading of the poetic does not imply that the poetic is therefore given over to a simple univocity or determinacy. Consequently, if Heidegger's language is to be construed literally rather than metaphorically, then the sense of literality at stake similarly cannot be such as to imply univocity or determinacy either. Here we should understand the sense of literality at issue as one that demands our attentiveness to language itself—understanding the literal in something like its original sense as that which concerns the letter or the word—and so the focus on literality can be seen as a way of remaining true to Heidegger's own insistence, for instance, in "Art and Space," that we must listen *to language*[55] and that we must do so even in our own speaking.

What comes to the fore here is a mode of speaking that is not metaphorical and that yet retains an essential vibrancy—what I have sometimes referred to as an *iridescence*[56]—that belongs to language as such (to language, one might say, as that "most delicate and . . . most suspended vibration"). Such vibrancy is not the same as mere ambiguity, nor does it stand as a mode of equivocity that remains merely within the contrast established by the pairing of equivocity with univocity. In the lectures on Hölderlin's *Remembrance*, Heidegger remarks that "so long as we remain within the language of 'univocity' [*Eindeutigkeit*] and 'equivocity' [*Vieldeutigkeit*] we grasp the word after the standards of 'logic.' But in truth any real word has its hidden and wide spaces of vibration."[57] Clearly, the vibrancy that Heidegger asserts as belonging to every word can itself be viewed as a form of equivocity or polysemy, of *Vieldeutigkeit*. So, this comment does not represent a rejection of the equivocal or polysemous as such. Rather, it can indeed be seen as an assertion of its primacy. Such a reading is confirmed by Heidegger's treatment of *Vieldeutigkeit* elsewhere in the later thinking.[58] Heidegger's rejection of metaphor thus goes hand in hand with his assertion of the essential vibrancy of language.[59] Yet this vibrancy, as is evident from Heidegger's characterization of the event itself, does not belong only to language. It is a vibrancy that belongs to the event and to being, to nearness and the dimension—a vibrancy that belongs to the word *and* to the thing. "It is enough here to consider just this," Heidegger says in the lectures on Hölderlin's *Remembrance*, "'things themselves,' before any so-called 'symbols,' are already poetized."[60] This is why the metaphorical has no role here and also why we may decide to draw on a certain conception of the literal[61]—because poetry is already given in the thing itself, as it is given in the event, in being, in the original and originary saying of language by which the thing is called forth, by which it is let into the open, by which it is placed.[62]

8.

Heidegger's rejection of metaphor might also appear to involve the rejection of the image. Certainly, image and metaphor are themselves often viewed as belonging together.[63] Yet there is surely a sense in which the image extends more widely than the metaphor alone. So when Heidegger presents us with the phrase *the house of being*, even if he does not present us with a metaphor, what he seems to offer is an image, even if the nature and status of that image can be put in question. In the brief passage quoted near the beginning of this discussion, Bachelard speaks of the "house image," and his own investigation of the house is framed within an inquiry into poetry and the poetic image—poetry being essentially concerned with the image.[64] The relation between metaphor and image (and that between image and poetry) is thus one that remains to be clarified.

It may be thought, however, that the matter is clear enough already. In the "Letter on 'Humanism,'" for instance, Heidegger denies that there is any transfer of the house image onto being.[65] In the *Ister* lectures he insists that "the rivers in Hölderlin's poetry are . . . in no way symbolic images that are merely more difficult to interpret in terms of degree" since "if that were the case, they would still remain essentially 'symbolic images.' Yet this is precisely what they are not."[66] Similarly, in the lectures on Hölderlin's *Remembrance*, Heidegger comments that "the masterkey of all poetics, the doctrine of image and metaphor, in the realm of Hölderlin's hymnal poetry, opens not a single door and brings us in no way into the open."[67] It would be easy to suppose that Heidegger does indeed treat the metaphor and the image together, rejecting both. Yet the passages like these, in which Heidegger is critical of images and the language of images (which is what we might suppose poetic language to consist in), typically involve the image only under a particular construal. So, in the *Ister* passage, it is the *symbolic* image that is rejected; in the *Remembrance* discussion, it is the image as tied to metaphor but also, once again, to *symbol* (and so to the idea of that which refers to something else, namely, a world beyond or behind—*Hinterwelten*);[68] in the "Letter on 'Humanism'" it is the *transfer* of the image (which may be thought already to be implied in the idea of the symbolic).

What is at issue here, so far as the image is concerned, is thus the image as tied to a movement beyond and away from the thing and so to the image construed *as symbolic*. It is thus that in the *Remembrance* lectures Heidegger concludes his discussion of image, symbol, and metaphor with the remark already quoted above, that "it is enough here to consider just this: 'things themselves,' before any so-called 'symbols,' are already poetized."[69] What then, of the image construed, not as symbol, but *as* thing or as belonging *with* the thing? The association of the poetic with the image ought to provoke a question concerning the image in the poetic, and in fact, Heidegger himself raises such a question, doing so in a way that does not imply the rejection of the image as such. In "The Nature of Language" he asks: "What, really, does 'figurative talk' [*bildliche Redewiese*] mean? We are quick to give the answer here, never giving it a thought that we cannot claim to have a reliable formulation so long as it remains unclear what is talk and what is imagery [*was Rede ist und was Bild*], and in what way language speaks in images, if indeed language does speak so at all."[70]

The figurative, which in the German is quite explicitly "of the image" (*bildlich*), or, as we might say, "imagistic," is itself usually taken to stand in contrast to the literal. But here that contrast also appears to be questionable—at least inasmuch as figurative talk is indeed imagistic and inasmuch as it remains unclear to what extent the image is indeed distinct from the symbol or may instead be said to belong with the thing. In "Poetically Man Dwells," Heidegger takes up the idea of the image, not as something symbolic or as transferred, but as something connected to the very possibility of appearing—appearing as the coming into the realm of the visible:

> Our current name for the sight and appearance of something is "image." The nature of the image is to let something be seen. By contrast, copies and imitations are already mere variations on the genuine image which, as a sight or spectacle, lets the invisible be seen and so imagines the invisible in something alien to it. Because poetry takes that mysterious measure, to wit, in the face of the sky, therefore, it speaks in "images." This is why poetic images are imaginings in a distinctive sense: not mere fancies and illusions but imaginings that are visible inclusions of the alien in the sight of the familiar. The poetic saying of images gathers the brightness and sound of the heavenly appearances into one with the darkness and silence of what is alien. By such sights the god surprises us. In this strangeness, he proclaims his unfaltering nearness.[71]

Poetry, Heidegger says, speaks *in images*, but presumably this does not mean that it necessarily speaks *in metaphors*. The image and the metaphor appear, on this account, to be distinct. The metaphorical is figurative, but the figurative is not always metaphorical, nor is it straightforwardly to be opposed to the literal. If one conceived of the metaphor differently—not as essentially a transfer or symbol but as itself an image understood as a genuine appearance—then the way would be open for a rethinking of the connection between the metaphorical and the figurative, between metaphor and poetry, and between metaphor and thinking.[72] Whether or not one can argue that such a possibility is implicit in Heidegger's approach,[73] it is nevertheless not the path Heidegger himself adopts. Metaphor is thus rejected, but the image as distinct from the symbol and the character of the poetic as oriented to such images seem to be affirmed.

The discussion of the image, then, while it may initially seem like something of a detour, actually turns us back toward what is central. Indeed, one might argue that the entire mode of thinking that is instantiated in Heidegger's later work is essentially oriented to the image—even in that it occurs *in images.*[74] Yet this focus on the image means something very specific: it is a mode of *seeing* that remains with things, allows things to appear, allows them to come into the open. The image that is at issue here is thus not the image as representation, not the image as symbol, not the image as it might be thought to operate in the metaphor understood as a form of transference, not the image as contrasted with that which is literal. Instead the image itself gathers, and if we take note of the way such gathering can be said to house and to place, perhaps we might even say that the image can be a home *for thinking.* Something of this is surely at work in Bachelard's thinking. For Bachelard, the investigation of the house is itself an investigation of the image, and in his work the image itself houses as much as does the house itself. Moreover, for Bachelard the image has nothing of the character of the metaphoric as the latter notion appears in Heidegger. Instead Bachelard claims that, in the engagement with poetry, we "are asked to consider an image not as an object and even less as the substitute for an object, but to seize its specific reality."[75] Moreover, it is precisely in virtue of its relation to the image that Bachelard declares poetry to be the origin of language.[76] The image possesses a dynamic and active character; it "reverberates"— like that which Heidegger attributes to language—and it is through the sonority of the image that the poet is said to speak "on the threshold of being."[77]

Heidegger says that poetry speaks in images "because poetry takes that mysterious measure, to wit, in the face of the sky." The taking of measure is, as we have already seen, directly tied to the dimension, to the opening of the Fourfold. It is a spacing and a placing—or, perhaps better, an entering into that spacing and placing, a gathering and a saying. The taking of measure does not address itself to what lies beyond, even though it does gather what is alien as well as what is familiar. But the place of this gathering is the very place of our own being as well as of the things that are gathered around us and in which the Fourfold is itself gathered. The character of Heidegger's thinking, of poetic thinking, as a thinking in images thus also returns us to the character of that thinking as a thinking of place. It is thus that the poetry that thinks can indeed be said to be the saying of the place of being, to be, in truth, the topology of being.

9.

Gadamer draws attention to the way in which Heidegger pushed against the constraints of traditional philosophical language in trying to find a vocabulary adequate to the direction in which his thinking was headed. Gadamer also draws attention to Hölderlin as playing a crucial role in the attempt to find such a vocabulary. Referring to the essays contained in his book *Heidegger's Ways*, Gadamer remarks that there he tried "to make it clear that the use of language in the later Heidegger does not represent a drifting off into poetry, but rather is situated completely in tune with the thinking which led him into a whole new line of questioning."[78] Here, Gadamer does not attempt to deny the poetic character of the later thinking but rather to argue against its treatment as merely a contingent affectation and to emphasize instead its character as a direct and necessary outcome of the radicalization of Heidegger's thinking in the period after *Being and Time*. The inquiry undertaken here has aimed to show that this radicalization is directly bound up with the turn toward topology—toward the saying of the place of being.

The turn toward place not only requires a different use of language—one that both draws upon and converges with the poetic—but also brings language itself directly into question. To think the being of language is to think the being of place. Thus saying *is placing* just as placing itself *is saying*. It is the necessity and intimacy of this relation that forces thinking toward poetic saying, and it does so, not because poetry involves some rhapsodic movement beyond, but precisely because it remains *here*, with things, in the very openness of the world: "Poetry does not fly above and surmount the earth in order to escape it and hover over it. Poetry is what first brings man onto the earth, making him belong to it, and thus brings him into dwelling."[79] Poetry, one might say, has its own being in the saying of the place of being, both in the saying and in the saying that responds to that saying. It is thus no surprise that the thinking of place has so often been concentrated among poets. We need not look only to Hölderlin in this regard. In English, in fact, it might seem as if the thinking of place has been the almost exclusive preserve of poets, of whom John Clare and William Wordsworth are only two of the most well-known examples.[80] Poetry is place-disclosing, and not only of particular places but of place itself and so of our own place, which is the place of being.

Yet what is also disclosed in poetry is language—poetry is indeed that which first makes language possible[81]—and so in poetry, the question of place and the question of language are shown as belonging together. The region of their belonging is topology. What poetry both reveals and instantiates is the nature of language *and* the nature of language *in its belonging to such a topology*. Significantly, however, and in contrast to the language to which philosophy is often taken to aspire, the language at issue here is not the language of completion or finality. Poetry exhibits no such completion, nor can it ever properly aspire to it. This might already be thought to follow from its inevitable polysemy—its iridescence and the iridescence of things, as explored above—but it does not follow from this alone. Because poetry is *a saying*, it is irreducible simply to *something said*. As such, it does not consist in something that, in being said, is thereby completed or finalized and so set behind us. The saying of the place of being that is "the poetry that thinks" is, as saying, something toward which we are constantly turned, something that always remains *before us*. Here we remain always on the way, just as we remain always on the way to language (the two ways are, in fact, one). What this means, however, is that the difficulty of language that Gadamer identifies as leading Heidegger toward the language of poetry and into the engagement with Hölderlin is not a difficulty that poetry, or Hölderlin, could ever enable Heidegger to overcome. The difficulty is one that belongs to language as such.

As language is the house of being, so language is itself the place of being, and thus the topology of being, which is the saying of the place of being, is also the saying of language. Moreover, saying and placing here appear as the same. One may say that this is partly what is captured in Heidegger's use of the term *Erörterung*, which can now be understood as precisely the placing that occurs in and through language, in and through which language is itself placed (exemplified in Heidegger's approach in "Language in the Poem," in which *Erörterung* is directly thematized).[82] In being on the way to language, we are also, therefore, on the way to the place that language is, which is to say that we are on the way *to place*. Indeed, in being on the way, we already find ourselves given over to place, for to be on the way is already to be turned toward place. And, more than this, to be turned toward place, even to be placed, is itself to be on the way. Heidegger comments that "the place, the gathering power, gathers in and preserves all it has gathered, not like an encapsulating shell, but rather by penetrating with its light all it has gathered, and only thus releasing it into its own nature."[83] Placing—place itself—is not some simple "remaining within" that holds what is gathered in an already determined locatedness. Instead, it is a gathering and a turning; it is a constant movement toward rather than a final coming to rest. The difficulty of language that leads Heidegger toward poetry is thus not a difficulty that belongs to language alone but rather a difficulty that belongs to language as placing, a difficulty that belongs *to place*. As such, however, it is not a difficulty to be overcome. Instead it is a difficulty that marks the continuing questionability of language and of place. It is this questionability that is opened up in the thinking of poetry and to which poetic thinking also responds. In responding, such thinking directs attention to its own place—to the place of saying and the saying of place—at the same time as it also heeds that place and the saying that belongs to it.

Notes

1. The hermeneutical character of the early thinking is most strongly present in the 1923 lectures collected in *Ontology: The Hermeneutics of Facticity*, and although the hermeneutical

is also present in *Being and Time*, it is less directly thematized in the later work, which has, in addition, a more strongly analytical orientation.

2. See Heidegger, "Dialogue on Language," 12.

3. On the topological character of Heidegger's thinking as a whole, see Malpas, *Heidegger's Topology*.

4. For more on their relation, see my discussion in Malpas, "Place and Situation"; see also Malpas, "Beginning of Understanding."

5. See Elden, "Heidegger's Hölderlin." Heidegger's increasing engagement with Hölderlin in the 1930s is undoubtedly tied to his disengagement from Nazism, but at the same time, it involves him in attempts to rethink terms that were also at issue in that engagement—including the idea of the "German" and of Germany. It is only as the war recedes in the late 1940s that Heidegger's thinking begins to grapple more directly and explicitly with topological themes, which had already emerged as explicit in the 1930s but which were often still addressed, at the earlier stage, in terms that invoked the nation, the people, and their role within a certain form of the history of being.

6. Heidegger, "Letter on 'Humanism,'" 239.

7. See Heidegger, "Letter on 'Humanism,'" 257–58.

8. Heidegger lectured on Hölderlin's "The Rhine" and "Germania" in 1934 and 1935 (Heidegger, *Hölderlins Hymnen "Germanien" und "Der Rhein"*). "Hölderlin and the Essence of Poetry," which first appeared in 1936, is derived from these lectures. In 1939 Heidegger presented what later appeared as the essay on Hölderlin's "As When on Holiday" (Heidegger, "As When on Holiday"). In 1941 and 1942, he lectured on Hölderlin's "Remembrance" (Heidegger, *Hölderlin's Hymne "Andenken"*), with an essay derived from this lecture appearing in 1943. In 1942 and 1943, he lectured on Hölderlin's "The Ister" (Heidegger, *Hölderlin's Hymn "The Ister"*). And in 1943 he gave a speech in Freiburg on Hölderlin's "Homecoming/To Kindred Ones" to mark the centenary of Hölderlin's death (Heidegger, "Homecoming/To Kindred Ones"). Heidegger was, of course, familiar with Hölderlin long before the lectures of the 1930s, having been an avid reader of the poet in his school days (see Heidegger, *Frühe Schriften*, 57–59) and having found a renewed enthusiasm for him during his period of military service in the last years of the First World War.

9. A number of the essays from *Vorträge und Aufsätze* also testify to Heidegger's ongoing engagement with Hölderlin; especially notable in this regard is "Poetically Man Dwells," in which the idea of "the house of being" is taken up in slightly different terms from those at work in the "Letter on 'Humanism.'" Hölderlin is also the focus of Heidegger's thinking in "Hölderlin's Heaven and Earth," presented in 1959, and "The Poem," from 1968.

10. Bachelard, *Poetics of Space*, xxxii.

11. Heidegger, "Letter on 'Humanism,'" 272.

12. Heidegger, "Letter on 'Humanism,'" 272.

13. The line alluded to here was first composed in 1947 and appears in Heidegger, "The Thinker as Poet," 12: "Poetry that thinks is in truth the topology of Being." The phrase "topology of being," which is here understood as the saying of the place of being, also appears in "Seminar in Le Thor 1969," 41, at which point reference is also made back to "The Thinker as Poet" and to the short essay (from the same year as the seminar), "Art and Space."

14. See Heidegger, *Being and Time*, especially §§ 19–21.

15. Unconcealment is not some abstract revealing that belongs nowhere in particular but is always itself placed. Indeed, the play of concealing and unconcealing belongs essentially to place; it is, one might say, the play of place itself.

16. The event is to be understood not merely as a temporal notion but as itself properly topological, as is evident in the discussion below. Joseph Fell describes the event as "the original understanding of place, clearing, abode, home, whole, or totality, worlded 'earth,' ground—all of which mean fundamentally the same" (Fell, *Heidegger and Sartre*, 204). The same is also true, I would argue, of the notion of the "moment" (das *Augenblick*), in *Being and Time*, of which the event can be seen as a development, and of the notion of the *kairos* (the "right" moment, in the sense of an "opening"—in Greek contrasted with *chronos*) that to some extent underpins both. One of the more general shifts in Heidegger's thinking (a shift that is essentially an explication of something already present in his thought) is toward an understanding of the topological character even of temporality itself. For more on the relation between *topos* and the idea of the moment as well as between *topos* and time, see Malpas, "Arendt and the Place of Thinking."

17. Heidegger, "Hölderlin and the Essence of Poetry," 56.

18. Heidegger, "Poetically Man Dwells," 214. The character of language as beckoning is taken up in more detail in Malpas, "Beckoning of Language."

19. In *Heidegger's Topology*, I summarily characterize the event as the "disclosive happening of belonging" as a way of drawing together the notions of appropriating (gathering/belonging), happening, and revealing/disclosing that all seem to be involved here—see Malpas, *Heidegger's Topology*, 217–18.

20. Heidegger, *Identity and Difference*, 37–38. Translation modified. The original translation by Joan Stambaugh has "appropriation" (or less often "event of appropriation"), rather than "event" for *Ereignis* (e.g., "to think appropriation as the event of appropriation") and instead of "thinking receives the materials" (where "materials" translates *Bauzeug*), Stambaugh has "thinking receives the tools" (*Bauzeug*, *Bau*, and *bauen* all figure in the original passage, although preserving this in the English translation is difficult, and neither Stambaugh's nor the modified translation given here attempts to do this).

21. Heidegger, "Letter on 'Humanism,'" 254.

22. Heidegger, "Poetically Man Dwells," 220.

23. Heidegger, "Poetically Man Dwells," 221.

24. Underlying both the English *dimension* and the German *Dimension* is the Latin *dimensio* ("measurement"), which in turn derives from *dimetiri* ("to measure out"), and so from *metiri* ("to measure"). The connection Heidegger makes here between dimension and measure is thus rooted in the terms themselves.

25. Heidegger, "Poetically Man Dwells," 227. The "building" at issue here is the same that is at issue in "Building Dwelling Thinking," but here it is revealed as the taking of measure. It is worth noting that in the "Letter on 'Humanism,'" building also appears, although there it is thinking that "builds upon the house of being" (Heidegger, "Letter on 'Humanism,'" 272).

26. Heidegger, "Nature of Language," 107.

27. Heidegger, "Hebel—Friend of the House," 100–101.

28. One might argue that this is indeed the very essence of spatiality, and it is largely what leads Günter Figal to argue for the spatial (or a mode of the spatial—what Figal calls *hermeneutical space*) as central to the possibility of hermeneutical experience (see Figal, *Objectivity*, 121–53). Figal, however, sees language as a dimension of this space (along with two other dimensions, which he names freedom and time—see *Objectivity*, 155ff.), whereas on this account, spatiality, or perhaps better, dimensionality (which, as I argue here, is itself directly tied to relationality), emerges as belonging together with language. Additionally, one might argue that inasmuch as dimensionality is both active and open, so it is itself also

closely bound to a mode of temporality and freedom, although not in the sense that the latter two are dimensions of the former.

29. Thus, in "A Dialogue on Language," Heidegger talks of the "boundary of the boundless." See Heidegger, "Dialogue on Language," 41; see also my discussion in Malpas, "Beckoning of Language."

30. Inasmuch as relation encompasses difference, so one might argue that in language is also found the difference of all differences, including even the ontological difference. In *Basic Concepts*, 41, Heidegger talks of the ontological difference—the difference between being and beings—as that in which we have "our domain of residence," prefiguring the idea of the "house of being," but in so doing, he also suggests the ontological difference as itself given in and through language. In "Language" (in Heidegger, *Poetry, Language, Thought*, 202–10), Heidegger addresses language in direct connection with difference (here written by Heidegger in hyphenated form as *Unter-Schied*), though in a way that goes beyond the thinking of the ontological difference alone and that draws difference into the same constellation of terms that includes the between and the dimension.

31. This might be thought to mark another point of difference from Figal's account in *Objectivity* (since there he argues that it is objectivity—standing over and apart from—that is basic to the possibility of encounter), except that Figal's notion of objectivity already carries a strong sense of activity within it.

32. Heidegger, "Letter on 'Humanism,'" 254–55.

33. Heidegger, "Poetically Man Dwells," 220.

34. Heidegger, "Letter on 'Humanism,'" 254.

35. Heidegger, "Art and Space," 306.

36. Heidegger, "Letter on 'Humanism,'" 254.

37. Heidegger, "Poetically Man Dwells," 220.

38. Heidegger, "Nature of Language," 106.

39. The date is significant—as is indicated in note 13 above, this is the same year in which Heidegger talks, in the Le Thor Seminar, of his thinking as a "topology of being," and the seminar makes direct reference to this essay in connection with the idea of such a topology.

40. Heidegger, "Art and Space," 307.

41. Heidegger, "Art and Space," 308.

42. "The question arises: Are places [*Orten*] initially and merely the result and consequence of making-space? Or does making-space acquire its peculiarity from the reign of gathering places? If this were the case, we would have to seek the peculiarity of clearing-away in the grounding of locality [*Ortschaft*] and ponder locality as the combined play of places" (Heidegger, "Art and Space," 308).

43. See Heidegger, "End of Philosophy," 57.

44. Heidegger, "Letter on 'Humanism,'" 272. See also Heidegger's comments in *Hölderlin's Hymne "Andenken,"* 39–40, in *Hölderlin's Hymn "The Ister,"* esp. 16–27 and 166, and in "Nature of Language," 100.

45. Heidegger, "Letter on 'Humanism,'" 272.

46. Heidegger, *Principle of Reason*, 48.

47. Joseph Kockelmans writes that "Heidegger's attitude in regard to metaphor is, at first sight at least, very paradoxical. For even though he claims that the language of the thinker cannot be interpreted in such a manner that metaphor would appear to be an important element in philosophical discourse, his later philosophy seems to be metaphorical through and through" (Kockelmans, "Heidegger on Metaphor and Metaphysics," 294).

48. Kockelmans comments that only Derrida seems to have taken this point seriously (in Derrida, "Retrait of Metaphor"). See Kockelmans, "Heidegger on Metaphor and Metaphysics," 306. Although, as I note below, Derrida's own position on the matter is also somewhat equivocal on this point, it nevertheless argues for a retention of some form of metaphoricity in Heidegger's thinking.

49. Jean Greisch argues, though for somewhat different reasons than those at issue here, that the issue of metaphor is directly implicated with the issue of place and, more particularly, with place as it appears in both the event [*Ereignis*] and in "discussion" or "placing" [*Erörterung*] (see especially Heidegger, "Language in the Poem," 159–60) and in the event [*Ereignis*]. See Greisch, "Les mots et les roses." See also Kockelmans's discussion of Greisch's reading in "Heidegger on Metaphor and Metaphysics," 302–6. The notion of "discussion" or "placing" [*Erörterung*] warrants some further comment here. The way Heidegger himself characterizes the notion explicitly draws out the topological implications present in the German. Thus, Heidegger asserts that the preliminary steps in any placing are the directing toward the place and then the heeding of the place (see "Language in the Poem," 159—Heidegger's further characterization here of place [*Ort/Ortschaft*] as *gathering* should also be noted). All of Heidegger's later thinking can be construed as just such a placing: both a directing toward and a heeding of place.

50. Heidegger, "Letter on 'Humanism,'" 272.

51. In this sense, one might also be led to suggest (though perhaps rather polemically) that one of the problems with many readings of Heidegger, early and late, is that *he is not read literally enough*. This is especially true of the topological vocabulary that he so often employs. Thus, we do not take sufficiently seriously the language of place and space as indeed topological and spatial, but instead treat it as if it actually referred to something else. The rub is that this may even be true of some of Heidegger's own readings of that language, at least early on. The tendency to deploy topological and spatial language, and yet to do so in a way that fails to attend to its topological and spatial character, is widespread in the contemporary literature on Heidegger, as well as in philosophy more generally and across many other disciplines and areas of inquiry. Thus, as I have argued elsewhere (see, for instance, Malpas, "Thinking Topographically"), the turn toward space and place that is so frequently cited as a characteristic feature of contemporary thought does not represent a new engagement with space and place as such but rather the deployment of a spatial and topological rhetoric in the service of already existing modes of critique that typically take the social and the political as their primary categories (almost always treating space and place as themselves political or social constructs). What thereby occurs is an obscuring and overlooking of the spatial and the topological in the very proliferation of an apparently spatial and topological language.

52. Derrida seems to take a view of literality that is more or less along these lines, resisting the treatment of Heidegger's language, and especially its key terms, as reducible to something either purely literal or purely metaphorical but nevertheless retaining some sense of metaphoricity in the very withdrawal of metaphor—in its "retrait." Derrida's approach seems partly to derive both from his own defense of metaphor within the discourse of philosophy (as developed in Derrida, "White Mythology") and from his rejection of the notion of that which is "proper to," with which he takes the literal to be at least connected (even if the two notions are not to be identified; see Derrida, "Retrait of Metaphor," 49. He also seems to associate the "literal" and the "proper" with a certain sense of univocity or monosemy, and the metaphoric with the polysemous). Yet as Derrida himself recognizes, some sense of the proper does indeed remain at work in Heidegger's thinking (it is most obviously present in

the notion of the event), even though Derrida contests this very notion (one is tempted to say that he contests its very propriety). Here Derrida's stance on literality and more importantly on the proper, like Heidegger's on metaphor, is itself directly related to a fundamental element within his more general philosophical position and to his critical engagement with Heidegger. What is at issue is the question of being: for Heidegger, the question of being is itself taken up in the question of language (and in the question of the *being of* language), whereas for Derrida it is in the face of the question of language that the question of being (especially inasmuch as this is indeed taken to be a question concerning *the proper*), to a large extent, falls away.

53. To some extent one might argue that this is Kockelmans's view (see Kockelmans, "Heidegger on Metaphor and Metaphysics," 316–17), except that Kockelmans makes no reference to the issue of literality but focuses only on the question of metaphor. It is also a view that can be seen as partly at work (in a slightly different way) in Derrida's reading and especially in his refusal of the notions of literality and propriety.

54. The idea of the metaphorical and the literal as correlative, rather than substantively distinct, seems to me to follow from Donald Davidson's view of metaphor as a particular use of language that always depends upon some prior sense of literality—a view that also involves the denial that there is anything that could be called metaphorical meaning. See Davidson, "What Metaphors Mean." Davidson's insistence on the primacy of literal meaning should not be construed as somehow turning metaphor into merely a secondary notion; rather, it preserves the character of metaphor as itself a distinctive use of language and not as some other domain of meaning within language.

55. Heidegger, "Art and Space," 307. It is such listening that underpins Heidegger's so frequent recourse to etymological consideration in his exploration of key terms and concepts. Attending to the origin of a term and the meanings buried in its history and prior usage is not only a way of freeing up our linguistic and conceptual preconceptions but also a way of bringing to the fore connections that may otherwise remain implicit in the terms and concepts at issue.

56. See Malpas, *Heidegger's Topology*, 37 and 249–50.

57. Heidegger, *Hölderlin's Hymne "Andenken,"* 15.

58. See Young, *Heidegger's Philosophy of Art*, 103–4.

59. Given that the two are connected, and given also that Heidegger sees the covering over of this vibrancy as one of the features of modernity—as part of the "emptying out" of language that is a feature of the current age—one might ask whether modernity is prone to an emptying out of language in the form of a striving for an impossible univocity and also in the form of a concurrent and persistent *metaphorization* (that the two appear together even though they also appear in tension with one another may itself be taken to reflect a deeper contradiction within modernity itself).

60. Heidegger, *Hölderlin's Hymne "Andenken,"* 40.

61. One of the few discussions that directly takes up the idea of literality as such is to be found in Barfield, "The Meaning of Literal." Barfield's approach is very different from that pursued here. Following a line of thinking that can be seen as implicitly deriving from Coleridge, Barfield argues against the view that metaphor arises out of literality (or out of what he calls the "born literal") and for the view that the fundamental relation of human beings to their world is essentially figurative. One might argue that the rethought conception of the literal advanced here, especially when connected with the idea of the

image as developed below (here Bachelard's position is particularly noteworthy), provides an alternative way of arriving at a similar conclusion to Barfield's even though in very different terms.

62. See Heidegger's discussion of Trakl's *A Winter Evening* in Heidegger, *On the Way to Language*, esp. 198–202.

63. This viewpoint seems to be present even in Kockelmans's discussion where the metaphoric and the figurative are treated as more or less the same—see "Heidegger on Metaphor and Metaphysics," esp. 297–98. As we shall see below, however, there is good reason to distinguish these, to treat metaphor as merely one form of figuration, and even to consider the possibility that the figurative and the literal may overlap.

64. See Bachelard, *Poetics of Space*, xi–xxxv.

65. Heidegger, "Letter on 'Humanism,'" 272.

66. Heidegger, *Hölderlin's Hymn "The Ister,"* 16–27 and 166.

67. Heidegger, *Hölderlin's Hymne "Andenken,"* 40.

68. Thus, in the discussion that immediately precedes Heidegger's rejection of the "masterkey of all poetics," he directly connects image, symbol, and the movement away from things: "We are tempted to say that Sun and wind are given as natural signs, and this then means something else: they are symbols. In talking and thinking in this way, we assume that the 'Sun' and 'Wind' are known in themselves. We believe that even earlier nations and peoples first came to know the 'Sun' and 'Moon' and 'Wind,' and then, in addition, used these alleged appearances of Nature as images for some world beyond" (Heidegger, *Hölderlin's Hymne "Andenken,"* 39–40).

69. Heidegger, *Hölderlin's Hymne "Andenken,"* 40.

70. Heidegger, "Nature of Language," 82.

71. Heidegger, "Poetically Man Dwells," 225–26.

72. It is just such a rethought conception of metaphor that is to be found in Davidson's "What Metaphors Mean," in which metaphor is a use of language (and not a type of meaning) directed at the opening up of an image. See also my discussion of the Davidsonian approach to metaphor in connection with Heidegger's thinking of art in Malpas, "Working of Art."

73. Greisch argues that Heidegger implicitly retains a commitment to a rethought conception of metaphor even as he also rejects metaphor (see Greisch, "Les mots et les roses"), although Greisch's account moves in a somewhat different direction than that suggested here.

74. Gadamer says of Heidegger that he was a thinker "who sees" and whose thinking took the form, not of a linear progression of ideas, but of a spatial exploration approaching the same thing from different angles and directions (see Gadamer, "Martin Heidegger—75 Years," 17). For Bachelard, of course, there is a sense in which thinking is itself essentially based in the image—the image, for him, "stems from the logos" (Bachelard, *Poetics of Space*, xix).

75. Bachelard, *Poetics of Space*, xv.

76. See Bachelard, *Poetics of Space*, xvi and xix.

77. Bachelard, *Poetics of Space*, xii.

78. Gadamer, "Reflections on My Philosophical Journey," 46.

79. Heidegger, "Poetically Man Dwells," 216.

80. See Heaney, "A Sense of Place," for an exploration of one mode of topology within English literature. For another such exploration (one that is both more far-reaching and

also attuned to Heidegger), see White, *The Wanderer and His Charts*. Heaney is a focus for some of my discussion in my *Place and Experience*. On White, see Malpas, "'Where Hegel Meets the Chinese Gulls'" (unpublished manuscript; available at https://www.academia.edu /6968611/_Where_Hegel_Meets_the_Chinese_Gulls_), which also discusses some of the themes explored above.

    81. See Heidegger, "Hölderlin and the Essence of Poetry," 60.

    82. The essay has the subtitle "Eine Erörterung von Georg Trakls Gedicht."

    83. Heidegger, "Die Sprache im Gedicht," 37. The passage begins: "Originally the word 'place' [*Ort*] meant the point of a spear [*Spitze des Speers*]. In it everything comes together. The place gathers unto itself, in the highest and in the extreme. Its gathering power penetrates and pervades everything." The translation here differs from that given in *Poetry, Language, Thought*, which compresses the first two sentences, omitting the reference to the spear, to give: "Originally the word 'site' suggests a place in which everything comes together, is concentrated" (see Heidegger, "Language in the Poem," 159–60). It is worth noting the way in which the English translation here itself serves to obscure the thematization of place, exemplifying the more general tendency to ignore or overlook the topological (whether in Heidegger's work or elsewhere).

Bibliography

Bachelard, Gaston. *The Poetics of Space*. Translated by Maria Jolas. Boston: Beacon, 1958.

Barfield, Owen. "The Meaning of Literal." In *The Rediscovery of Meaning and Other Essays*, 33–43. Middletown, CT: Wesleyan University Press, 1977.

Davidson, Donald. "What Metaphors Mean." In *Inquiries into Truth and Interpretation*, 245–64. Oxford: Clarendon, 1994.

Derrida, Jacques. "The Retrait of Metaphor." In *Psyche: Inventions of the Other*, vol. 1, edited by Peggy Kamuf and Elizabeth G. Rottenberg, 48–80. Stanford: Stanford University Press, 2007.

———. "White Mythology: Metaphor in the Text of Philosophy." In *Margins of Philosophy*, 207–72. Translated by Alan Bass. Chicago: University of Chicago Press, 1982.

Elden, Stuart. "Heidegger's Hölderlin and the Importance of Place." *Journal of the British Society for Phenomenology* 30, no. 3 (1999): 258–74.

Fell, Joseph. *Heidegger and Sartre: An Essay on Being and Place*. New York: Columbia University Press, 1979.

Figal, Günter. *Objectivity: The Hermeneutical and Philosophy*. Translated by Theodore D. George, Albany: State University of New York Press, 2000.

Gadamer, Hans-Georg. "Heidegger—75 Years." In *Heidegger's Ways*, 15–28. Albany: State University of New York Press, 1994.

———. "Reflections on My Philosophical Journey." In *The Philosophy of Hans-Georg Gadamer*, edited by Lewis Edwin Hahn, 3–63. Chicago: Open Court, 1997.

Greisch, Jean. "Les mots et les roses: La métaphore chez Martin Heidegger." *Revue des sciences philosophiques et theologiques* 57, no. 3 (1973): 433–55.

Heaney, Seamus. "A Sense of Place." In *Preoccupations, Selected Prose, 1968–1978*, 131–49. London: Faber and Faber, 1980.

Heidegger, Martin. "Art and Space." In *The Heidegger Reader*, edited by Günter Figal, 305–9. Translated by Jerome Veith. Bloomington: Indiana University Press, 2009.

———. "As When on Holiday." In *Elucidations of Hölderlin's Poetry*, 67–100. Translated by Keith Hoeller. Amherst, NY: Humanity Books, 2000.

———. *Basic Concepts*. Translated by Gary E. Aylesworth. Bloomington: Indiana University Press, 1998.

———. *Being and Time*. Translated by John Macquarie and Edward Robinson. New York: Harper and Row, 1962.

———. "Building Dwelling Thinking." In *Poetry, Language, Thought*, 143–62. Translated by Albert Hofstadter. New York: Harper and Row, 1975.

———. "A Dialogue on Language." In *On the Way to Language*, 1–56. Translated by Peter D. Hertz. New York: Harper and Row, 1971.

———. "The End of Philosophy and the Task of Thinking." In *On Time and Being*, 55–73. Translated by Joan Stambaugh. New York: Harper and Row, 1972.

———. *Frühe Schriften*. GA 1. Edited by Friedrich-Wilhelm von Herrmann. Frankfurt: Klostermann, 1978.

———. "Hebel—Friend of the House." *Contemporary German Philosophy* 3 (1983): 89–101. Translated by Bruce V. Foltz and Michael Heim.

———. "Hölderlin and the Essence of Poetry." In *Elucidations of Hölderlin's Poetry*, 51–66. Translated by Keith Hoeller. Amherst, NY: Humanity Books, 2000.

———. "Hölderlin's Heaven and Earth." In *Elucidations of Hölderlin's Poetry*, 175–208. Translated by Keith Hoeller. Amherst, NY: Humanity Books, 2000.

———. *Hölderlin's Hymne "Andenken."* GA 52. Edited by C. Ochtwadt. Frankfurt: Klostermann, 1982.

———. *Hölderlins Hymnen "Germanien" und "Der Rhein."* GA 39. Edited by S. Ziegler. Frankfurt am Main: Klostermann, 1980.

———. *Hölderlin's Hymn "The Ister."* Translated by William McNeill and Julia Davis. Bloomington: Indiana University Press, 1996.

———. "Homecoming/To Kindred Ones." In *Elucidations of Hölderlin's Poetry*, 23–50. Translated by Keith Hoeller. Amherst, NY: Humanity Books, 2000.

———. *Identity and Difference*. Translated by J. Stambaugh. Chicago: University of Chicago Press, 1969.

———. "Language in the Poem." In *On the Way to Language*, 159–98. Translated by Peter D. Hertz. New York: Harper and Row, 1971.

———. "Letter on 'Humanism.'" In *Pathmarks*, edited by William McNeill, 239–76. Translated by Frank A. Capuzzi. Cambridge: Cambridge University Press, 1998.

———. "The Nature of Language." In *On the Way to Language*, 57–100. Translated by Peter D. Hertz. New York: Harper and Row, 1971.

———. "The Poem." In *Elucidations of Hölderlin's Poetry*, 209–20. Translated by Keith Hoeller. Amherst, NY: Humanity Books, 2000.

———. "Poetically Man Dwells." In *Poetry, Language, Thought*, 211–29. Translated by Albert Hofstadter. New York: Harper and Row, 1975.

———. *The Principle of Reason*. Translated by Reginald Lilly. Bloomington: Indiana University Press, 1996.

———. "Seminar in Le Thor 1969." In *Four Seminars*, 35–63. Translated by Andrew Mitchell and Francois Raffoul. Bloomington: Indiana University Press, 2004.

———. "The Thinker as Poet." In *Poetry, Language, Thought*, 1–14. Translated by Albert Hofstadter. New York: Harper and Row, 1975.

———. *Vorträge und Aufsätze*. GA 12. Frankfurt-am-Main: Klostermann, 1985.

Kockelmans, Joseph. "Heidegger on Metaphor and Metaphysics." In *Martin Heidegger: Critical Assessments*, vol. 3, edited by Christopher Macann, 293–320. London: Routledge, 1992.

Malpas, Jeff. "Arendt and the Place of Thinking: Finitude, Time, and *Topos*." In *Philosophy Today*, forthcoming (available at https://www.academia.edu/8325368/_Where_are_we_when_we_think_Hannah_Arendt_and_the_Place_of_Thinking).

———. "The Beckoning of Language." In *Hermeneutic Heidegger*, edited by Ingo Farin and Michael Bowler, 203–21. Evanston: Northwestern University Press, 2016.

———. "The Beginning of Understanding: Event, Place, Truth." In *Consequences of Hermeneutics*, edited by Jeff Malpas and Santiago Zabala, 261–80. Chicago: Northwestern University Press, 2010.

———. *Heidegger's Topology*. Cambridge, MA: MIT Press, 2006.

———. *Place and Experience*. Cambridge: Cambridge University Press, 1999.

———. "Place and Situation." In *The Routledge Companion to Philosophical Hermeneutics*, edited by Jeff Malpas and Hans-Helmuth Gander, 354–66. London: Routledge, 2014.

———. "Thinking Topographically: Place, Space, and Geography." *Il cannocchiale: rivista di studi filosofici* 42, no. 1–2 (2017): 25–54.

———. "'Where Hegel Meets the Chinese Gulls': Place, Word, and World in the Work of Kenneth White." Unpublished manuscript; available at https://www.academia.edu/6968611/_Where_Hegel_Meets_the_Chinese_Gulls_.

———. "The Working of Art." In *Heidegger and the Thinking of Place*, 237–50. Cambridge, MA: MIT Press, 2010.

White, Kenneth. *The Wanderer and His Charts: Exploring the Fields of Vagrant Thought and Vagabond Beauty*. Edinburgh: Polygon, 2010.

Young, Julian. *Heidegger's Philosophy of Art*. Cambridge: Cambridge University Press, 2001.

JEFF MALPAS is Distinguished Professor at the University of Tasmania and Visiting Distinguished Professor at Latrobe University. He is coeditor of *Reading Heidegger's Black Notebooks* and author of *Heidegger's Topology* and *Place and Experience*.

2 Heidegger and Trakl

Language Speaks in the Poet's Poem

Markus Wild

HEIDEGGER'S *ON THE Way to Language* is a collection of six essays arranged in chronological order, running from "Language" (1950) to the final piece, "The Way to Language" (1959). The collection is not an easy read, and it contains one of Heidegger's arguably most difficult texts, namely "The Language in the Poem: A Discussion of Georg Trakl's poetic work" (1952).[1] It is the aim of this chapter to offer a comprehensive account of Heidegger's approach to language and to Trakl's work. There are, however, three features found in the Heidegger literature that stand in the way of a comprehensive account, namely *exegetical internalism, exegetical subsumption,* and *exegetical oppositionalism.* In the first part of this chapter, I will explain what I mean by these three features. In the second part, I will offer an account of Heidegger's approach to language and Trakl's poems as they appear in the first two essays of *On the Way to Language.*

1. Clearing the Path

Some interpreters choose to trace their way to *On the Way to Language* by starting with Heidegger's take on language in *Being and Time.* Only then do they guide us through the writings of the 1930s and the 1940s.[2] This can be called *exegetical internalism,* since the interpretation of the later Heidegger begins with traces of the early Heidegger. I will choose a different and, I think, more promising exegetical approach, which I will call *exegetical externalism.* The basic idea is to locate Heidegger's often startling claims in relation to other discussions while responding to clues and hints contained in Heidegger's text.

It is well known that Hölderlin is incomparably important for Heidegger's thought, and it comes as no surprise that every other poet Heidegger writes about (Homer, Sophocles, Goethe, Novalis, Mörike, Hebel, Stifter, Rilke, George, Benn) is directly or indirectly compared to Hölderlin. However, there is one important exception: Trakl. Although Hölderlin is quoted in virtually all of Heidegger's poetry analyses, in the essays on Trakl, Hölderlin is neither mentioned nor quoted. I take it that Trakl is not measured against Hölderlin because he stands right next to him, on equal grounds, as the following biographical reminiscence suggests: "In those days of expressionism, these realms [*language, poetry, art*] were constantly before me—but even more so, and already since my student days before the First World War, was the poetic work of Hölderlin and Trakl."³ Trakl stands offside; he is standing apart: "All that Georg Trakl's poetry expresses remains centered around and focused on the wandering stranger. He is, and is called, 'he who is apart [*der Abgeschiedene*].'"⁴ In stark contrast to the interpretation of the other poets, Trakl is not read as someone offering statements that concern aspects of art, poetry, and philosophy. Trakl does not represent a link in the steady development of Heidegger's thought on poetry.⁵ We should, therefore, refrain from subsuming Trakl among the other poets. I call this idea *exegetical subsumption*.

Another problem one encounters on the path to Heidegger's later writings is the idea, found in the literature, that Heidegger is opposing some traditional conception of truth, language, poetry, or thinghood in order to replace it. Here is an example: "Arguing *against the traditional understanding of language* (as a means of inner expression, as a human activity, and as representational), Heidegger construes poetic language as an intimate correspondence to this radiant presencing of things."⁶ According to this view, Heidegger argues against the traditional conception of language, which claims that language is an expression of mental states (language as expression), a tool used by human beings or a human activity (language as human practice), and the representation of worldly affairs (language as representation).⁷ I call this stance *exegetical oppositionalism*. But this view amounts to a confusion between distinguishing different views and opposing or overcoming them. It is certainly correct that Heidegger takes the traditional conception to be inadequate for language as such, for language as language. Nevertheless, he thinks that this traditional conception is still *correct*: "No one would dare to declare incorrect, let alone reject as useless, the identification of language as audible utterance of inner emotions, as human activity, as a representation by image and by concept. The view of language thus put forth is correct [*richtig*]."⁸ Therefore, Heidegger does not think that the traditional conception is wrong and does not argue against it. Rather, he thinks that the traditional conception suffers from a serious shortcoming: it prevents us from thinking about language as such.⁹ The problem is not that language does not really display the three features just mentioned (expression, practice, representation). The problem is that we tend to think that this is all there is to language. Thus, if Heidegger writes that the "view of language thus put forth is correct [*richtig*]," he is not opposing this view but is, rather, looking for its deeper significance. A deeper understanding concerns language as such and is captured in the claim that "language speaks." Moreover, oppositional exegesis of Heidegger blocks us from asking pertinent questions concerning the relationship between the expressive, practical, and representational functions of language, on the one hand, and language as such, on the other.[10] I submit that there are three topics in Heidegger's text "Language":

1. What are the metaphysical surface features of human language? Answer: Expression, practice, and representation.
2. What is language *as* language? Answer: Language speaks, and it speaks "as the peal of stillness" (*Die Sprache spricht als das Geläut der Stille*).[11]
3. What is the relation between the second and first questions? How does one get from the second to the first?

If you think that Heidegger argues *against* the traditional conception of language, you cannot take seriously the correctness of the answer to question 1 and you cannot make sense of question 3. Yet question 3 figures quite prominently in Heidegger's text. So it would be preferable to adopt a point of view that makes sense of Heidegger's writing. Let me try to render the structural features even more salient by locating Heidegger's later kind of writing within the tradition of classical rhetoric. Questions 1 and 2 are associated with two distinct levels of linguistic style in Heidegger's writing. Question 1 roughly conforms to the plain style (*genus humile*) and question 2 to the grand style (*genus sublime*). The plain style is suitable for instruction and argumentation; it uses conversational language and makes spare use of tropes. The grand style is an elevated and striking style, appropriate for eminent and important subject matter, and it employs daring metaphors, archaic expressions, and poetic license. The plain style is, of course, the preferred style of philosophical prose. Grand style, on the other hand, is traditionally associated with elegy and tragedy. Philosophers highly critical of traditional metaphysics, however, have a strong leaning toward grand style, as the writings of Nietzsche and Derrida illustrate. The essays in *On the Way to Language* make use of both styles; they are instances of mixed style (*genus mixtum*). When Heidegger switches to the sublime rhetorical mode, the purpose is no longer argumentation and instruction but elevation and transformation. Departing in this way, he makes language come into its own. This elevated play with language has two purposes: first, in it, language speaks for itself, thus illustrating the claim that language speaks; and, second, it aims at a transformation of the meaning of the statements and questions uttered in plain style. The point of this second aim is that the reader is supposed to *hear* the (basically) correct idea that language is expression in a novel way. The ultimate goal is to transform the reader.

The distinction between these two levels of style harbors important consequences for the philosophical interpretation of Heidegger's later writings. The plain-style-assertive parts can and should be evaluated by the norms of clarity and argumentative rigor. The grand-style-evocative parts, however, should be judged by their ability to transform and enrich the plain-style-assertive sentences, by their ability to let us better understand complex linguistic phenomena, such as Trakl's poetry, and by their transformative power.

2. Taking the Path

In the second part, I want to achieve a proper understanding of Heidegger's claim that language speaks. I proceed in three steps. First, I ask what Heidegger means by the claim on the plain-style level. Second, I defend the claim that there is such a thing as hearing language as language and that the poem is the place to look for it. Third, I attempt to come to grips with Heidegger's purpose in his engagement with Trakl's poetry.

Language Speaks

In the first essay, Heidegger famously claims: "Language is: language. Language speaks."[12] At first sight, the claim that language speaks seems to be either pointless (since it states a tautology) or plainly false (since it is human beings that speak languages). Heidegger was, of course, well aware of this fact. Nevertheless, he further sharpened the peculiar nature of his claim by emphasizing that he means the claim in both of the following senses: first, what language does is speaking (language *speaks*), and second, language is the one that speaks (*language* speaks).[13] The second part of the claim does not imply that human beings do not speak. Rather, the point is that language speaks too. Speaking is what language does. Regarding the first part of the claim, however, Heidegger mentions the objection that, according to the ordinary view of language, speech consists in the activation of the organs that produce sound and in the audible expression and communication of minds. There are, thus, two objections against the claim that language speaks: first, there is no speaking without organs for producing sound and audible expression; second, speaking is essentially tied to minds. Since languages have neither organs nor minds, the claim that language speaks seems not so much pointless or wrong as rather meaningless. So, what is Heidegger up to?

According to *exegetical externalism*, it is wise to relate Heidegger's peculiar claim to other discussions by picking up clues in Heidegger's text. I will consider two different clues in *On the Way to Language*:

1. "As against the identification of speech as a merely human performance, others stress that the word of language is of divine origin. According to the opening of the Prologue of the Gospel of St. John, in the beginning the Word was with God."[14]
2. "To say and to speak are not identical. A man may speak, speak endlessly, and all the time says nothing. Another may remain silent, not speak at all and, yet, without speaking, says a great deal."[15]

Before I start, it will be useful to have an idea of what I am arguing for in the pages that follow. Heidegger boldly claims that every great poet writes just one poem. This, I will call "the poet's poem." He also claims that language speaks. However, there is no such thing as a poet's poem in the sense one finds poems in a poet's collected work. In what sense, then, can language speak in the poet's poem? I will, first, argue that, analogous to a special interpretation of divine discourse, the great poet's work is the deputized discourse of the poet's poem. It utters poetic words representing the illocutionary power of the poet's poem. In this sense, the poet's poem speaks without consisting of words or marks. Moreover, one way that we can listen to language speaking is by listening to the poet's poem by way of the actual poems of the poet. And, in grasping the poem, we engage with language as language by abstracting from any implications, intentions, purposes, and special knowledge about some domain, as well as about our general knowledge about persons, the language, and the world we inhabit. In this sense, language speaks in the poet's poem.

Let's start with the first clue. For the sake of argument, assume the existence of a personal deity. A traditional answer explains that God, lacking hands and mouth, cannot literally speak but can do so only in a figurative sense. However, speech act theory allows for a distinction between the locutionary act (uttering words) and the illocutionary act (such as asking, commanding, or promising). In ordinary circumstances the illocutionary act is performed by virtue of a locutionary act. Now, consider a lawyer bringing a charge on behalf of a firm. The lawyer is the mouthpiece that utters the firm's charge. Again, consider the ambassador of the United States issuing a warning against some regime. In this case, it is rather the president, and not the ambassador, who issues the warning. The subject of the locutionary act (performed by the lawyer or the ambassador) is distinct from the subject of the illocutionary act (performed by the firm or the president). One can, thus, *deputize* the locutionary act. Again, if you follow up on someone else's remark by saying, "That goes for me too," you *appropriate* the illocutionary force of the other's utterances without performing the utterance in question. Prophets can be viewed, so to speak, as God's lawyers or ambassadors, and prophetic discourse as deputized divine discourse. Moreover, the scriptures can be understood as divinely appropriated human discourse. In this sense, God speaks without words or marks.[16]

Now we can pick up the second clue. In more mundane circumstances (and closer to Heidegger's text), we readily recognize a difference between uttering and saying. Uttering words is not identical with saying something, because what I say when I say something is not the utterance of sounds, rather it is something that I mean or that the words mean. Moreover, one can say something without uttering words at all. For example, you can say something by pointing, by remaining silent, by displaying facial expressions, by waiting, by breathing, by posting a sign, or by leaving a token. Heidegger's example of a person remaining silent yet saying a great deal without speaking is an example of a person performing an illocutionary act without uttering any words. Once you extend the realm of language to include pointing, remaining silent, displaying facial expressions, waiting, breathing, posting a sign, or leaving a token, you can go several steps further.[17] First, Heidegger claims that listening is part of speaking: since language is understood as a communicative action (speaking), the hearing of and listening to what is said and spoken is part of language. In speech act theory, the perlocutionary act presupposes the listening on the receiver's end. Second, beyond what takes place in the communicative situation, speaking and listening coevolve simultaneously while we are speaking. In other words, there is a constant and constitutive feedback between our speaking and our listening. Finally, there is not only a listening *while* but also a listening *before* we speak. This third step is important in Heidegger's argument since it allows Heidegger to claim that "we do not merely speak the language—we speak by way of it. We can do so solely because we always have already listened to the language. What do we hear there? We hear language speaking."[18]

There are, I think, at least five ways of making sense of Heidegger's third step, namely, in terms of language rules, language as thought, linguistic lapses, language as perception, and language in poetry. I do not claim that Heidegger has these five ways in mind. Rather I simply elaborate on Heidegger's third step by pointing to these five ways of making sense:

1. Think of language as an immensely complex game governed by certain rules. When we say something, we perform a move in a language game. In speech act theory, locutionary and illocutionary acts (in contrast to perlocutionary acts) are conceived as being constitutively related to linguistic and social conventions. Thus, before we speak, we have to be aware of the linguistic and social conventions constitutive of speaking.

2. Regard thought as a kind of inner speech, either simply as inner speaking or as a model for thinking. Much of our thought can be considered as internalized speech. There is, thus, an underlying unity to our thinking, namely, overt language use. In this sense, we hear language speaking before we speak.

3. Heidegger says that we speak in the most proper sense when we fail to speak[19]—for example, when we fail to retrieve a word from memory (tip of the tongue phenomenon), when we are looking for the appropriate expression, when we try to find the right word in a delicate situation, or when we are struggle with the right word. To be sure, in all these cases, we are listening to language.

4. Heidegger holds that language "speaks by saying, this is, by showing."[20] Heidegger claims that language is basically a kind of showing, not in the

sense that language is a collection of signs, but, rather, in the sense that language is the foundation for the very existence of signs. Showing, according to Heidegger, is "reaching into all regions of presences, summoning from them whatever is present to appear and to fade."[21]

5. Language speaks as language when we listen to eminent uses of language, such as we find in poetry. In poetic language, one is aware of the sound of language (including phonetic, phatic, and rhetic acts corresponding to the verbal, syntactic, and semantic aspects), forgotten meanings, ambiguities, puns, rhymes, alliterations, assonances, colors, rhythms, and other patterns. In contrast to ordinary language use, the language in poems has the power to make us listen to language as if words were uttered for the first time, as if we were to learn language again.

Since the last point is evidently connected with Heidegger's engagement with poetry, I want to explore it in more detail. My aim is, still, to understand the idea that language speaks, especially in the poem.

The Poet's Poem

The word *poem* (*Gedicht*) has several meanings in Heidegger's work. Heidegger distinguishes between two meanings of the concept *poem*: the ordinary or general concept refers to the abstract concept of the poem, encompassing the features all poems have in common; the emphatic concept refers to an outstanding poem, a poem that marks our destiny.[22] "Hölderlin's poem," of course, is a poem in the emphatic sense. Since Hölderlin wrote many poems, what does Heidegger mean by "Hölderlin's poem"? There is a third meaning of the concept *poem*. For Heidegger, every great poet writes really only one poem, or more precisely, "Every great poet creates his poetry out of one single poem."[23]

This bold thesis of the "poet's poem" involves three additional claims. First, a *normative* claim: the measure of the greatness of a poet is the extent to which one is able to stay committed to the poem. Second, an *ontological* claim: the poet's poem is neither one excellent piece of work among the poet's creations nor the totality of the creations; rather, the poet's poem "remains unspoken"; it remains silent. The poet's poem is, as it were, the living source of the poetic creation. Or, as Heidegger puts it, the poet's poem is the "gathering power" (*versammelnde Kraft*) of the poetry. Third, a *hermeneutic* claim: it is the task of the reader or interpreter to locate the site or location (*Ort*) of the poet's poem. The site or location of the poet's poem is the place where "everything comes together." On the one hand, the reader has to start from the readings of stanzas, lines, phrases, and words in order to get a grip on the poet's poem (*Erläuterung*). On the other hand, the reader must already have some initial apprehension of the poet's poem in order to grasp the lines (*Erörterung*). The dialogue (*Zwiesprache*) with a poet's poem spans this reciprocity of consideration (*Erörterung*) and elucidation (*Erläuterung*). The site or location of a great poet's poem is a gathering power, a ground-swell that permeates everything the poet creates in the form of the poet's poem.

Before I argue for the bold thesis of the poet's poem, I want to motivate its initial, intuitive plausibility. Heidegger is very explicit about the bold thesis that all great poets create poetry out of one single poem. It seems hard to assess the bold thesis in its general form. Let's start with the more modest form. Does the bold thesis apply to Trakl's poetry? I think it does.

Trakls literary production is usually grouped into four phases or stages. The first phase embraces his more epigonal work until 1909. The creations of the second stage (1909–12) are collected in the volume *Gedichte* (published in 1913), which marks Trakl's breakthrough toward his own personal voice. In his third phase (1913–14), Trakl accomplishes his unmistakably hermetic, hypnotic, and obsessive "Trakl tone."[24] The poetry of this stage is collected in the volume *Sebastian im Traum* (published in 1915, after the author's early death). The final stage commences in early 1914, when the tone and imagery of Trakl's poetry withdraws from the self-enclosed and moves toward the more monumental style—hills transform into mountains, the mockingbird (*Amsel*) into the eagle (*Adler*)—of his final publications in the journal *Der Brenner* in 1914 and 1915. Heidegger is aware of the development of the "Trakl tone" because the bulk of Heidegger's quotes from Trakl's work (roughly 70%) stems from the third period, with occasional reviews and previews to the second and fourth period, respectively.

Trakl's poetry has often been described as hermetic, hypnotic, and obsessive. The obsessive and repetitive quality of his vocabulary and imagery is especially remarkable. Walter Killy observed that "each new sad-beautiful image encountered . . . is somehow already known and already read."[25] Trakl's repetitive deployment of words and similes is one distinguishing mark of the lyric discourse of modernity, namely the establishment of an independent linguistic world carried by an abundance of internal cross-references rather than the transmission of unequivocal meanings. This palpable feature of Trakl's work provides the reader with an important clue as for its interpretation: the poems are not self-contained entities; they are relational creatures that make sense only within the whole web and kaleidoscopic landscape of Trakl's literary world.[26] There are at least two reasons for calling Trakl's literary world a landscape. First, the most frequently encountered words in Trakl's poems refer to elements of a central European landscape, including *hill, forest, cultivated field, tree, water, pond, river, bird*, or *game*.[27] Second, Trakl's poems present what might be called a temporal landscape, since in his literary world the reader simultaneously encounters different temporal stages of the poet's personality. Many poems of the first section of Trakl's second collection, *Sebastian im Traum*, exhibit this kind of personal temporal landscape (most explicitly, the poem "At the Mönchsberg"). Heidegger's essays on Trakl display an accurate awareness of the repetitive character of the vocabulary and imagery in Trakl's work. Heidegger also takes the geographical and temporal landscape of Trakl's world into account.

These important features of Trakl's work motivate the thesis that Trakl creates his poetry out of one single poem.[28] However, does the bold thesis hold for great poetry in general? It seems to be difficult to assess the bold thesis in its general form. Now, think of the poetic work of poets such as Keats, Eliot, Dickinson, Whitman, Stevens, Baudelaire, Rimbaud, Valéry, Benn, Rilke, Celan, and Montale. They all, I submit, possess a certain tone and a voice of their own, which is an indicator of the bold thesis. Moreover, this suggests that the bold thesis indeed does make sense on a more general level. I even think that the normative claim has a certain plausibility. The German nineteenth-century poets Eduard Mörike, C. F. Meyer, and Hugo von Hofmannsthal wrote poems of great power and beauty, demonstrating an individual voice. Unfortunately, they very often fail in realizing their voice in their actual works. I do not, however, see why every great poet has to display the kind of unity of voice one encounters in Whitman, Trakl, or Valéry. Goethe is, I think, a perfectly good counterexample.

Thus, I conclude that the bold thesis has some plausibility. But what is this site or location (*Ort*) of the poet's poem supposed to be? It is the center of a poet's poetical creation, and yet it is a fictional entity, since there is, in a way, no such thing as the poet's poem. Let me elucidate this thought by following the method of exegetical externalism, or, more precisely, applying an analogy with the center of gravity of an ordinary physical object and fictional persons.

In Newtonian physics, a center of gravity (or mass) is the mean location of a distribution of mass in space. When an object is supported at this center, it remains in static equilibrium. Consider a broomstick. It has a center of gravity. If you are balancing it, you can tell quite accurately whether it would start tipping over or remain in equilibrium. Why does the broomstick not fall over? Because your finger is lodged at its center of gravity. This is an explanation, but it is not a causal explanation because the center of gravity has no causal force whatsoever. The center of gravity is neither a material entity, since the only physical property it possesses is spatio-temporal location, nor an abstract object (like numbers or propositions), since abstract objects do not have a precise spatio-temporal location. The center of gravity is, thus, a fictional entity. Yet, in contrast to fictional entities in model explanations, the center of gravity is a real feature of an object, even if it is a fictional entity. One can even change the center of gravity: chip off a little piece from the broomstick and you change the spatio-temporal character of its center.[29]

Now, consider fictional characters in novels. They are persons without spatio-temporal location. Open up *Anna Karenina* and you will learn a lot about the heroine. Some information is explicitly contained in the text, and the reader gathers some information by implication (for example, Tolstoy mentions neither Anna's navel nor her first encounter with a train, but surely she has a navel and has encountered a train for the first time somewhere sometime—and we can be sure that Anna does not have three hands). There are, however, questions about Anna that cannot be answered. Does she have a birthmark on her left shoulder? Has she ever eaten boar stew? Has she ever cut her middle finger? The problem is not that we just do not know; there are no answers to these questions. Indeterminacy is a defining property of fictional characters, and this strongly distinguishes them from spatio-temporal entities, such as physical objects or human beings.

Centers of gravity have only the properties they were endowed with by the physical theory that constitutes them. Fictional characters have only those features that are explicitly mentioned in the novel, implied by the novel's plot, or implicated by our special knowledge of the writer's context (Anna never took a plane to Italy) or our general background knowledge about persons, language, and the world we inhabit (Anna never ate fire). I want to suggest that Heidegger's notion of the poet's one single poem can be understood along the lines just elaborated. It is a fictional entity that constitutes, as it were, the center of gravity (the gathering site) of a great poet's creation. Despite its being a fictional entity, a creature of our mind, it possesses perfectly real features, features one can read from the poet's written work. Just as in the case of fictional characters, the poet's poem does not have a spatio-temporal location. In stark contrast to fictional characters (and this is the most important point), in locating the poet's poem, the reader can only rely on the written word of the poet. Propositions implied by the poem's lines and stanzas or implied by our special knowledge of the writer's context or by our general background knowledge about persons, language, and world do not count.

This important feature guides Heidegger's interpretation of poetry, especially Trakl's work. The fact that one can only rely on what is said in the poet's poem for the purpose of locating (*Erörterung*) the site (*Ort*) of the poet's poem is expressed in Heidegger's assertion that "what is spoken purely is the poem." The poet's poem is spoken purely because all one can rely on are the poet's words and images. Heidegger explains: "What is spoken purely is that in which the completion of the speaking that is proper, to what is spoken is, in its turn, an original."[30] What is this supposed to mean? In everyday situations, in the sciences, and in novels, what is spoken is always already involved in a huge net of implications, intentions, purposes, special knowledge about a domain, and general knowledge about persons, language, and the world we inhabit. In contrast, what is purely spoken is spoken just as if it were said for the first time, as if we were learning language again, as if we could engage with language in abstraction from the whole net of implications, intentions, purposes, and special and general knowledge. When we abstract from implications, intentions, purposes, special knowledge about a domain, and general knowledge about persons, language, and the world we inhabit, we encounter the speaking as language. Thus, language speaks when it speaks purely. And, according to Heidegger, we encounter language as language in poetry.[31]

Now some strands of my argument can be pulled together. I started out this discussion by looking at two particular clues in *On the Way to Language*: "As against the identification of speech as a merely human performance, others stress that the word of language is of divine origin" and "to say and to speak are not identical."[32] Moreover, I noted that there are two objections against Heidegger's slogan "language speaks." First, there is no speaking without organs for producing sound and audible expression. Second, speaking is essentially tied to minds. Since languages have neither organs nor minds, the claim that language speaks seems not so much pointless or wrong as meaningless. I think I have given sense to the meaning that language speaks (and especially so in poetry). However, every argument, example, and analogy I have employed so far in order to make sense of this claim seems to presuppose some sort of mind involved in speaking—in the case of God, it is the divine mind; in the case of Anna Karenina, Tolstoy's mind; in the case of the poet's poem, Trakl's mind.

The Emphatic Reader and the Apartness of the Poet's Poem

Now, what shall we do with the claim that *language* speaks? Or more precisely, what shall we do with the claim that language speaks in the speaking of the great poet's poem? Again, the logical possibility we encountered in the case of divine speech is useful. On the one hand, prophetic discourse is *deputized* divine discourse; on the other hand, the scriptures are divinely *appropriated* human discourse. Our example for appropriation was the following: if you follow up on a remark by someone else by uttering, "That goes for me too," you *appropriate* the illocutionary force of the other's utterances without performing the utterance in question.

I would like to suggest that the speaking of language in the speaking of a great poet's poem is discourse appropriated by the reader. If you follow up the work of a poet by uttering, "That goes for me too," you appropriate the power (the illocutionary force) of the poet's words without performing them. What the reader performs is the poet's one single poem. Reading the work of a great poet is, according to the bold thesis, locating the poet's one single poem. This does not mean that the poet's poem is in the mind of the reader. Remember the example of the center of gravity: despite its being a fictional entity, a creature of our minds, a center of gravity possesses perfectly real features, features you can read from the physical properties of an object. And the same holds for the poet's poem: despite its being a fictional entity, it possesses perfectly real features, features you can read from the poet's written work.

Thus, if the great poet's work is the deputized discourse of the poet's poem and if the poet's poem is the reader's appropriation of the poet's poem, who is speaking, after all? Heidegger calls it here *"Zwiesprache,"* discourse, or literally "double-speaking." As we have seen, the dialogue (*Zwiesprache*) with a poet's poem spans the reciprocity of consideration (*Erörterung*) and elucidation (*Erläuterung*), and within this frame of dialogue, it is not clear who is the subject performing the poet's poem. It thus seems natural to maintain that, in this case, language itself speaks, just as in the saying "one word leads to another" (*ein Wort gab das andere*).[33]

There is, thus, a certain insistence that the reader is central to Heidegger's understanding of poetry. The idea that language speaks in the poem only makes sense if we take language to speak in the speaking of a great poet's poem as discourse appropriated by the reader. In a way, readers let the poem of a great poet become their own voice. I think that Hannah Arendt has best understood this aspect of Heidegger's approach to poetry. In 1953, Arendt set out (in a letter dated July 15, 1953) to defend Heidegger's interpretation of Trakl against criticisms by Hugo Friedrich. What might appear to Friedrich (and numerous other philologists) as "doing violence" to the text is, in reality, comparable to the contortions one finds in paintings by Cézanne and Picasso. According to Arendt, Heidegger places himself at the very center of the work in order to elucidate it in an animated speech. Heidegger is thus able to recognize the inherent space of what cannot be said, which is distinct in each great work and which gives rise to the work itself as well as its internal structure. Where Friedrich seems to detect violence, Arendt sees vitality. Nevertheless, she surmises that there is a danger that the interpreter may be rendered more significant than what is to be interpreted and that this might indeed have happened in Heidegger's exploration of Trakl. Arendt's notion that Heidegger places himself at the very core of Trakl's poetry in order to develop his poems through expressive language appears to me, therefore, to be a promising way forward.[34]

We might envisage the reading of great poets to offer us "life's second chance."[35] When we grow up and integrate into our social environment, we acquire habits of seeing, speaking, and judging. In other words, we acquire a second nature. That second nature is shaped by habituation, education, and learning. Acquiring a character, thus, requires that one, for example, develop dispositions based on habits. The particular nature of these dispositions will in turn depend on a specific cultural context as well as on certain hopes one projects into the future. Indeed, it is part of our very nature that we acquire this second nature.

Not all, though, may be content with the particular shape of their second nature. They discover reading, for example, and then might gradually turn into *emphatic* readers. Reading becomes a way of being socialized a second time around, with assistance by a poet's linguistic world and the solidarity and community with the literary characters and figures of speech as well as with the creators and specialists of this world of language. One might call such individuals the inhabitants of a linguistic world. The emphatic reader comes to inhabit a world of language and poetry. Such a reader seeks to reform and replace the influence of parents and teachers, education and personal context, and language and time. In short, reading emphatically creates a second chance to develop one's second nature.

Once we feel personally touched by this linguistic world, we seek to understand why and how this happens. We read our way deeper into the linguistic world and get to know more about who created it. Gradually, we come to see things through the lens of this world, with the eyes of the poet. As soon as we have made the poet's world of language our own, we can carry it with us. We start to describe the smaller and larger events that happen around us in the terms of this world. Some of the descriptions will help us, while others repel us; some hit a right note, and others miss their target. Most of all, we start discovering our own environment and ourselves through these descriptions. We might indeed recognize new things or familiar ones in a new light. It is possible that what we see through these descriptions will not please us, and in the best possible scenario, these descriptions will then transform us. If we are careful enough, we will also grasp the place where the poet and the work originate and which gives rise to its particular character. We come to locate ourselves in this place and literarily undertake to become the poet.

We find the "unsaid of what is said," namely, the poet's poem of which Heidegger speaks, the moment we gather in that "secret site" where we can describe ourselves through the linguistic world. That which remains unsaid in what is said remains so simply as long as the emphatic reader has not yet rendered the linguistic world of the poet one's own. The has never uttered (to the self or to others) what the poet speaks of. Sometimes we say about a verse, "Though it speaks to me, I do not understand it." Wittgenstein expressed this sentiment about Trakl. Yet, it can only speak to us if what *we* do not know before we do know *it* has already taken hold of us. Sometimes we also say, "It resonates with something in me." Possibly, we dislike what has been touched in us and what we discover among the descriptions the poet leaves to our disposal. We surrender the linguistic world and shut ourselves out. In the ideal case, however, these descriptions transform us. Then we resonate with what speaks to us.

Heidegger certainly resonates with what he takes to be the central feature of Trakl's poem. As I have already mentioned at the beginning, the site of Trakl's poem, the source of his creation, is "apartness" (*Abgeschiedenheit*).[36] Now, I want to change from a plain-style explanation of Heidegger's basic claims in *On the Way to Language* to the grand-style paraphrase of Heidegger's account of the site of Trakl's poem. The word *apartness* is taken from the last poem in Trakl's collection *Sebastian im Traum*: "Song of the departed" or "Song of he who stands apart" (*Gesang des Abgeschiedenen*). According to the normative claim mentioned above, the more Trakl speaks of our apartness, the more profound the quality of his work; according to the ontological claim, all of Trakl's poems belong to the unspoken, silent poem that trades on apartness; and according to the hermeneutical claim, any elucidation of Trakl's poetical lines should relate to apartness. Heidegger starts his reading of Trakl's poem with the sentiment, "Something strange is the soul on the earth" (*Es ist die Seele ein Fremdes auf Erden*). Against the interpretation of the Brenner circle, Heidegger refuses to read *soul* in a Christian or Platonic fashion. In other words, he does not think that the soul is a stranger on Earth because the soul is not of the material or mundane realm. This reading strikes me as entirely correct. This is not to deny Trakl's repeated reference to Christian vocabulary and imagery. The soul is not accidentally a stranger on Earth. The soul is a stranger essentially, an errant, a wanderer on Earth, or so Heidegger claims. The soul looks for a site or location in order to dwell on Earth. For Heidegger, apartness in Trakl's poetry is closely linked to spirit, since "apartness is active as spirit" and "apartness itself is the spirit."[37] Trakl's spirit, or so Heidegger argues, is not something rational or intellectual or spiritual, in the religious sense, but is, rather, associated with the image of the flame: "Spirit is flame."[38] The spirit as flame is both a gentle and a destructive force; it is "both gentleness and destructiveness."[39] The spirit in this sense is the driving force of the soul: "The spirit chases, drives the soul to get underway to where it leads the way."[40] By the light of the spirit (flame "glows and shines"),[41] the soul produces a vision of its place on Earth. This is, as the line "Something strange is the soul on the earth" says, the place of an errant, of a wanderer. Having no place stands, of course, for apartness. The soul as an errant embodies both the one standing apart (since it is a stranger) and the one departing (since it is a wanderer). This "flaming vision" that drives the soul "is pain"—not pain as a sensible, bodily state, but the pain of being apart or departed. Apartness equals apartness from the earth as it is represented in the central European landscape evoked in Trakl's poetry. Apartness sums up apartness from one's own past (childhood), which is present as the temporal landscape in Trakl's work. Finally, apartness amounts to being apart from others, who are represented in the characters of the sister and the brother. Pain is thus "the animator" of the soul's strangeness on earth. As soon as the soul starts dwelling on earth, pain is located. This is the reason that the most important line of the poem entitled "A Winter Evening" (the poem Heidegger interprets in the opening essay of *On the Way to Language*) runs: "Pain has turned the threshold to stone."

As we have seen above, some of the motives and words upon which Trakl obsessively dwells (such as soul, spirit, spiritual, flame, pain) flow together in the idea of apartness. But it is not clear whether Heidegger holds that all great poetry is located in apartness or whether this marks only the site of certain poets' poems. I think that, just as in the case of the bold thesis, Heidegger wants to claim that apartness is the true site of every great poem and, yet, that the poets will articulate apartness in different ways. Just as in the case of the bold thesis, however, this might be true for some great poets, even if it does not seem to me that it needs to be true for all great poets (again, Goethe comes to mind). Rather, Heidegger's claim has to be that those poets who create their work out of one single poem develop different articulations of apartness. For example, Mörike's poem "Seclusion" (*Verborgenheit*) should serve as an entry point to Mörike's apartness, which will not be articulated as spirit and flame but, rather, as "openness" and "dream." Another example is Robert Walser's poetic work (including prose and verse). One of Walser's most characteristic poems is "Aside" (*Beiseit*):

> I take my daily walk
> This leads not far or wide
> And home; then without talk
> Or sound I'm put aside.[42]

The title of the first printed version (1899) was "Saying" (*Spruch*), and the last word was *freed* (*befreit*). Later, Walser replaced this last word with *aside* and chose the same word as the new title. Thus, in the case of Walser, it seems abundantly obvious that the articulation of apartness or asideness in this poet's poem has to revolve around hidden sources of being free or, rather, freed.

I have been emphasizing the idea that apartness sums up apartness from one's own past. This holds, I suggested, for poets such as Trakl, Mörike, and Walser. In his Trakl interpretation, Heidegger refers at one point to childhood. I would like to suggest that we relieve this passage of its time-honored connotations and, instead, appreciate it as a directive for the emphatic reader. The reader departs (removes oneself) by trying to inhabit Trakl's poem and, in the process, is rendered a stranger. Hence, the soul exists on this earth only as a stranger. Heidegger makes the following remark about the converging character of the place where Trakl's poem resides. Given that *to read* means to gather and to collect, this converging place "carries mortal nature back to its stiller childhood, and shelters that childhood of the kind, not yet borne to term, whose stamp marks future generations. The gathering power of apartness holds the unborn generation beyond all that is spent, and saves it for a coming rebirth of mankind out of earliness."[43]

It seems to me that here Heidegger describes the process of emphatic reading whereby the reader might be socialized once more. The reader becomes an infant again by setting the self up for a missed opportunity of acquiring a new way of seeing, speaking, and judging. This second chance offered to one's second nature is described in terms of "unborn" (*Ungeborenes*) or "the coming resurrection" (*kommende Auferstehung*) and the result of the initial socialization as "worn-out second-hand life" (*Abgelebtes*) and as "evil" (*Böses*). What is buried is less the childhood of psychoanalysis than the opportunities missed in acquiring one's second nature. This does not exclude turning back to examine one's childhood, akin to the psychoanalytical vein. Nevertheless, different ways of investigating one's personal life history might be equally appropriate here, such as we find in Jean Paul (in the description of his autobiography), in Stifter (in his fragmentary reminiscences), and in Proust (in *La Recherche*).

Heidegger advises the emphatic reader about how to relate to the linguistic world of this particular poetic work. The reader is called upon to approach and appreciate radical openness (of whose character one must, as yet, be unsure) and to seek the inherent nature of that for which one is destined. If we truly come to inhabit the linguistic world of the poem (i.e., the poet's poem) and in turn are ourselves transformed, it is clear why it should be exclusively destined for us and why it should weave the destiny in which we find ourselves. Put differently, poetry merely comes into its own once it speaks to a reader who will eventually dwell in it and render its linguistic world one's own.

At the beginning of this essay, I distinguished two theatrical levels of Heidegger's essays in *On the Way to Language*: the plain style and the grand style. When Heidegger switches to the sublime rhetorical mode, the purpose is not to argue and instruct but to elevate and transform. The ultimate purpose is transformation of the reader. As Wallace Stevens puts it: "I think that his [the poet's] function is to make his imagination theirs [the reader's] and that he fulfills himself only as he sees his imagination become the light in the minds of others."[44] A poem addresses an individual so that one might turn into an emphatic reader of the poem oneself. And in this sense language speaks in the poet's poem.

Notes

1. "This interpretation of Trakl's poem, it seems to me, is one of Heidegger's richest texts: subtle, overdetermined, more untranslatable than ever. And, of course, one of the most problematic" (Derrida, *Of Spirit*, 86).

2. "Heidegger's concern for the experiment as it relates to the question of language culminates in his final essay concerning language, 'The way to language'" (Powell, "Way to Heidegger's 'Way to Language,'" 180).

3. According to a letter by Heidegger from December 15, 1952, Heidegger encountered Trakl's poem in the journal *Der Brenner* from 1912. Ludwig von Ficker (1880–1967), the editor of *Der Brenner* and mentor of Trakl, was present when Heidegger gave his talk on Trakl's poem for the first time (Arendt and Heidegger, *Briefe*, 81). Heidegger opened his talk on Trakl

with a short note indicating that he had read *Der Brenner* in 1912 and bought Trakl's *Gedichte* in 1913. (Cf. Heidegger and von Ficker, *Briefwechsel*, 8.)

4. Heidegger, *On the Way to Language*, 170.

5. Heidegger, *On the Way to Language*, 170. Mitchell: "What Heidegger's later interpretations of the poets present us with, then—in the readings of Rilke (1946), Trakl (1950, 1952), and George (1957–1958)—is a steady development and deepening of this thought of relationality and thus of the connections between word and world" (Mitchell, "Heidegger's Poetics of Relationality," 217).

6. Mitchell, "Heidegger's Poetics of Relationality," 225. My emphasis.

7. Heidegger, *On the Way to Language*, 170.

8. Heidegger, *On the Way to Language*, 191. (Cf. Heidegger, *Poetry, Language, Thought*, 195–96, and Heidegger, *On the Way to Language*, 121.)

9. Heidegger, *Poetry, Language, Thought*, 206.

10. Heidegger, *Poetry, Language, Thought*, 206.

11. Heidegger, *Poetry, Language, Thought*, 205.

12. Heidegger, *Poetry, Language, Thought*, 198. Translation modified.

13. Heidegger, *Poetry, Language, Thought*, 195.

14. Heidegger, *On the Way to Language*, 190.

15. Heidegger, *On the Way to Language*, 122.

16. Cf. Wolterstorff, *Divine Discourse*.

17. Heidegger, *On the Way to Language*, 123.

18. Heidegger, *On the Way to Language*, 124.

19. Heidegger, *On the Way to Language*, 113.

20. Heidegger, *On the Way to Language*, 121.

21. Heidegger, *On the Way to Language*, 125.

22. Heidegger, *Elucidations*, 210.

23. Heidegger, *On the Way to Language*, 160. Translation modified.

24. Heselhaus, *Deutsche Lyrik der Moderne von Nietzsche bis Yvan Goll*, 328.

25. Killy, *Über Georg Trakl*, 41. From the 1950s on, we find observations of the "ascetic tendency of [Trakl's] language" (Leitgeb, "Die Trakl-Welt," 19) and his "stenographic system" (Schneider, *Der bildhafte Ausdruck*, 123). Michael Hamburger famously called this quality "self-plagiaristic" (Hamburger, *Proliferation of Poets*, 204). Brigitte Peucker has argued that the repetitive character of Trakl's imagery and vocabulary can be read as a phase of the Freudian compulsion to repeat in order to gain mastery over his predecessors and over his poetic materials. This is an instance of what Harold Bloom has called the undoing of the writer from whom one borrows (cf. Peucker, "Poetry of Repetition").

26. In his interpretation of Trakl's poem "Kaspar Hauser Lied," Gunther Kleefeld aptly remarks: "Any attempt to illuminate the enigmatic verse of the fourth stanza of the 'Kaspar Hauser Lied' must take into account the connotative relations which inhere between this imagery and Trakl's work as a whole. One must, in other words, refer once again to recurrent parallel imagery in other poems." (Kleefeld, "Kasper Hauser and the Paternal Law," 64).

27. Cf. Wetzel, *Konkordanz zu den Dichtungen Georg Trakls*.

28. They motivate the claim, though they do not justify it. The justification of the claim naturally derives from the reading of Trakl offered by Heidegger.

29. Cf. Dennett, "The Self as a Center of Narrative Gravity."

30. Heidegger, *Poetry, Language, Thought*, 192.

31. What I have been arguing for is nicely and powerfully expressed in Wallace Stevens's prose and poetry: "A poem need not have a meaning and, like most things in nature, often does not have" (Stevens, *Collected Poetry and Prose*, 914). And the poem "The Motive for Metaphor" (1947) says: "You like it under the trees in autumn, / Because everything is half dead. / The wind moves like a cripple among the leaves / And repeats words without meaning" (Stevens, *Collected Poetry and Prose*, 257).

32. Heidegger, *On the Way to Language*, 190, 122.

33. Cf. Paul Valéry: "Un poète . . . n'a pas pour fonction de ressentir l'état poétique: ceci est une affaire privée. Il a pour fonction de le créer chez les autres" (Valéry, *Oeuvres*, 1321).

34. Arendt and Heidegger, *Briefe*, 316.

35. Cf. Edmundson, *Why Read?*

36. Heidegger, *On the Way to Language*, 172.

37. Heidegger, *On the Way to Language*, 185.

38. Heidegger, *On the Way to Language*, 193, 180.

39. Heidegger, *On the Way to Language*, 179.

40. Heidegger, *On the Way to Language*, 180.

41. Heidegger, *On the Way to Language*, 181.

42. Cf. Walser, "Aside."

43. Heidegger, *On the Way to Language*, 186.

44. Stevens, *Collected Poetry and Prose*, 660–61.

Bibliography

Arendt, Hannah, and Martin Heidegger. *Briefe 1925–1975*. Edited by Ursula Ludz. Frankfurt am Main: Klostermann, 1998.

Dennett, Daniel. "The Self as a Center of Narrative Gravity." In *Self and Consciousness: Multiple Perspectives*, edited by F. Kessel, Pamela M. Cole, and Dale L. Johnson, 103–15. Hillsdale, NJ: Psychology Press, 1992.

Derrida, Jacques. *Of Spirit*. Chicago: University of Chicago Press, 1989.

Edmundson, Mark. *Why Read?* New York: Bloomsbury USA, 2004.

Hamburger, Michael. *A Proliferation of Prophets*. New York: St. Martin's Press, 1984.

Heidegger, Martin. *Elucidations of Hölderlin's Poetry*. Translated by Keith Hoeller. New York: Humanity Books, 2000.

———. *On the Way to Language*. Translated by Peter D. Hertz. New York: Harper and Row, 1971.

———. *Poetry, Language, Thought*. Translated by Albert Hofstadter. New York: Harper and Row, 1971.

Heidegger, Martin, and Ludwig von Ficker. *Briefwechsel 1952–1967*. Stuttgart: Klett-Cotta, 2004.

Heselhaus, Clemens. *Deutsche Lyrik der Moderne von Nietzsche bis Yvan Goll*. Düsseldorf: Bagel, 1961.

Killy, Walter. *Über Georg Trakl*. Göttingen: Vandenheock & Ruprecht, 1967.

Kleefeld, Gunter. "Kaspar Hauser and the Paternal Law: The Dramaturgy of Desire on Trakl's Kaspar Hauser Lied." In *The Dark Flutes of Fall: Critical Essays on Georg Trakl*, edited by Eric Williams, 38–84. Columbia: Camden House, 1991.

Leitgeb, Josef. "Die Trakl-Welt: Zum Wortbestand der Dichtungen Georg Trakls." *Wort im Gebirge* 3 (1951): 7–39.

Mitchell, Andrew J. "Heidegger's Poetics of Relationality." In *Interpreting Heidegger: Critical Essays*, edited by Daniel O. Dahlstrom, 217–30. Cambridge: Cambridge University Press, 2011.

Peucker, Brigitte. "The Poetry of Repetition: Trakl's Narrow Bridge." In *The Critical Cosmos: Modern German Poetry*, edited by Harold Bloom, 123–37. New York: Chelsea House, 1989.

Powell, Jeffrey. "The Way to Heidegger's 'Way to Language.'" In *Heidegger and Language*, edited by Jeffrey Powell, 180–200. Bloomington: Indiana University Press, 2013.

Schneider, Karl L. *Der bildhafte Ausdruck in den Dichtungen Georg Heyms, Georg Trakls und Ernst Stadlers*. Heidelberg: Carl Winter, 1954.

Stevens, Wallace. *Collected Poetry and Prose*. Edited by Francis Kermode. New York: Library of America, 1997.

Valéry, Paul. *Oeuvres*, vol. 1. Edited by J. Hytier. Paris: Gallimard, 1957.

Walser, Robert. "Aside." Translated by Michael Hamburger. *Modern Poetry in Translation* 3, no. 8 (2007): 120.

Wetzel, Heinz. *Konkordanz zu den Dichtungen Georg Trakls*. Salzburg: Müller, 1977.

Wolterstorff, Nicholas. *Divine Discourse: Philosophical Reflections on the Claim That God Speaks*. Cambridge: Cambridge University Press, 1995.

MARKUS WILD is Professor of Philosophy at the University of Basel. He is working on early modern philosophy, philosophy of mind, and philosophy of literature.

3 Toward a Hermeneutic Interpretation of Greeting and Destiny in Heidegger's Thinking

Diego D'Angelo

Introduction

This study aims to problematize a conceptual connection Heidegger establishes in his later thought: the connection between the "destiny [*Geschick*] of Being" and the greeting (*Grüßen*) of the gods and of the holy. An analysis of Hölderlin's poetry is crucial in the development of a better understanding of this topic, for Hölderlin is the poet who was, in Heidegger's view, destined to be "sent . . . into the essence of poetic activity."[1] In German, there is a close kinship between the verb *to send* (*schicken*) and the noun *destiny* (*Geschick*); in keeping with this kinship, destiny itself is not some stable substance that "sends" something else. It is rather the sending itself or the gathering (indicated through the prefix *Ge-*) of the sending. Destiny is not to be conceived as something that does something else but as the epochal arrival of an individual (in this case, the poet) that belongs to the history of Being in an eminent way. Such belonging is made possible because the poet is sent by destiny into the essence of poetic activity, that is, into being the peculiar, historical variation of the poetic that a single poet and his works incarnate.[2] In this way, the poet and his poetry become destiny.

Such sending or destiny is conditioned. The poet, sent by destiny or as destiny, must himself be "originally greeted" (*ursprünglich gegrüßt*).[3] If sending or destiny (*Geschick*) is indeed endowed with some kind of "original greeting" (*ursprüngliches Grüßen*), then understanding this notion is crucial to understanding Heidegger's thoughts about destiny, poetry, and the history of Being. Another reason that the relation between greeting and sending plays a pivotal role in Heidegger's thinking is that it bears on the relation between language and historical Being. Although this leads to the more general question as to the relation between language and Being in Heidegger, for the following analysis this question must remain in the background.

A central point emerges from Heidegger's confrontation with Hölderlin on the question of greeting, as described above: the greeting obtains an ontological primacy over destiny. Greeting is considered to be the condition of possibility for the poet to be sent into the original abode of his poetry, which is afforded by the history of Being. The poet has to be greeted in order to find the historical position proper for his poetry. But because the poetry of the poet who was sent is also said to be an opening of the destiny of Being itself, this transcendental lineage can be traced even further. Only through the "signs" (*Zeichen*) in the poet's poetry is it possible for beings (τὰ ὄντα) to gather (*sich sammeln*) in a particular configuration of Being—in other words, in an epoch of Being.[4] *Geschick* (destiny), then, is nothing but sending (*Schickung*) via the signs of the poet.

In Heidegger's view, such sending is possible only if the poet is able to receive and pass on the signs or "hints" (*Winke*) of the gods. This takes place in poetry, for poetry operates with and becomes meaningful through such signs. This receiving and passing on of signs and hints is the institution of "what remains" (*was bleibt*), as Heidegger says, referring to a Hölderlinian verse: "*was bleibet aber, stiften die Dichter.*" Each question about the presence or absence of being (*Anwesen und Abwesen*) in a singular configuration of the history of Being, thus, rests upon an interpretation of these signs, signs the poet interprets, signs of himself as an exemplary figure, signs of the gods, and, most of all, signs of the holy.[5] If this is indeed so, one needs a hermeneutic of these signs, hints, and greetings to understand the concept of sending in its relation to the history of Being. The aim of this contribution is to provide such a hermeneutic. It is, however, clear that in Heidegger's considerations of the history of Being, the greeting (and all that is related to it) is but one possibility of philosophically representing the role of the poet in the instantiation of Being. Other descriptions are possible, but for the very nature of poetry itself—that is, the role that signs play in poetry—an investigation of the greeting aims at showing a general structure that underlies the history of Being. Outside of Heidegger's philosophy, the question of the theoretical meaning of the greeting—and, more generally, of the idea of the history of Being—is beyond the scope of the present analysis, which aims only at an immanent reconstruction of key concepts of Heidegger's philosophy.[6]

My analysis is divided into four sections, all of which will deal mostly with the texts in which Heidegger explicitly interprets Hölderlin's poetry, since here the connection between greeting and destiny is most clearly stated. The aim of the first section is to explain the role greeting (*Grüßen*) plays in Heidegger's interpretation of Hölderlin's poetry by contrasting the classical semiotic interpretation of this concept with a hermeneutical understanding that is to be achieved through the reading of Heidegger's and Hölderlin's texts themselves. Contrary to a common reading of Heidegger, I claim not only that greeting is an aspect of Hölderlin's poetry that Heidegger adopts in his interpretation but also that greeting serves as a key concept of Heidegger's philosophy itself. If this can be established, greeting cannot be taken as a mere metaphor. Instead, it yields genuine and original philosophical content. In my analysis, this content will turn out to be both phenomenological and hermeneutical. In order to achieve a phenomenological and hermeneutical understanding of greeting, I first give an abstract definition of this concept.

In the second section, I discuss the dynamic structure of the greeting in more detail and concreteness in order to describe its role in the relation between poets and human beings. I call its role in the relation between poets and human beings "second-order greeting." In my analysis, greeting can be established as the link between past and future in the gathering (*Versammlung*) of the present "now."

In the third section, I address the question of where the greetings come from. The holy is the first "greeting" instance, and, therefore, its greeting is the "inceptual greeting." The greeting is the encounter and the union of human beings and gods in the "wedding feast" (*Brautfest*). It is significant that Heidegger discusses this as the union of the "ideal" with the "real" in the greeting itself.

In the last section, I aim to establish the central claim already anticipated in this brief introduction: that the ontology of gathering in the history of Being rests on a hermeneutic of greeting. Greeting in the original sense, as established by the first three sections, is the joining of the real and the ideal, the past and the future, in the unity of a sending or destiny of Being.

The overall scope of this contribution consists in showing how an understanding of the meaning of Being's destiny presupposes an understanding of the poetical greeting. Being "greets" the poet and, in this way, opens up its own historical destination, in which man can dwell. The following contribution takes up therefore an element of Heidegger's interpretation of Hölderlin that is prima facie only of secondary importance and makes it the center of analysis. On the one hand, such a reading of Heidegger's philosophy can help in assessing the resonance the concept of greeting has had for other thinkers (such as for Jacques Derrida);[7] on the other hand, as an immanent interpretation of Heidegger, this approach serves to show that the language of the poet (which is a central topic of Heidegger's philosophy) is to be understood as a kind of greeting and that the whole history of Being can be conceived as a sending made possible by this very greeting itself.

1. The Poetic Function of Semiotic Concepts

One common reading of Heidegger's engagement with themes like greetings, hints, and signs takes Heidegger's usage of them to be derivative of Hölderlin's poetry. In this kind of reading, the themes are mere poetic metaphors with no genuine philosophical content. These metaphors have no philosophical role and are merely inherited from the literary texts Heidegger interprets. The interpretation of greetings, hints, and signs as mere metaphors or literary symbols is, however, either tautological or unsustainable. If we treat greetings, hints, and signs in a classical philosophical way—that is to say, as semiotic figures that have the structure of *aliquid stat pro aliquo* (the structure of the representation, of the surrogate)—then the metaphor, too, is a semiotic figure with the very same structure. In a traditional semiotic understanding of these notions, the claim that greetings, hints, and signs are metaphors amounts to a statement that semiotic figures are semiotic figures, which is tautological and uninformative.

The reading of greetings, hints, and signs as mere metaphors is also problematic when we try to understand greetings and hints from the point of view of Hölderlin's poetry and Heidegger's thought rather than from the perspective of classic semiotic theory. Understanding greetings and hints from a Heideggerian perspective means taking up these themes in a hermeneutic way provided by an immanent reading of Hölderlin's texts. In the lectures on Hölderlin's hymn "The Ister," Heidegger denies every interpretation of poetic elements as symbolic images of some other reality: "We are claiming that Hölderlin's river poetry, indeed his hymnal poetry as a whole, is not concerned with symbolic images."[8] If this is true—and we'll grant that it is for the sake of the following confrontation with Heidegger's interpretation of Hölderlin—then no poetic element can be a metaphor either. Greetings and hints are not some kinds of representatives or vehicles serving to transport an idea, a μετα-φέρειν. Some other reality, such as a landscape or some biographical element, is not simply transposed into poetry with the help of metaphors, nor is it symbolized through the words of the poet. If one takes notions such as greeting to be meaningful philosophical concepts, more complex questions arise. In order to discuss these questions, the concepts of greeting and of the hint must be understood, not in the classical, semiotic way, but in a genuinely hermeneutical way—that is, the meaning of these concepts has to be gathered from a reading of Heidegger's and Hölderlin's texts themselves, not by an appeal to the classical (metaphysical) definition of the sign as *aliquid stat pro aliquo.*

One reason for this impossibility to understand such concepts in the classical way is that poetry itself speaks about and uses signs, greetings, and hints; the poet chooses these elements and makes them themes of the poetry itself and does not just *use* them, presupposing their meaning. Hölderlin's poetry is (among other things) poetry about greetings, hints, and signs, so it is philosophically interesting to discover the genuine content of the notions of greeting, hint, and sign at play in those texts.

But there is more to it. In Heidegger's interpretation, not only is greeting a theme for Hölderlin's poetry, but Hölderlin's poetry is itself a kind of greeting.[9]

Greetings, thus, are not a kind of *stat pro*, standing for something else. They have an entirely different structure, a structure that is in itself twofold: poetry as such is a kind of greeting, but poetry is also about greeting. This is another way of saying that, for Heidegger, Hölderlin is the poet whose poetry is about poetry itself; he is the poet of the poets. This self-referentiality would be impossible to grasp via an interpretation whereby greeting has a representative, *stat pro* structure. Rather, greeting itself is essentially self-referential.

Only because of their self-referential character do sign and other concepts related to it have an important role to play in Hölderlin's poetry. As expressed in the hymn "The Ister," signs are even necessary: "A sign is needed / Nothing else / plain and simple."[10] The poem also says that "the heavenly" (*die Himmlischen*) needs the sign in order to appear. It is only thanks to the sign that the gods can "feel themselves warm by one another"[11]—that is, that they can first gather and meet. Because what remains is granted by the poets, however, we can assume that the poet and his poetry—and, most of all, the signs of such poetry—condition the possibility of the gods belonging together (i.e., the gods also need the poet and his poetry).[12] The nearness of "the heavenly" to one another is established by their "communication" with and through the poet.

Therefore, signs are necessary because without them the gods could not be "summoned" (*herbeigerufen werden*) and gather themselves. "Through the sign," Heidegger explains in the lecture on "The Ister," "the heavenly find their way to the unity of their being united."[13] This unity is possible only thanks to a relation to Being. But this relation is in turn possible through the language of the poet and through his signs:

> This Other who is needed is . . . the sign. So that the gods "feel themselves warm by one another," they must be able to feel something in general. "Of themselves," however, they "feel nothing." The gods are "without feeling," "of themselves," that is, remaining within their own essence, they are never able to comport themselves toward beings. For this, a relation to Being is required (i.e., to the "holy" that is "beyond" them), Being as shown to them through the Other who is the sign. Were it not for this sign and its showing and its sharing among one another, then the heavenly would remain without any possibility of having feeling for an Other or of being with one another.[14]

The other who is a sign is but the poet himself. Heidegger interprets Hölderlin's verse "we are a sign that is not read" not to describe human beings in general.[15] Rather, *we* refers to the poets in particular. The poet himself is a sign among others and has a relation to Being (because the poet indicates Being in his poetry). Therefore, he can grant the gods a relation to Being so that they can comport themselves toward beings in the first place. For this ontological reason, Heidegger can claim that the gods *need* the mortals. The *Dasein* of human beings as such always already has a relation to Being and to its meaning. Hence, the heavenly need their mediation in order to enter in the truth of Being. Only through the signs of the poet can the gods have a relation to Being and to its truth.

If, then, signs mediate the relation of the gods to Being and to its truth, we can also see that a sign understood in this manner is no sign in the traditional semiotic meaning of a *stat pro*, which creates a representative connection between a material thing (the sign) and an ideal meaning that does not show itself directly. In Heidegger's interpretation of Hölderlin, the metaphysical dualism between material sign and ideal meaning transforms itself into an ontological dynamic, a dynamic more complex than the traditional understanding of signifying elements. The sign is needed, it is necessary in order for the heavenly (heaven but also the gods and the ideal) to comport themselves to the terrestrial (*das Irdische*, but also the earth, earthly beings in the sense of "*die Erde*"). The sign is a bridge in Heidegger's sense of the word. The bridge does not simply connect the riversides but lets them come to appear for the first time as what they are.[16] The gods can be gods only when something else is not god, and, in the same way, mortals are only mortals in contrast to something that does not die; the mortals are only mortals before the immortals, or before the gods. In Heidegger's reading of Hölderlin, this dialectic relation is made possible by the sign. The sign thus determines the relation between mortals and immortals, terrestrial and heavenly. But in order for this mediation to be possible, not just any sign is needed. According to Heidegger's interpretation, we need a sign made by a "demigod"—that is, by the poet himself. The poet as a demigod is mediation *par excellence*: in his very essence, he mediates between gods and mortals.[17]

Further analysis of the signs given by the demigod (i.e., the poet) requires a consideration of the concept of greeting, which plays a central role not so much in "The Ister" as in Heidegger's lectures on "Andenken" ("Remembrance"), of which we have no English translation at this point.[18] Here, in much the same way as in the lectures on "The Ister," Heidegger claims that the words of the poet cannot be metaphors or symbols for something "real" outside the poetry or for aspects of the poet's biography. Therefore, the pivotal point of "Remembrance" lies in the line where the poet wishes to greet the land and the seashore. As Heidegger says, "we cannot believe what we are hearing: is not everything here turned into its very opposite?"[19] Heidegger here refers to the verse "But go now and greet."[20] This greeting is not only the pivotal point of "Remembrance" but the "secret of remembrance" itself.[21] This means that the greeting has to be understood, in its essence, as a kind of remembrance. It denotes the poet both "thinking backward," for example, when he thinks of his own past sojourn at the seashore, and "thinking forward" (*Hindenken*), because what is remembered "surpasses our present" and "suddenly stands in the future."[22]

This temporal entanglement is the essence of greeting, to which the opening stanza of *Andenken* refers. The greeting happens in such a way that the poet, through the greeting itself, moves into (*rückt ein*) another time-space (*Zeitraum*). The movement into another time-space is possible only if the former time-space is left behind, though not forgotten. As something left behind but not forgotten, the former time-space is also coming (*kommend*): it stays "before us" in the remembrance of times past. The greeting, therefore, bears a relation to the past time-space (I must have been at the seashore in order to greet it), to the present time-space (from which I am greeting the seashore at the present moment), and to the future, as the greeting is "coming" to that which is greeted.[23] This spatio-temporal greeting is a "going with the wind" that is, at the same time, a remaining. Only because the poet remains where he is can he send his greetings, through the wind, to, for example, the beautiful Garonne and to the gardens of Bordeaux.[24] This intertwining of going and remaining is possible because the greeting "makes known" (*gibt kund*) the one who greets, namely the poet, and it also remains close to the poet; it remains the poet's greeting. The greeting bears the poet himself as the one greeting, but the poet cannot simply go along with the greeting; he has to remain behind. Nonetheless, the greeting is directed to the one who is greeted. The greeting thus travels through the entire expanse of a time-space. It does not diminish the distance between all involved but, rather, endows it with poetic meaning.

Yet, in Heidegger's interpretation, this dynamic of greeting is still more complicated than that. There is not only a movement from the one who greets to the one greeted but also a kind of countermovement from the greeted to the greeting one: "the greeted inclines toward the greeting one because he thinks towards him."[25] Heidegger brings out this feedback structure most succinctly in the phrase "in the greeting of the poet, the greeted is meant for the poet."[26] In German, this phrase reads: "*Im Gruß des Dichters denkt ihm das Gegrüßte zu.*"[27] The use of the verb *zudenken*, literally *thinking-to* or *thinking-toward*, is quite peculiar. The one greeted is thought of by the poet while the one greeted also thinks of the poet. The greeted is "destined" for the poet, if we take *destined* as a possible translation of "*zugedacht sein*," being thought-to or supposed-to. In other words, it is meant or *intended for* the poet (and therefore destined for him) insofar as it is *intended by* the poet. The remembrance of the beautiful Garonne and of the gardens of Bordeaux comes to the fore by itself and from itself. It is not caused by the poet but is directed to the poet interpellated by the greeting.

Greeting also has an essentially ontological determination. The one greeted, as greeted, becomes what he is in himself. Through the greeting, he receives his own essence: "the greeting is a letting-be of things and men."[28] Mediating between the greeter and the greeted, greeting brings both together in the "intimacy" (*Innigkeit*) of their essence,[29] just as the bridge does in Heidegger's famous example already quoted. In this, the greeted first assumes its proper essencing.[30] Through the greeting, the greeted is made capable of returning to its ownmost essence, of manifesting itself as what it is, namely as something past that continues in the present and stretches out into the future.[31] In Heidegger's interpretation, this coming to being and return to propriety must be considered in ontological terms: greeting takes place in poetry; in poetry, greeting lets the truth of Being itself be. According to Heidegger, greetings let the greeted be a being for the first time. Now we can see why: greeting reciprocally relates the greeter to the greeted and, therefore, also relates both the greeter and greeted to their past and future. In this temporal connection, it establishes their most fundamental ontological relation.

The only way to understand the temporal intertwining of the greeting that Heidegger finds in "Remembrance" is to avoid reducing greeting to some metaphor for something other than itself. The greeting is not a symbol for the memorial work of the poet that—in the traditional view—perpetuates (and therefore eternalizes) the deeds of heroes. Greeting is not a form of memory at all. Its structure is not that of a simple "holding on" to something past but, rather, that of a projecting of the past into the future. As in our everyday understanding, greeting opens up the possibility of a dialogue between two or more persons. In the reverse situation, too, when a greeting is said in parting from someone, it frequently expresses the hope to meet the other again in the future. When it does express the hope *not* to meet the other again, however, it is equally a hope directed toward the future.

Opening a future this way, through greeting, does not happen by chance or incidentally. Both the possibility of such an opening and the way in which this opening takes place are codetermined by the past. The greeting one does not just follow the past or a poet's own memory. The poet makes the past present (*vergegenwärtigen*), and, by way of becoming present, the past, too, now awaits a coming fulfillment. Poetry is not a reminder of the past. Poetry that does not "remember" (in the sense Heidegger and Hölderlin give to *andenken*) merely "reminds." Poetry that reminds remains tied up with the present because the poet reminds us now of what happened in the past, yet the relation to the past is only extrinsic, without relating this past to the future. In contrast, the structure of remembrance in the sense of "Andenken" is essentially different. In Heidegger's ontological interpretation, it has the spatio-temporal structure of the greeting.

Now we can catch a glimpse of why the analysis of greeting is so important for Heidegger in this lecture course on "Remembrance." The temporal structure and the particular dynamics of greeting provide an extraordinary paradigm for describing poetic remembrance in its own founding (*stiftende*) function. Consider the following example: if I were giving a lecture in an auditorium and greeted someone, I would have to turn toward the person I greet. She would also have to turn toward me. Otherwise (in the case that she does not in any way respond to my greeting), it would not be a greeting at all but only some kind of gesture received and understood by no one. In turning toward someone, we have an expectation, namely, that the attention of the one who is greeted will turn toward the greeter in reply to the greeting. This relation, which is itself founded by the greeting, presupposes that a certain distance remains between the greeter and the greeted. They may remain near, but in order to be near each other and not simply one and the same thing, they have to remain at a distance.[32]

In order for a reply to be possible, necessary conditions must be fulfilled. The greeter and greeted must be at a distance from one another, though they must also enter into a relationship established by the greeting. In order to institute such a relation, the greeter and greeted must come to share a common past. If you and I knew each other, we would also greet each other. Though greeting is, first of all, a relation between persons, in Hölderlin's verse greeting also takes place when the poet greets the beautiful river. The greeter and greeted must know each other in some way in order for a greeting to take place. They must, at least, know about the existence of each other. But in what sense does the beautiful Garonne *know* the poet? Obviously not in the usual sense of this word, as if the river would be said to, say, hold some form of justified belief. Rather, the poet and the river share a common past: they are related by past experience. Therefore, the present experience of the greeting poet can interact with the past experience of the poet from the time he has seen the river. A shared past is the condition of possibility for the greeting to happen and to open a space for the future.

2. The Greeting of the Poet

In any discussion of the greeting of the poet, it is imperative to recognize that the word *of* indicates both a subjective and an objective genitive. The poet greets and is also greeted. Here is how Heidegger describes the complicated structure of the greeting: "To it [i.e., to the greeting] belongs a threefold structure: first, that the holy greets, so that gods and men are greeted; second, that gods and men are greeted in this way; in the end, that gods and men, as greeted in this way, can from this moment on greet each other again and can remain by each other precisely by way of this greeting."[33]

Hölderlin may, upon these grounds, interpret greeting as the "wedding feast" (*Brautfest*) between gods and men. But this wedding between gods and men takes place only when the greeting is not a direct greeting between them. It has to happen through some kind of medium, for instance, through the signs of the poetry and through the poet's writing. In this section, I focus on the greeting between poets and men, and the following section will be devoted to greetings directed *toward* poets. We will see thereby, though indirectly, the role of the holy in the process of greeting.

The poet does not greet only once. Greeting, rather, defines the poet; a poet is one who greets (*ein Grüßender*). The poet's poetry (as remembrance) is a greeting: "To being a poet belongs the greeting. For this reason the greeting one must hint to the essential richness of the greeted."[34] At the same time, however, the poet is only a poet because he was himself greeted in the first place.[35] Heidegger distinguishes an "inceptual greeting" (*anfängliches Grüßen*)[36] that is directed to the poet, from what I call a second-order greeting. This second-order greeting happens in the signs given in the poet's poetry. The first, inceptual greeting conditions this second-order greeting. Thus, the poet can greet only after a relation between him and something in the world has been established. This happens through an original greeting that is directed toward the poet.

According to Heidegger, the second-order greeting of the poet brings "everything that has been greeted in its unity."[37] This unity is not based on similarity with regard to external characteristics. Rather, the element that establishes the unity of everything greeted by the poet is precisely the fact of being greeted by the poet. This kind of unity consists in the fact that everything has a relation to the poet. Since everything has become related to the poet, everything is gathered by his greeting. But if the poet has been greeted in the first place, then the things of the world are not just gathered around him, as if he were exterior to them. He, as the poet having already been greeted by the world, is among the things greeted. Moreover, he is in their center.

Second-order greeting, as a greeting by the poet, is remembrance. It does not have the less complex structure of a simple reminder of the past. Remembrance gathers the past by sending the past to the future and presenting this past as a sending. Indeed whatever is greeted, in that it is greeted *now*, is not simply past but having been (*ge-wesen*); it is past (*gewesen*), but, at the same time, it continues to hold sway (*west*), although from "afar."[38] What, then, are those past events—or things past—that are greeted and thus sent into the future? It is the wedding feast of gods and men, which had its original place and time in ancient Greece.[39] It is this event that is past yet that continues to manifest itself: "In the greeting 'the brown women' are mentioned. The holidays of the South are meant here. The southern land is Greece. The greeting is directed to the Greek feast, i.e., to the encounter of men and gods that took place in ancient Greece. If the essence of greeting is to let what is greeted be as what it is, then this greeting elevates the past feast [i.e., the encounter of gods and men in ancient Greece], as past [*gewesen*] to its own essencing [*Wesen*]."[40]

What is greeted shows itself in the greeting. The greeting lets it be what it is. Such a "letting be," which allows the greeted to show itself as what it is, is possible by virtue of the temporal structure of the greeting discussed above. Whatever is greeted turns to the one who greets and thus remains in the present as something past. The greeted remains as itself because only in the greeting is the "appropriate remaining" (*gemäße Bleiben*) possible.[41] The German word *gemäß* can be translated both as *appropriate* and as *measured*, so the question arises: How is this "appropriate remaining" or "measured remaining" to be understood? What is the measure of such remaining? The measure can be no external criterion but has to come from the things themselves (that the greeting allows to be) and to remain because of the greeting. What remains and continues to be has its proper measure in itself. This is a peculiar measure of the greeting: what is greeted remains in accordance with itself as a past that continues to manifest itself in its remembrance and in the greeting of the poet.

Yet, *that* the poet can be greeting is conditioned by a greeting that the poet himself has received. This is what Heidegger calls "inceptual greeting," and it is toward this that I now turn my analysis.

3. The Holy and the Greeting

Who or what greets in the inceptual greeting? In his hymn "As when on a holiday," Hölderlin calls the element that greets inceptually "the holy."[42] In this poem we can read:

> But now day breaks! I awaited and saw it come, And what I saw, may the holy be my word.[43]

The *holy* is the word for what the poet sees coming. The poet sees the holy as day breaks, as the light of the day comes and the shadows of the night fade. What the poet sees is, thus, twofold: the coming into presence of the day and the withdrawal of the night. The language of the poet is capable of showing and making known both the coming-into-presence and the withdrawal. The poet is messenger (*Bote*), as Heidegger says, of that "in which men and things can show themselves for the first time."[44]

The reason that this space of "letting something show itself" is called "the holy" (*das Heilige*) becomes clear if we observe the word itself and its meaning—though Heidegger himself does not purse this. The word *Heil* means, among other things, *the whole*, an intact and unwounded totality. The word is used most often in relation to the human body to mean *healthy* or, with a similar English word, *wholesome*.[45] The process of healing (*Heilung*) is, thus, a process of making whole. The meaning of *Heil* was enlarged, in the historical development of the German language, to apply not only to processes of healing but to things in general.[46] The holy is an instance that thus precedes every possible appearance of something. It is what defines the appearing as "wholesome," as an integral and coherent whole. It, therefore, implies the form of the totality of what shows itself. This totality, however, also withdraws itself.

Heidegger's interpretation of the word *nature* in Hölderlin's hymn "As when on a holiday" points to this withdrawal. For Heidegger, *nature* has the same meaning as the Greek word φύσις, which Heidegger understands as *growth*.[47] It signifies sprouting, opening up, and rising, but also the decay and death proper to the movement of nature. From a lyrical perspective, Heidegger sees this word as synonymous with *the holy*. In fact, the two words are interchangeable.[48] Heidegger says that "Hölderlin names nature the holy" and that "the holy is the essence of nature."[49] The essential relation between the holy and nature consists in the fact that both have this double structure of showing and withdrawing, of emerging and drawing back. The holy is "wholesome," without faults. Yet, the holy, too, comprises decay and death. Such "holy" togetherness of appearing and concealing, therefore, conditions the possibility of all differences that constitute particulars. The holy grants "its bounded presence to all differentiations."[50] The holy as wholesome unity is the undifferentiated instance that makes all differences possible by letting them be.

If we now turn to the main argument of our inquiry with this in mind, we can better understand what is at stake in the notion of greeting that Heidegger is developing in these lectures: greeting as inceptual is a greeting from the holy, or from the original unity of showing and concealing. As *heil*, as *wholesome*, the holy is the undifferentiated unity, but this unity can, by way of greeting, let all differences be, making them manifest. The greeting of the holy is essentially the beginning (*der Anfang*). The temporal structure and the complex phenomenological dynamic of greeting are the original differentiation of the "wholesome" unity. This differentiation is the sending (*Schickung*) of the holy determining itself and differentiating itself from itself according to the modalities of the greeting. The wholesome unity differentiates itself in accord with the measure given by the greeting and its temporal structure.

Heidegger says that "the inceptual greeting is the concealed essence of history. The inceptional greeting is *the* event, is *the* beginning."[51] The inceptual greeting is the event and the beginning because it is that place where the wholesome unity of nature opens up and unfolds by sending itself into a future and into a past, following the temporal structure of the greeting.

Yet the opening also generates a differentiation between the *real* and the *ideal*. What is astonishing about some passages in Heidegger's lecture on Hölderlin's hymn "Remembrance" is that we can find explicit considerations of these contrasting terms. This is no remainder of metaphysical dualisms and fruitless oppositions otherwise overcome by Heidegger's philosophy. For Heidegger, the greeting indicates the central dynamics of Hölderlin's poetry, the "becoming-real of the ideal and the becoming-ideal of the real," as some kind of "terrible but divine dream";[52] in the following pages, we will come back to an explanation of why this dream is terrible and divine. Heidegger develops this further: "Insofar as we have to say the becoming-ideal of that which was real in the past, and as we have to say this real itself as the past in the intimacy of its essence, such saying can only be a greeting."[53] Here we again find the temporal structure of the greeting, but it is now *expressis verbis* related to the difference between ideal and real.

We have seen that the possibility of sending the past into the future is essential to greeting as Heidegger describes it. The greeting makes the past into something that has been (*ein Ge-wesenes*) and that becomes manifest as such. I claim that this dynamic of greeting is the very same dynamic of Hölderlin's poetry as a whole. This may serve to shed some light on the following paragraph:

> In the free imitation of art, i.e., in the founding [*Stiften*] that art achieves, there is something like a terrible but divine dream. But why are we confronted with the dream in this context, where we are speaking about the founding of a realm, the establishing [*Gründung*] of history? The dream cannot signify here simply the unreal in the sense of the mere vanishing and not-being. On the contrary: the dream indicates the becoming-real of the possible in the becoming-ideal of the real. The real returns in its recollection while the possible (as coming) binds the expectation. This, taken together, is a dream in the place where art founds history. The dream brings the fullness of the possible that is not yet appropriated and preserves the transfigured recollection of the real.[54]

The movement of "the becoming-real of the possible in the becoming-ideal of the real" is the founding of history. Yet it is a dream. *Dream* is not, however, an antonym to *reality*; it is something that "preserves" the real. The dreaming proper to poetry is the founding of history insofar as what comes (*das Kommende*)— in other words, the direction to the future proper to the expectation of the possible—belongs to the dream itself. If we want to find an antonym to *dream*, we should think, instead, of *recollection*. Recollection as remembrance (*Andenken*) lets that which was once real (the past, *das Gewesene*) become present (*wesen*) as a past that has, in turn, become ideal through poetry (*das Ge-wesen*e). What Hölderlin calls Greece and what the primal object of remembrance is (i.e., the past), is necessarily ideal: it is not an echo of a vanished reality but something that opens up only in remembrance. It is, therefore, present only in thought (*Denken*), as the ideal content of thought. In thinking remembrance, the past becomes a phenomenon in Husserl's sense, with its inherent "noematic" essentiality. The presencing past is necessarily a content of thought.[55]

4. Toward a Hermeneutic of Greeting and Destiny

The poet, defined by his own second-order greeting, is a messenger of the inceptual greeting of the heavenly. Already in Plato, we find this idea of the poet as ἑρμηνεύς, that is, as someone who delivers the message of the gods. In Heidegger's interpretation, on the other hand, we have a more detailed analysis of the transition from the gods to the poets: the poet, who is a demigod, receives inceptual greeting from "angels" (ἀγγελοι),[56] who are messengers themselves. An angel's greeting "comes out of the gaiety that allows everything to be at home."[57] Insofar as the angel's greeting is bound to the idea of being at home, the messengers are "angels of the house".[58] they show the space (*Raum*) that people can make into their house, the space they can call home. To humans, home means to be in the "historical space" of the peoples.[59] The greeting of the messengers, in other words, opens up a space for dwelling. Yet angels are not simply beings that exist in between gods and men. Rather, "with the name 'angels' the being of those who were previously called 'gods' is now said more purely."[60] By their essence, the gods are those who greet. They must give the inceptual greeting so that the open can reach humans, so that humans can dwell in that opening that is, at the same time, the foundation of history.

A founding movement comes out of the holy, and this movement brings the "opening" (also called in these lectures "gaiety" and "*das Heitere*"). This original opening is that "which first 'imparts,' or 'grants,' the open to every 'space' and every 'temporal space.'"[61] This founding movement is the movement of greeting, and it happens between messengers, poets, and humans. The opening of time and space (of "time-space"[62]) takes place in a twofold manner. Both aspects of this manner are mediated by greeting. First, opening is made possible by the greeting of the gods, directed at the poets. Second, every opening would remain impossible for humans without greeting's mediation and the signs given by the poet in his poetry (i.e., a second-order greeting). Such greeting is directed toward humans and occurs in language. Yet it is an inceptual greeting that establishes history.

The movement of greeting individuates and differentiates things. It allows things to become what they are in their singular individuation and in their differentiation from one another. In this, the movement is historical in its essence. "Gaiety" or the "clearing" is also the simple event of opening up in the history of Being. We can, however, separate the "holy," the source of this movement, from the opening up of Being: the opening up is an opening up that happens inside what is "whole" or "wholesome": that is, the holy itself, which is not individuated or differentiated in itself. Only because the greeting individuates and differentiates things can Heidegger appeal to destiny (*Geschick*): the sending is the movement of the determination of history as an essential destiny.

The "gaiety" is the historical differentiation of the holy. This differentiation happens along the two axes already discussed: first, along the difference (which is at the same time the entanglement) between future and past, and then along the difference/entanglement between the real and the ideal. The gaiety is, first of all, *one* space of possibilities that is not realized but that belongs to *one* epoch in the history of Being. The gaiety is the differentiation of reality and possibility; therefore, it is the individuation of *a* time-space in *a* particular epoch of Being. It determines what space and time mean as, for example, in our epoch, they are interpreted as mathematical and physical. The interpretations of our epoch represent, however, only one manner in which the inceptual greeting can be understood in its historicity. The opening up of an epoch in the history of Being (as a sending of Being in an individualized time-space) is mediated by the second-order greeting of the poet. This greeting is, in turn, only a "greeting passed along" (*Weitergrüßen*) from the inceptual greeting between gods (or angels) and poets. The gods themselves remain hidden and withdrawn because, when something is disclosed, something else remains undisclosed and the gods are the concealed *par excellence*. The holy as "wholesome" allows for the double movement of opening up and remaining undisclosed: "To prepare joyfully for the greeting messengers, who bring the greeting of the still-reserved treasure, is to prepare for the fitting nearness for their approach—this is what determines the vocation of the homecoming poet. The holy does indeed appear. But the god remains distant. The time of the reserved discovery is the age when the god is absent. . . . However, since the find is near, although in a reserved manner, the absent god extends his greeting in the nearing of the heavenly ones. Thereby 'god's absence' is also not a deficiency.[63]

The holy shows itself in the opening up, while its wholesomeness remains hidden.[64] This withdrawal announces the presence of the gods precisely in their absence because they greet the poet and then withdraw. Withdrawal belongs to the opening up. Insofar as something opens up, something has to remain hidden, as we already pointed out before. The gods remain hidden in poetry. They disappear while greeting.

Heidegger often takes recourse to semiotic elements when describing his metaphysics of the gods. This semiotic aspect in Heidegger's metaphysics is, however, grounded in the things themselves. As the ones who greet, the gods behave precisely as signs.[65] They announce something, and by "announcing," as "signifiers," they remain withdrawn. The poet himself, in receiving the greeting of the gods, is not directed toward the gods themselves but to what the gods make known. The gods disclose the wholesomeness of the holy in the entanglement of showing and concealment. By virtue of their essence, the gods are always already "absconded" (*entflohen*). This concealment of the "still-reserved treasure" is necessary because in pure light no one can see anything.[66] Only via the absence of the gods does it become possible for something to show itself. Things can show themselves by escaping the pure light and casting shadows. In this way, beings (τὰ ὄντα) can gather (λέγειν), singularize and differentiate themselves.

As a way of concluding, we can say with Heidegger and Hölderlin that only through the greeting of the poet and the hermeneutical (ἑρμηνεύειν) interpretation of the signs of the messengers (Ἑρμῆς) is it possible for things to be present at all. If this is so, then greeting is precisely the opening up of the destiny of Being: Being sends (*schickt*) itself to the poet in the form of greetings, and the poet opens up the dimension in which humans dwell—that is, the historical destination (*Schickung*) of Being to humanity.

Notes

1. Heidegger, *Erläuterungen zu Hölderlins Dichtung*, 150; English translation: *Elucidations of Hölderlin's Poetry*, 171.

2. Here and throughout the text, I reference "the poet" in male gender, in line with Heidegger's understanding of Hölderlin as the eminent poet. It is only for easier readability that I refrain from adding alternative pronouns.

3. Heidegger, *Erläuterungen zu Hölderlins Dichtung*, 150; English translation: *Elucidations of Hölderlin's Poetry*, 171. In the course of this article, we will pay attention to the concept of *greeting* as it is developed by Heidegger in his interpretation of Hölderlin. This concept has, as I will explain in what follows, two different mediating functions. It mediates between the holy and the poets and between the poets and men. In different texts, Heidegger uses different concepts that deal with the same phenomenon. We can read, for example, in *Holzwege* that "das Wort des Sängers hält noch die Spur des Heiligen" (Heidegger, *Holzwege*, 274; English translation: "The singer's words stay on the track of the sacred," Heidegger, *Off the Beaten Tracks*, 204). There, the "trace" seems to correspond to what I call, in the following, "the inceptional greeting." On the concept of *trace* in this context, see Fédier, "Die Spur des Heiligen," 1991. Heidegger seems to use the concept of *sign* to indicate the second-order greeting, or what he also calls the *"Weiterwinken"* (Heidegger, *Hölderlins Hymnen "Germanien" und "Der Rhein,"* 35).

4. Poets, like metaphysicians, can "articulate the next or coming understanding of Being" (Richardson, *Heidegger*, 214). The changing historical articulation of Being is not historicism or relativism since, as Werner Marx has argued, Being itself is essentially unified (Marx, *Heidegger and the Tradition*, 167–68).

5. The question of Heidegger's alleged "theology" of the 1930s has already been discussed at length, but even a cursory inquiry into this topic would go beyond the limits of this article. The central point that is relevant for our interpretation is underlined by John Caputo: "But it is clear to everyone but Heidegger's most fanatic disciples that he is clearly Hellenizing and secularizing a fundamentally biblical conception of the history of salvation. He was in the most literal sense building a rival *Heilsgeschichte* to the biblical one that he had discovered in his New Testament studies" (Caputo, "Heidegger and Theology," 280). On this topic see also Fehér, "Der göttliche Gott."

6. One question that I must set aside here concerns how "violent" Heidegger's interpretation of Hölderlin is. For alternative philosophical interpretations of *Andenken*, see Gadamer, "Thinking and Poetizing," as well as Henrich, *Course of Remembrance*. Bernard Freydberg compares these three interpretations of *Andenken* in his "On Hölderlin's 'Andenken.'"

7. On Derrida's reading of the concept of greeting and his association of *salut* in the sense of greeting and *salut* in the sense of sanity (and hence of the holy), see Derrida, *Religion*, in particular the essay "Faith and Knowledge."

8. Heidegger, *Hölderlins Hymne "Der Ister,"* 30; English translation: *Hölderlin's Hymn "The Ister,"* 26.

9. See Heidegger, *Hölderlins Hymne "Andenken,"* 52: "da dies Sagen [scil.: des Dichters] ein Grüßen ist."

10. Heidegger, *Hölderlins Hymne "Der Ister,"* 5; English translation: *Hölderlin's Hymn "The Ister,"* 5.

11. Heidegger, *Hölderlins Hymne "Der Ister,"* 5; English translation: *Hölderlin's Hymn "The Ister,"* 5.

12. See Heidegger, *Hölderlins Hymne "Der Ister,"* 186; English translation: *Hölderlin's Hymn "The Ister,"* 149.

13. Heidegger, *Hölderlins Hymne "Der Ister,"* 194; English translation: *Hölderlin's Hymn "The Ister,"* 157.

14. Heidegger, *Hölderlins Hymne "Der Ister,"* 194; English translation: *Hölderlin's Hymn "The Ister,"* 157.

15. Heidegger, *Was heißt Denken?,* 6; English translation: *What Is Called Thinking?,* 10.

16. See Heidegger, "Bauen, Wohnen, Denken," 145–62; English translation *Building, Dwelling, Thinking.*

17. For the topic of the poet as a demigod, see Heidegger, *Hölderlins Hymne "Der Ister,"* 153; English translation: *Hölderlin's Hymn "The Ister,"* 123.

18. This *Vorlesung* is currently being translated by Julia Ireland and William McNeill.

19. "Allein wir trauen kaum unserem Ohr. . . . Schlägt hier nicht alles in sein Gegenteil um?" (Heidegger, *Hölderlins Hymne "Andenken,"* 42).

20. Heidegger, *Elucidations of Hölderlin's Poetry,* 103.

21. "Das Geheimnis des Andenkens" (Heidegger, *Hölderlins Hymne "Andenken,"* 49).

22. "Da das Erinnerte sich über unsere Gegenwart hinwegschwingt und plötzlich in der Zukunft steht" (Heidegger, *Hölderlins Hymne "Andenken,"* 54). This entanglement is the general structure of time in the history of Being. See Heidegger, *What Is Called Thinking?,* 76: "One still supposes that the handed-down [what remains in history of previous epochs] is something we have really [*eigentlich*] behind us, whereas it rather comes towards us, since we are delivered over and destined to it."

23. The analysis of the future is embedded into the "kairological time" of the future god. On this point, see Heidegger, *Phänomenologische Interpretationen zu Aristoteles,* 137; English translation: *Phenomenological Interpretations of Aristotle,* 102.

24. For an analysis of this element, see Henrich, *Course of Remembrance,* 155–61.

25. "Das Gegrüßte selbst neigt sich, auf den Grüßenden hindenkend, diesem zu" (Heidegger, *Hölderlins Hymne "Andenken,"* 54).

26. Heidegger, *Hölderlins Hymne "Andenken,"* 55.

27. Heidegger, *Hölderlins Hymne "Andenken,"* 55.

28. "Das Grüßen ist ein Seinlassen der Dinge und der Menschen" (Heidegger, *Hölderlins Hymne "Andenken,"* 50).

29. Heidegger, *Hölderlins Hymne "Andenken,"* 53.

30. "Ist in seine Wirktlichkeit gehoben" (Heidegger, *Hölderlins Hymne "Andenken,"* 52).

31. On the question of *Seinlassen* in relation to essence (what-being) and existence (that-being), see Haugeland, "Letting Be."

32. Richard Schaeffler puts emphasis on this point: "Der Gruß stiftet Beziehung, ohne die Vorbehaltenheit des Grüßenden preiszugeben. Das gilt schon unter Menschen. Wer den

anderen grüßt, stiftet Beziehung, aber er wahrt zugleich Abstand zu dem, den er grüßt"
(Schaeffler, "Der 'Gruß des Heiligen,'" 80).

33. "Dazu [i.e., zum Grüßen] aber gehört zumal das Dreifache: einmal, dass das Heilige
grüßt, damit Götter und Menschen gegrüßt werden; zum anderen, dass Götter und
Menschen also Gegrüßte sind; zuletzt, dass Götter und Menschen als die so Gegrüßten
seitdem selbst einander wieder grüßen und in solchem Grüßen aneinander sich halten
können" (Heidegger, *Hölderlins Hymne "Andenken,"* 70).

34. "Zum Dichtersein dieses Dichters gehört jetzt dieses Grüßen. Deshalb muss der
Grüßende auch dem Wesensreichtum des Gegrüßten zuwinken" (Heidegger, *Hölderlins
Hymne "Andenken,"* 62).

35. "Der Dichter ist nicht nur der Grüßende, sondern *zuvor schon* der Gegrüßte"
(Heidegger, *Hölderlins Hymne "Andenken,"* 62).

36. "Ein anfängliches Grüßen" (Heidegger, *Hölderlins Hymne "Andenken,"* 68).

37. "Das Grüßen bringt alles Gegrüßte in seine Einheit zusammen" (Heidegger,
Hölderlins Hymne "Andenken," 56).

38. Heidegger, *Hölderlins Hymne "Andenken,"* 81.

39. Karl Jaspers has claimed that Hölderlin's schizophrenia plays a role with regard to
the "actual presence" of the mythical world in Hölderlin's poetry between 1801 and 1805.
I cannot deal in more detail with this question, but I agree with Jaspers's interpretation that
the schizophrenia may be a factor in Hölderlin's poetry, although that does not depreciate its
poetical value. See Jaspers, *Strindberg und Van Gogh,* 98–113.

40. "Im Gruß werden aber 'die braunen Frauen daselbst' genannt. Die südlichen Feiertage
sind gemeint. Das südliche Land steht für das Griechenland. Das griechische Fest, die im
Griechentum gewesene Entgegnung der Menschen und Götter, wird gegrüßt. Wenn das
Grüßen darin sein Wesen hat, das Gegrüßte sein zu lassen in dem, was es ist, dann hebt
dieses Grüßen das gewesene Fest als das Gewesene in sein Wesen" (Heidegger, *Hölderlins
Hymne "Andenken,"* 84).

41. "Das gemäße Bleiben" (Heidegger, *Hölderlins Hymne "Andenken,"* 113).

42. Heidegger, *Hölderlins Hymne "Andenken,"* 70.

43. For this translation, see Heidegger, *Elucidations of Hölderlin's Poetry,* 69.

44. Heidegger, *Erläuterungen zu Hölderlins Dichtung,* 16; English translation: *Elucidations
of Hölderlin's Poetry,* 35, translation modified. This quotation refers to Heidegger's term *Die
Heitere* (gaiety), but given the whole of Heidegger's text, it becomes clearer that this concept
(if it is a concept) is synonymous with the "holy" (see Heidegger, *Erläuterungen zu Hölderlins
Dichtung,* 18; English translation: *Elucidations of Hölderlin's Poetry,* 37: "This pure opening
which first 'imparts,' that is, grants, the open to every 'space' and to every 'temporal space,'
we call gaiety [*die Heitere*] according to an old word of our mother tongue. . . . 'The highest'
and 'the holy' are the same for the poet: gaiety."

45. The ethical and moral connotations of this word in English have been let aside in the
following analysis. The word is used in the following text as a semantic interpretation for *das
Heilige* in a more literal sense—that is, precisely in the sense of something *unwounded.*

46. See on this the entries "Heil," "heil," and "heilig" in the *Deutsches Wörterbuch von J.
und W. Grimm.*

47. Heidegger, *Elucidations of Hölderlin's Poetry,* 79.

48. "But the name 'nature,' as the fundamental poetic word, is already overcome in the
hymn 'As When on a Holiday.' This overcoming is the consequence and sign of a saying

that starts from a more primordial point. . . . But why must 'the holy' be the poet's word?" (Heidegger, *Elucidations of Hölderlin's Poetry*, 80–81).

49. Heidegger, *Elucidations of Hölderlin's Poetry*, 82.
50. Heidegger, *Elucidations of Hölderlin's Poetry*, 85.
51. "Dieser anfängliche Gruß [ist] das verborgene Wesen der Geschichte. Dieser anfängliche Gruß ist *das* Ereignis, ist *der* Anfang" (Heidegger, *Hölderlins Hymne "Andenken,"* 70).
52. "Das Realwerden des Möglichen im Idealwerden des Wirklichen," "ein furchtbarer aber göttlicher Traum" (Heidegger, *Hölderlins Hymne "Andenken,"* 121). On the topic of the relation between the real and the ideal with a particular focus on imagination (as a gathering, poetical force), see Sallis, *Force of Imagination*, and Sallis, *Gathering of Reason*.
53. "Sofern das Idealwerden des vormals Wirklichen und dieses als das Gewesene in der Innigkeit seines Wesens gesagt werden muss, kann dieses Sagen nur ein Grüßen sein" (Heidegger, *Hölderlins Hymne "Andenken,"* 129).
54. "In der freien Kunstnachahmung, will sagen, in dem von der Kunst vollzogenen Stiften gibt es so etwas wie einen furchtbaren aber göttlichen Traum. Was soll das Traumhafte hier, wo es sich um das Stiften eines Reiches handelt, um Gründung der Geschichte? Das Traumhafte kann hier nicht das Unwirkliche im Sinne des bloßen Entschwindens und Nichtseins meinen; im Gegenteil: das Traumhafte betrifft das Realwerden des Möglichen im Idealwerden des Wirklichen. Das Wirkliche geht zurück in die Erinnerung, indem das Mögliche und zwar als das Kommende die Erwartung bindet. Dieses in einem ist dort, wo die Kunst die Geschichte stiftet, ein Traum. Der Traum bringt die noch nicht angeeignete Fülle des Möglichen und bewahrt die verklärte Erinnerung an das Wirkliche" (Heidegger, *Hölderlins Hymne "Andenken,"* 121).
55. "Das bisher Wirkliche [wird] ideal und [west] in der Erinnerung an" (Heidegger, *Hölderlins Hymne "Andenken,"* 122).
56. See Heidegger, *Elucidations of Hölderlin's Poetry*, 35.
57. Heidegger, *Elucidations of Hölderlin's Poetry*, 36.
58. Heidegger, *Elucidations of Hölderlin's Poetry*, 36.
59. Heidegger, *Elucidations of Hölderlin's Poetry*, 35.
60. Heidegger, *Elucidations of Hölderlin's Poetry*, 39.
61. Heidegger, *Elucidations of Hölderlin's Poetry*, 37.
62. On this concept see especially Heidegger, *Contributions to Philosophy*, 259ff.
63. Heidegger, *Elucidations of Hölderlin's Poetry*, 46.
64. On the topic of the remaining of the holy, see Duque, *Residuos de lo sagrado*, 47–63.
65. See Gourdain, "Heidegger et le 'dieu à venir.'"
66. "And if," said I, "someone should drag him thence by force up the ascent which is rough and steep, and not let him go before he had drawn him out into the light of the sun, do you not think that he would find it painful to be so haled along, and would chafe at it, and when he came out into the light, that his eyes would be filled with its beams so that he would not be able to see even one of the things that we call real?" (Plato, *Republic*, VII, 515e–516a).

Bibliography

Caputo, John. "Heidegger and Theology." In *The Cambridge Companion to Heidegger*, edited by Charles B. Guignon, 326–44. Cambridge: Cambridge University Press, 1993.

Derrida, Jacques. *Religion* (with Gianni Vattimo). Stanford: Stanford University Press, 1998.

Duque, Félix. *Residuos de lo sagrado. Tiempo y escatología en Heidegger, Levinas, Hölderlin y Celan.* Madrid: Abada Editores, 1997.

Fédier, François. "Die Spur des Heiligen." In *Auf der Spur des Heiligen. Heideggers Beitrag zur Gottesfrage*, edited by Günther Pöltner, 3–19. Wien/Köln: Böhlau, 1991.

Fehér, Istvan. "Der göttliche Gott. Hermeneutik, Theologie und Philosophie im Denken Heideggers." In *Das Spätwerk Heideggers. Ereignis—Sage—Geviert*, edited by Damir Barbarić, 57–78. Würzburg: Königshausen & Neumann, 2007.

Freydberg, Bernard. "On Hölderlin's 'Andenken': Heidegger, Gadamer, Henrich—A Decision?" In *Research in Phenomenology* 34 (2004): 181–97.

Gadamer, Hans-Georg. "Thinking and Poetizing in Heidegger and in Hölderlin's 'Andenken.'" In *Heidegger Toward the Turn: Essays on the Work of the 1930s*, edited by James Risser, 145–62. Albany: State University of New York Press, 1999.

Gourdain, Sylvaine. "Heidegger et le 'dieu à venir': s'il y a l'etre, pourquoi dieu?" In *Klesis. Revue Philosophique* 15 (2010): 89–103.

Haugeland, John. "Letting Be." In *Dasein Disclosed*, edited by Joseph Rouse, 232–61. Cambridge, MA: Harvard University Press, 2013.

Heidegger, Martin. "Bauen, Wohnen, Denken." In *Vorträge und Aufsätze*, GA 7, 145–62. Frankfurt am Main: Klostermann, 2000.

———. "Building, Dwelling, Thinking." In *Poetry, Language, Thought*. Translated by Albert Hofstadter. New York: Harper, 1971.

———. *Contributions to Philosophy (From Enowning).* Translated byParvis Emad, Kenneth Maly. Bloomington: Indiana University Press, 1999.

———. *Elucidations of Hölderlin's Poetry.* Translated by Keith Hoeller. New York: Humanity Books, 2000.

———. *Erläuterungen zu Hölderlins Dichtung.* GA 4. Frankfurt am Main: Klostermann, 1981.

———. *Hölderlins Hymne "Andenken."* GA 52. Frankfurt am Main: Klostermann, 1982.

———. *Hölderlins Hymne "Der Ister."* GA 53. Frankfurt am Main: Klostermann, 1984.

———. *Hölderlins Hymnen "Germanien" und "Der Rhein."* GA 39. Frankfurt am Main: Klostermann, 1980.

———. *Hölderlin's Hymn "The Ister."* Translated by William McNeill and Julia Davis. Bloomington: Indiana University Press, 1986.

———. *Holzwege.* GA 5. Frankfurt am Main: Klostermann, 1977.

———. *Off the Beaten Tracks.* Translated by Julian Young and Kenneth Haynes. Cambridge: Cambridge University Press, 2002.

———. *Phänomenologische Interpretationen zu Aristoteles. Einführung in die phänomenologische Forschung.* Frankfurt am Main: Klostermann, 1985.

———. *Phenomenological Interpretations of Aristotle: Initiation into Phenomenological Research.* Translated by Richard Rojcewicz. Bloomington: Indiana University Press, 2001.

———. *Was heißt Denken?* Tübingen: Niemeyer, 1997.

———. *What Is Called Thinking?* Translated by Jesse Glenn Gray. New York: Harper and Row, 1968.

Henrich, Dieter. *The Course of Remembrance and Other Essays on Hölderlin.* Stanford, CA: Stanford University Press, 1997.

Jaspers, Karl. *Stringberg und Van Gogh. Versuch einer pathographischen Analyse unter vergleichender Heranziehung von Swedenborg und Hölderlin.* Berlin: Springer, 1926.

Richardson, John. *Heidegger*. New York: Routledge, 2012.

Sallis, John. *Force of Imagination*. Bloomington: Indiana University Press, 2000.

———. *The Gathering of Reason*. New York: State University of New York Press, 2005.

Schaeffler, Richard. "Der 'Gruß des Heiligen' und die 'Frömmigkeit des Denkens.'" In *Auf der Spur des Heiligen. Heideggers Beitrag zur Gottesfrage*, edited by Günther Pöltner, 23–42. Wien/Köln: Böhlau, 1991.

DIEGO D'ANGELO is Postdoctoral Research Fellow and Lecturer at the University of Würzburg, Germany. He is author of *Zeichenhorizonte. Semiotische Strukturen in Husserls Phänomenologie der Wahrnehmung* (Springer, forthcoming).

4 Later Heidegger's Naturalism

Tristan Moyle

Introduction

In the following essay, I sketch the framework for a naturalistic interpretation of later Heidegger. By *naturalistic interpretation* I do not mean a reduction of his concepts to the more basic vocabulary of natural science. Far from it. Instead, in a rough approximation, I intend something like what we might think of as Feuerbach's naturalization of Hegel or Aristotle's naturalization of Plato. Here, *naturalizing* means tracing abstract, speculative content, content that appears quite puzzling and unworldly, back to a vocabulary that is rooted in ordinary, concrete, natural existence. In application to later Heidegger, I adopt this methodological stance in relation to sentences such as these: "Da-sein is owned by be-ing . . . as en-*owned*, Da-*sein* itself becomes *more its own* and the self-opening ground of the self,"[1] and "Being owned over into enowning . . . amounts to an essential transformation of the human from 'rational animal' (*animal rationale*) to Da-sein."[2]

There are countless others. One of the attractions of researching later Heidegger is the sense that his work contains deep, rich insights; one of the frustrations is that these insights have not been recognized by the wider philosophical community, which is no doubt put off by sentences such as these. This essay seeks to rectify this, as best it can. Of course, we do not have two philosophers, with one naturalizing the other, but only one, Heidegger, looked at in two ways. The result is an interpretive stance that is more hermeneutic than scholastic, with all the advantages and disadvantages that flow from this. But there is something about the later work that invites the adoption of such a stance; in any case, if our ability to communicate to non-Heideggerians is at all valuable, then we are under an obligation to pursue these more treacherous endeavors.

So much for the methodological approach. I also intend "Later Heidegger's Naturalism" in a more substantive sense. Let us distinguish, in broad brushstrokes, three forms of naturalism (there are many others): scientific naturalism, ethical naturalism, and aesthetic naturalism. What they have in common is the refusal of supernaturalism, the idea that there exists a supernatural being, beings, or powers, outside the natural world, that have dealings, causal or otherwise, with this world. But the naturalism of each form is very different. Scientific naturalism is the view that all natural phenomena are identical to, or metaphysically constituted by, physical entities. There is nothing more to the mental, biological, or social realms than the arrangement of these sorts of entities. This metaphysical stance often goes hand in hand with the methodological claim that any kind of access to the real must be anchored in the impersonal stance of scientific investigation. By *ethical naturalism* I mean, specifically, the naturalism of McDowell (I am ignoring the other, very different kinds). According to McDowell, we ought to contest the concept of nature as it is deployed within scientific naturalism rather than acquiesce in the view that only entities that can be subsumed under causal law are able to count as natural. This contestation amounts to a "partial re-enchantment of nature."[3] The re-enchantment is grounded in a focus on second nature. Our first nature, our animal, biological propensities, constrains the shape of our second nature, but nonetheless our second nature takes the form it does because of our upbringing (our *Bildung*). Our *Bildung* is the "framework within which [worldly] meaning comes into view"; the human capacity to resonate to the meaning we find in things is not "mysterious" but is grounded in the "normal coming to maturity of the animals that we are."[4] McDowell also describes his naturalism as Aristotelian or Greek naturalism. The reason for this is that he takes *Bildung* to be a central concept in Aristotle's ethics. Our ethical upbringing habituates our moral vision in such a way that the wise person is able to see, directly, what the practical situation demands. But McDowell generalizes the point. The culturally and linguistically structured form of our *Bildung* goes all the way down, informing even the actualizations of our natural, perceptual powers. It is because we always see it through the inherited, sociocultural prism of a tradition that the natural world appears to our eyes as already meaningful and ordered—in other words, as partially "enchanted."[5]

I take later Heidegger's work to offer the framework for a radicalization of ethical naturalism. I call this picture *aesthetic naturalism*, although I could also have described it as *romantic naturalism* because it has deep affinities with the realistic intuitions of either the Jena Romantics themselves or with those loosely connected with the movement, such as Herder, the early Schelling, Wilhelm von Humboldt, and Feuerbach. But I use these labels primarily to orient my interpretation rather than to make specific historical claims. Aesthetic naturalism, like ethical naturalism, contests the scientistic conflation of the natural with the scientifically verifiable, but it offers a more satisfying rectification of the concept of nature because the re-enchantment it enacts goes much deeper. When Heidegger talks of Being, or worse, Beyng, this can look like supernaturalism. But I argue (in the first section) that what he is referring to ought to be taken as a power of our nature, our second nature. The activity of this power brings our species-nature to completion in familiar ways. This power, more specifically, is rhythm (second section); if I may scrutinize a remark in Heidegger's Heraclitus seminar, rhythm is the form by which language approaches the human being. When we are appropriately informed in this way, our *Bildung* opens our eyes to the "speaking" of the things themselves (third section). This inspired modality of experience, which occurs when the power of Being is activated in an *Ereignis* experience, can happen across the full range of our passive and active natural powers. Nature, and natural beings, in what I think of as an austerely animist view of things, appear as if animated, in stark contrast to the scientific view of nature as disenchanted.[6] This is the more complete and satisfying re-enchantment that Heidegger's naturalism provides. In contrast to McDowell's ethical naturalism, the framework by which meaning comes into view is fittingly received as a gift from nature itself. I close by situating Heidegger's aesthetic naturalism even further from its contemporary counterparts. I suggest that it offers a view of the world that prepares us for the gods or god, taking the concept of preparation as indicating epistemic conditions that are centered on "aesthetic faith" (fourth section).

1. Being and Human Nature

The first plank of the interpretation is the claim that we ought to understand Being as a power of human nature. To this suggestion, I can imagine a quick counterargument, which might be called the *metaphysical humanist objection*. Metaphysical humanism is the view that humanity is at the center of things.[7] The objection would be that such a naturalizing approach is ineliminably humanistic because, foregrounding human nature, it reduces Being to the human being. We know that this is unacceptable because Heidegger insists that we need to ask about the "relation of being to the essence of the human being."[8] The error of all forms of metaphysical humanism, or subjectivism, is that they fail to register that the *humanitas* of man consists in his being "more than merely human," that is, "more essentially [than being human] in terms of his essence."[9] The truth, contrary to metaphysical humanism, is that our "proper dignity" lies in our relation to Being; to attend to the dimension that governs our essence is to "honor" Being rather than to vindicate human civilization or culture.[10] Of course, Being is not an isolated absolute. Being needs human beings to receive the gift that it gives; in attending to this gift, human beings complete, fulfill, their nature. Each belongs to the other. The quick counterargument to an interpretation of Being as a power of human nature is that it necessarily covers over this crucial mutual belonging of Being and humanity.

The objection can be parried, however. Let us call later Heidegger's position *antihumanism* (he also tentatively describes it as humanism in an "extreme sense").[11] A form of antihumanist naturalism is entirely possible. Aristotle, suitably interpreted, provides a good model. According to Aristotle, there is a power of our nature (intelligence, *nous*) that, when engaged, completes our essence. This inner activity of intelligence, our "authoritative and better element," which each of us "would actually seem to *be*,"[12] is either "something divine, or the divinest of the things in us."[13] That is, we become the animals we are, fulfilling our species-essence, by attaining a state whose functioning represents a transcendence of the human. Furthermore, our relation *to* this inner activity, Aristotle remarks, ought to be one of "devotion." The thinker rightly "cherishes" and "honors" the "more than human" power of their innermost nature.[14] These Greek terms (*cherishing, honoring*, etc.) are conventionally used in relation to the virtue of piety (*to hosion*).[15] The thinker displays piety, but of a distinctive kind; this is a "piety of thought" (the echoes of Heidegger are self-evident), in which the thinker devotes the self to (i.e., honors) "thinking itself." Indeed, this is not all. Aristotle remarks, puzzling commentators, that the gods benefit in turn the thinker who devotes the self to what they themselves love.[16] How can Aristotle talk of the gods intervening in human affairs, given what we know of his philosophical theology? Sarah Broadie argues that we can understand the concept of divine benefit along the following lines. Divine benefit is not material prosperity or good fortune, which are external goods of little use to the thinker. Rather, the benefit or favor Aristotle is getting at is the gift of "rational inspiration." The reward of the piety of thought is a bestowal of cognitive insight, manifest in those eureka moments when everything falls into place and a problem is solved.[17]

This is not the place to evaluate Broadie's reading of Aristotle, although the affinities to Heidegger are striking. The point is that we have is a form of naturalism that, when suitably interpreted, focuses on the inner activity of a natural disposition and that nonetheless is able (at least, up to a point) to accommodate an antihumanist perspective. We are a kind of animal whose nature it is to transcend that very nature. This transcendence occurs when a distinctive power of our nature is engaged. The best life is one that cherishes this power. What matters, then, is the mode of relation between the human being and the appropriating power of its nature. *This* decides whether we end up with humanism or antihumanism. Is this power at our disposal, or are we at its disposal? A naturalistic interpretation of Heidegger rules nothing out at this stage. Naturalism, in sum, does not entail humanism.

2. Rhythm as the Measure of Man

I wish to make a bold claim. If later Heidegger had a motto, it would be this: "All hail Rhythm!" Being, that is, is a power of human nature, and this power is rhythm. According to this view, to attend thoughtfully to the dimension of the truth of Being that governs the essence of the human being is to honor and cherish rhythm. To enact rhythm is to realize the "proper dignity" of humanity (this can happen in different modes, corresponding to the different natural powers). I will try to justify this interpretation in two ways: by citing textual evidence and by highlighting the way the claim provides a singularly illustrative schema for grasping later Heidegger. The textual evidence is dealt with in this section; the schema is sketched throughout the rest of the chapter.

First, the textual evidence. In a seminar on Heraclitus, conducted between 1966 and 1967, Heidegger makes the following remark, referring to the work of the musicologist Georgiades:

> He has spoken excellently about language. Among other things, he asks about rhythm, and shows that ῥυσμός [*Rysmos*, Ionic form for rhythm] has nothing to do with ῥέω (flow), but is to be understood as imprint (*Gepräge*). In recourse to Werner Jaeger, he appeals to a verse of Archilochos, Fr. 67a. . . . The verse reads . . . "Recognise which rhythm holds men." Moreover, he cites a passage from Aeschylus' *Prometheus*, to which Jaeger likewise has referred and in which the ῥυσμός . . . has the same meaning as in the Archilochos fragment . . . (Prometheus 241). Here Prometheus says of himself, "In this rhythm I am bound." He, who is held immobile in the iron chains of his confinement, is "rhythmed," that is, joined. Georgiades points out that humans do not make rhythm; rather, for the Greeks, the ῥυθμός [*Rythmos*] is the substrate of language (*das Substrat der Sprache*), namely the language that approaches us. Georgiades understands the archaic language in this way. We must also have the old languages of the fifth century in view in order to approximate understanding of Heraclitus. . . . In the sentences of the archaic language, the state of affairs speaks, not the conceptual meaning (*In den Sätzen der archaischen Sprache spricht die Sache und nicht die Bedeutung*).[18]

Rhythm, first, ought to be understood as character or imprint (*Gepräge*) and not flux or flow; second, rhythm is the substrate of language; third, in the archaic language, the "matter" itself speaks rather than the meaning.[19] In relation to the first claim, already in a lecture on Stefan George, delivered in 1958, Heidegger notes that rhythm, *rhythmos*, does not mean flux or flowing but form. Rhythm is "what is at rest, what forms the movement of dance and song, and thus lets it rest within itself."[20] What he means is that rhythm represents the coming to rest in itself or the gathering itself into form of that which lacks natural fixity (as, for example, a dancing body "resolves" into a pattern or figure of movement). Jaeger makes this very point, alongside his comments on Archilochus: it is not flow, he remarks, but pause, the steady limitation of movement, that lies beneath the Greek discovery of rhythm in music and dancing.[21] Heidegger (and Jaeger) are most likely thinking of Plato, who explicitly develops the familiar connection between rhythm and the movement of dance and song. In the *Laws*, we are told that "whereas animals have no sense of order and disorder in movement ('rhythm' and 'harmony,' as we call it), we human beings have been made sensitive to both and can enjoy them. This is the gift of the same gods whom we said are given to us as companions in dancing."[22]

But the message of Heidegger's remark in the Heraclitus seminar, with its reference to the archaic lyric poets, is that, for the ancient Greeks, at least before Plato, the rhythm of dance and song is secondary. The original meaning of ῥυθμός is ethical and refers, in a broad sense, to the form of a person's character.[23] But this is not yet a conception of character as a state or condition whose formation is under the agent's self-conscious, voluntary control, as it is by the time of Aristotle's *Nicomachean Ethics*.[24] To be "rhythmed" is to be brought into form or held in bounds and, in being bound in this way, for one's distinctive character to take shape. This is noted by poets other than Archilochus. Theognis, for example, also counts ῥυθμός among humanity's distinctive traits: "Never praise a man before knowing clearly his feelings (ὀργή), his disposition (ῥυθμός), his character (τρόπος)."[25] Indeed, there is a residue of this archaic sense of ῥυθμός even in Aristotle. "What kind of talking," he asks (incidentally, a few lines after quoting Theognis), is able to "transform" the "rhythm of [a person's] life"? It is not possible, Aristotle claims, "for words to dislodge what has long since been absorbed into one's character-traits."[26] One's rhythmic disposition, in the archaic sense, then, appears to be a measure that is neither an external, heteronomous imposition on the agent nor a subjective form that this agent self-knowingly produces. Rather, ῥυθμός is a normative constraint that comes both from within and from without a person's being.

In the Heraclitus passage, Heidegger does not explain the transition from rhythm considered as an ethical disposition to the idea that rhythm represents the substrate of language. But we are able to connect the dots. Language is the second nature of human beings. Our first nature provides us with certain biological propensities, often shared with other animals. But being brought up within a language, becoming encultured, involves, among other things, the shaping and molding of ethical character. This upbringing (*Bildung*) in language-using animals is grounded in ῥυθμός. So what Heidegger seems to be saying is that the linguistic form of life that *in*forms our existence is rhythmic, in its essence. By holding our existence in this way, it is the rhythm of language that gives us our distinctive character (*Gepräge*). This is a decidedly non-metaphysical conception of language. Here, language is not considered merely as an instrument for the communication of thought and feeling; language is not possessed by human beings. Rather, the rhythm of language "approaches us," that is, holds sway over us, appropriates us. The ease with which the concept of ῥυθμός fits into Heidegger's conception of language, as demonstrated in the Heraclitus passage, should not surprise us. We know that the "most appropriate mode of appropriating," indeed, the "mode in which Appropriation speaks," is the "saying" of language.[27] This saying is a movement or "way" that "form[s] a way" and "clears a path."[28] However, this movement, through which language speaks, is not arbitrary or haphazard but normatively binding; it has precisely the order in movement, the purposefulness without purpose, that ῥυθμός displays. Indeed, in a lecture on Georg Trakl, in 1953, Heidegger comes close to making this exact point.[29] But by 1966, he is explicit: it is through rhythm that the "matter" of language "speaks."

We need to know, of course, *how* exactly the ῥυθμός of language, our second nature, informs our character. I say more about this in the next section. Before we get to this, let us consider another reason that thinking of Being as ῥυθμός might be considered singularly appropriate. We know that Being (*Seyn*) essentially unfolds as the event of appropriation (*Ereignis*). We know that the "it" that gives Being, in the *Ereignis*, is Being itself. Being is at once the giver, the activity of giving, and that which is given. The source of Being, in other words, is not some*thing*, such as a cause or an all-perfect, supreme entity. We also know that Being holds sway as *Ent-eignis*, as the withdrawal and concealing of Being. Expropriation is an essential form of the mystery of *Ereignis*; it marks the way in which Being holds itself in reserve. Finally, in being appropriated by Being, people are brought into their ownmost essential being. To be appropriated in this way is for a human being to achieve a kind of freedom.[30] These points are uncontroversial; what Heidegger means by them is less so. But consider the way in which the concept of rhythm is apt as a concrete schema for grasping these abstract ideas. Rhythm *gives*. The gift of rhythm is impersonal; no transcendent, personal giver gives rhythm. Rather, rhythm *gives itself*. In being brought into rhythm, the human being is bound or held. This is a form of normative and not causal constraint. Yet no principle of reason lies at the heart of this mysterious gift. Rhythm has no "Why?" Simply, *there is* rhythm. When gripped in this way, in an *Ereignis* experience, the sublime beauty of rhythm brings the thankful, inspired, dancing animal, receiving its gift, into the dimension of its innermost essence.

In all, one might say that the concept of rhythm forces itself upon us when we try to make sense of the *Ereignis* (especially when combined with Heidegger's own remarks on the matter). The resulting picture is naturalistic—in fact, almost Feuerbachian—but this is naturalism of a distinctively antihumanist kind. The proof of the pudding, though, is in the eating. It is to the implications of this naturalistic picture concerning the relation between human beings and rhythm, assuming it is generally correct, that I now turn.

3. Later Heidegger's Factical Ideal

Thinking, after the Turn, "abandons subjectivity."[31] It is tempting to take this proposition, allied with the fact that we do not have a detailed description of ordinary human experience in the later work, as indicating that the Turn marks a turn *from* ordinary, human experience. But the one does not necessarily follow from the other. To abandon subjectivity is to deepen and recast our grasp of human experience, not to jettison it in favor of Being itself. We ought to take more seriously Heidegger's assertion that Being itself could not be experienced without a more original experience of the essence of man.[32] This original experience of the essence of man can only take place within the bounds of ordinary (or, more precisely, extraordinary) concrete experience. It is common knowledge that Heidegger focuses on the creative activities of poets and great thinkers after the pragmatism of *Being and Time*. But we have been led by the lack of a detailed, systematic, phenomenologically nuanced description of *Ereignis* experience (i.e., the sort of personal, transformative experience during which we dwell in the truth of Being) into overcorrecting our focus to Being itself. The advantage of using the concept of rhythm as the guiding thread of our interpretation is that it functions to prevent this excessive drift from human to Being, without neglecting the insights that necessitated the abandonment of subjectivity. The presencing of rhythm is nothing, after all, but *as* and *how* it occurs in the life of human beings.

The discussion can be oriented by reference to a concept Heidegger introduces in *Being and Time*: a "factical ideal." A factical ideal is a "definite ontical way of taking authentic existence," one that underlies any "ontological Interpretation of Dasein's existence."[33] This ontical way of taking authentic existence is, one might say, an immediate, concrete interpretation of the world-historical situation (or factical life context) one finds oneself in. We do not have later Heidegger's factical ideal, but we *do* have a skeletal "ontological Interpretation" of this ideal, as laid down in abstract concepts such as "it gives," the "truth of Being," the "event of appropriation," and so on. The factical ideal is missing, in other words, but we ought to take this lack as unfinished business rather than as a principled omission. What is required is a reconfiguration of the factical ideal and not its abandonment along with subjectivity.

I propose, as a hypothesis, that we take the following passage from Nietzsche as crystallizing later Heidegger's factical ideal. This will help further orient the discussion. Nietzsche describes, with astonishing clarity, the fundamental elements of the experience of inspiration:

> Does anyone . . . have a clear idea of what poets in strong ages called *inspiration*? . . . If you have even the slightest residue of superstition, you will hardly reject the idea of someone being just an incarnation, mouthpiece, or medium of overpowering forces. The idea of revelation in the sense of something suddenly becoming visible and audible with unspeakable assurance and subtlety, something that throws you down and leaves you deeply shaken—You listen, you do not look for anything, you take, you do not ask who is there; a thought lights up in a flash, with necessity, without hesitation as to its form,—I never

had any choice. . . . A perfect state of being outside yourself. . . . An instinct for rhythmic relations that spans wide expanses of forms—the length, the need for a rhythm that spans wide distances is almost the measure of the force of inspiration. . . . All this is involuntary to the highest degree, but takes place as if in a storm of feelings of freedom, of unrestricted activity, of power, of divinity.[34]

We have no better description of an *Ereignis* experience. This is nothing other than the (extra)ordinary "event" of inspiration. Being is the source of inspiration, but it ought not to be taken as some*thing*, an opaque X working behind the scenes. To reflect *on* Being *is* to turn our attention *to* the "meaning-giving process"—mediated by the experience of inspiration—*as* that very process gives itself to us. This is the focus of later Heidegger's work. And we can see what is, for Nietzsche, the measure of the force of inspiration: rhythm. In this "perfect state of being outside [itself]," gripped by rhythm, inspired Dasein becomes full of the truth in the archaic sense of being freely "open to" the truth as "it speaks." To dwell *in* the truth of Being is for the truthful, inspired one to be in a position to repeat the words of Heraclitus: listen not to me but to the *logos*. But to say this is *not* to abandon the immanent domain of human experience. This domain remains the center ground (and not *Being itself*). What is brilliant about later Heidegger is that he provides the conceptual tools, the categories, for deepening and systematizing the sort of factical experience that Nietzsche merely gestures toward in this passage.

Let us consider how this systematization might work. There are a variety of active and passive natural powers. We have the passive power to see and active powers to move our bodily limbs, to deliberate and act morally, and to engage in theoretical cognition. A range of modes of operation are associated with these powers. These modes lie on a scale, from the active exercise of our powers all the way through to their passive actualization. Thinking, the formation of judgment, for example, involves the active exercise and synthesis of our concepts, in thoughts of the form x is y. Further down the scale lies the entertaining of suppositions; further down still daydreaming or idle fantasy. At the opposite end lies mere actualization. Our perceptual powers, for example, are passively actualized. We have no choice; we cannot help what we see, even though we might decide to scan the horizon or open our eyes. But the operation of our sensibility is not devoid of rationality. On the contrary, we come to see that x is y. This experience, in which our concepts are involuntarily actualized, entitles us, rationally, to form beliefs on the basis of what we perceive. So, running alongside the operation of our natural powers is a parallel scale of operation of conceptual capacities. A specific mode of operation of a natural power is also, in other words, a specific mode of operation of a conceptual capacity.[35] To exercise the power of bodily movement is also to exercise a practical concept, and so on.

The operations of even our passive natural powers are structured by concepts because we are animals that have the *logos*, that is, we acquire language, our second nature, as part of our upbringing (*Bildung*). This second nature acts as a kind of linguistically mediated cultural repository or tradition, one that acts as a prism through which we see and engage with the world, down to the very workings of our natural sensibility. Now, in relation to this picture, there is, in modern analytic philosophy, generalizing in a rather crude way, what we might call an ideological commitment to an exemplary or paradigmatic mode of operation of our natural powers. This is their *exercise* in acts of judgment.[36] Exercise of our capacities (which might also occur in practical, deliberative contexts) is taken as a sort of regulative ideal: it is the mode of engagement that is believed to represent the capacity human beings have for autonomous freedom. Free spontaneity, in this picture, is being in self-conscious, voluntary control of one's thinking (or acting). But this *is* mere ideology. Later Heidegger provides an alternative factical ideal, one that abandons the metaphysical subjectivism that this picture inchoately endorses. We can set out the alternative as follows.

There is a hidden, fundamental mode of operation of our natural powers, aside from their actualization and exercise, a sort of hidden, unifying root from which *exercise* (understanding) and *actualization* (sensibility) emerge as two stems. This hidden root is what Heidegger refers to in the Heraclitus passage as the ῥυθμός of language. When our natural powers are affected by rhythm, in an *Ereignis* experience, the concepts that structure them are neither passively actualized nor actively exercised but spontaneously animated. The conceptual content of this sort of experience has an imperative form ("Do *x*!"); its verbal representation is given in the hortative mood. Things appear, in an inspired experience, as if they are speaking to us. This can happen across the full range of our natural powers. Let us apply this framework, for illustrative purposes, to the active powers, that is, to the bodily, moral, and intellectual powers.

§1. *Bodily Powers.* When the bodily power is affected by rhythm, things in the world (if the agency is object directed) or the body itself (if the agency occurs for its own sake) appear as if speaking to the agent. For example, when a rock climber is in the zone, the foothold appears to say, "Adjust your toe *like so!*" Inviting a response, it admonishes, "Decelerate your swing!" The rock face appears as if *it wants* the agent to *x* or to *y*. The rock climber no doubt has the intention, "Climb the V7." But it is the overarching and ongoing unity of practical reasoning that strikes the inspired climber. In this experience, there is an involuntary animation of the climber's practical concepts—not their voluntary exercise.[37] This is not acting in flow, as if the climber's bodily movements are detached from rationality, so that, when asked, "Why did you adjust your foot?" the climber might simply reply, "It just felt right."[38] Rather, an expert climber will cite a reason, whose content will have conceptual form. But the climber takes the idea to have come *to* the self. To be inspired is to undergo, not a state of Dionysian flux, but an austere, Apollonian lucidity, as clear as the mountain air. In these moments, when one's practical rationality is guided by ῥυθμός, one's movements are shaped by a form of purposefulness that is yet external to the autonomous subject. An event of Being happens *to* the mindful agent, an event whose command *the body* expresses.

§2. *Moral Powers.* The world that speaks in a different, higher register is also the moral and intellectual world, the object of our moral and intellectual powers. The *phronimos*, the ethically wise individual, when in the zone, with the power of moral deliberation (*bouleusis*) fully engaged, catches the inner voice of conscience. Attuned to its whisper, a decision (*prohairesis*) settles in the soul. The *phronimos* makes this choice, but it is a choice that *comes to one*, that impresses and forces itself *upon one*: "Return the letter!" or "Save your friend!" Here, the imperative content of the moral perception is categorically, not hypothetically, structured. "You *must* save your friend!" or "This is your *duty*!" Inspired in this way, the conscience of the *phronimos* is shaped by the ῥυθμός of the moral situation as it calls. In such an inspired state, which is far from being a state of affective flux, a person, in whom the truth of Being dwells, attains "truth, of a practical sort"[39] (1139a27).

§3. *Intellectual Powers.* A thought "lights up in a flash," Nietzsche remarks, "com[ing] when 'it' wants and not when 'I' want."[40] The nature of this paradigmatic event returns us to the analysis of Book X of the *Nicomachean Ethics*. Absorbed thinkers, when in the zone, let the concepts themselves speak. A thought presses itself upon us: "This way!" When we are struck by a thought while we are grappling with a complex problem, we suddenly realize *how* to do something. But this sudden flash of inspiration is not the rapid, inner execution of *what* one knows how to do—or of content that is subsequently matched in outward expression. Rather, when ῥυθμός engages the theoretical powers, it points us in a direction and "clear[s] a path." When Being speaks, it does not point to an already well-trodden path but to a new one, as a path is cleared through a snow-covered field.[41] Nietzsche is quite right that it is a "superstition of the logicians" to say that the "it" is just that "famous old I." But that the "subject 'I' is the condition of the predicate 'think'"[42] remains, precisely, a foundational assumption of recent philosophy, which later Heidegger's work invites us to challenge. There is more to the process of thinking than the voluntary exercise of our concepts.

The kinds of activities occurring in modes §1–3 appear "involuntary to the highest degree" but also take place as if in a "storm of feelings of freedom, of unrestricted activity." Let us say, in Heidegger's terms, that these activities, as such, display a relation of "needful usage" (*Brauchen*).[43] On the one hand, the agent appears as if used by ῥυθμός. The necessity (or compulsive involuntariness) of proper usage, in which a human is maintained by Being, is a use that "handles" or "fit[s] itself to the thing" in order to summon it to its essential nature.[44] On the other hand, ῥυθμός "needs" the site of human thought for its realization, whether this is mediated through our bodily, moral, or cognitive powers. Yet, being summoned into its ownmost nature by the call of ῥυθμός, the event of inspiration also "establishes the free scope of freedom in which free human nature may abide."[45] The free, unrestricted activity in which the agent spontaneously engages is the activity of a thing that has been released (by ῥυθμός) into the essence of its innermost nature. Later Heidegger's notion of freedom is compatibilist, then, but of a distinctive and original kind. Freedom arises when one's uninhibited activity is determined by one's nature, but such determination is precisely not a form of metaphysical or humanist *self*-determination.

Let us return to the beginning. When Heidegger remarks that, for example, "Being owned over into enowning . . . amounts to an essential transformation of the human from 'rational animal' (*animal rationale*) to Da-sein," the transformation he is referring to can seem quite mysterious. It is tempting to think of this as some sort of fantastic, radical change in our metaphysical constitution. But it is possible to domesticate Heidegger's rhetoric. If we see Heidegger's picture through naturalistic eyes, then he is pointing to a kind of paradigm shift in what we take to be the exemplary forms of human, factical life. To conceive of a human as an *animal rationale* is to conceive of one as, first and foremost, a biological organism with a variety of attributes, including the distinctive attribute of *logos* possession, used, instrumentally, to represent and communicate thought and feeling. But to conceive of a human as Dasein is to transform our factical ideal; it is to conceive of a human as, first and foremost, the "inspired animal," the animal that can listen to the heartbeat of the world. That is, it is to lay down and systematize the exemplary forms of factical existence sketched from §1–3. To live in this way is to "learn to live in the speaking of language," as Heidegger urges us to do.[46] In this sort of life, one receives the stamp (*Gepräge*) of Being. This is the kernel of later Heidegger's aesthetic or romantic naturalism. In order to achieve this transformation—as difficult as it may be—we do not have to take one step out of mundane, material, human existence.

4. The Aesthetic-Practical Argument from Inspiration

A problem, in Heidegger's opinion, with the conception of humanity as *animal rationale* is that the human being is conceived as a living thing alongside plants and animals. On the one hand, beings of nature are "most clearly akin to us," given our "bodily kinship" with them. But, on the other hand, "it might also seem as though the essence of divinity is closer to . . . our ek-sistent essence."[47] Heidegger spells out the sort of proximity he has in mind. After Being has been experienced in its truth, the holy (*Heilige*) begins to radiate. The radiating of the holy, in turn, prepares a dimension within which the god or gods can appear: "Only from the truth of Being can the essence of the Holy be thought. Only from the essence of the Holy is the essence of divinity to be thought. Only in the light of the essence of divinity can it be thought or said what the word 'God' is to signify."[48]

Heidegger comments in an interview, in 1966, that "we cannot think [the god] into being here; we can at most awaken the readiness of expectation." This preparation of readiness is, furthermore, "connected with the fact that what I name with the word Being . . . requires humans for its revelation, preservation and formation."[49] One might imagine that a purported naturalistic interpretation of Heidegger would struggle with these passages. However, on the contrary, the naturalism of the factical existence sketched from §1–3, although it is resolutely secular, nonetheless invites a sort of supernaturalism to grow from its soil. Nietzsche's precise words are so telling: "If you have even the *slightest* residue of superstition, you will hardly reject the idea of someone being just an incarnation." That is to say, the categorical structure of the experience of inspiration, more than any other experience, provokes the further thought of a divine giver of this gift. The point is that this provocation has rational warrant. The category *gift*, with similar concepts such as *thankfulness*, implies at least two things. First, when we are struck by a thought, in a eureka moment, this ought not to be taken, phenomenologically speaking, as the effect of a causal impression. One cannot receive a gift from a brute cause, whether conceived as a psychological mechanism or as an environmental stimulus. Second, as an experiential state, this gift cannot be a gift from another person (even if that person helps us to this insight); nor, because of its law-like form, can this gift be given to oneself. One is entitled, then, rationally, to interpret an *Ereignis* experience as a sort of divine benefit (as Aristotle seems tempted to do in Book X).

So, when Heidegger remarks that "only from the truth of Being can the essence of the Holy be thought," we can take this as the stipulation of an epistemic condition. Let us call this Heidegger's aesthetic-practical argument from inspiration. The point is that this is not a theoretical proof of divinity; it is a possible stance, taken on aesthetic-practical grounds. One is entitled to believe in the existence of the divinities (or God) as a kind of aesthetic-practical postulate of our aesthetic consciousness. That is, we take postulates such as these to set out what *must* be the case if we are to comprehend, in the fullest sense, the "facts" of the experience of inspiration. But this is not a proof along the lines of "it is certain that gods (or God) exist" but rather in the sense of something like "*I* am (aesthetically) certain that the gods (or God) exist." The perfections of these dark gods (whatever they are) will, of course, be restricted by the requirements of the aesthetic-practical purview. This stance—let us call it *aesthetic faith*—I take to be what Heidegger means by "the Holy." Inspired Dasein is entitled to enter the dimension of aesthetic faith, given the facts of aesthetic consciousness, and, furthermore, on the basis of this faith, to postulate the existence of supernatural beings as conditions for this consciousness. There are intimate threads of epistemic support, then, tying the various stages identified by Heidegger (truth of Being, the holy, the gods, etc.). He is certainly not advocating a return to some kind of mysticism or irrationalism. But the standpoint of aesthetic faith, favored by the poets, does not *have* to be taken. The thinker is able to prepare—and tarry within—the naturalistic soil of faith. Here, ῥυθμός, the gift of our nature, remains solely worthy of worship. But this *is* naturalism of a radically different kind from the aggressively atheistic naturalism that is part and parcel of contemporary scientism. Heidegger, in laying down an alternative factical ideal, is challenging the ideological grip that scientism has on our concept of nature rather than relinquishing it in favor of a supernaturalistic conception of Being.

A final thought. The concept of the *Ereignis* is Janus faced. It has a microstructure (which I have analyzed as an *Ereignis* experience) and a world-historical, sociocultural macrostructure (which I have not discussed). The approximate connection between these two faces is relatively clear. The work of the inspired thinker creates a site for Being to appear and thus for an epoch of Being to be established. But Heidegger's technical vocabulary at the level of the macrostructure is ripe for naturalization. We need to see linkages between concepts such as *Weltanschauung*, world formation, and niche construction. The thinker, inspired by ῥυθμός, is a person who makes sense, that is, who renders things intelligible in a productive sense, as a spider spins its web or a bird builds its nest. This philosophical labor of the concept engineer, refashioning our view of how things hang together, must be seen as part of the natural history of our species. Only when both aspects of the *Ereignis* are developed will this sketch of later Heidegger's naturalism be complete.

Notes

1. Heidegger, *Contributions to Philosophy*, 211.
2. Heidegger, *Contributions to Philosophy*, 3.
3. McDowell, *Mind and World*, 85.
4. McDowell, *Mind and World*, 87–88.
5. McDowell, *Mind and World*, 184–85.
6. The contrast would be with naive animism. This distinction deserves further comment. I mention it here only to put it to one side.
7. Heidegger, "Letter on Humanism," 245.
8. Heidegger, "Letter on Humanism," 245.
9. Heidegger, "Letter on Humanism," 260.

10. Heidegger, "Letter on Humanism," 251.

11. Heidegger, "Letter on Humanism," 261.

12. Aristotle, *Nicomachean Ethics*, 1178a3.

13. Aristotle, *Nicomachean Ethics*, 1177a17.

14. Aristotle, *Nicomachean Ethics*, 1179a23–28.

15. Aristotle, *Nicomachean Ethics*, 447.

16. Aristotle, *Nicomachean Ethics*, 1179a29.

17. Aristotle, *Nicomachean Ethics*, 441, 448–49.

18. Heidegger, *Heraclitus Seminar*, 55.

19. I put to one side the connection Heidegger makes between rhythm and the jointure of Being. But it does point in interesting ways toward Heidegger's "The Anaximander Fragment" and so to the concepts of *justice* and *historical fate*. On this, see the closing comments on the "macrostructure" of the *Ereignis*.

20. Heidegger, "Words," 149.

21. Jaeger, *Paideia*, 126.

22. Plato, "Laws," 1345, lines 652–54. Note that this claim could act as a foundation for philosophical anthropology. It has, additionally, a significant degree of empirical support. See Schachner, "Auditory-Motor Entrainment."

23. Jaeger makes this point (*Paideia*, 126), as does Benveniste, *Problems in General Linguistics*, 287.

24. Aristotle, *Nicomachean Ethics*, 1114a9.

25. Theognis, "Elegy and Iambus," 343, lines 963–64.

26. Aristotle, *Nicomachean Ethics*, 1179b17–18.

27. Heidegger, "Way to Language," 135.

28. Heidegger, "Way to Language," 113, 129–30.

29. Heidegger, "Language in the Poem," 160.

30. Heidegger, "Time and Being," 8–10, 12, 23.

31. Heidegger, "Letter on Humanism," 249.

32. Cited (GA 55, 293) in Haar, *Heidegger and the Essence of Man*, ix.

33. Heidegger, *Being and Time*, 358.

34. Nietzsche, *Ecco Homo*, 126–27.

35. McDowell, *Mind and World*, 77.

36. McDowell, *Mind and World*, 13.

37. Nor is absorbed engagement to be interpreted as the *unreflective* but voluntary exercise of our practical concepts. This is McDowell's position. See *Mind, Reason, and Being-in-the-World*, 53. The problem with this position is that it distorts the phenomenology.

38. This is Dreyfus's position, the dialectical opposite of McDowell's. According to this view, engaged agency is detached from the agent's rationality. See *Mind, Reason, and Being-in-the-World*, 28. Later Heidegger offers us a middle path between these alternatives.

39. Aristotle, *Nicomachean Ethics*, 1139a27.

40. Nietzsche, *Beyond Good and Evil*, 17.

41. Heidegger, "Way to Language," 129.

42. Nietzsche, *Beyond Good and Evil*, 17.

43. Heidegger, "On the Question of Being," 308.

44. Heidegger, *What Is Called Thinking?*, 187.

45. Heidegger, *What Is Called Thinking?*, 133.

46. Heidegger, "Language," 210.

47. Heidegger, "Letter on Humanism," 248.

48. Heidegger, "Letter on Humanism," 267.

49. Heidegger, "Only a God Can Save Us," 107.

Bibliography

Aristotle. *Nicomachean Ethics*. Edited by Sarah Broadie. Translated by Christopher Rowe. Oxford: Oxford University Press, 2002.

Benveniste, Émile. "The Notion of 'Rhythm' in its Linguistic Expression." In *Problems in General Linguistics*, 281–88. Translated by Mary Elizabeth Meek. Coral Gables, FL: University of Miami Press, 1971.

Haar, Michel. *Heidegger and the Essence of Man*. Translated by William McNeill. New York: State University of New York Press, 1993.

Heidegger, Martin. *Being and Time*. Translated by John Macquarrie and Edward Robinson. Oxford: Blackwell, 1995.

———. *Contributions to Philosophy (From Enowning)*. Translated by Richard Rojcewicz and Daniela Vallega-Neu. Bloomington: Indiana University Press, 2012.

———. *Heraclitus Seminar*. Translated by Charles Seibert. Evanston: Northwestern University Press, 1993.

———. "Language." In *Poetry, Language, Thought*, 185–207. Translated by Albert Hofstadter. New York: Harper and Row, 1971.

———. "Language in the Poem." In *On the Way to Language*, 159–98. Translated by Peter Hertz. New York: HarperCollin, 1971.

———. "Letter on Humanism." In *Pathmarks*, 138–76. Translated by William McNeil. Cambridge: Cambridge University Press, 1998.

———. "Only a God Can Save Us." In *The Heidegger Controversy*, edited by Richard Wolin, 91–116. Cambridge: MIT Press, 1993.

———. "On the Question of Being." In *Pathmarks*, 291–322. Translated by William McNeil. Cambridge: Cambridge University Press, 1998.

———. "Time and Being." In *On Time and Being*, 1–24. Translated by Joan Stambaugh. New York: Harper and Row, 1972.

———. "The Way to Language." In *On the Way to Language*, 111–38. Translated by Peter Hertz. New York: HarperCollin, 1971.

———. *What Is Called Thinking?* Translated by J. Glenn Gray. New York: Harper and Row, 1968.

———. "Words." In *On the Way to Language*, 139–58. Translated by Peter Hertz. New York: HarperCollin, 1971.

Jaeger, Werner. *Paideia*. Vol. 1. Translated by Gilbert Highet. Oxford: Oxford University Press, 1986.

McDowell, John. *Mind and World*. Cambridge, MA: Harvard University Press, 1998.

Nietzsche, Friedrich. *Beyond Good and Evil*. Edited by Rolf-Peter Horstmann and Judith Norman. Cambridge: Cambridge University Press, 2002.

———. *Ecce Homo*. Edited by Aaron Ridley and Judith Norman. Cambridge: Cambridge University Press, 2005.

Plato. "Laws." In *Plato: Collected Works*, edited by John Cooper, 1318–1616. Translated by
Trevor Saunders. Cambridge: Hackett, 1997.

Schachner, Adena. "Auditory-Motor Entrainment in Vocal Mimicking Species."
Communicative & Integrative Biology 3, no. 3 (May–June 2010): 1–4.

Shear, Joseph K., ed. *Mind, Reason, and Being-in-the-World: The McDowell-Dreyfus Debate*.
London: Routledge, 2013.

Theognis. "Elegy and Iambus." In *Greek Elegiac Poetry*, 166–385. Translated by Douglas
Gerber. Cambridge, MA: Harvard University Press, 1999.

TRISTAN MOYLE is Senior Lecturer in Philosophy at Anglia Ruskin
University, Cambridge, UK.

II.
HEIDEGGER'S *PHYSIS*

5 Why Is Heidegger Interested in *Physis*?

Thomas Buchheim

Translated by Diego D'Angelo

Φύσις APPEARS IN Heidegger's thought—perhaps one should say it *arises* in his thought—around 1926, with his reception of pre-Socratic philosophy in the lecture course *Basic Concepts of Ancient Philosophy*.[1] More precisely, it appears in the deconstruction (undertaken in these lectures and elsewhere) of the word *metaphysics* into its components. Following this, the problem of φύσις slowly disappears from Heidegger's thinking in the 1940s. Or rather, it remains only as a memory, as a remembrance of philosophy's golden age.[2] The essay "On the Essence and Concept of φύσις,"[3] written in 1939, must, then, be considered the high point of the presence of φύσις in Heidegger's thought. It is a zenith, yet one can already see the future decline in his interest.

In the φύσις essay, Heidegger already clearly sees the central place of φύσις in the inceptual Greek conception of philosophy found particularly in Heraclitus, Parmenides, and Anaximander. At this point in his career, Heidegger's attempt to grasp this first beginning of the history of being and to repeat it in another inceptual moment was still in full force. This other beginning was supposed to lead the essence of truth into a transformed unconcealment of the being of beings. Yet if Heidegger was so well under way in thinking φύσις as an event of being, why does it take him until 1939 to approach and interpret the "last echo"[4] of original pre-Socratic φύσις in Aristotle—instead of remaining with the inceptual essence of φύσις that he had already conquered before? Why does he slip back, so to speak, into the mishaps of metaphysics under the yoke of λόγος in Aristotle?

Heidegger published the essay "On the Essence and Concept of φύσις" for the first time in 1958,[5] almost twenty years after having written it. At that time, Heidegger was more concerned with twisting (*Verwindung*) metaphysics than with overcoming (*Überwindung*) it.[6] Twisting metaphysics first takes a step back (*Schritt zurück*) into understanding the completion of its origin. Unlike overcoming metaphysics, it does not aim at leaving metaphysics behind through a reversal of ontology.[7] In the period between writing and publishing the essay on φύσις, which also is the period in which Heidegger reconceives the favorable relation to metaphysics, he adds a few notes on the history of Being; he inserts these in between slash marks in the 1940s (or so I believe). These notes make clear that Heidegger considered φύσις and its discussion in Aristotle as the pivotal origin of metaphysics in its entirety. Thus at the end of the essay, he writes: "Because φύσις in the sense of the *Physics* is one kind of οὐσία and because οὐσία itself stems in its essence from φύσις as projected in the beginning, therefore ἀλήθεια belongs to Being and *therefore* presenting into the open of the ἰδέα (Plato) and into the open of the εἶδος κατὰ τὸν λόγον (Aristotle) is revealed as *one* characteristic of οὐσία; *therefore* for Aristotle the essence of κίνησις becomes *visible* as ἐντελέχεια and ἐνέργεια."[8] Without φύσις as the paradigmatic οὐσία, and without the revelation of οὐσία out of inceptual φύσις, being (οὐσία) would have become visible neither as ἐνέργεια for Aristotle nor as εἶδος for Plato. These fundamental metaphysical determinations of being can be attributed to φύσις as the origin of metaphysics, as it were, even though these determinations are by no means without possible alternatives. Such alternatives to these determinations of being would, however, not abide within the destiny (*Geschick*) of the being of metaphysics. In this and other supplemental texts, Heidegger thinks back into the history of being by recollecting (*Andenken*). Heidegger had, indeed, declared such recollecting the urgent task of his thinking from the mid-1940s on.

In retrospect, it seems that Heidegger published the essay "On the Essence and Concept of φύσις" only in 1958 because it is in this text that the origins of the metaphysical history of being can become recognizable immediately. In 1939, he still wrote an explication of φύσις on the basis of an interpretation of Aristotle. At the time, he thought that the original essence of φύσις was conceptually exposed in Aristotle, like an echo that can still be heard, an echo well documented in the form of Aristotle's extensive treatise, the *Physics*. Heidegger's thesis at the time was that in Aristotle's relatively detailed text, with its transparent argument, it would be possible to conceptually grasp, as an echo, something of the true and original essence of φύσις (about which we do not have any longer text): "The first coherent and thoughtful discussion ('first' because of its way of questioning) of the essence of φύσις comes down to us from the time when Greek philosophy reached its fulfillment. It stems from Aristotle and is preserved in his φυσικὴ ἀκρόασις. . . . But even so, this first thoughtful and unified conceptualization of φύσις is already the last echo of the original (and thus supreme) thoughtful projection of the essence of φύσις that we still have preserved for us in the fragments of Anaximander, Heraclitus, and Parmenides."[9] We are thus faced with Heidegger's attempt to reassure himself and to certify his interpretation of the earliest projection of φύσις through an insistent analysis of its Aristotelian echo.

This could, perhaps, also explain why Heidegger decided, at first, not to publish this attempt.

Therefore, I will first examine the question of whether Heidegger's interpretation is possible and justified: Does Aristotle's treatment of the concept of φύσις as ἀρχὴ κινήσεως in fact reflect something of the original sense of φύσις for the pre-Socratic thinkers in the way Heidegger understands them? In examining this question, we will come to understand what it is about φύσις that Heidegger is actually interested in. Then, I will try to explain something of Heidegger's hopes for a "metontology," which he connects with the concept of φύσις in the late 1920s and in the 1930s. I will also show how his hopes are slowly but steadily undermined by the κρύπτεσθαι φιλεῖ of φύσις. In closing, I will indicate how, considered in this manner, it is φύσις itself that leads Heidegger to a mere recollective thinking (*andenkendes Denken*) of the history of metaphysics instead of the intention to bring about a transformation of ontology within this history.

1. Aristotle's Echo of φύσις as the Original Happening of Being

What are, then, the most important—and, for the Heideggerian research, always controversial[10]—initial features of Heidegger's interpretation of φύσις in Aristotle? What are, namely, those features that he interprets as an echo of Heraclitus and other thinkers? The four most notable claims are as follows. I would like to examine them carefully in sequence:

1. φύσις is a kind of οὐσία (φύσις-is-οὐσία claim).[11]
2. φύσις has what it takes to indicate "beingness" in general or "the being of beings as such and as a whole" (οὐσία-is-φύσις claim).[12]
3. οὐσία qua φύσις of a single being is at the same time somehow the being of beings as such and as a whole (claim to unitary reduction).
4. φύσις not only is "in itself" the essential possession of a singular being but is likewise its being from and to this essence (framing-of-essence claim).

1. The φύσις-Is-οὐσία Claim

It seems clear that Aristotle says nowhere in *Physics* B 2 that φύσις is οὐσία or a kind of οὐσία. But it is also clear that Heidegger does not claim that Aristotle *says* this somewhere explicitly. Rather, he understands some of Aristotle's statements to identify the being or the beingness of certain things with φύσις. Therefore and in this respect, things are οὐσία. Heidegger, in other words, distinguishes (a) things as a particular οὐσία (singular substance) and (b) the οὐσία of one or more than one thing (relational substance). Only οὐσία in this second sense is identified with φύσις when Heidegger claims that φύσις is οὐσία or a kind of οὐσία.

By now, almost everyone who is at all versed in Aristotle knows that Heidegger cannot be more right with this interpretation. In fact, from the *Metaphysics* and many other of Aristotle's texts, it becomes clear that, first, he makes precisely the distinction Heidegger made, and, second, he even identifies the πρώτη οὐσία of material substances, or relational substances in the sense of claim (b), with their φύσις as ἀρχή.[13] Consequently, φύσις is a particular kind of the οὐσία of things, just as Heidegger says—φύσις is the οὐσία of a particular kind of thing, or φύσις is a particular kind of οὐσία.

Another question is how explicitly Aristotle says this in the text of *Physics* B 1. It would, however, be inappropriate to be more wary of this than of the question itself. For in *Physics* B 1, Aristotle does identify φύσις with the word that, according to the *Metaphysics*, represents the πρώτη οὐσία in all things—with εἶδος. Precisely because φύσις is, above all, the εἶδος of physical things, it cannot be anything but a kind of οὐσία. Yet another question is whether Aristotle expresses this in the passage Heidegger most commonly quotes in order to make his point. The passage in question is *Physics* B1, 192b 32–34: "φύσις, then, is what has been said [sc. ἀρχὴ κινήσεως ἐν ᾧ ὑπάρχει πρώτως καθ'αὑτό]; and anything which has a source of this sort, has φύσις. And all these things are οὐσία; for [it is] some underlying subject, and within an underlying subject φύσις always exists."[14]

I translated the controversial statement in such a way as to make both opposed possibilities of interpretation easily recognizable: The first interpretation claims that φύσις is only *in* an underlying subject but is not itself an underlying subject of any kind.[15] According to the second interpretation, φύσις also is *in* an underlying subject. But, in addition, φύσις is *itself* an underlying subject or a certain type of underlying subject. This second interpretation is rejected as "clearly wrong" without hesitation and without further argument by our modern standard editions (Ross among others).[16] The sentence, it is argued, has to be punctuated after *subject*. Then, the clause "it is an underlying subject" or, better, "each is an underlying thing of some sort" would refer to the things mentioned beforehand, which are all οὐσία and in which there is a φύσις or a similar principle of movement.

In order to defend Heidegger's account, we can say that in 1939 he was still reading the text of Bekker (although the new standard edition was published by Ross in 1936), which follows the classical variant and does not punctuate but reads the statement in one stroke: "because φύσις is always a kind of underlying subject and in an underlying subject." It is, however, also possible to raise a number of linguistic and philosophical concerns about Ross's interpretation, which nobody has called into question since then.[17] In Ross's interpretation, the subject changes from the sweeping plural "all these things are οὐσία" to the singular "for it is some underlying thing." This change is obviously possible, but one would perhaps expect an ἕκαστον or something similar in order to disambiguate the sentence. Moreover—and this, in my opinion, is much more important—the sentence in question must give an *explanation* for the claim that all these things are οὐσία. But if each one of these things is an underlying thing anyway, and is also named to demarcate this, then each thing is οὐσία already. There would be no need to call φύσις, as something that is in each thing, into play. To the contrary, in this case, φύσις could simply be one of the many properties of the underlying thing to which it belongs at each time, and this thing would still be οὐσία. In the contemporary standard reading proposed by Ross, it is impossible for the sentence to serve as a justification with respect to φύσις. Third, the little word τι—*a determined* or *a certain* or *a kind of*—is quite superfluous in its indefinite usage as *some*. If any random thing were meant here, one would expect to find ὁτιοῦν instead of τι as a more explicit expression of this idea.

Be this as it may, there are independent philosophical arguments *in favor* of Heidegger's interpretation beyond the interpretation of that dubious sentence. These arguments show that, in Aristotle's conception, φύσις itself is in a certain sense an "underlying subject" and that, *precisely because* of this, everything that has a φύσις must be οὐσία. In the *Metaphysics* (unlike the *Categories*), there are several passages where Aristotle differentiates the concept of "underlying subject" in such a way as to encompass relational substance—in other words, the "first substance," form, or φύσις. One such passage can be found in the third chapter of Book VII, where Aristotle begins his discussion of the concept of substance: "To a special degree οὐσία seems to be the primal underlying subject. In one way one can understand matter as something of this kind, in another way the form (μορφή), and in still another the 'from-both' [*das Aus-Beiden*]."[18] Of particular interest for our question is the distinction Aristotle makes in *Metaphysics* Θ, chapter 7, between the predication of a substantial term (relational substance) pertaining to a purely "hyletic substrate," on the one hand, and the predication of a property pertaining to something that is in turn an underlying substantial thing, on the other: "Thus where one predicates in this way [as in the sense mentioned last: predication of a property of an underlying substantial thing], the ultimate element is an οὐσία; but where one does not predicate in this way, and that which is predicated is a determined εἶδος, or a 'this one,' the ultimate element is matter and mere hyletic οὐσία."[19] Aristotle, thus, thinks that one often has to understand the predicated εἶδος or the primal substance of a thing as "this one." In these cases, the claim to εἶδος as underlying shifts away, as it were, from the material base of the object—as we can assume—to the predicated substantial term. The predicated substantial term is to be designated as the substance of the whole object. On the classical reading of the text in the *Physics*, this conception would serve as a perfect explanation for the claim that everything that has a φύσις has to be οὐσία—namely, because φύσις (qua substantial form or εἶδος) is, in a certain sense, the underlying subject of the whole thing in which φύσις is.[20] What remains of the thing as a whole can then only be matter or "hyletic οὐσία" elevated, as it were, to a separate and determined οὐσία as soon as φύσις comes into play. This seems to correspond exactly to Aristotle's conception, and, at the same time, it is exactly Heidegger's interpretation of the text. I conclude that it is much more favorable still to remain with Bekker's version of the Greek text. In any case, one must accept Heidegger's first claim, that φύσις is a kind of οὐσία, no matter whether one follows Ross's or my interpretation of the passage in question.

2. The *οὐσία-Is-φύσις Claim*

Heidegger's second claim is that φύσις, although primarily understood as the ἀρχὴ κινήσεως of only physical things, not only has what it takes to designate an οὐσία *bounded*, as it were, within physical things but also extends beyond that, to "the being" of all things and, in general, of all beings as such and as a whole.

This is a two-stage claim. The first half certainly can be ascribed to Aristotle and can even be demonstrated from *Physics* B 1. This first claim is evident: οὐσία qua φύσις of those things that are determined by φύσις, each time such determination happens, amounts to something more than linking φύσις to only *one* such thing; things determined by φύσις always and necessarily constitute chains and connections of generation in which the things are integrated. This is precisely because φύσις is integrated into these things in their very substance. Thus, beyond being bound to a particular thing determined by it, φύσις is "the being" of all such beings that lie within these generative associations. This is because φύσις causes or "principiates" these beings in this way. The cause of the being of a thing cannot, for Aristotle, lie within this very thing. It must in every case amount to something more than the thing itself. Therefore, if φύσις is the cause or the principle of the being of a thing, it cannot, by being contained in it, be exhausted.

This is precisely what Heidegger shows in his essay by way of analyzing *Physics* B 1. There is no need to address this in detail. In addition, however—and this concerns the second stage of the problem—Heidegger points to a revealing passage in *Metaphysics*[21] where the principle or the principles of all beings in general are defined as principles "of a certain φύσις." I quote the passage in context:

> There is a science which studies being *qua* being, and what by itself belongs to it. This science is not the same as any of the so-called particular sciences, for none of the others deals generally with being *qua* being; they divide off some portion of it and study the attributes of this part, as do for example the mathematical sciences. But since it is for the first *principles* and the *most ultimate* causes that we are searching, clearly they must be principles of a certain φύσις in itself. Hence if *these* principles were investigated by those also who investigated the elements of existing things, the elements must be elements of being

not incidentally, but *qua* being. Therefore it is of being *qua* being that we too must grasp the first causes.[22]

Here, Aristotle says that the science he has in mind, as science of being as such, must be the most general science of all but that it can also be determined by its aim to expose the most ultimate causes and principles of all beings. These principles "must be principles of a certain φύσις," for there are no "principles" or "causes" that are *not* principles of something determinate and, therefore, principles of a certain φύσις. That of which the principles are principles serves as the factual and determinate anchor, as it were, for the most general structures of Aristotelian ontology.[23] Yet because the being of beings, which belongs to everything in the most general way, is constituted by elements that have the character of principles or causes, the science of being must, despite its generality, be the science of something determinate. The source of determination for its elements and principles is explicitly called "a certain φύσις," and it is clear that what is meant by these principles of the science of being is that which principles are in relation to being as such and that this is οὐσία.

Such evidence from *Metaphysics* could be multiplied by closer inspection, even if such reference are unobtrusive and scarce.[24] We must, therefore, admit that Heidegger is correct in this second claim at its second stage: Aristotle not only thinks φύσις (at least in the *Metaphysics*) is a kind of οὐσία but also thinks, inversely, that οὐσία is a certain φύσις or is φύσις itself in a certain sense. There can be no doubt about this, and yet it comes as no surprise given the profound knowledge of Aristotle's texts that Heidegger demonstrates in his lecture courses.

3. The Claim to Unitary Reduction in οὐσία and φύσις

Although it is central for Heidegger's philosophy in its totality and for Aristotle's metaphysics, the third claim is especially difficult to prove. The claim is that the οὐσία of a being (and consequently its φύσις *qua* οὐσία) must, in some way, be the being of beings as such as well as the being of beings as a whole. Only then, in Heidegger's view, is it relevant to metaphysics at all.

Here, we have to concede that φύσις as ἀρχὴ κινήσεως καὶ στάσεως ἐνυπάρχουσα is best suited to represent or to manifest the οὐσία of singular things *and* the being of beings in general and as a whole *within* these singular things. The concepts of ἐνέργεια or ἐντελέχεια, which Heidegger analyzes at length, are to succeed in the traversal from "beings" to "beings as a whole." Several passages from *Metaphysics* are particularly suited to establishing the association between the being of singular things and the being of beings in their totality. The first passage comes from book Θ, chapter 8. Heidegger most certainly knew this passage and had it in mind, though he does not quote it in the essay: "Thus it is obvious by this argument that actuality is prior to potentiality with respect to οὐσία;

and that in point of time, as we have said, one actuality presupposes another right back to that of the prime mover in each case."[25] This means that φύσις qua actuality must be a principle for movement *internal* to the actual. But precisely because it is internal, this principle must continually relocate the ground of its own actuality in the direction of something primary. φύσις qua reality, together with its always already given ἐνέργεια, thus constitutes an interconnection of the universe through reciprocal movement, which depends on a primarily moving principle. Thus the οὐσία of a thing is its φύσις, and also φύσις is a principle of movement that stems from another actual thing but that is also itself actual. From these two ideas, it follows that the being of beings as a whole manifests itself nowhere else but in the being actual of singular things.

This interconnection is further attested in passages from books Λ and I. These passages have considerable metaphysical import for Aristotle, although their ontological relevance is hardly ever discussed in the literature. These passages are little known, and their meaning is often misconstrued because readers fail to see that they are necessary for metaphysics. It is this necessity that Heidegger had more clearly in his view than any other interpreter of Aristotle. A first passage explains that, although at first sight it seems as if an external principle would *increase* the number of principles, it is possible to reduce the principles to a certain minimal number only because of the existence of external principles of movement:

> And since not only things which are inherent in an object are its causes, but also certain external things, e.g. the moving cause, clearly "principle" and "element" are not the same; but both are causes. Principles are divided into these two kinds, and that which moves a thing or brings it to rest is a kind of principle and οὐσία. Thus analogically there are *three* elements and *four* causes or principles; but they are different in different cases, and the proximate moving cause is different in different cases. Health, disease, body; and the moving cause is the art of medicine. Εἶδος, a particular kind of disorder, bricks: and the moving cause is the art of building. . . . And since in the sphere of physical things the moving cause of man is man, while in the sphere of objects of thought the moving cause is the εἶδος or its contrary, in one sense there are only *three* causes and in another four. For in a sense the art of medicine is health, and the art of building is the εἶδος of a house, and man begets man; but besides these there is that which as first of all things moves all things.[26]

Here, one can see clearly how the internal principles can be further reduced through the constitutive role played by the external principle of movement. The trick with φύσις, and in general every ἐντελέχεια, is that the external cause of movement is at once the forming principle. Thus, as we just learned from *Physics* B 1, φύσις is also an internal principle of the physical substance. But such a substance must be produced through a material basis with the aid of external causes. In the principle of φύσις, then, both the steretic opposites to form and matter, at least in nuce, are already contained. Thanks in particular to φύσις as ἀρχὴ κινήσεως καὶ στάσεως, Aristotle establishes the οὐσία of a being as the exponent of the being of beings as such and as a whole. In the *Metaphysics* (but already in the *Physics*, as Heidegger shows), this technique is used to form a proposition such as the following: ἐκ τοιαύτης ἄρα ἀρχῆς ἤρτηται ὁ οὐρανὸς καὶ ἡ φύσις. Thanks to this principle [sc. the νόησις from 1072a30], heaven and φύσις are conjoined together.[27] Thus φύσις, as οὐσία of transient things, both presupposes *and* employs a principle of movement in every substantial φύσει ὄν. But all other things that exist either stem from φύσει ὄντα or adhere to φύσει ὄντα. The φύσει ὄντα constitute, as it were, the warps in the texture of beings as a whole. And beings can be a "whole" only because the "whole" is structured through the φύσει ὄντα.[28]

I want to introduce another relevant passage. This passage is of great interest because one recognizes here that Aristotle, by applying the concept of φύσις to the highest kinds of beings (the infamous categories), can succeed in making these last distinct branches of beings relate to each other. Moreover, he can succeed *only* in this way. By following their φύσις as a guiding thread, Aristotle makes the highest kinds or categories submit to being, including the being of beings as a whole. He is particularly proud of this discovery, for this discovery is the anti-Platonic bedrock in his thinking:

> That the one, then, in every genus is a definite φύσις, and in no case is its φύσις just this—viz., unity, is evident; but as in colours the one itself which we must seek is one colour, so too in the sphere of οὐσία the one itself is one οὐσία. And that in a sense unity means the same as being is clear from the fact that it follows the categories in as many ways, and is not comprised within any category, e.g. neither in substance nor in quality, but is related to them just as being is; and from the fact that in "one man" nothing more is predicated than in "man", just as being too does not predicate anything apart from the "what" or the quality or the quantity; and also the "being-one" is nothing more than "being a particular thing"[29]

The *different* kinds of beings, each of which must have a fundamental φύσις as criterion and principle of unity, can be further reduced to a superior principle only insofar as both φύσις is a principle of movement in each kind *and* movement serves as an external principle for all that is. If this were not so, there would be only a final, irreducible multiplicity of types of branches or kinds of beings and there would not be a being of beings as such and as a whole. There would exist only particulars, of which there would be only unrelated sciences without a metaphysics as science of beings as such and in general. Aristotle has seen and stated this clearly. Therefore, it is unjustified to accuse Heidegger of over-interpreting or wrongly interpreting one of Aristotle's fundamental insights.

Heidegger, however—and this I, too, judge critically—takes this single passage from *Physics* B 1 as a sufficient expression of Aristotle's entire metaphysical enterprise. Even more problematic, perhaps to the point of intolerability for the unprepared reader, is that Heidegger translates the passage in an unacceptable way. This is precisely because he reduces Aristotle's whole metaphysical theory to the first chapter of *Physics* B 1. By giving such a translation, Heidegger does violence not only to his own language but also to the Greek language—and, not to mention, to Aristotle's use of language. But every reader of Heidegger knows that the violation of language and the disturbing way that he translates are systematically grounded in his thinking. For Heidegger, language is both the refuge of abraded traditions and the cradle of thinking from which new beginnings are possible. The possibility of these new openings demands destruction to overcome language.

4. The Framing-of-Essence Claim

In the light of the aforesaid, what is the real and central attraction Heidegger finds in the Aristotelian φύσις and in φύσις in general? That φύσις is both οὐσία of a given present at hand *and* what *is coming* from something neither present at hand (*vorhanden*) nor present (*anwesend*) through movement; that φύσις is *a trace of the not present at hand in the being of the present at hand*. But what is a *trace*? It is an indication perceived or, better, *read*, and it is an indication of something that is not present. Thus the importance of the relation between λόγος (truth) and φύσις for Heidegger.

Conceived or comprehended as φύσις, each physical being is present at hand or present from and because of something not present at hand. Nobody will raise a doubt that precisely *this* is the most important meaning and the reason for its very use, everywhere the word φύσις or φύεσθαι is used significantly by the pre-Socratics or in archaic Greece. Who would want to doubt that?

I would like to quote at least one significant case in point. I would like to do this because, as far as I can see, no one has discovered and interpreted this text with regard to φύσις (not even Heidegger), although this passage is one of the best to show the essential feature of this word. Pindar presents the word φύσις at the beginning of the sixth *Nemean Ode* with the greatest poetic awareness, using it to express that φύσις is the abounding present trace of the immense background of gathering and origin. These are the verses: "There is one race of men, one race of gods; and from a single mother we both draw our breath. But all allotted power divides us: man is nothing, but for the gods the bronze sky endures as a secure home forever. Nevertheless, we bear some resemblance to the immortals, either in greatness of mind or in φύσις, although we do not know, by day or by night, towards what goal fortune has written that we should run."[30]

The big question of what φύσις means in these lines can find an answer, in my understanding, only through the fact that "the secure home" of the sky, where the gods live, always "endures" and always remains the same, whereas man neither is nor has something enduring in order to gather his powers. Mind (νοῦς) and nature (φύσις) are the two ways of gathering both greatness and penetrating power. Both rely upon a not-present-at-hand and invisible background, without which the moment of expression could not have the divine extent pertaining to it, as Pindar says, at least occasionally. The invisibility of the not-present-at-hand background, nevertheless necessary to such magnificent achievement is brought out even more by the idea that despite human achievements, we don't see where things are coming from or wither they go. And this is precisely the essence of φύσις—and, in its own way, of νοῦς, too—according to Pindar's poetical staging of the word.

The not present at hand, of which each φύσις carries a trace, must not always lie in the past. Precisely if φύσις is not only the ontological constitution (*Seinsverfassung*) of a thing but also—as Aristotle sees it—the internal principle of movement and cause of such constitution, the not present at hand is, in the actual imprint of a thing determined by φύσις, also the future something coming about through φύσις. Thus the not present at hand is also everything from which something may come. φύσις is the trace of the not present at hand, both with respect to its origin in something else and with respect to its moving toward something else. Nobody has seen this with more clarity than Aristotle himself, as he expresses in *Physics* B 1 and in his *Metaphysics* as well, in Θ 8 and many other places. I can therefore spare myself further demonstration through detailed analysis that Heidegger's fourth claim is correct as well. This is the claim that φύσις means not only the essence or being of a thing it possesses at that moment and in actuality, but also a framing of essence or a setting to that essence spanning backward into the past and forward into the future. The φύσις of the being (οὐσία) of a thing determined by φύσις arises from itself, from the φύσις, but also returns toward itself, toward φύσις, and this happens in a way that is reflected in the manner in which a particular thing possesses φύσις. "Everything which is generated," Aristotle states in the *Metaphysics*, "moves towards a principle and towards its end."[31] Therefore, if a thing already holds its principle, qua φύσις, in itself, then it moves toward that which it already is, its being or its οὐσία. "Understood as becoming, φύσις is therefore treading [toward itself or] toward φύσις." This is a quotation from the *Physics* at the end of B 1, and Heidegger regards it as particularly important. Something can move toward itself, and thus remain ahead of itself, only if it *lacks* itself in some way. Φύσις, as an internal principle of movement and of becoming, must be characterized by incompleteness and lack—that is, by στέρησις. Heidegger even claims that it is this στέρησις, inscribed as *becoming*, that for Aristotle renders the active completion that is attractive to physical beings—completion promoting itself, as it were. There are some remarkable quotations that can show this as well, although Heidegger does not cite them: for example, "Hence, just as teachers think that they have achieved their end when they have exhibited their pupil performing, so it is with nature."[32] Let us conclude by summarizing this point once more: φύσις in some way indicates both the past and the future being (*Sein*) of being (*Seiende*) determined by it. And this cannot be irrelevant for Heidegger's ontological projects from *Being and Time* onward. Should we go so far as to claim that the φύσις "of the Greeks"—as Heidegger himself loves to express it—is the paradigm of a *self-temporalizing* being of beings?

2. Fundamental Metontology, Invigorated by Greek φύσις, of the Greeks

All genuine philosophical concepts are, in Heidegger's understanding, "formal indications." These concepts don't mean that which they relate to, but they are "a pointer to the fact that anyone who seeks to understand is called upon by this conceptual context to undertake a transformation of themselves into their Dasein."[33] For Heidegger, this transformation into *Dasein* means to open oneself to the occurring of a confrontation with the concept and its possibilities, relating to the whole of the world. This is what Heidegger himself has been doing with the concept of φύσις since 1928: he wants to be himself, as it were, a φύσις for the being of beings and for its transformative temporalization; he wants to temporalize and ground a new or another beginning from the originality of the first beginning with the φύσις of the Greeks, to put himself in the place of that beginning and to repeat it. At that time, Heidegger believes that the ontological occurring of φύσις as being of beings, as such and as a whole, holds a future within itself. For this reason, in the lecture course *The Fundamental Concepts of Metaphysics*, from which I quoted the definition of formal indication, after the introduction and the analysis of the concept of metaphysics and after quoting from Heraclitus's fragment 123, Heidegger says:

> The prevailing of beings as a whole intrinsically strives to conceal itself. Commensurate with this, a peculiar confrontation is associated with this prevailing, a confrontation in which φύσις is revealed. . . . The separation of these two meanings of φύσις: beings themselves and the being of beings, and the history of these meanings and their development culminate in Aristotle, who precisely grasps questioning concerning the φύσει ὄντα as a whole (φύσις in the first sense) and the question concerning οὐσία, the being of beings (φύσις in the second sense), in one, and designates this questioning as πρώτη φιλοσοφία . . . First Philosophy, philosophy in the proper sense. Philosophizing proper asks after φύσις in this dual sense: after beings themselves and after being.[34]

Heidegger wants to take up such philosophizing when he now wants to "undertake" such "separation" in the "confrontation" with the concept of φύσις, a separation directed toward the future. In order to achieve this, anybody who wishes to understand this concept must transform into Dasein. And this is what Heidegger tries to achieve in this lecture course and, in general, in these years. Through a confrontation with the historical essence of φύσις, φύσις itself must be induced to a new temporalization of itself.

This would be possible, more precisely, in the way Heidegger describes it in 1929 in "On the Essence of Ground":

> In such a way that those beings that are surpassed also already pervade [*pervade*: this word always designates φύσις in Heidegger, T.B.] and attune that which projects.... Dasein would be unable to be pervasively attuned by beings as the being [*Seiendes*] that it is, and thus would be unable, for example, to be embraced, captivated, or permeated by them; it would be altogether deprived of any leeway for this, were it not for the fact that an irruption [*Aufbruch*] of world, and be it only a glimmer of world, accompanies such being absorbed by beings.[35]

Yet *irruption* (*Aufbruch*) is Heidegger's translation for the Greek word ὁρμή, which for Aristotle differentiates things that are through φύσις from those that are by way of τέχνη: only the physical beings have an irruption to their own being in themselves. Thus Heidegger wants to listen to this irruption in itself and, along with his own being and its own way of temporalizing itself in relation to beings, awaken himself and other listeners so that Dasein may be grounded anew in the projection (*Entwurf*): "In accordance with its essence, the projection of possibilities is in each case richer than the possession of them by the one projecting. The ready possession of possibilities belongs to *Dasein*, however, because, as projective, it finds itself in the midst of beings. Certain other possibilities are thereby already withdrawn from *Dasein*, and indeed merely through its own facticity. Yet precisely this withdrawal of certain possibilities pertaining to its potentiality for being-in-the-world—a withdrawal entailed in its being absorbed by beings—first brings those possibilities of world-projection that can 'actually' be seized upon toward *Dasein* as its world."[36]

This function of the steretic withdrawal, bringing closer certain possibilities, is clearly a sign of φύσις. According to Heidegger's interpretation, φύσις can convey the being of beings only because φύσις itself withholds that very being through a specific "becoming-absent" (*Abwesung*) of itself. But let us continue to read Heidegger's considerations from "On the Essence of Ground": "Such withdrawal lends precisely the binding character of what remains projected before us the power to pervade [*Walten*, again Heidegger's word for φύσις, T.B.] within the realm of Dasein's existence."[37]

It becomes clear here that in Heidegger's opinion Dasein is world projecting (i.e., temporalizing) by comporting itself according to the way of φύσις: faithful to the φύσις κρύπτεσθαι φιλεῖ and through the κρύπτεσθαι—that is, through the withdrawal that is inscribed in φύσις itself, φύσις reveals the being of beings in the unconcealment of a world.

3. Drowning in Withdrawal and the Saving Anchor of Recollection

In the lecture course *Metaphysical Foundations of Logic* (1928),[38] about a year and a half before writing about the essence of ground, Heidegger discovers for himself Heraclitus's fragment 123: φύσις κρύπτεσθαι φιλεῖ. And as is his methodic whim, he himself tries to transform this idea in his own thinking. Thus in the above-mentioned essay "On the Essence of Ground," appearing in a *Festschrift* for Edmund Husserl on occasion of his seventieth birthday (1929), and—as he quotes the fragment anew—in the lecture course *Fundamental Concepts of Metaphysics* (1929–30),[39] Heidegger's interest in this fragment goes on for a while with repeated quotations and interpretations that aim at integrating ever more strictly the moment of concealment into the unconcealing movement of φύσις. It appears, for example, in the lecture course *The Essence of Truth: On Plato's Parable of the Cave and Theaetetus*[40] and then again in 1935, in *Introduction to Metaphysics*. This last mention comes with a certain turning of events, though, which is to come to the fore in the 1939 essay on the concept and nature of φύσις, which has been the focus of our attention. Heidegger—if I may say it all at once—gradually relinquishes the idea of a new temporalization of being arising from a retreat into Greek φύσις and from its character of withdrawal. The early translations of fragment 123 (φύσις κρύπτεσθαι φιλεῖ) and its transformations into Heidegger's own thinking had a certain optimistic tone about them, as unconcealment was seen as made possible by φύσις and as coming from φύσις itself, as arising from the being of beings, and Heidegger hinted even at a *new* unconcealment. Yet in *Introduction to Metaphysics*, Heidegger for the first time describes the emergence (*Aufgehen*) of φύσις as of the kind of concealment and therefore as an instance that produces seeming and error: "We conclude our elucidation of the opposition—and this also means the unity—of being and seeming with a saying of Heraclitus (fragment 123): φύσις κρύπτεσθαι φιλεῖ: being (emerging appearance) intrinsically inclines toward self-concealment. Being means: to appear in emerging, to step forth out of concealment—and for this very reason, concealment and the provenance from concealment essentially belong to being. Such provenance lies in the essence of being, of what appears as such. Being remains inclined toward concealment, whether in great veiling and silence, or in the most superficial distorting and obscuring."[41]

The κρύπτεσθαι φιλεῖ of φύσις, the *primacy* of self-concealment over revealing into unconcealment, eats away like a cancer. Heidegger's all-too-vivid purposed new grounding of the world from the old root of metaphysics (i.e., φύσις) is gradually brought to despair and fades away. The "great veiling and silence" is expanding. Accordingly, as early as 1939 we reach the point of maximum despair over the essence and continuing presence of metaphysics. This is what Heidegger expresses at the end of our essay "On the Essence and Concept of φύσις": "φύσις κρύπτεσθαι φιλεῖ. 'Being loves to hide itself.' What does this mean? It has been suggested, and still is suggested, that this fragment means being is difficult to get at and requires great efforts to be brought out of its hiding place and, as it were, purged of its self-hiding. But what is needed is precisely the opposite. Self-hiding belongs to the predilection [*Vor-liebe*] of being; i.e., it belongs to that wherein being has secured its essence." Who would pledge himself to cut loose such a blockage of being in self-hiding? "And the essence of being is to unconceal itself, to emerge, to come out into the unhidden—φύσις. Only what in its very essence unconceals and must unconceal itself, can love to conceal itself. Only what is unconcealing can be concealing."

This means, then, that unconcealment could perhaps itself be concealing. But who can assess this? And on the basis of what? "And therefore the κρύπτεσθαι φιλεῖ is not to be overcome, not to be stripped from φύσις [but precisely this is what Heidegger tried to do and required, condensed to the formulation 'stripped of concealing,' for the new grounding of the world in his metontology, T.B.]. Rather, the task is the much more difficult one of allowing to φύσις, in all the purity of its essence, the κρύπτεσθαι that belongs to it."[42]

How can one leave to φύσις its κρύπτεσθαι, that which it exercised all along in the event and in the history of metaphysics? First, one has to release any attempt of oneself taking over the happening of concealing and unconcealing; one has to leave it to φύσις. Second, it is necessary, as Heidegger says elsewhere, to let metaphysics achieve itself, to let it *arrive* and to learn to experience it as self-concealing of φύσις, before one can conceive of ways to get out of metaphysics or to overcome it. Indeed, this is what Heidegger (although quite secretly) tried to do in those years, beginning in 1935 or 1936: to sense the essence of metaphysics as the concealing of being. Although metaphysics lacked the force to ground a world anew, nevertheless it is beginning to understand this lack of power as a destiny of concealing. It arrives at the thought that it is being itself, and therefore φύσις itself, and therefore the emerging unconcealment itself, that, in unveiling beings, not only manifests itself to please us, but also, in the farthest-reaching revelation of beings, in concealing unconcealment or unconcealing concealment, withdraws from sight again and again. Φύσις in the historical accomplishment of metaphysics, acquires something fatal for Heidegger, becomes a fate and a prison that we—we humans—have no power to escape from on our own.

Thus the star of φύσις begins to sink in the late 1930s and early 1940s; the word disappears almost completely from the vocabulary of Heidegger's philosophizing or becomes the recollection of a questionable destiny of being.[43] I close my considerations with an archetypal image of φύσις that Heidegger drew at the beginning and that is indeed closest to the Greek φύσις of the beginning: the image of the root. Heidegger's use of such an image in 1949 in his "Introduction to 'What Is Metaphysics?'" shows how φύσις helps metaphysics in the work of hiding itself in beings, instead of opening possibilities for a new grounding of being and of granting a first irruption in that direction:

> The tree of philosophy grows out of the soil in which metaphysics is rooted. The ground and soil is the element in which the root of the tree lives, but the growth of the tree is never able to absorb this soil in such a way that it disappears in the tree as part of the tree. Instead, the roots, down to the subtlest tendrils, lose themselves in the soil. The ground is ground for the roots, and in the ground the roots forget themselves for the sake of the tree. The roots still belong to the tree even when they abandon themselves, after a fashion, to the element of the soil. They squander themselves and their element on the tree. As roots, they do not turn toward the soil—at least not as if it were their essence to grow only into this element and to spread out in it. Presumably, the element would not be the element either if the roots did not live in it.[44]

The tree is philosophy; the roots metaphysics; the ground (and soil) is the concealing-unconcealing essencing of the truth of being; the element of the soil is being qua being. In the tree the ground of metaphysics can't show itself. Instead the element, nourishing the roots of the tree, is (through the roots) directed toward the growth of the tree turned away from the soil. The tree reaches so deeply into the soil that no possibility remains to understand the "wherefrom" of this attachment. Element, roots, and tree are but a single hiding of the origin of metaphysics.[45]

Notes

1. Heidegger, *Grundbegriffe der antiken Philosophie*, GA 22, 35ff, 149ff, 170ff, 216ff; English translation: Heidegger, *Basic Concepts of Ancient Philosophy*, 28ff, 124ff, 142ff, 174ff.

2. Cf. Heidegger, *Der Satz vom Grund*, in particular 113–14; English translation: "Heraclitus wants to say: To being there belongs a self-concealing. . . . Today we say: being proffers itself to us, but in such a way that at the same time it, in its essence, already withdraws. This is what the term 'history of being' means. Nothing has been arbitrarily concocted under this term, but what has already been thought is thought more decisively. When one recollectively thinks upon the history of being, a history that is difficult to bring into view, this history of being first comes to light as such. When we say that being proffers itself to us while it, in its essence, also withdraws, then of course this means something still different than what Heraclitus' fragment and Aristotle's sentences designate" (Heidegger, *Principle of Reason*, 64f).

3. Following the indications of the translator in the original edition (*Il Pensiero* III, 2, 130), this text was conceived to be presented and discussed in a seminar at the University of Freiburg in 1940. Of the original version there remains only a typewritten copy by Heidegger's brother. This copy contains in slashes the addenda that were not read at the time, as the translator confirms. I think these are reflections by Heidegger himself, which he added later as his brother made a copy of the text in the 1940s.

4. Heidegger, "Vom Wesen und Begriff der φύσις," 242; English translation: "On the Essence and Concept of φύσις," 186.

5. In the italian journal *Il Pensiero*: "Dell'essenza e del concetto della φύσις."

6. Cf., e.g., Heidegger, "Zur Seinsfrage," 416; English translation: "In order to respond to a recovery of metaphysics, thinking must for this reason first clarify the essence of metaphysics. To such an attempt, the recovery of metaphysics initially appears to be an overcoming that merely brings exclusively metaphysical representation behind it, so as to lead thinking into the free realm attained by a recovery from the essence of metaphysics. But in this recovery, the enduring truth of the metaphysics that has seemingly been rejected first returns explicitly as the now appropriated essence of metaphysics" ("On the Question of Being," 314).

7. Cf. Heidegger, "Die seinsgeschichtliche Bestimmung des Nihilismus," 368; English translation: "Thinking to encounter follows Being in its withdrawal, follows it in the sense that it lets Being itself go, whereas for its own part it stays behind. Then where does thinking linger? No longer where it lingered as the prior, omitting thought of metaphysics. Thinking stays behind by first taking the decisive *step back*, back from the omission—but back to where? Where else than to the realm that for a long time has been granted to thinking by Being itself—granted, to be sure, in the veiled figure of the *essence* of man" ("Nihilism as Determined by the History of Being," 255). Cf. also Heidegger, "On the Question of Being."

8. Heidegger, "Vom Wesen und Begriff der φύσις," 301; English translation: "On the Essence and Concept of φύσις," 230.

9. Heidegger, "Vom Wesen und Begriff der φύσις," 242; English translation: "On the Essence and Concept of φύσις," 186.

10. See especially the review by Karl-Heinz Ilting, "Sein als Bewegtheit."

11. See especially Heidegger, "Vom Wesen und Begriff der φύσις," 260, 299; English translation: "On the Essence and Concept of φύσις," 199, 228.

12. See especially Heidegger, "Vom Wesen und Begriff der φύσις," 299; English translation: "On the Essence and Concept of φύσις," 228. Cf. 281 (English 212) with 193b 2–6 and 259 (English 199) with 192b 30ff.

13. See for example Aristotle, *Metaphysics* Z 17, Δ 4.

14. Cf. Heidegger, "Vom Wesen und Begriff der φύσις," 259–61; English Translation: "On the Essence and Concept of φύσις," 199–200.

15. For this reading one has to add in German and English, but not in Greek, the "it is" we have in brackets in order to complete the clause.

16. So states Ross in *Aristotle's Physics*, vol. II, 501, referring to E. Laas, who first proposed this interpretation in 1863.

17. At least some of the earliest commentators, such as Thomas Aquinas, regard as obvious a reading of the text similar to Bekker's and Heidegger's: "et talia sunt omnia subiecta naturae: quia natura est subiectum, secundum quod natura dicitur materia; et est in subiecto, secundum quod natura dicitur forma" (*In. phys. Comm.*, n. 146; ed. Marietti, 75).

But here the reference to the meaning of φύσις as matter should not be necessary or intended in order to justify for φύσις itself the status as a kind of underlying subject.

18. Aristotle, *Metaphysics* Z 3, 1029a 1–3; depending on the possible reading and way of comprehending this passage, one can consider the following: Z 13, 1038b 4–6 and H 1, 1042a 26–32.

19. Aristotle, *Metaphysics* 1049a 34sq.

20. This explanation is much more conclusive than even the classical reading of the text, since according to this interpretation φύσις, on the one hand, qua matter, constitutes the material substrate of the φύσει ὄντα, and on the other hand, qua form, is actual within in this matter (this would approximately match the interpretation by Thomas Aquinas quoted above). In this classical reading, the double meaning of φύσις as matter and as form would be anticipated. Heidegger himself understands that this is unsatisfactory: the interpretation of φύσις as matter is rejected by Aristotle with its interpretation as form, because this second interpretation can overcome and include the first one.

21. Aristotle, *Metaphysics* Γ 1, 1003a 27: see Heidegger, "Vom Wesen und Begriff der φύσις," 299; English translation: "On the Essence and Concept of φύσις," 229.

22. Aristotle, *Metaphysics* Γ 1, 1003a 21–32.

23. One of the results of this connection is that in Aristotle's view, the being of physical things, like the being of principles and most ultimate causes, must be ἐνέργεια. We cannot deal with this question here.

24. See Buchheim, "Functions of the Concept of *Physis*." Particularly interesting in this context is section I.2; see the following.

25. Aristotle, *Metaphysics* Θ 8, 1050b 9–6.

26. Aristotle, *Metaphysics* Λ 4, 1070b 22–35.

27. Aristotle, *Metaphysics* Λ 7, 1072b 14.

28. Cf. furthermore Aristotle, *Metaphysics* Λ 10, 1075a 12–24.

29. Aristotle, *Metaphysics* I 2, 1054a 9–19. Translation modified.

30. Pindar, *Nemean Ode* VI, 1–8.

31. Aristotle, *Metaphysics* Θ 8, 1050a 7f.

32. Aristotle, *Metaphysics* Θ 8, 1050a 17–19.

33. Heidegger, *Grundbegriffe der Metaphysik*, GA 29–30, 430. English translation: *Fundamental Concepts of Metaphysics*, 297.

34. Heidegger, *Grundbegriffe der Metaphysik*, GA 29–30, 51f; English translation: *Fundamental Concepts of Metaphysics*, 34.

35. Heidegger, "Vom Wesen des Grundes," 166f; English translation: "On the Essence of Ground," 128.

36. Heidegger, "Vom Wesen des Grundes," 167; "On the Essence of Ground," 128–29.

37. Heidegger, "Vom Wesen des Grundes," 167; "On the Essence of Ground," 129. Translation modified.

38. Heidegger, *Metaphysische Anfangsgründe der Logik*, GA 26, 281; English translation: *Metaphysical Foundations of Logic*, 217.

39. Heidegger, *Grundbegriffe der Metaphysik*, GA 29–30, 41f; English translation: *Fundamental Concepts of Metaphysics*, 27.

40. Heidegger, *Vom Wesen der Wahrheit*, 13f; English translation: *Essence of Truth*, 9.

41. Heidegger, *Einführung in die Metaphysik*, GA 40, 121–22; English translation: *Introduction to Metaphysics*, 120–21.

42. Heidegger, "Vom Wesen und Begriff der φύσις," 300–301; English translation: "On the Essence and Concept of φύσις," 229–30.

43. To my knowledge, up to now the only scholar to point out this well-considered disappearance of nature, of φύσις, from Heidegger's thought in the early 1940s was Hartmut Buchner, under the title of a "farewell or recovery [*Verabschiedung oder Verwindung*] of the metaphysical concept of nature in favor of an opening of world in general." He presents his claims in an extensive discussion of a section from the *Contributions* (GA 65, n. 155). Cf. Buchner, "Natur und Geschick von Welt," particularly 46–52.

44. Heidegger, "Einleitung zu 'Was ist Metaphysik?'" 366. English translation: Heidegger, "Introduction to 'What Is Metaphysics?'" 278.

45. This contribution first appeared as "Was interessiert Heidegger an der φύσις?" in *Heidegger und die Griechen*. Translated by Diego D'Angelo.

Bibliography

Aristoteles. *Aristotelis Metaphysica*. Recognovit W. Christ, nova impressio correctior. Leipzig: Teubner, 1934.

———. *Aristotle's Physics*, rev. ed. Introduction and commentary by William. D. Ross. Oxford: Clarendon, 1936. Special ed. 1998.

Buchheim, Thomas. "The Functions of the Concept of *Physis* in Aristotle's *Metaphysics*." *Oxford Studies in Ancient Philosophy* 20 (2001): 201–34.

———. "Was interessiert Heidegger an der φύσις?" In *Heidegger und die Griechen*, edited by Michael Steinmann, 141–63. Frankfurt am Main: Klostermann, 2007.

Buchner, Hartmut. "Natur und Geschick von Welt." In *Destruktion und Übersetzung. Zu den Aufgaben von Philosophiegeschichte nach Martin Heidegger*, edited by Thomas Buchheim, 39–54. Weinheim: VCH, 1989.

Heidegger, Martin. *Basic Concepts of Ancient Philosophy*. Translated by Richard Rojcewicz. Bloomington: Indiana University Press, 2008.

———. *Einführung in die Metaphysik*. GA 40. Edited by Petra Jaeger. Frankfurt am Main: Klostermann, 1983.

———. "Einleitung zu 'Was ist Metaphysics?'" In *Wegmarken*, GA 9, edited by Friedrich-Wilhelm von Herrmann, 365–85. Frankfurt am Main: Klostermann, 1976.

———. *The Essence of Truth: On Plato's Cave Allegory and Theaetetus*. Translated by Ted Sadler. London: Continuum, 2002.

———. *The Fundamental Concepts of Metaphysics: World, Finitude, Solitude*. Translated by William McNeill and Nicholas Walker. Bloomington: Indiana University Press, 1995.

———. *Die Grundbegriffe der antiken Philosophie*. GA 22. Edited by Franz-K. Blust. Frankfurt am Main: Klostermann, 1993.

———. *Die Grundbegriffe der Metaphysik. Welt—Endlichkeit—Einsamkeit*. GA 29–30. Edited by Friedrich-Wilhelm von Herrmann. Frankfurt am Main: Klostermann, 1983.

———. *Introduction to Metaphysics*. Translated by Gregory Fried and Richard Polt. New Haven, CT: Yale University Press, 2000.

———. "Introduction to 'What Is Metaphysics?'" In *Pathmarks*, 277–91. Translated by William McNeill. Cambridge: Cambridge University Press, 1998.

———. *The Metaphysical Foundations of Logic*. Translated by Michael Heim. Bloomington: Indiana University Press, 1984.

———. *Metaphysische Anfangsgründe der Logik im Ausgang von Leibniz*. GA 26. Edited by Klaus Held. Frankfurt am Main: Klostermann, 1978.

———. "Nihilism as Determined by the History of Being." In *Nietzsche*, vol. 2. Translated by Frank A. Capuzzi. San Francisco: Harper and Collins, 1991.

———. "On the Essence and Concept of φύις in Aristotle's *Physics* B, 1." In *Pathmarks*, 183–231. Translated by William McNeill. Cambridge: Cambridge University Press, 1998.

———. "On the Essence of Ground." In *Pathmarks*, 97–136. Translated by William McNeill. Cambridge: Cambridge University Press, 1998.

———. "On the Question of Being." In *Pathmarks*, 291–322. Translated by William McNeill. Cambridge: Cambridge University Press, 1998.

———. *The Principle of Reason*. Edited by Reginald Lilly. Bloomington: Indiana University Press, 1991.

———. *Der Satz vom Grund*. 4th ed. Pfullingen: Neske, 1978.

———. "Die seinsgeschichtliche Bestimmung des Nihilismus" [1944–46]. In *Nietzsche*, vol. 2, 301–63. Pfullingen: Neske, 1961.

———. *Vom Wesen der Wahrheit. Zu Platons Höhlengleichnis und Theätet*. GA 34. Edited by Hermann Mörchen. Frankfurt am Main: Klostermann, 1988.

———. "Vom Wesen des Grundes." In *Wegmarken*, GA 9, edited by Friedrich-Wilhelm von Herrmann, 123–77. Frankfurt am Main: Klostermann, 1976.

———. "Vom Wesen und Begriff der φύσις. Aristoteles Physik B 1." In *Wegmarken*, GA 9, edited by Friedrich-Wilhelm von Herrmann, 239–303. Frankfurt am Main: Klostermann, 1976.

———. "Dell'essenza e del concetto della φύσις. Aristotele, Fisica B 1" [Vom Wesen und Begriff der φύσις. Aristoteles Physik B 1]. *Il Pensiero* III, 2–3 (1958). Translated into Italian by Giorgio Guzzoni.

———. "Zur Seinsfrage." 1955. In *Wegmarken*, GA 9, edited by Friedrich-Wilhelm von Herrmann, 385–427. Frankfurt am Main: Klostermann, 1976.

Ilting, Karl-Heinz. "Sein als Bewegtheit. Zu Heidegger, Vom Wesen und Begriff der φύσις. Aristoteles Physik B 1." *Philosophische Rundschau* 10 (1962): 31–49.

Pindar. *Pindari Carmina cum Fragmentis*, pars I Epinikia post B. Snell edidit H. Maehler. Leipzig: Teubner, 1980.

———. *Pindari Carmina cum Fragmentis*, pars altera Fragmenta Indices edidit B. Snell. Leipzig: Teubner, 1964.

THOMAS BUCHHEIM is Professor for Metaphysics and Ontology at the University of Munich. Historically he has worked on Pre-Socratic Philosophy, on Aristotle, on Schelling, and on Kant. He is author of *Die Vorsokratiker. Ein philosophisches Porträt, Unser Verlangen nach Freiheit, Aristoteles—Eine Einführung in seine Philosophie*.

6 Being as *Physis*

The Belonging Together of Movement and Rest in the Greek Experience of Physis

Guang Yang

1.

Together with λόγος and ἀλήθεια (unconcealment or truth), Heidegger considers φύσις to be a fundamental term in Greek philosophy. The naming force of this word is said to enable a primordial experience of Being that also marks the beginning of Western thought. Such an originary experience holds an undifferentiated togetherness of various essential moments of Being or of its synonym, φύσις. According to Heidegger's Being-historical (*seinsgeschichtlich*) narrative in the 1930s and 1940s, the richness and originality of Being was obscured by the metaphysical understanding of Being initiated by Plato's doctrine of ideas. Counteracting the disempowerment and demotion of Being, Heidegger, in texts of this period, attempts to restore the unencumbered power of φύσις, that is, to save φύσις, or better, to let φύσις "save itself."[1] In his view, φύσις as Being can refer to beings as a whole as well as to the "emerging-abiding sway"[2] of Being as such, another name for the eventful appropriation (*Ereignis*) of Being in its complex movement. Heidegger's recourse to the origin of philosophy by means of reawakening the disclosing force of the basic words (*Urworte*) of Greek thinking is embedded, however, in his grand discourse on the first beginning and other beginning of Western history. Particularly in the recently published *Black Notebooks*,[3] this narrative has no doubt obscured the force and subtle novelty of his interpretation of φύσις, giving rise to a politicized reading of the problematic. But to directly link Heidegger's thinking of φύσις to National Socialist ideology or even to take the former as an element of the latter would obviate from the very beginning all possibilities of engaging with this theme philosophically.[4]

Instead of generalizing assumptions about the archaic belonging together of φύσις, λόγος, and ἀλήθεια as different names for Being in the context of Heidegger's history of Being, the following reflections will take up the idea of rest or repose (στάσις, ἠρεμία), rarely discussed in the literature, in its intimate relation to movement. I attempt to show that Heidegger's nuanced inquiry into the primordial Greek experience of φύσις cannot be reduced to the one-sided emphasis on an ontological movement as the emerging event of Being. Rather, the unique intertwining of movement and rest and their unitary relation will prove an often overlooked, yet most compelling, point in Heidegger's thinking of φύσις. The Aristotelian notion of force or possibility (δύναμις), which Heidegger has interpreted at length in his well-known essay on *Physics* B 1 and other lecture courses, will thus be linked with his interpretation of φύσις. The reigning power Heidegger associates with φύσις will not be construed in the Being-historical and ontological sense; it will rather be understood, in more phenomenological fashion, as a natural, kinetic force uniting movement and rest. Describing the interplay of δύναμις and rest attempts to shed new light on Heidegger's understanding of the movement of φύσις and Being.

2.

Heidegger's essay on *Physics* B 1 is different in both tone and style from the lecture course *Introduction to Metaphysics*—held four years earlier in the middle of a turbulent period for Heidegger—spelling out his understanding of Being qua φύσις in the context of the history of Being.[5] In *Physics* B 1, except for invoking the non-metaphysical φύσις of the pre-Socratics at the beginning and the end of the essay, Heidegger aims mainly at bringing to light how the essential fullness of early Greek φύσις is echoed for the last time in Aristotle's *Physics*.[6] But how exactly does the primordial experience of pre-Socratic φύσις reverberate in Aristotle's text? Heidegger's anti-metaphysical reading is carried out in the essay through his interpretation and his unorthodox translation of *Physics* B 1. The essay challenges the derivative and restrictive oppositions between Being and becoming, Being and seeming, and others, drawing on the pre-Socratic thinkers and Greek poets in a way similar to Heidegger's interpretation in *Introduction to Metaphysics*. The overarching problem of an originary sense of Being takes shape as the question of how to think of Aristotle's static ontology of substance as dynamic. Ontologically and phenomenologically at once, this leads Heidegger to the phenomenon of movement. And more significantly, in the Greek word φύσις, as a verbal substantive, Heidegger sees the possibility of articulating and grasping the volatile and elusive movedness of beings that is essentially inscribed into their being rather than attributed to them as a merely accidental feature. In fact, the ontological "movedness" (*Bewegtheit*) constitutes both the very being of entities undergoing change and the essential way (*Weise*) of Being as such.[7]

Among the many layers of meaning ascribed to the word φύσις in *Physics* B 1,[8] one aspect seems to stand out for Heidegger: in contrast to an ontic designation of entities as natural beings, φύσις indicates the origin and intrinsic principle (ἀρχή) of movement and rest in physical things (φύσει ὄντα).[9] In other words, φύσις means the invisible ground and force by virtue of which natural things are able to emerge and at the same time conceal themselves, just as the beingness (οὐσία) underlies all beings in Aristotle's first philosophy. Such a two-fold, enabling and yet withdrawing force can be equated with the power of Being, which is characterized as the staying, enduring power of Being's sway (*Walten*) in *Introduction to Metaphysics*.[10] And yet, to make this thought plausible, it seems more fruitful to reinscribe this ontological power in Aristotle's account of the structure of movement of natural things. These entities—not necessarily always linked to the general ontological principle of φύσις—form the basis of Aristotle's analysis,[11] in particular with respect to his definition of movement in relation to δύναμις and ἐνέργεια, ὕλη and μορφή. It is not enough to describe φύσις as a manifestation of being because the locus of such manifestation is a particular entity that can be, but needs not be, moving.

What commentators readily overlook is the inconspicuous word *rest* in the formulation whereby φύσις functions as origin or beginning (ἀρχή) of both movement and rest. If it is, φύσις constitutes an inner force bringing motion and rest into "an originary unity,"[12] providing the hidden drive for the disclosing and withdrawing event inherent in the sending of Being (*Seinsgeschick*) in the Heideggerian sense.[13] Such a unitary relation between movement and rest resonates with the unitary belonging together of oppositions according to Heraclitus's conception of λόγος.[14] But if both movement and rest are constitutive of the manifestation of φύσις, its primordiality depends not only on the possibility of living beings to *themselves* move but also on their capacity to rest.[15] And in contrast to the specific definition of δύναμις in *Metaphysics* Θ as a source of change,[16] φύσις is considered in the *Physics*, as Heidegger says, to be an ordering origin (*ausgängliche Verfügung*), "such that each thing that changes has this ordering within itself."[17] Heidegger's use of the word *ordering* (*Verfügung*) here suggests that the origin is not an accidental and external initiation of the movement, a starting point that can be left behind once the entity sets in motion. Rather, that here is such a continuing ordering distinguishes natural beings from artifacts (ποιούμενα). Heidegger quotes and explains the example of a doctor who is ill and regains his health by treating himself, highlighting the contrast between φύσις and τέχνη: "The origin and ordering of regaining health is not being a doctor but being human, and this only insofar as the human being is a ζῷον, a living being that lives [*lebt*] only inasmuch as it 'is a body' ['*es leibt*']. As even we say, a healthy 'nature,' capable of resistance, is the real origin and ordering ['*Verfügung*'] of regaining health. Without this ἀρχή, all medical practice is in vain."[18]

τέχνη thus cannot be successful without the support of the underlying yet reigning power of φύσις. φύσις is therefore prior in the resulting dichotomies listed by Heidegger, such as nature vs. skill or nature vs. history. But how does the originary belonging together of movement and rest relate to the φύσις of natural things capable of moving and resting of their own accord? Heidegger's account of this question proceeds by first establishing the intimate relation between rest and movement: "Rest is a kind of movement; only that which is able to move can rest."[19] A triangle is unmoved, to follow Heidegger's example, but it does not rest. In contrast, when a tree or a cow stands still, it *is* nonetheless in movedness (*Bewegtheit*), the essence of which does not exclude but include rest. However, this argument can be reversed: it is only thanks to the capacity to stand still and to rest that φύσις qua ἀρχή can "rule"[20] (*walten*) from within the natural beings as an ordering principle over movement. A withering tree, standing there at rest, undergoes change and "moves," to use another of Heidegger's examples. This already points to an equal importance of rest and movement in Heidegger's account of φύσις. Yet Heidegger's analysis is modeled on the Aristotelian analogy between φύσις and τέχνη, and rest is explained within the terminological parameters set by Aristotle. Heidegger even speaks of the rest of artifacts constituted by the resultative state of "having-been-produced,"[21] while movedness is said to refer only to the activity of production under way.

As a result of this analogy, τέχνη as cause of movement is confounded with φύσις as origin of the self-movement and inherent rest of natural things. But beyond this analogy, which commentators have tried to make plausible,[22] it is interesting to note that the concept of rest becomes increasingly important in Heidegger's thinking. Even though movement is the guiding and dominant principle in the tensional structure of φύσις, there is an originary Greek experience of rest that, according to Heidegger, informs and anchors the conception of movedness. In this vein, *Contributions to Philosophy* draws a distinction between "metaphysical" and "physical" rest: rather than "absence" and "a limit case of motion," rest, understood metaphysically in its genuine sense, means "the highest concentration of movedness."[23] Heidegger is here shifting emphasis from motion to rest, if one considers that he used the same expression, "a limit case of motion" (*Grenzfall der Bewegung*), to characterize rest in its inferior relatedness to motion in one of the lecture courses on Aristotle in Marburg.[24] But this is just the position he now rejects. If the "limit case of motion" constitutes the very structure of metaphysical rest, it is no longer merely a transitory phase of movement, a static beginning that needs to be overcome and left behind. Although one finds this idea often in Heidegger scholarship,[25] metaphysical rest is more than simple absence of movement. Rather, it is rest that "includes" and "gathers" (*sammelt*) the possibility of movement, thereby "disclosing" it:[26] it takes something other than movement in order to store it up, as it were, to keep the movement in reserve, such that a moving being can gather itself into its full self in tranquil repose. Rest is revealed as a more fundamental capacity, distinguished from movements in the narrow, ontic sense of an activity and moving process.

In Heidegger's view, the highest movedness consists exactly in a gathering of movements that achieves rest.²⁷ In such preeminent, ontological, or metaphysical rest, movements are concentrated. But despite its primacy, rest continues to manifest itself only in an essential contrast with and correlation to movement. In their manifestation, their intractable relationship must be thought as reciprocal dependence on each other. φύσις is not dissolving but heightening the tension of movement and rest, gathering it into an eminent unity. It is neither movement nor rest but such complex and intertwining togetherness that is missing in artifacts and mechanical products. Modeling his interpretation of φύσις on τέχνη, Heidegger is thus running the risk of obscuring his own pivotal insight.

Heidegger also illustrates the intertwining of movement and rest with the help of the Aristotelian notion of ἐντελέχεια and a specific kind of movement, such as seeing. Seeing, taken as activity, or as "standing in the work" (ἐνέργεια),²⁸ exemplifies the peculiar overlapping of movement and rest. From Heidegger's description of the calm holding and "having" (ἔχει)²⁹ of oneself during the process and at the end of one's movement or action, one can again infer that rest cannot be reduced to movedness and that the tension between movement and rest does not privilege movement but is reciprocal and mutual. If, in Heidegger's reading, the ontic tension between concrete movements and rest is transferred to the ontological level, Being likewise would take on the bivalent character of remaining at rest and emerging into presence at once. However, this insight is threatened again when Heidegger traces the gathering force of rest back to the Aristotelian concept of τέλος qua εἶδος in his commentary on *Physics* B 1. This ultimately embeds rest in the classical distinction between ὕλη and μορφή. The latter of which, not in the static sense of form but as "placing into the appearance,"³⁰ is said to have priority over the former and to therefore manifest φύσις in a higher degree. In his reflections on the relation between φύσις and τέχνη, Heidegger aims, inter alia, at recovering the full and primordial sense of τέχνη. τέχνη in this sense does not mean modern technology and machination overpowering and exploiting nature.³¹ To the extent that Heidegger takes φύσις as but a key to other notions, he obscures what is, by his own account, its central insight.

If one were to follow Heidegger's interpretative strategy, the originary sense of φύσις embracing both movement and rest, ὕλη and μορφή, being and becoming, would again be reduced to the eidetic, restrictive understanding of being. While φύσις as a phenomenon of both movement and rest stands at the threshold and limit of ontology, it is incorporated and collapsed into the Heideggerian account of Being, leveling the specific meanings of φύσις as natural force and elements.³² And yet there are several layers of complication in Heidegger's interpretation of Aristotle and his reflection on τέχνη that do not fit into the teleological hylomorphism or into Heidegger's endeavor to appropriate the unappropriable alterity of φύσις into his ontology. Rather than affirming or rejecting

Heidegger's interpretation as a whole, the task is to discern those complications in Heidegger's arguments, opening up a transgressive interpretation.

3.

The Aristotelian scheme of ὕλη and μορφή corresponds to another pair of concepts, δύναμις and ἐνέργεια. Accordingly, ὕλη can be thought of as a force and a potential (δύναμις)—or, following Heidegger's characteristic translation, as "being appropriate for" (*Eignung*)[33]—that is directed at and inclined toward μορφή as its realization and fulfillment. From this perspective, movement (κίνησις) is understood as the imperfect δύναμις coming to its end, such that the "not yet" (*Noch nicht*)[34] of the merely appropriate is overcome, ὕλη taking the shape of μορφή. Over the course of movement, δύναμις, the holding itself in reserve within itself, would be completely exhausted. An entity's "being appropriate" would fulfill itself as δύναμις comes forth to complete presence. This contradicts, however, the idea of φύσις as origin governing movement and rest, as reservoir of sustaining force that cannot be exhausted by the existence of natural things and their actual movements. In the light of this originary sense of φύσις, it is indeed necessary to reconsider the role of ὕλη, δύναμις, and the motionless aspect of nature.[35]

In *Physics* B 3, where Aristotle offers a general account of the doctrine of four causes (αἰτία), the *causa materialis* (ὕλη) is described as the "out of which" (ἐξ οὗ),[36] for instance the bronze for the bringing forth of a statue. If we compound the concept of material cause as the "out of which" with Heidegger's interpretation of φύσις as origin (*Ursprung*), the primordiality of φύσις would then manifest itself in the ὕλη disengaged from the one-sided inclination toward form. Origin in this context does not mean a mechanical cause. Rather, it provides the possibility as such, which enables the differentiation between cause and effect.[37] Against the backdrop of Heidegger's reflections on the origin of artworks, the concealment of earth and its hyletic repose are considered as an indispensable yet undisclosable moment of φύσις constituting the reverse side of the emergence of truth involved in the origination of works of art. In this sense, φύσις would be the mysterious and inexplicable surplus or "excess" (*Übermaß*)[38] that exceeds the model of τέχνη and hence the subjectivist understanding of artworks as human products and accomplishments.

From his Being-historical perspective, however, Heidegger would not readily agree with the straightforward identification of φύσις with the natural element of earth often suggested by commentators of *The Origin of the Work of Art*.[39] For Heidegger, φύσις is a mark of the holistic occurrence of truth and Being and hence is not to be confused either with the totality of things in nature or with a single natural element. On the other hand, it does not designate a formal, abstract determination of physical things either. In other words, the force of φύσις precedes the conceptual division between the formal and the material.[40] To mediate the eventful and ontological character of φύσις with the ontic notion of nature as physical things, an understanding of δύναμις different from the one sketched above is needed: φύσις can be thought as an innate force (δύναμις) of natural things, out of which movements such as growing can be originated and initiated. φύσις would then transgress all "being appropriate" and indeed constitute an "excess" to any such delimited understanding of movement. Regarding Heidegger's philosophy of art, the source and ground of movement can be traced back to the earth. As a force the "twofoldness of phusis"[41] comes to the fore in the manifestation of the earth in its strife with the world.

The pivotal question of *The Origin of the Work of Art* once more concerns the notion of origin. If art indeed is "a third thing" besides artists and artworks,[42] their genuine underlying origin, whence does it derive its originary power sustaining the circle between artist and work of art, transcending the paradigm of production and product defined by τέχνη? My approach to this question will be to try to show that the force of art holding sway (*waltend*) in works of art is—at least with respect to the belonging together of movement and rest—rooted in φύσις. It is the reigning power of φύσις that shapes both the intimate strife between world and earth and the tensional unity of movement and rest. To begin with, it is interesting to note that Heidegger speaks of the "resting-within-itself"[43] (*Insichruhen*) of things and artworks several times, which an inadequate, metaphysical concept of *thing* would do violence to. The matter-form schema, though not originary enough to capture the essence of art, does, however, offer a point of departure for reflections on the constancy and unity of a thing. In contrast to the standing and self-holding Heidegger associates with εἶδος in the essay on φύσις, the constancy of things in the artwork essay depends on the massive materiality of a thing, such as the granite block, "resting in itself,"[44] despite the unity of things still being grasped with the Aristotelian concept of a composite unity, a union of matter and form.[45] This leads to the distinction between the shoe-equipment reposing in its unitary form and reliability (*Verläßlichkeit*) and a granite block at tranquil rest within itself: the latter "takes shape by itself" (*eigenwüchsig*),[46] while the repose of the shoes as equipment is derivative—it does not rest out of itself. By extension, a striking parallel emerges between the self-sufficiency of works of art and natural things growing on their own. However, rather than developing this idea, Heidegger introduces instead the idea of truth as disclosure of Being in works of art. It is this idea that defines the essence of art and occurs in works of art governing the world of historical people.[47]

Along with the Being-historical determination of the origin of art, the ὕλη-μορφή schema transforms itself into the strife between earth and world.[48] As anticipated above, this strife also relates to φύσις in the ontological and verbal sense of presencing as such. Heidegger's description of the temple and φύσις is telling in this regard: "Standing there, the building rests on the rocky ground. This resting of the work draws out of the rock the darkness of its unstructured yet unforced support. . . . The steadfastness of the work stands out against the surge of the tide and, in its own repose, brings out the raging of the surf."[49] Far from indicating a merely passive, inert raw material to receive a form stamped and imposed on it, Heidegger describes the earthy ground (rock) as a steady element holding itself and counterweighing the motion of other elements in nature and time. In his interpretation of *Antigone*, Heidegger attributes to earth a certain "indestructible" power that seems to be able to resist—"from out of the superiority of the calm [*aus der Überlegenheit der Ruhe*]"[50]—the emergence of restless human toil. But Heidegger's focus is not just on the elemental force of earth. In the artwork essay, he rather incorporates it into the all-embracing event of the emerging φύσις that "lights up"[51] the earth. In the emerging event, world as an open expanse of meanings and relations is set up by the temple and at the same time drawn back to the historically loaded earth that Heidegger further associates with the "home-land."[52] What interests us, however, is less such non-metaphysical rediscovery of earth in a historical context than the question of how the belonging together of world and earth in their strife is channeled into the intimate unity of movement and rest. Heidegger makes this point quite directly:

> The setting up of a world and the setting forth of earth are two essential traits belonging to the work-being of the work. Within the unity of that work-being, however, they belong together. This unity is what we seek when we reflect on the self-sufficiency of the work and try to express in words the closed, unitary repose of this resting-in-itself. . . . what we have made visible in the work is by no means a repose but rather a happening. . . . When rest includes motion, there can be a rest which is an inner collection of motion. Such rest is, therefore, a state of extreme agitation [*höchste Bewegtheit*]—presupposing that the kind of motion in question requires [*fordert*] such rest. The repose of the work that rests in itself is, however, of this sort. We will come, therefore, into the proximity of this repose if we can manage to grasp the movement of the happening in the work-being of the work as a unity.[53]

First of all, it is of some importance to note that the self-sufficiency of art here is based, not on the Kantian aesthetic idea of disinterestedness,[54] but on a unique gathering of movement in the repose of works of art. Such unitary togetherness mirrors the doubly structured φύσις, whose verbal form φύειν names "the emerging that reposes in itself," as Heidegger says in *Introduction to Metaphysics*.[55] With regard to Heidegger's example of the Greek temple, it is the massive marble and rock that grants the possibility of its repose. Moreover, the self-hiding (κρύπτεσθαι) of φύσις in fragment 123 of Heraclitus is transferred here to the self-secluding of earth refraining from any attempt to disclose it.[56] In other words, earth indicates the "drive of the emerging and rising of all things," or φύσις as that which at the same time "keeps itself secluded."[57] In distinction from a raw material appropriate for a certain productive τέλος, the potential and force (δύναμις) of earth that holds itself in reserve would not be used up even after the "setting-up" of a world in a work of art. On the contrary, the opening up of a worldly expanse in art that lets earth appear as such is, in turn, dependent on the impenetrable and inanimate materiality of earth, such as the dark pigment in Van Gogh's painting, which, according to Heidegger's interpretation, supports the life world of the peasant woman. On this account, one may speak of earth as a "trans-historical"[58] dimension of the sensible works of art, which can be seen as balancing the Being-historical aspect of art in Heidegger's sense.

The tensional belonging together of movement and rest also retrieves Heraclitus's idea of πόλεμος, which Heidegger calls strife (or struggle, *Streit*).[59] Far from destructive dispute, the strife between world and earth brings the opponents into intimate (*innig*) togetherness and so constitutes one essential moment of the dynamic phenomenality unique to works of art. Furthermore, "the repose of the work that rests in itself thus has its essence in the intimacy of the struggle."[60] The intimacy of the struggle can be illustrated precisely by the gathering and concentration of movement in rest: "In the intense agitation [*der gesammelten Bewegnis*] of this conflict presences repose [*Ruhe*]. It is here that the self-subsistence, the resting-in-itself [*Insichruhen*] of the work finds its ground."[61] In this way, the oppositional movement and the discord between the struggling contestants is contained and collected into the harmonic intimacy of the contesting forces. Just this belonging together of movement and rest is reflected in a work of art resting in itself. In the lecture course on Hölderlin, from almost the same period as *The Origin of the Work of Art*, the mysterious intimacy (*Innigkeit*) of nature as unity of "conflictual turning" (*Widerwendigkeit*)[62] of oppositional powers is used to characterize Being itself. Similar to the intimacy of strife in *The Origin of the Work of Art*, the intimate, unitary togetherness of counterturning (*gegenwendig*) forces relates movement and tranquil rest, the latter here called but "the semblance [*Schein*] of absence of movement."[63] Aligning the characterization of nature as intimacy with the gathering of movement in rest of works of art, we can come to the conclusion that the inscrutable union of movement and rest in art consists ultimately in the uncanny power of φύσις prevailing both ontically in the material and ontologically as an intrinsic, self-secluding, yet gathering force.

4.

The previous part of this essay has sought to show that the overwhelming power of φύσις can be found in art. It is for this reason that it transcends the Aristotelian conceptual pair of matter and form. And yet, as some commentators have already pointed out,[64] Heidegger's view of art still subscribes to the priority of ἐνέργεια over δύναμις to the extent that the essence of art found in the "actual work" is defined as "what is at work in the work [*im Werk am Werk*], in terms, that is, of the happening of truth."[65] "At work in the work" is precisely the turn of phrase Heidegger uses to translate ἐνέργεια in the essay on φύσις.[66] Even the strife between world and earth could be seen as a reformulation of the hylomorphism of Aristotle. On this account, one could argue that the moment of repose discussed above and the unfathomable force of φύσις are indeed inferior to the unconcealing movement of truth as the actualization of what is merely potential in nature.

On the other hand, the unbridgeable and tensional rift (*Riss*) between world and earth, which works of art also display, cannot be totally identified with the sketch or "outline" (*Umriss*) and "figure" (*Gestalt*)[67] derived from the Aristotelian μορφή—there is even a tendency in Heidegger research to see the dynamics of history as "movement toward realizing a form (μορφή)."[68] The moment of repose in art cannot be narrowed to the eidetic determinacy, either. Once disassociated from the teleological formation, the material side of works of art turns out to be a natural force that cannot be taken simply as a privation or a deficient mode, a "not yet." Rather, it constitutes a dimension indispensable for the manifestation of art. To put the same point in a more phenomenological manner, the earthy and dark background of a work of art, an early painting by Van Gogh, for example, remains inconspicuous, indeterminate, and unmeasured as potentiality in contrast to the lit-up foreground where the life world indicated by human figures and other outlined things comes to salience.[69] Works of art, considered in this manner, would provide a site where an open and undecidable play between presence and absence, measure and unmeasure (*Unmaß*), takes place. In fact, the withholding of earth together with its quiet reserve in a work of art can be read as an indicator of the originary excess of art rooted in φύσις, which requires and stimulates the worldly and epistemological appropriation at once but never gives over to it completely. Thus φύσις marks the limit of accessibility but at the same time holds open the possibilities of historical appropriation and therefore can withstand fateful "decision" in the Being-historical sense.[70] Moreover, it attests to the primordiality of art also in the sense that the source of the conflicting movements in art works, contrary to τέχνη and technical products, refers back to its innate force rather than to external causes, for φύσις as origin of movement and rest is an inexhaustible source to which both can return again and again.

To sum up, Heidegger has brought to light the significance of the phenomenological belonging together of movement and rest in his interpretation of the Greek φύσις and his writing on art. In both cases, φύσις has proven to be, disregarding to a certain extent Heidegger's ontological interpretation, the cryptic force (δύναμις)[71] uniting movement and rest, manifesting itself in the intense concentration of movement in rest. If our stress on the tranquil moment of φύσις is based on a different conception of δύναμις loosened from the Aristotelian schema to which Heidegger seems to more strictly adhere, then we are confronted with the question of how such a seemingly unmoved "quiet power of the possible" (*stille Kraft des Möglichen*)[72] is related to movement as its actualization—a rest not attracted to movement in any determinate way would appear to simply become nonmovement and therefore cease to be rest. But with regard to the twofold unity of φύσις as origin of both movement and rest, it seems to be plausible to maintain a certain degree of independence of potentiality from its actualization (ἐνέργεια),[73] to which the self-sufficiency of rest testifies. Moreover, quiet resting would keep its self-sufficiency even in the midst of movement, in nature as well as in art, for art, wrested from nature, is hidden but also "found in nature."[74]

Notes

1. Heidegger, *Basic Concepts of Ancient Philosophy*, 28: "φύσις σώζεται." See also Aristotle, *Metaphysics* A 3, 983b 13. The context of this lecture course of 1926, where Heidegger speaks of φύσις, is certainly different from those later texts.

2. Heidegger, *Introduction to Metaphysics*, 15.

3. See, e.g., Heidegger, *Ponderings II–VI*, 156.

4. See Ireland, "Naming Φύσις," 315–46. Ireland's discussion of the political significance of φύσις in Heidegger's thinking did not draw on the most important text on this topic at all, namely Heidegger's essay on *Physics* B 1 in *Pathmarks*.

5. Against Heidegger's ontological equation of Being with the early Greek φύσις, see, e.g., Hadot, *Veil of Isis*, 307.

6. See Heidegger, "On the Essence and Concept of Φύσις," 186.

7. See Heidegger, "On the Essence and Concept of Φύσις," 189, 216. Heidegger makes a distinction here between ontic movement and ontological movedness. On the verbal sense of Being as movedness, see, e.g., Capobianco, *Heidegger's Way of Being*, 25; Bröcker, *Aristoteles*, 62–66.

8. Three "presuppositions" underlie, according to Thomas Sheehan, Heidegger's interpretation of φύσις in this essay on Aristotle: a thoroughgoing "Greek naturalism," "kineticism," and the phenomenological aspect of φύσις ("Nihilism," 285–87). For our purpose the second "presupposition" is especially relevant.

9. See Aristotle, *Aristotle's Physics*, B 1, 192b 13–14: ἐν ἑαυτῷ ἀρχὴν ἔχει κινήσεως καὶ στάσεως.

10. See Heidegger, *Introduction to Metaphysics*, 67. It seems to me that in Heidegger's thinking the word *Macht* (power) is more liable to be connected to *violence* (Gewalt), whereas *Kraft* (force) can be used in mostly neutral and nonpolitical contexts. The question at issue here is whether the swaying power of φύσις has political implication as Julia Ireland suggests. On relation of *Walten* to *Gewalt*, see Derrida, "L'oreille de Heidegger," 407–9; Ziarek, *Language after Heidegger*, 198–200.

11. See Wieland, *Aristotelische Physik*, 245.

12. See Heidegger, *Introduction to Metaphysics*, 64.

13. See Heidegger, *Principle of Reason*, 65.

14. See Diels and Kranz, *Fragmente der Vorsokratiker*, vol. 1, DK 22, B 111. The Greek word for *rest* in this fragment is ἀνάπαυσις.

15. On the capacity of rest in relation to movement, see Gadamer, "Griechen," 291.

16. See Aristotle, *Metaphysics* Θ 1, 1046a 10–11: ἀρχὴ μεταβολῆς ἐν ἄλλῳ.

17. Heidegger, "On the Essence and Concept of Φύσις," 191.

18. Heidegger, "On the Essence and Concept of Φύσις," 196.

19. Heidegger, "On the Essence and Concept of Φύσις," 189.

20. Heidegger, "On the Essence and Concept of Φύσις," 190.

21. Heidegger, "On the Essence and Concept of Φύσις," 192.

22. Brogan, "Intractable Interrelationship," 43–56.

23. Heidegger, *Contributions to Philosophy*, 152. The word *metaphysical* has no derogatory connotation here, as it usually has in later years.

24. Heidegger, *Basic Concepts of Ancient Philosophy*, 167.

25. See, e.g., Sadler, *Heidegger and Aristotle*, 63.

26. Heidegger, "On the Essence and Concept of Φύσις," 217. The English translator chose not to translate literally another key German verb in this passage, *auffangen* (to catch, contain, or collect), but rendered it into English as a cognate with *gather* (*sammeln*).

27. Incidentally, in the Chinese Daoist tradition rest is often considered to be superior to movement. Heidegger quoted once chapter 15 of *Dao De jing*, in which the ambivalent relationship between movement and rest is described vividly. See Heidegger, *Reden und andere Zeugnisse eines Lebenswegs*, 618; Waley, *Way and Its Power*, 160, 176 (chapter 26), where "rest" or "quietness" is called "lord and master of activity."

28. Heidegger, "On the Essence and Concept of Φύσις," 217. On the difference between ἐνέργεια and other kinds of motions, see Ackrill, "Aristotle's Distinction," 121–41.

29. Heidegger, "On the Essence and Concept of Φύσις," 218.

30. Heidegger, "On the Essence and Concept of Φύσις," 212.

31. See Heidegger, *Basic Questions of Philosophy*, 154–55.

32. Regarding critical reflections on Heidegger's ontological approach to φύσις, see Figal, *Gegenständlichkeit*, 377–78. On φύσις and the elemental sense of nature, see Sallis, *Force of Imagination*, 147–62.

33. Heidegger, "On the Essence and Concept of Φύσις," 219.

34. See also Aristotle, *Metaphysics* Θ 6, 1048b 8–9.

35. On the unmoved side of nature, see Sallis, *Force of Imagination*, 151–52, where Sallis speaks of the "quiet" and "changeless" in nature and elements.

36. Aristotle, *Physics* B 3, 194b 24.

37. See Brogan, "Aristotle's Doppel ἀρχή," 126.

38. Heidegger, *Four Seminars*, 38. The "excess" of φύσις refers to the overabundance of what presences in this seminar.

39. See, e.g., Sallis, "Heidegger's Poetics," 181; Thomä, *Zeit des Selbst und die Zeit danach*, 714–15.

40. See Heidegger, *Nature, History, State*, 24. One should take into consideration that the texts in this volume are not Heidegger's own notes for the lecture course.

41. Brogan, *Heidegger and Aristotle*, 81.

42. See Heidegger, "Origin of the Work of Art," 1–4.

43. See, e.g., Heidegger, "Origin of the Work of Art," 8–10, 21, 26.

44. Heidegger, "Origin of the Work of Art," 9.

45. See Aristotle, *Metaphysics* 7, 1037a 32: σύνολος; Heidegger, "Origin of the Work of Art," 52.

46. Heidegger, "Origin of the Work of Art," 10.

47. See Heidegger, "Origin of the Work of Art," 16–19, 21.

48. On Heidegger's discovery of earth transcending the Aristotelian concept of ὕλη, see Sinclair, *Heidegger, Aristotle and the Work of Art*, 135–67.

49. Heidegger, "Origin of the Work of Art," 21.

50. Heidegger, *Introduction to Metaphysics*, 164.

51. Heidegger, "Origin of the Work of Art," 21.

52. Heidegger, "Origin of the Work of Art": "der heimatliche Grund." The hyphen in *home-land* is added by me.

53. Heidegger, "Origin of the Work of Art," 26.

54. On Heidegger's criticism of aesthetics in general, see Young, *Heidegger's Philosophy of Art*, 8–14.

55. Heidegger, *Introduction to Metaphysics*, 106.

56. See Diels and Kranz, *Fragmente der Vorsokratiker*, vol. 1, DK 22, B 113.

57. Dastur, "Heidegger's Freiburg Version," 128.

58. Espinet, "Kunst und Natur," 65. In this respect, I disagree with Julian Young, who argues that the materiality of art can sometimes be ignored and concealed. See Young, *Heidegger's Philosophy of Art*, 48.

59. See Heidegger, "Origin of the Work of Art," 22.

60. Heidegger, "Origin of the Work of Art," 27.

61. Heidegger, "Origin of the Work of Art," 33.

62. Heidegger, *Hölderlin's Hymns "Germania" and "The Rhine,"* 232.

63. Heidegger, *Hölderlin's Hymns "Germania" and "The Rhine,"* 233.

64. See Sinclair, *Heidegger, Aristotle and the Work of Art*, 168; Michail Pantoulias, "Heideggers Ontologie des Kunstwerks," 158.

65. Heidegger, "Origin of the Work of Art," 33.

66. See Heidegger, "On the Essence and Concept of Φύσις," 217. On ἐνέργεια, see also the appendix to "Origin of the Work of Art," 53.

67. Heidegger, "Origin of the Work of Art," 38, 54.

68. Guignon, "Being as Appearing," 49.

69. On *measure* and *unmeasure* (*Unmaß*), see Heidegger, "Origin of the Work of Art," 48.

70. See Heidegger, "Origin of the Work of Art," 31, 38.

71. In an earlier lecture course on Aristotle's concept of force (δύναμις), Heidegger talks about the force of "material nature," in *Aristotle's Metaphysics* Θ 1–3, 61.

72. Heidegger, "Letter on 'Humanism,'" 242.

73. For Sheehan, however, the significance of δύναμις consists completely in its dependence on ἐνέργεια, whereas I am trying to deconstruct such one-sided dependence. See Thomas Sheehan, "On the Way to Ereignis," 152–53. Agamben takes up Heidegger's interpretation of δύναμις and unfolds it in relation to impotentiality (ἀδυναμία). See Agamben, "On Potentiality," 181.

74. Heidegger, "Origin of the Work of Art," 43. Heidegger is citing here the German artist Albrecht Dürer. Work on this essay was sponsored by School of Humanities, Tongji University, Shanghai Pujiang Program (Phenomenology and Eastern Aesthetics of Nature 17PJC106).

Bibliography

Ackrill, J. L. "Aristotle's Distinction between Energeia and Kinesis." In *New Essays on Plato and Aristotle*, edited by Renford Bambrough, 121–41. London: Routledge and Kegan Paul, 1965.

Agamben, Giorgio. "On Potentiality." In *Potentialities: Collected Essays in Philosophy*, 177–85. Translated by Daniel Heller-Roazen. Stanford: Stanford University Press, 1999.

Aristotle. *Aristotle's Physics*. Edited by W. D. Ross. Oxford: Clarendon, 1936.

———. *Metaphysics*. Edited by W. D. Ross. Oxford: Clarendon, 1924.

Bröcker, Walter. *Aristoteles*. Frankfurt am Main: Klostermann, 1964.

Brogan, Walter A. "Aristotle's Doppel ἀρχή: φύσις und κίνησις." In *Heidegger und die Griechen*, edited by Michael Steinmann, 123–39. Frankfurt am Main: Klostermann, 2007.

———. *Heidegger and Aristotle: The Twofoldness of Being*. Albany: State University of New York Press, 2005.

———. "The Intractable Interrelationship of *Physis* and *Techne*." In *Heidegger and the Greeks: Interpretive Essays*, edited by Drew A. Hyland and John P. Manoussakis, 43–57. Bloomington: Indiana University Press, 2006.

Capobianco, Richard. *Heidegger's Way of Being*. Toronto: University of Toronto Press, 2014.

Dastur, Françoise. "Heidegger's Freiburg Version of the Origin of the Work of Art." In *Heidegger toward the Turn: Essays on the Work of the 1930s*, edited by James Risser, 119–44. Albany: State University of New York, 1999.

Derrida, Jacques. "L'oreille de Heidegger. Philopolémologie (Geschlecht IV)." In *Politiques de l'amité*, 343–419. Paris: Édition Galilée, 1994.

———. *Politiques de l'amité*. Paris: Édition Galilée, 1994.

Diels, Hermann, and Walther Kranz, ed. *Die Fragmente der Vorsokratiker*. 2 vols. Berlin: Weidmannsche, 1960.

Espinet, David. "Kunst und Natur. Der Streit von Welt und Erde." In *Heideggers Ursprung des Kunstwerks. Ein kooperativer Kommentar*, edited by David Espinet and Tobias Keiling, 46–65. Frankfurt am Main: Klostermann, 2011.

Figal, Günter. *Gegenständlichkeit. Das Hermeneutische und die Philosophie*. Tübingen: Mohr Siebeck, 2006.

Gadamer, Hans-Georg. "Die Griechen." In *Gesammelte Werke*, vol. 3, 285–97. Tübingen: Mohr Siebeck, 1987.

Guignon, Charles. "Being as Appearing: Retrieving the Greek Experience of *Physis*." In *A Companion to Heidegger's Introduction to Metaphysics*, edited by Richard Polt and Gregory Fried, 34–57. New Haven, CT: Yale University Press, 2001.

Hadot, Pierre. *The Veil of Isis: An Essay on the History of the Idea of Nature*. Translated by Michael Chase. Cambridge, MA: Harvard University Press, 2006.

Heidegger, Martin. *Aristotle's Metaphysics Θ 1–3: On the Essence and Actuality of Force*. Translated by Walter Brogan and Peter Warnek. Bloomington: Indiana University Press, 1995.

———. *Basic Concepts of Ancient Philosophy*. Translated by Richard Rojcewicz. Bloomington: Indiana University Press, 2007.

———. *Basic Questions of Philosophy Selected "Problems" of "Logic."* Translated by Richard Rojcewicz and Andre Schuwer. Bloomington: Indiana University Press, 1994.

———. *Contributions to Philosophy (Of the Event)*. Translated by Richard Rojcewicz and Daniela Vallega-Neu. Bloomington: Indiana University Press, 2012.

———. *Four Seminars*. Translated by Andrew Mitchell and François Raffoul. Bloomington: Indiana University Press, 2003.

———. *Hölderlin's Hymns "Germania" and "The Rhine."* Translated by William McNeill and Julia Ireland. Bloomington: Indiana University Press, 2014.

———. *Introduction to Metaphysics*. Translated by Gregory Fried and Richard Polt. New Haven, CT: Yale University Press, 2000.

———. "Letter on 'Humanism.'" In *Pathmarks*, edited by William McNeill, 239–76. Cambridge: Cambridge University Press, 1998.

———. *Nature, History, State: 1933–1934*. Translated by Gregory Fried and Richard Polt. London: Bloomsbury, 2015.

———. "On the Essence and Concept of Φύσις in Aristotle's *Physics* B 1." In *Pathmarks*, edited by William McNeill, 183–230. Cambridge: Cambridge University Press, 1998.

———. "The Origin of the Work of Art." In *Off the Beaten Track*, 1–56. Translated by Julian Young and Kenneth Hayes. Cambridge: Cambridge University Press, 2002.

———. *Ponderings II–VI: Black Notebooks, 1931–1938*. Translated by Richard Rojcewicz. Bloomington: Indiana University Press, 2016.

———. *The Principle of Reason*. Translated by Reginald Lilly. Bloomington: Indiana University Press, 1991.

———. *Reden und Zeugnisse eines Lebensweges, 1910–1076*. Edited by Hermann Heidegger. Klostermann: Frankfurt am Main, 2000.

Ireland, Julia. "Naming Φύσις and the 'Inner Truth of National Socialism': A New Archival Discovery." *Research in Phenomenology* 44 (2014): 315–46.

Pantoulias, Michail. "Heideggers Ontologie des Kunstwerks und die antike Philosophie. Heraklit und Aristoteles." In *Heideggers Ursprung des Kunstwerks. Ein kooperativer Kommentar*, edited by David Espinet and Tobias Keiling, 139–59. Frankfurt am Main: Klostermann, 2011.

Sadler, Ted. *Heidegger and Aristotle: Question of Being*. London: Athlone, 1996.

Sallis, John. *Force of Imagination: The Sense of the Elemental*. Bloomington: Indiana University Press, 2000.

———. "Heidegger's Poetics: The Question of Mimesis." In *Kunst und Technik. Gedächtnisschrift zum 100. Geburtstag von Martin Heidegger*, edited by Walter Biemel and Friedrich-Wilhelm von Herrmann, 175–88. Frankfurt am Main: Klostermann, 1989.

Sheehan, Thomas. "Nihilism: Heidegger/Jünger/Aristotle." In *Phenomenology: Japanese and American Perspectives*, edited by Burt C. Hopkins, 273–316. Dordrecht: Kluwer Academic, 1999.

———. "On the Way to Ereignis: Heidegger's Interpretation of Physis." In *Continental Philosophy in America*, edited by Hugh J. Silverman, 131–64. Pittsburgh: Duquesne University Press, 1983.

Sinclair, Mark. *Heidegger, Aristotle and the Work of Art: Poiesis in Being*. New York: Palgrave Macmillan, 2006.

Thomä, Dieter. *Die Zeit des Selbst und die Zeit danach. Zur Kritik der Textgeschichte Martin Heideggers. 1910–1976.* Frankfurt am Main: Suhrkamp, 1990.

Waley, Arthur. *The Way and Its Power: A Study of the Tao Te Ching and Its Place in Chinese Thought.* New York: Grove, 1977.

Wieland, Wolfgang. *Die Aristotelische Physik.* Göttingen: Vandenhoeck & Ruprecht, 1962.

Young, Julian. *Heidegger's Philosophy of Art.* Cambridge: Cambridge University Press, 2001.

Ziarek, Krsyztof. *Language after Heidegger.* Bloomington: Indiana University Press, 2013.

GUANG YANG is Associate Fellow at School of Humanities, Tongji University Shanghai. He is author of the book *Versammelte Bewegung at Mohr Siebeck, Tübingen.*

7 The End of Philosophy and the Experience of Unending *Physis*

Claudia Baracchi

1. End of the Millennium

In the wake of German idealism, and markedly after Nietzsche's ardent meditation, a vast segment of Western philosophy has engaged in a confrontation with
the metaphysical tradition, calling for the unhinging of its presuppositions and
authority. The story is well known—or at least it is one of the stories that can be
told about philosophy at the end of the millennium. The philosophical discourse
of the last century (if, in fact, such a discourse is singular) has prominently and
coherently endeavored to call an order of things crystallized through a millenary
domination into question. It has, indeed, endeavored to subvert order as such
and its hierarchical logic—that is, logic tout court, implicated in the dynamics
of power as, at once, power's sublime precipitate and foundation. In a broad, sustained, and variegated set of discussions, metaphysics has been exposed in its
ideological dimensions and crypto-political valences. From classical phenomenology to Frankfurt critical theory and from philosophical anthropology to the
thinking of difference (in inflections as diverse as may be, for instance, in Derrida, Deleuze, and Irigaray), the past century has undertaken to dismantle the
dichotomies constitutive of the so-called history of metaphysics. These dichotomies include soul and body, intelligibility and sensibility, mind and nature, sky
and earth, thought and extension, theory and practice, voice and phenomenon,
life and death, and philosophy and biography. We could say that the overall effort
has been oriented to the overcoming of divisions and the composition of disso-
ciations and, hence, to the possibility of healing and regeneration.

After Hegel, then, and radicalizing his pronouncement, the century has proclaimed "the end of metaphysics" (the end of the epoch of Western philosophy as
metaphysics)—an end that would coincide with a beginning, with a new (other)
inception, so much so that precisely such an end would harbor, as an undisclosed
seed, the task of thinking yet to come. This vast movement decisively hinges on
the figure and language of Martin Heidegger and finds a number of program-
matic formulations in his work, most notably in *Das Ende der Philosophie und die*

Aufgabe des Denkens ("The End of Philosophy and the Task of Thinking"). This work first became available in French in 1964 and was published in German in 1969.[1] With lapidary precision, this brief text announces the end of philosophy as we know it, that is, as the academic discipline focused on knowledge (its conditions and exercise) and ultimately resolving itself into the sciences. In its pursuit of knowledge, in the end, philosophy comes to be superseded by scientific procedures and paradigms. To the extent that it has accomplished its task, reached its own completion, and, hence, exhausted its historical function, philosophy is at an end.

Yet, once such a diagnosis is formulated and its argumentation refined and refracted through a multitude of idioms, what does it imply? What should rigorously follow from it? Beyond the often-baroque taste for paradox and conceptual contortion, beyond the frequently spectacular provocations characterizing recent philosophical discourse, what would be the import of subjecting philosophy to such a critical scrutiny and urging a regeneration of thinking in light of its belonging in and to life? Why should it concern those who study and teach philosophy (its canon, history, transmission, and perpetuation) in schools and universities? Why should it matter to anyone who may care for thinking? I pose such questions assuming that the seismic movements that traversed the last century deserve to be taken seriously, undergone as genuinely compelling, and not taken as a mere divertissement. I assume, that is, that the painstaking deconstruction of metaphysical dichotomies does not amount to a sterile joke, to a display of intellectual virtuosity as legitimate as self-referential and, thus, of no consequence whatsoever.

Before focusing more closely on the essay by Heidegger mentioned above, I should put forth at least a couple of further considerations. At stake in the broad movement of the past century is the possibility of experience. The century is deeply concerned with the elusiveness and dispersion of experience in its irreducibility to the outcome of conceptual operations. Both the phenomenological elaboration of *Erlebnis* (the lived experience constituting the affective underground, shadowy and shifting, of the living subject) and the focus on *Erfahrung* (the term privileged by Heidegger in the attempt to distance his discourse from the questions of subjectivity and of life) articulate experience as radically exceeding the order of the empirical and experimental. This entails a thorough reassessment of the logic that opposes (and subordinates) experience to intellection, and, thus, *a posteriori* knowledge to the freedom and absoluteness of the *a priori*. To the extent that experience is subjected to conceptual knowledge, constitutively secured to and ordered by the concept, the encounter with beings and with the world is compromised, to say nothing of the experience (the *pathos*) of the event. Conversely, in the undoing of the conceptual constructs opposing empiricism and idealism, experience comes to name a primordial exposure that does not amount to knowledge (although it makes knowledge possible), a relatedness that illuminates, a confrontation in which the elements in play first manifest themselves and become originally accessible.[2] In this sense, experience names a coming to know indeterminately prior to cognition and unfolding in openness, availability, and vulnerability. Such contact takes place within the expanse disclosed through the grounding experience (*Grunderfahrung*) of *physis* as such.[3]

On an altogether different register, Walter Benjamin also seizes the improbability and fragility of experience. In the short 1933 essay "Experience and Poverty," he diagnoses the structural impoverishment and diminution of experience in the wake of World War I and the concomitant political-economic upheavals.[4] Situated in a field of forces incommensurable and out of control, where masses of men and women suffer the strains of hunger and totalitarianism, the individual is, as such, alienated from the structure and rhythm of everyday life, deprived of a living adherence to ordinary conditions and circumstances, which recede from awareness and become literally imperceptible. Taking up both Heidegger's analyses and Benjamin's intuition of the desensibilization at the heart of modern life, Giorgio Agamben further develops the contemporary impossibility (indeed, the "destruction") of experience. He underlines the disappearance of the subtle and inconspicuous and, concomitantly, the prevalence of the spectacle—loud, traumatic, and over the top.[5]

Along with a widespread sense of urgency regarding the questions of experience and sensibility, the polemical discourse pervading the nineteenth and twentieth centuries yields its most suggestive articulations in confronting basic themes in the philosophy of history. With Heidegger in particular, the last century learns to turn to the past in a questioning mode and to experience its mystery and ultimate irretrievability (broadly speaking, the problems of temporality). But undergoing the enigma of the past also means broaching the question concerning our genealogy and origin—the meaning itself of the pronoun *we*.[6] The task, thus, involves confronting our provenance while the experience of the past becomes opaque and obscure. The task entails wondering how we became what we are, through what vicissitudes and trajectories, and, above all, through what manners of forgetfulness and disappearance, through what discontinuities and precipitations back into latency. That is, we must wonder how we came to find ourselves here, where we are, by what paths, conscious as well as unconscious, dimly lit or altogether dark. For the past (individual as well as collective) is saturated with that which has never been seen and has yet to take place. In mostly submerged movements, it nurtures and dictates the future.

Today more than ever, Heidegger seems an unlikely point of reference for issues in the philosophy of history, and in many respects his comprehension of the political implications of his work appears hopelessly confused if not awkwardly inarticulate. Nevertheless, it can hardly be denied that his readings often reenergize ancient and long silent texts in ways utterly relevant to the problems mentioned.

2. Place

"The End of Philosophy and the Task of Thinking" announces the end of Western philosophy and, after a concise delineation of its history, develops a meditation on that which is to come and remains to be thought in this epochal shift. The essay develops in a precarious balance on its threshold. The end of philosophy can only be perceived in the experience of a distance, of a non-coincidence with respect to that which the philosophy of the West has become (an academic subject matter, the discipline of knowledge losing itself into the scientific paradigm). Yet, on the other hand, such alienation does not simply amount to extraneousness, as if the end were observed from without or after the fact. The end is *ongoing* and *immanent* in the exercise of philosophy. Heidegger's reflection oscillates between inside and outside, between what is fulfilled and what remains as an assignment to be carried out, verging on completion and confronting an infinite task. In this oscillation, the limit (the threshold) thickens, expands, and reveals itself as a matter of place. The end is the place (*Ort*) experienced in the movement of trespassing and traversing: "The old meaning of the word 'end' means the same as place: 'from one end to another' means from one place to another."[7] Thus, the end of philosophy is its "there," "where" philosophy is properly situated. However, "that in which" philosophy unfolds points to that which exceeds philosophy and, in fact, provides the conditions for it. Heidegger concludes: "The end of philosophy is the place, that place in which the whole of philosophy's history is gathered in its most extreme possibility. End as completion means this gathering."[8]

In its exposure to that which exceeds it, philosophy has always been ending—that is, it has always been at an end. Its ability or inability to acknowledge this determines the mode and implications of its end—whether the end becomes the locus of decomposition or of regeneration. For, in its denial and oblivion of that which indeterminately exceeds it, in its defensiveness and self-enclosure, philosophy is at an end in the degenerative sense. And yet precisely in this turning back upon itself lies the possibility of bursting itself open, of experiencing itself as traversed by the exorbitant and unmasterable. In accomplishing its forgetful movement of closure, philosophy brushes the possibility of casting light on its own forgetfulness. The possibility of such a nascent remembrance carries radically disruptive implications vis-à-vis the history and exercise of philosophy. Again, the end is revealed as the locus of both calcification and unbound possibility, of utmost conclusion and the promise of radical openness.

It should be observed that the end of philosophy does not merely amount to a realization of the historicity (i.e., multiplicity and finitude) of philosophical discourses. To be sure, philosophy has always met an end (that which exceeds it) and retraced its exposure to (and contention with) excess precisely in revising itself. Philosophy meets an end in engendering articulations of truth necessarily finite, multiple, and mutable that follow upon each other in the concatenation of the epochs. The historicity of philosophical discourses, in their virtual discontinuity with respect to one another, grants the continuity and continuation of philosophy as a tradition, lineage, and spiritual register. At issue here is not, however, the historicity of any particular philosophical discourse but rather the historicity of philosophy as such. The theme of the end carries a more radical indication: the announcement of the historicity of philosophy itself. It announces that philosophy is a tradition that had a beginning and will see an end precisely to the extent that it neither coincides with nor exhausts thinking.[9] Indeed, why would the questioning ethos that came to be and developed in determinate spatiotemporal circumstances be unending?

After all, the essay opens precisely by casting light on contemporary philosophy in its derivativeness: philosophy in its institutional form, philosophy as the body of knowledge canonized, preserved, and transmitted in Western universities. "To the extent that philosophical thinking is still attempted," Heidegger notes, "it only attains an epigonal renaissance and variations of it."[10] And although the end of philosophy need not mean "a cessation of its way of thinking,"[11] it still announces that philosophy has come to a limit from which it can only turn back upon itself. The openness of the speculative labor, the encounter with the matter at stake, is over. At issue, as we pointed out, is the possibility of accessing, of experiencing "the things themselves" and their necessity—and that means the possibility of being determined in or by undergoing this occurrence.

3. Experience

Thus, Heidegger intimates that the distinctive project of metaphysics is presently withering away, for circumstances do not require it anymore. In this connection we find the analysis of philosophy merging with the sciences and the diagnosis of the abysmal emptiness at the heart of the fullness of this epoch. Heidegger follows the course from Aristotle to Galileo, to the age of cybernetics that has enfolded the globe in the communicative World Wide Web. Here, the pursuit of knowledge is exposed in its ancillary role, acquiescent to the demands of efficiency and productivity. While formally paying homage to the language of being, the sciences speak in the dissipation of being and, therefore, in the eclipse of beings. The all-steering, all-informing science of cybernetics grants unlimited communication, but its content is increasingly insubstantial, dispensable, or even altogether lacking. What is being said in informatics, what its formalizations speak of, is no longer evident. Once again, at stake is the estrangement from the matter of experience, the matter to be undergone and thought—the "things themselves" that Aristotle assimilated to "phenomena" and to the "truth itself," which would "necessitate" a certain thinking and acting posture.[12] As Heidegger puts it, in a characteristically ambivalent turn to Plato (the one who inaugurates the epoch of philosophy as metaphysics and, at once, abides irreducible to it): "When we ask about the task of thinking, this means in the scope of philosophy to determine that which concerns thinking, that which is still controversial for thinking, and is the controversy. This is what the word *Sache* [thing, matter] means in the German language. It designates that with which thinking has to do in the case at hand, in Plato's language *to pragma auto* [the thing itself] (see *Letter VII*, 341c 7)."[13]

Heidegger proceeds, then, to examine the more recent calls "to the things themselves" by Hegel and Husserl. Bringing together the Greek forefather and the German predecessors, he draws the defining ventures of the history of metaphysics in a few broad strokes.[14] But the point is manifestly *not* securing the matter itself to the presence granted by subjective (and ultimately scientific) presentation, whether through the movement of the *idea* in speculative dialectic or the gift of originary intuition in phenomenology. The point would be, rather, letting the matter itself, in its unresolved and even disturbing dimensions, haunt thinking—or, more precisely, call for thinking. And possible indications for such a development to come may be found in the dimly lit receptacles of the past. It might be a matter of retrieving a discrepancy between the beginning and ending of the philosophy of the West—a forgotten non-coincidence, a "concealed" history[15] revealing unheard-of potentialities buried (undeveloped and unexpressed) in the ancient inception: "But is the end of philosophy in the sense of its evolving into the sciences also already the complete actualization of all the possibilities in which the thinking of philosophy was posited? Or is there a *first* possibility for thinking apart from the *last* possibility that we characterized (the dissolution of philosophy in the technologized sciences), a possibility from which the thinking of philosophy would have to start, but which as philosophy it could nevertheless not expressly experience [*erfahren*] and take over?"[16]

Here, the intertwining of problems pertaining to, on one hand, experience (the belonging and contact with things, the access to and openness of beings) and, on the other hand, history (the transmission of philosophical discourse, the temporal/ecstatic as well as hermeneutic difficulties of what goes under the name of tradition) is formulated.

This is crucial and can hardly be emphasized enough: the language of experience (*Erfahrung*) is both pervasive and pivotal in this essay and, more precisely, in the elaboration and interrogation of the task of thinking. Experience names the approach to that which remains as yet unthought in our history and, hence, the absolute proximity of experiencing and thinking. The open that allows the appearing of all that appears is from the start indicated as a matter of experience. And experience should not be understood empirically: "Only by virtue of luminosity can that which is radiant show itself, that is, radiate. But luminosity in its turn rests upon something open, something free, which it might illuminate here and there, now and then. Luminosity plays in the open and strives there with darkness. . . . We call this openness, which grants a possible letting appear and show, 'clearing' [*die Lichtung*]. . . . The forest clearing [*Waldlichtung*] is experienced [*erfahren*] in contrast to dense forest, called *Dickung* in our older language."[17]

Such would be the *Sache*, indeed the *Ur-sache*,[18] yet to be thought, yet to be perceived primordially in the becoming radically mysterious of experience. It is of the utmost significance that, at this juncture, Heidegger should refer to Goethe's thought of the primal phenomenon (*Urphänomen*). Goethe's thought not only casts the question of origin ultimately in sensible terms—that is, neither beyond nor behind that which gives itself sensibly[19]—but also, and most decisively, insists that it must be accepted (received) as the absolute limit of contemplation. It is the limit past or above which nothing else should be sought. *Urphänomen* is the ultimate *Sache* of a contemplation (*theôrein*) that, in seeking the primordial provenance of the phenomenon, never turns away from phenomenality.[20]

Heidegger is even more explicit in emphasizing experience as the axis around which his thinking effort gravitates. He deliberately turns to archaic Greek sources in a quest for a pre-philosophical comprehension of experience outside of metaphysics. Thus, he draws upon Parmenides, who stands at the very inception of Greek philosophy, in order to cast light on words that lay out that which still persists unthought in and by philosophy. The unthought is not unspoken, yet the spoken indication remains unheeded—as if inaudible, unreadable:

> *chreô de se panta puthesthai*
> *êmen Alêtheiês eukukleos atremes êtor*
> *êde brotôn doxas tais ouk eni pistis alêthês.*[21]

Heidegger renders the ancient verses as follows:

> *du sollst aber alles erfahren:*
> *sowohl der Unverborgenheit, der gutgerundeten, nichtzitterndes Herz*
> *als auch der Sterblichen Dafürhalten, dem fehlt das Vertrauenkönnen auf*
>   *Unverborgenes.*[22]

Heidegger's translation could be translated into English thus:

> But you should experience all:
> the untrembling heart of unconcealment, well-rounded,
> as well as the opinions of mortals, lacking the ability to trust the unconcealed.

Parmenides would have spoken that which was nevertheless not thoroughly unfolded in thinking: "*Alêtheia*, unconcealment, is named here. It is called well-rounded because it is turned in the pure sphere of the circle in which beginning and end are everywhere the same."[23] But it should be highlighted that the task of thinking is rendered by Heidegger in terms of experiencing, *erfahren*: "*chreô de se panta puthesthai*" becomes "you should experience all." The Greek *puthesthai*, the aorist infinitive of *punthanomai*, is usually translated as "learning" (just like *manthanô*, which appears on line 31 as *matheseai*, "you will learn"), but designates "apprehending," especially in relation to the posture of inquiry and the overall circumstances of the quest (not unlike *erôtô* and *ereunaô*, albeit with a broader semantic range). It belongs in an especially ancient group of words related to the root *bheu-dh-*, which has corresponding forms in numerous languages—suffice it to mention the Sanskrit *bódhati* (from which, in Pali, comes the past participle *buddha*), "being awake, alert, attentive, comprehending," but also (attested in the Avestan *baodaiti*) "sensing, feeling, perceiving," and hence also "observing, noting."[24] Experience involves perceptual openness, the vibrant intensification of sense in all its senses, the utmost concentration of sensibility accompanied by keen awareness. This is synthetically conveyed in German by the participial or adjectival form *sinnend*. Heidegger notes: "The meditative man [*der sinnende Mann*] is to experience [*erfahren*] the untrembling heart of unconcealment."[25] He then elucidates what is said in the phrase "the untrembling heart of unconcealment": "It means unconcealment itself in what is most its own, means the place of stillness [or silence] [*Ort der Stille*] that gathers in itself what first grants unconcealment. That is the clearing of the open."[26] And again: "We must think *alêtheia*, unconcealment, as the clearing that first grants being and thinking, their presencing to and for each other. The quiet heart of the clearing is the place of stillness [or silence] from which alone the possibility of the belonging together of being and thinking, that is, presence and apprehending [*Anwesenheit und Vernehmen*], is first given."[27]

In the Parmenidean poem, the disciple is set on the way to "all experiencing" (*panta puthesthai*). The task announced and barely initiated here is experiencing everything, from the silent, unmoving, hospitable center of all that moves to the loud and ever-changing crowd of phenomena coming to take place there. There is no argumentation, no further reference or discursive ground: in such an experience, discourse comes to an end, its techniques and logico-syntactic constructs meet their ultimate limit. Such an experience can only be trusted. Only thus can discourse find rest in that which indeterminately exceeds and perturbs it. And it is this trust (*pistis*), this ability to confide and entrust oneself to the uncontrollable, that, according to the poem (line 30), constitutes the ultimate challenge for the mortal tribe—as if the philosopher inaugurating an epoch had prophetically caught a glimpse of the epoch in its end as well as the *inability* to trust that would in the end become perspicuous. Trusting what one perceives, what comes forth of its own accord and presents itself in its outline, seems to be the most elusive, most arduous endeavor.

In the *puthesthai*, one may also discern the etymological familiarity with the knowing attributed to the Pythia—the knowing conveyed by and through the Delphic priestess in its depth and ecstatic *pathos* yoking together gods and human beings.[28] Such togetherness involves undergoing incalculable distance and discontinuity. What is properly human is protected in an experience of dispossession. In the openness to that which exceeds the human and human affairs, the human is filled, nourished, most properly positioned with respect to the other, whether human or nonhuman, other-than-human, inhuman. In contrast with this ground experience and with the fullness of the word springing from it,[29] Heidegger underlines the empty formalism that paradoxically defines the age of universal communication. It is the impoverishment and hollowness of the word in the epoch of the end of metaphysics, that is, the epoch of cybernetics and "world-civilization."[30]

What Heidegger may have thought of the cultural and political significance of the work of thinking is unclear. Even in his late, comprehensive statements, he is oblique at best and often polemical vis-à-vis the language of ethics, politics, and the human sciences, which he finds complicit with metaphysics.[31] The luminescent pronouncements in the essay under consideration remain to an extent shut, impervious to efforts at drawing out and unfolding what is folded there. Nonetheless, a shift is evidently at stake. As unthinkable as it is immense, it is the shift to another world: "We are thinking of the possibility that the world-civilization that is just now beginning might one day overcome its technological-scientific-industrial character as the sole criterion of the human being's world sojourn."[32] In the openness of experience and its unpredictable gifts, in the relinquishing of communication without content and without community (globalization without world), the contact with and among things would perhaps be regenerated and the world come alive again in arcane solidarity. What is certain is that experience thus understood is not simply given by nature. It is naturally possible, but it requires work, focused practice, the discipline intimately connected with creativity and every manner of cultivation, refinement, and sharpening.

4. Exercise

Parmenides's poem, then, prescribes "experiencing all," and most remarkably experiencing "the untrembling heart of unconcealment": in Heidegger's words, the "place of stillness [or silence]" wherein "being and thinking" ("presence and apprehending") belong together.[33] This means that thinking is never formal, that is, empty, never emancipated from the matter of thinking. At once committed to and guided by being (by the matter to be thought), thinking articulates being: "The possible claim to a binding character or commitment of thinking is grounded in this bond. Without the preceding experience [*Erfahrung*] of *alêtheia* as the clearing, all talk about committed and non-committed thinking remains without foundation."³⁴ Only in following things as they present themselves does thinking attain any authoritativeness: it is binding in virtue of being bound. And only through the primordial experience of the bond of thinking and being in the clearing can questions such as these arise at all: "Whence does Plato's determination of presence as *idea* have its binding character? With regard to what is Aristotle's interpretation of presencing as *energeia* binding?"³⁵ Heidegger remarks: "Strangely enough, we cannot even ask these questions, always neglected in philosophy, as long as we have not experienced [*erfahren*] what Parmenides had to experience [*erfahren*]: *alêtheia*, unconcealment."³⁶

In the earlier essay "Plato's Doctrine of Truth," Heidegger had insisted that while archaic Greek thinking seized upon what is said in the word *alêtheia*, Plato inaugurated the reduction of truth to propositional value (i.e., to certainty).³⁷ Primordially apprehended (experienced) as disclosedness, *alêtheia* became *orthotês*, correctness, *adaequatio intellectus et rei*—the correspondence between a proposition and its content. In the 1964 essay, however, Heidegger no longer explains such a shift chronologically. The dimness of originary disclosure is now presented almost as an anthropological constant, carrying the same inevitability and natural necessity:

> The natural concept of truth does not mean unconcealment, not even in the philosophy of the Greeks. It is often and rightly pointed out that the word *alêthes* is already used by Homer only for the *verba dicendi*, for statements, thus in the sense of correctness and reliability, not in the sense of unconcealment. But this reference means only that neither the poets nor everyday linguistic usage, nor even philosophy, see themselves confronted with the task of asking how truth, that is, the correctness of statements, is granted only in the element of the clearing [*Lichtung*] of presence.³⁸

The task still remains thinking/experiencing *alêtheia* as the primal condition for the truth of statements. But the alienation from such an experience is not a contingent shortcoming, a mistake that the Greeks could have avoided. There is no temporal sequence of progressive loss and estrangement from an originary insight into *alêtheia*. Truth in the propositional sense holds sway from the start, as if atemporally and immediately:

> We must acknowledge the fact that *alêtheia*, unconcealment in the sense of the clearing of presence, was originally experienced [*erfahren*] only as *orthotês*, as the correctness of representations and statements. But then the assertion about the essential transformation of truth, that is, from unconcealment to

correctness, is also untenable. Instead we must say: *alêtheia*, as clearing of presence and presentation in thinking and saying [*als Lichtung von Anwesenheit und Gegenwärtigung im Denken und Sagen*], immediately comes under the perspective of *homoiôsis* and *adaequatio*, that is, the perspective of adequation in the sense of the correspondence of representing with what is present.[39]

It is so *natural*, so immediate, to understand truth "in the traditional 'natural' sense as the correspondence of knowledge with beings" that, after the first mention of naturalness, Heidegger drops the quotation marks around the word.[40] The propositional sense of truth (the concern with exactness of discourse, with sincerity or insincerity) may be experienced as natural. Yet interrogating the natural, indeed, recognizing the natural as remarkable, proves singularly fruitful:

> How is it that *alêtheia*, unconcealment, appears to the human being's natural experience [*das natürliche Erfahren*] and speech *only* as correctness and dependability? Is it because the human being's ecstatic sojourn in the openness of presencing is turned only toward what is present and the presentation of what is present [*nur dem Anwesenden und der vorhandenen Gegenwärtigung des Anwesenden*]? But what else does this mean than that presence as such, and together with it the clearing that grants it, remains unheeded? Only what *alêtheia* as clearing grants is experienced [*erfahren*] and thought, not what it is as such.[41]

The glowing expanse in which the world takes place recedes so that the world may come forth. More ancient than Greek antiquity and its archaic prolusion, so simple and evanescent as to remain unspoken in the words of philosophers and poets alike, the condition for presence and absence, manifestation and obscuration, is itself obscured so that beings may be seen, sensed, and thought in their appearing and disappearing. What gives also retreats, so that the given may be perceived, known, manipulated, and, at the limit, claimed as human made.[42] What the Greeks *necessarily* failed to think, so that they could think what they did think, made possible a venture now at an end: "This remains concealed. Does that happen by chance? Does it happen only as a consequence of the carelessness [*Nachlässigkeit*] of human thinking? Or does it happen because self-concealing, concealment, *lêthê*, belongs to *alêtheia*, not as a mere addition, not as shadow to light, but rather as the heart of *alêtheia*?"[43]

Implicated in such a necessary concealment is nothing other than the structure of the human being itself. The "natural experience" of human beings involves the "ecstatic sojourn in the openness of presencing" and the turn "only toward what is present."[44] Dwelling in the open, exposed to whatever comes to pass there, human beings are enraptured by the beings they encounter: the shimmering expanse, in which beings come to be and from which they fade away, mostly escapes them and is silently, unconsciously assumed. That "in which" everything comes to be (or not) abides nearly nameless. Yet, it provides the *there* of every birth and becoming, of every giving and absence. It implicitly accompanies the abundance and generosity of origin.[45]

The human being is irresistibly attracted to the beings that present themselves, inevitably driven to care for things. Early on, Heidegger names this structure *care [Sorge]*. Care, a fundamental trait of the human being, is that because of which the Greeks said the word but did not hear what is said in it. The derivativeness of truth as the conformity of judgment and being escaped them. Inebriated by the brilliance and variety of present beings, deafened by the resounding of *logos*, the Greeks failed to hear the silence at the heart of words, to see the withdrawal in the midst of phenomenal surfacing. Yet, at the end of philosophy and the epoch the Greeks opened, at this pointed place of completion and utmost concentration, it becomes possible, at the limit, to draw closer to that which was neglected—to heed the call to think (and this means to experience, live through, and sustain) the silent opening that grants, the region more ancient than the opposition of appearing and disappearing, of disclosure and closure, older even than the light that lets appear and disappear.

Heidegger brings the essay to a close with a twofold gesture. He turns to the Greek inception, as if discerning there another beginning, and, in so doing, points to still intact resources in the language of care. After diagnosing at length the failure, necessary and fecund, of Greek antiquity, Heidegger suggests that we must attend to it anew and otherwise, for it may not be exhausted in its giving. In the end, we are urged to turn to the past as that which is yet to be heard—as that which, as yet unheard, has not yet come to pass. At stake is exercising *Sorge* with respect to that which, far from imposing itself in its conspicuity, withdraws and eludes us, bringing our attention precisely to that which recedes and abides dimly lit or altogether obscure. The language of *Sorge* is revealed in a semantic twist: from the existential structure of concerned absorption in the world at hand, to the exercise of precision in receptivity, fine-tuning of sensibility, safeguarding that which is always on the verge of dispersion. Our forgetful way of losing ourselves in the midst of shining beings harbors the resource by virtue of which we could somehow access that which is forgotten and lost. Thinking in the end of philosophy is, thus, crucially connected with the renewal of words. In the 1969 interview with Richard Wisser, Heidegger notes that the thinking he pursues "demands a new care with language" (*verlangt eine neue Sorgfalt der Sprache*) and not the proliferation of neologisms as he believed earlier (notably in the *Beiträge*). In "The End of Philosophy and the Task of Thinking," just following the reference to Aristotle's *Metaphysics* that concludes the essay, Heidegger warns: "This sentence demands careful reflection" (*Dieses Wort verlangt eine sorgfältige Besinnung*).[46] The issue here is not simply traversing the ancients in a thrust to "the other beginning" (which constitutes a central movement in the

Beiträge) but, rather, hearing the alterity in them, the other beginning already folded in their fateful saying.

But what leads Heidegger, even beyond Parmenides, to Aristotle? What is the context of this concluding quotation? This move strikes one as surprising, especially in light of the assertion, a few pages earlier, that "since Aristotle it has become the matter [*Sache*] of philosophy as metaphysics to think beings as such ontotheologically."[47] Yet it appears that Aristotle realized with considerable subtlety the implications of Parmenides's pronouncement about "well-rounded unconcealment,"[48] and his texts retain precious indications of the experience of *alêtheia*—the "place of stillness and silence" from which "being and thinking"[49] stem. As we shall see, the two thinkers are much more attuned than a superficial historiographic narrative would allow.

Near the end of the discussion, Heidegger critically assesses his own efforts toward the task of thinking. This line of self-questioning will lead to the decisive (if concise) confrontation with Aristotle. The hypothetical critic asks:

> But is not all this unfounded mysticism, or even bad mythology, in any case a ruinous irrationalism, the denial of *ratio*?
>
> I ask in return: What does *ratio, nous, noein*, apprehending, mean? What do ground and principle and especially principle of all principles mean? Can this ever be sufficiently determined unless we experience *alêtheia* in a Greek manner as unconcealment and then, above and beyond the Greek, think it as the clearing of self-concealing [*als Lichtung des Sichverbergens*]? As long as *ratio* and the rational still remain questionable in what is their own, talk about irrationalism is unfounded. The technological-scientific rationalization ruling the present age justifies itself every day more surprisingly by its immeasurable effect. But this effect says nothing about what first grants the possibility of the rational and the irrational. The effect proves the correctness of the technological-scientific rationalization. But is the manifest character of that which is, exhausted by what is demonstrable? Does not the insistence on what is demonstrable block the way to that which is?
>
> Perhaps there is a thinking that is more sober-minded than the incessant frenzy of rationalization and the intoxicating quality of cybernetics. One might aver that it is precisely this intoxication that is extremely irrational.[50]

At issue, then, is loosening the hold of the logic of demonstration and demonstrability—showing the extent to which its primacy and foundational claims are unfounded, unbalanced, and even unwell. Thinking is not reducible to the procedures of reason and the production of knowledge. However, "we all still need an education [*Erziehung*] in thinking, and first of all, before that, knowledge of what being educated [*Erzogenheit*] and uneducated [*Unerzogenheit*] in thinking means."[51] At this juncture, Heidegger turns to Aristotle's *Metaphysics*.

5. Aristotle

The text Heidegger quotes is in treatise Gamma at 1006a6–8, and it reads: "For it is uneducated not to have an eye for the case in which it is necessary to look for a demonstration and the case in which it is not necessary."[52] Aristotle then continues: "On the whole, demonstration of everything is impossible (for it would go on to infinity, so in this way as well there is no demonstration)."[53] The passage concerns the question of *nous*, that is, the question of silence (*nous* without *logos*)[54]—silence in the midst of *logos*, immediacy both inseparable from and inassimilable to the questioning and ordering mediation of *logos*.[55] Aristotle is exceedingly clear about the irreducibility of the two terms. The fact that later on, most notably in the Scholastic (con)versions of Aristotle, *logos* and *nous* are progressively conflated (the latter being resolved into the former) is far from innocent, and it signals that the ability, however inceptive, to listen to the ineffable faded away and that this decisively curved the unfolding of our history. And yet even Willem van Moerbeke could not reliably render *nous* with one single Latin term. Even he, celebrated among translators for his elegance and unbending rigor, had to resort to a double rendition: *nous* is *intellectus* and *intuitus*—the capacity for "reading into" things in an immediate glance, out of an intimacy with them, open to their sudden lighting up. *Nous* sustains a mode of wisdom (*sophia*) more primordial than the operation of *logos* in its demonstrative demeanor (*sullogismos, epistêmê*).[56] It is significant that Heidegger's essay should close on this note: it points in the direction of that which, at the end of philosophy, remains to be thought—that which, in its aliveness, was not only forgotten but, more pointedly, never unfolded. What remains to be thought (and this means experienced) is the silence of that which is not subject to demonstration, to which no question corresponds, which can only be received, taken in, undergone. This way of thinking is radically other than scientific/rational operations. Indeed, it constitutes the more ancient condition of the latter. Heidegger's gesture situates antiquity (in the figure of Aristotle) at the heart of the thinking to come.

In this way, the end of philosophy is illuminated as what exceeds philosophy qua discourse, however "inceptive" or "immanent."[57] Prior to any determination and any question concerning *what* (what something is), the end of philosophy points to the fragile and yet undeniable advancing of beings, the disarming and yet ineliminable acknowledgment *that* they are. We note here the intertwinement of the themes of affirmation and sensibility, *aisthêsis*. In the Aristotelian (as well as Platonic) elaborations, sensibility (the openness to and of phenomena) is closely connected with the most accomplished knowing, which is not that of *logos*. Without getting into the extremely complex discussions of the relation between noetic and sensible perceptions, it must be said that, though irreducible to each other, they are consistently co-implicated in the emergence and apprehension of universals. And this means that sensory perception, typically in the mode of trust (*pistis*), is never extraneous to the constitution of the assumptions (principles) on which every demonstration (*apodeixis*) rests.[58] For the apodictic procedure casts light on that which is, in any case, already given; it confers further evidence on the articulations of the given. In a sense, sensation names the communion and communication (the exchanges) constitutive of the open, its being connected with itself in a pervasive and propagating motility.

Heidegger is not inclined to deploy the word *aisthêsis* liberally. It is a term that he finds thoroughly implicated in the history of metaphysics.[59] And yet his discussion of the end of philosophy is constellated by references to the phenomenological turn "to the things themselves," and it lingers on the convergence of thinking and seeing, on a vision that receives and lets be. But turning to the things themselves, to their sensible glow, implies a further sensibilization. The radiant manifestation of things exposes the open, the disclosive expanse always already in play if manifestation is at all to take place. Such a turn to things, then, keeps philosophy at an end, at its limit—compels philosophy to confront its other, which can only be received, accepted, and affirmed on the ground of such a passivity (and passivity may only be a strange ground indeed). The end of philosophy is always already signaled in the claim of the things themselves. And the task of thinking lies in this call (to the things themselves and, at once, to the open that grants their unfolding in their being). Where Heidegger encounters the unthought in Aristotle, we could venture to say that the end of philosophy *is* the task of thinking and that such a task is crucially a matter of sensibility. That is to say, the task glimpsed in this end involves a careful cultivation of sensibility, for such care and refinement may provide access to what remains to be thought. But this marks a definitive rupture with respect to the philosophical order of conceptual mastery and willful construction: "For it is not yet decided in what way that which needs no proof in order to become accessible to thinking is to be experienced."[60] And "only the peculiar quality of what demands of us above all else to be granted entry [*zugelassen zu werden*] can decide about that."[61]

"The task of thinking," Heidegger concludes, "would then be the surrender of previous thinking to the determination of the matter [*Sache*] for thinking."[62] The task would crucially be a matter of learning how to receive—and learning here bespeaks disciplined cultivation. It is a matter of learning how to receive that which is given, handed down undisclosed; how to cast in ever new guises that which is transmitted and reaches us, undiminished in its energy, in the midst of an unsettling epochal shift. It is likewise a matter of learning how to receive the decision and determinacy coming, as it were, from the outside and needing neither rational foundation nor proof in order to compel assent.[63] In the end, it is a matter of learning to affirm excess—to experience exceeding singularity in the minute and unspectacular scansions of the everyday, in the infinite variations of the ordinary, in the nearly imperceptible vibrations of becoming.

The beginning abides pervaded, agitated by a potentiality unconsciously operative, unquiet, unbound. Hence the task of catching a glimpse, in the past (in that which, of the past, is manifest), of the energy and vibrant force of a future, not yet manifest—almost a foreign body, or a seed released into an indeterminately protracted incubation. Heidegger's gesture is subversive precisely because, beyond all historiographic postures and the taxonomies of the "history of ideas," it undertakes to seize the new in the least ideological, least predictable way and to retrieve the new in the ancient—the new (exorbitant and undisclosed) enclosed within the ancient disclosure. There will have been, then, nothing obvious in the past, and evidence may be the locus of the deepest and most hidden enigma. The new would (perhaps) demand to be pursued not so much (or not at all) in a movement of estrangement from the old but (perhaps) in old receptacles, unexplored and, therefore, ageless. Because of this, philosophy, its history, which is *this* history, the history of *us*, even understood in its uniqueness and originality, is not one. Even avoiding all comparative approaches, arguably superficial in their certitude that there are *philosophies* (in the plural) to be compared, and surreptitiously hegemonic in bringing other cultures to the Greek paradigm—even beyond considerations of this kind, the problem remains of how we are to understand geospiritual and psychocultural categories such as Greece, the West, and Europe. Thus, the situation manifests itself in its complexity. History, tradition, and hence identity become refracted and multiplied. What holds for every individual, for whom the archaeological excavation always comes to uncover darkness, holds for collective organisms. Thus, even this past, of which the present is the vessel, cannot be reduced to the so-called history of metaphysics, with the disasters of which metaphysics is the cause, or perhaps only the symptom. Even this past is agitated from within by a thinking that cannot be brought back to the rational foundation, by that which indeterminately exceeds calculation and its maneuvers. Indeed, what persists unheeded does not, thereby, amount to nothing.

Philosophy is, therefore, at an end in various ways: (1) it is at an end, as we saw, insofar as philosophical discourses are historical and, in their finitude, constantly come to be and are superseded by others; (2) it is at an end in that philosophy is itself historical—that is, it is a tradition with a beginning and (like everything that has a beginning) an end precisely because it neither coincides with nor exhausts thinking tout court; and (3) finally, and more pointedly, philosophy is and always has been at an end precisely in its unresolved confrontation with the other and its many names (sensibility, immediacy, nondiscursive knowledge, *logos* itself to the extent that it is irreducible to logic, etc.). But acknowledging and remaining mindful of this aspect of philosophical life means interrupting its history and, more to the point, its academic practice. Here, memory entails a radical discontinuity with respect to the path that philosophy has taken, which leads to the end of metaphysics. The authoritativeness, or even plenitude, of the word is at stake. For more than a century in our universities, the twilight of metaphysics (and of the dichotomies attributed to it, above all between *praxis* and *theôria*, acting and thinking) has been announced. And, yet, to this day we hardly see any signs of transformation in the direction of a way of thinking able to touch life and be touched by it—of a thinking at once shaped through action and transformative of action, and therefore of all practices, academic and not. The overcoming of the rift between *praxis* and *theôria* seems to be a safely theoretical matter. Consequently, much of what is said in such places as our classrooms, however rhetorically seductive and unparalleled in erudition, tends to remain empty, incapable of touching the world. For in order to touch the world, the insightful word would have to become life, action, body.

The reference to *Metaphysics* Gamma, and particularly to Aristotle's admonition that it is fundamental (indeed, infinitely more grounding than any demonstrative ground) to recognize when it is pertinent to look for a demonstration and when it is not, constitutes an urgent indication. It calls for exercising receptivity, for the ongoing learning to seize the indemonstrable, which is the principle and beginning itself, on the basis of which every demonstrative truth may subsequently be argued for and discursively assessed. The Aristotelian posture demands a perceptual refinement, the development of an attitude of trust as the disposition appropriate to that which is indemonstrable and syllogistically unknowable. In Plato, as well, such a trusting stance is ultimately the register of our openness to the sensible.

Thus, well beyond the pronouncements regarding the overcoming of metaphysics and its fractures, the Heideggerian gesture puts forth, however reticently, an invitation to deepen the work of perception, to infuse it with attention and wakefulness. Somehow phenomenological in tenor, the indefatigable interrogation of phenomena (that is, of the things of this world, of our conditions and surroundings) would be at stake. Declaring the problematic character of metaphysics or even deconstructing metaphysics, exposing and explicating its intrinsic textual strategies, is not enough. Or, more precisely, what is called for is a deconstructive gesture that, by traversing texts and hermeneutical practices, would frequent sensible things and nurture a confidence in them; an investigation of sense, within and across sense, acknowledging sense as the authoritative guide of thinking; a thoughtful inclination to trust, to entrust oneself to what is neither oneself nor one's own; a heightened awareness of the bodily root, of a belonging in the arc of the earth most certainly exceeding any literalism—for belonging to the earth definitely does not amount to any form of territorial or identity fixation or nostalgic primitivism and in no way excludes the nomadic and migratory dynamism variously inscribed in individual as well as collective histories.

It would be a matter of dwelling in the proximity of that which, in some way, shows itself—of the terrible exercise of patience and hesitation, of the ability to wait, letting oneself be overcome by that which comes to be. Such an exercise is what is, here, called *experience*. But, of course, in this way the word *experience* comes to be quite remote from the modern philosophical jargon that explains experience by reference to the rational subject and sensibility by reference to intelligibility. Experience has become mysterious. It demands alertness, wakefulness of the senses in the dissipation of purely rational points of reference, and the rigor that sustains study and concentration, while all around nothing stands still. And one may wonder whether and to what extent it might be akin to contemplation in the archaic and simple sense of *theôria*, which is not simply resolved into theoretical/scientific observation. Clearly the practice and development of such a discipline would be at odds with the present time. This epoch, as many have noted, is structurally hostile to experience, to the point of making experience virtually impossible.

But it is evident that the work of perceptual education cannot be contained within the framework of traditional phenomenology and, in fact, destabilizes its configurations. Therefore, various questions emerge urgently. These questions concern the strange, composite unity of thinking and sensibility, whose difference must be affirmed in light of their inseparability. How does thinking live and give itself in life? How does thinking sink into bodily sensing, drawing upon it for guidance and orientation? In what guises does the integration of irreducible modes let itself be imagined? These questions bear decisively on the problem of the human, on the unfathomed depth in which even the most exorbitant contemplative practice is rooted. Investigating the human substratum involves following not only its broad movements, the political and anthropological developments, but also the infinitesimal, individual, radically singular facets. It involves traversing the human phenomenon in its open range from the vertex of transcendence to the most minute and ephemeral worldly involvement, from phenomenological reduction to the irreducibility of that which always becomes and changes, in a transit of life in action and its ever-unique faces.

The upheaval of the "end of metaphysics" unveils the possibility, indeed, the vital urgency, of such developments. To tend to the belonging together of *praxis* and *theôria*, to experience the depth and enduring enigma of such a unity, means to protect the theme of the overcoming of dualism and preserve it from becoming a vacuous formula. It means to attempt (no doubt inadequately, but to attempt nonetheless) to correspond with the questions the last century has sent forth. They reach out for a response.

Notes

1. The essay first appeared in a French translation by Jean Beaufret and François Fédier, in "Kierkegaard vivant" (Paris: Gallimard, 1966). The German text was issued only three years later, in Heidegger, *Zur Sache des Denkens*. Although with frequent variations, I will follow the English translation appearing in Heidegger, *Basic Writings*. I have discussed aspects of this essay in "A Vibrant Silence."

2. Heidegger, "Einleitung in die Phänomenologie der Religion."

3. Heidegger, *Grundbegriffe der Metaphysik*.

4. Benjamin, "Erfahrung und Armut," 313–18.

5. Agamben, *Infanzia e storia*.

6. This is consistently evident throughout the trajectory of Heidegger's thinking. In the introductory remarks to his course on Plato's *Sophist* (winter semester 1924–25), he notes: "This past, to which our lectures are seeking access, is nothing detached from us, lying far away. On the contrary, we are this past itself. And we are it not insofar as we explicitly cultivate the tradition and become friends of classical antiquity, but instead, our philosophy and science live on these foundations, i.e., those of Greek philosophy, and do so to such an extent that we are no longer conscious of it: the foundations have become obvious. Precisely in what we no longer see, in what has become an everyday matter, something is at work that was once the object of the greatest spiritual exertions ever undertaken in Western history. . . . To understand history cannot mean anything else than to understand ourselves—not in the sense that we might establish various things about ourselves, but that we experience what we ought to be. To appropriate the past means to come to know oneself as indebted to that past. The authentic possibility to be history itself resides in this, that philosophy discover it is guilty of an omission, a neglect, if it believes it can begin anew, make things easy for itself" (Heidegger, *Plato's Sophist*, 7).

7. Heidegger, "Ende der Philosophie," 63.

8. Heidegger, "Ende der Philosophie," 63. The thinking of place receives further nuances in Heidegger's notes on *Ort* in the discussion of Georg Trakl's poetry—a discussion clearly resonating with the later essay under consideration here. Place is here evoked in its strange and estranging traits. We are reminded that *Ort* originally indicates the tip of the spear and, therefore, a point of convergence, the highest and most extreme point that gathers attracting and, thereby, shelters. However, place does not shelter in the manner of containment. It shelters, rather, by penetrating. It gathers and permeates what is gathered with its own light. It, thus, lets what is gathered be, unfold in its being. In this sense, *Ort* would be a matter neither of extension nor of containment. Instead, it would name the expansive luminosity and dynamic orientation wherein what comes to be may genuinely unfold. The end, thus, emerges as the place of coming to light. It also indicates the place of estrangement and placeless concentration, the incandescent tip, the stranger's strange place, discontinuous with respect to the measurable, quantifiable space of modernity. See Heidegger, "Sprache im Gedicht."

9. In *Was heißt Denken?*, by reference to Socrates, Heidegger iconically captures the chasm between thinking and the history of philosophy as the literary history of the progression from *doctrina* to *scientia* to the contemporary sciences. While Socrates maintained himself within the current of thinking (the draw toward the infinitely

provocative, withdrawing source of thinking), later philosophers drew away from that call, as fugitives seeking refuge from a draw too compelling and overwhelming.

10. Heidegger, "Ende der Philosophie," 63.

11. Heidegger, "Ende der Philosophie," 63.

12. Aristotle, *Metaphysics*, 984a 18, 986b 31, 984b 10.

13. Heidegger, "Ende der Philosophie," 67.

14. Despite its rhetorical felicity, or precisely because of it, Heidegger's narrative of the unitary history of Western philosophy is consistently problematic. It identifies metaphysics with Platonism and, hence, identifies the twilight of philosophy with the reversal of Platonism. By *Platonism*, Heidegger means the decision to seize each being in its look or idea, to understand the sensible by reference to the beyond sensible, and, therefore, to privilege knowledge and the theoretical posture against action, experience, and sensibility. Such an order of priorities would be inverted in Nietzsche's thought of the will to power. In its completion, metaphysics would relinquish the ancient posture of disinterested contemplation and unveil its will to know as will to produce and master beings. However, even a rather hasty consideration of the Platonic (let alone Aristotelian) texts reveals a primacy of ethico-political concerns that, alone, suffices to raise doubts about Heidegger's emphasis on disinterestedness, knowledge for its own sake, and contemplative detachment. Indeed, a love of knowing severed from life in the *polis*, involvement in action, and belonging in the flow of becoming is altogether unlikely in the Greek perspective. As for Platonic "idealism," we should seriously consider the radical meaning of the word *idea*: the look, outward aspect, or profile of something and, therefore, the being of that something, its distinctive cipher and cause. In its thrust toward that which would comprehend and exceed the sensible, the language of the Greek beginning preserves its sensible root and reminds itself of the primordiality of sense. While such strands of Heidegger's reading seem less than compelling, and indeed troubling, what remains persuasive in his scheme is the diagnosis of the sameness underlying all inversion and opposition. A given epochal configuration is not simply overcome by countermovement, let alone antagonism. The inversion of metaphysics still operates within the scope of metaphysics, uncovers possibilities latent in it, promotes its fuller manifestation. In Heidegger's idiom, science is still Platonism, and so are Marxist materialism and Nietzsche's iconoclastic gestures. Metaphysics (Platonism) completes itself in its own inversion, that is, as the realization of a concrete historical order through science and technology. (Let it be noted in passing that, for all its emphasis on the techno-scientific problem, Heidegger's analysis and Heideggerian parlance in general prove dramatically unable to acknowledge the relevance of the economic phenomenon.)

15. Heidegger, "Ende der Philosophie," 65.

16. Heidegger, "Ende der Philosophie," 65.

17. Heidegger, "Ende der Philosophie," 71–72.

18. Heidegger, "Ende der Philosophie," 72.

19. Heidegger, "Ende der Philosophie," 72.

20. Goethe, *Schriften zur Naturwissenschaft*, vol. 4, 71–72.

21. Heidegger, "Ende der Philosophie," proem, lines 28–30.

22. Heidegger, "Ende der Philosophie," 74.

23. Heidegger, "Ende der Philosophie," 74.

24. Chantraine, *Dictionnaire étymologique de la langue grecque*, 955.

25. Heidegger, "Ende der Philosophie," 75.

26. Heidegger, "Ende der Philosophie," 75.

27. Heidegger, "Ende der Philosophie," 75.

28. Chantraine, *Dictionnaire étymologique de la langue grecque*, 953. The connection between *punthanomai* and Puthô, the ancient name of Delphi, is attested in various sources: an oracle reported by Pausanias (*Description of Greece* 10.18.2), Sophocles's *Oedipus Tyrannos* (70 and 603), and Plutarch (*Opuscula moralia: De E apud Delphos*, 385b). Consider also the proximity with *puthmên*, conveying the sense of that which lies deep down, at the bottom or basis.

29. In the seminal 1953 lecture "Fonction et champ de la parole et du langage en psychanalyse," Lacan distinguishes the "full word" from the empty one. Echoing the Hegelian dialectic of recognition, he illuminates the symbolic structure of communication: one who speaks receives one's own utterance from the listener, in the sense that the subjective function of the word requires alterity as its condition. Thus, the word uttered finds its sense in the listening of the other broadly understood and is as such always already an answer. In contrast to such a word, full and fulfilled in an open, desirous relatedness, the empty word is severed and self-enclosed: it is the word of narcissistic certainty and self-reference.

30. Cybernetics names the all-encompassing turn to format, formatting, and informatics. The encounter with beings is diminished to a frictionless, formal account, and the pathos of singularity (the *pathos* of the event) to an abstract universal project. Here, Heidegger envisions the Westernization of the planet. The Western will to power assimilates the wandering earth to its own project: "End of philosophy means: beginning of world-civilization [*Weltzivilisation*] grounded in Western-European thinking" (Heidegger, "Ende der Philosophie," 65). *Weltzivilisation* signifies the domination of the media, the trance-like absorption within the televised and tele-visible sign (vision from afar, alienated from sensibility and sensuousness), and hence growing desensibilization and coarser, occluded, and increasingly obtuse receptiveness. In this respect, every effort at sensory education and sensual refinement carries genuinely revolutionary implications.

31. In the 1963 television interview with Thai monk Bhikkhu Maha Mani (broadcast by channel SWR), Heidegger ventures to outline the traits of the thinking to come. The task of thinking requires an "altogether new method," involving only "the unmediated dialogue from human being to human being." Such a method can only be attained through a "long exercise" (*Einübung*) and "practice" (*Übung*) of "seeing in thinking." Presently, because of our history and educational system, this can be achieved by "few," but it can be conveyed to others in a "mediated fashion" and, in principle, can be achieved by all human beings. The task of thinking is, thus, illuminated in its pedagogical dimension and conditions. In the interview with Richard Wisser (broadcast on September 24, 1969, by channel ZDF, on Heidegger's eightieth birthday), Heidegger leaves the question of the fate of thinking suspended. Underlining the simultaneous simplicity and difficulty of thinking in the overcoming of metaphysics, he multiplies the signs of tentativeness: his own attempt would be a mere preparatory contribution, and even one who perhaps will take up the task of thinking will have to be hesitant, to submit to the incommensurable. The concluding words are those Heinrich von Kleist wrote in a letter to his sister Ulrike in 1803, which Heidegger copied in a notebook: "I step back before one who is not yet here and bow, a millennium in advance, before his spirit." A similar emphasis on waiting and readiness is ubiquitous in the 1966 Spiegel interview ("Nur noch ein Gott kann uns retten"): preparing for the manifestation of a god, thinking announces itself in fostering alertness, wakefulness, vigilance. There is no trace here of the earlier project of bringing philosophical guidance to bear on political institution and of reconfiguring the university if not the world as such: these late statements only let transpire the dedicated cultivation of a transformation in

thinking—a work whose connections with the world are opaque and reticently protected. But what is disheartening here as well as elsewhere is the insistence on the privileged relationship between Germany and Greece, such that Western humanity, as even "the French confirm," when beginning to think, must speak German; Heidegger, "Spiegel-Gespräch mit Martin Heidegger," 679.

32. Heidegger, "Ende der Philosophie," 67.

33. Heidegger, "Ende der Philosophie," 75.

34. Heidegger, "Ende der Philosophie," 75.

35. Heidegger, "Ende der Philosophie," 75.

36. Heidegger, "Ende der Philosophie," 75.

37. "Platons Lehre von der Wahrheit," 203–38. The essay, written in 1940, was first published in *Geistige Überlieferung*, Das Zweite Jahrbuch (Berlin: H. Küpper, 1942), 96–124. It develops the line of reflection initiated with the 1930–31 lecture course "On the Essence of Truth" and the essay by the same title ("Vom Wesen der Wahrheit," *Wegmarken*, cit., 177–202). It is clear, however, that this research further unfolds the meditation on truth in *Being and Time* (§ 44) and will keep haunting Heidegger's later work.

38. Heidegger, "Ende der Philosophie," 77–78.

39. Heidegger, "Ende der Philosophie," 78.

40. Heidegger, "Ende der Philosophie," 76.

41. Heidegger, "Ende der Philosophie," 78.

42. See the earlier characterization of beings "as knowable, handled, and worked upon [*als Erkennbares, Behandeltes, Bearbeitetes*]" (Heidegger, "Ende der Philosophie," 62).

43. Heidegger, "Ende der Philosophie," 78.

44. Heidegger, "Ende der Philosophie," 78.

45. In Plato's *Timaeus*, *chora* indicates that "in which" beings come to be and linger for their allotted duration, and that "from which" they perish (49e–50a, 50c–d). Interrupting all thinking ordered by the dichotomy of sensibility and intelligibility, *chora* names the mystery of the unspoken yet altogether necessary *there* of all creativity and generation, of all beings and ontology itself. Making, bringing forth, the overflowing expansiveness of origin as such, in their very occurrence imply the there—which amounts to neither space in its geometric homogeneity nor even to place in the sense of embodied *topos*. It is the vibrating field of the lives of beings, of ongoing pulsations, exchanges, and transformations—"moving" and "being moved," "sweeping along," "shaking and being shaken" (48a–b, 52a–c, 52d–53a). In the *Timaeus*, *chora* also designates maternal receptivity, sustenance, nourishment, and protection (49a–b, 50b, 51a, 52d). Concerning the open of the clearing, where everything "becomes present and absent" ("Ende der Philosophie," 72), Heidegger says that it "would not be the mere clearing of presence, but the clearing of presence concealing itself, the clearing of a self-concealing sheltering [*Lichtung der sich verbergenden Anwesenheit, Lichtung des sich verbergenden Bergens*]" (78–79). Indeed, "does not a sheltering and preserving rule in this self-concealing of the clearing of presence, from which alone unconcealment can be granted?" (78).

46. Heidegger, "Ende der Philosophie," 80.

47. Heidegger, "Ende der Philosophie," 76.

48. Heidegger, "Ende der Philosophie," 74.

49. Heidegger, "Ende der Philosophie," 75.

50. Heidegger, "Ende der Philosophie," 79.

51. Heidegger, "Ende der Philosophie," 80.

52. Heidegger, "Ende der Philosophie," 80; Aristotle, *Metaphysics*. The Greek text reads: *"esti gar apaideusia to me gignoskein tinon dei zetein apodeixin kai tinon ou dei."* Heidegger's translates: *"Es ist nämlich Unerzogenheit, keinen Blick zu haben dafür, mit Bezug worauf es nötig ist, einen Beweis zu suchen, in bezug worauf dies nicht nötig ist."* It is worth noticing that Heidegger renders *gignoskein,* "to know," "to recognize," as "having an eye for," "discerning at a glance." The intertwining of the question of indemonstrable first principles, the problem of infinite regress, the impossibility of demonstrating everything, and the difference between knowledge and demonstration is an absolutely vital preoccupation for Aristotle. He returns to it in various contexts and registers. Suffice it to recall here the paradigmatic elaboration in *Metaphysics* alpha elatton (994b9–31). *Metaphysics* 1006a6–8, on the desirable education in thinking and the appropriateness or inappropriateness of demonstration, is mirrored in *Nicomachean Ethics* Alpha (1094b22–28; see also, in the same treatise, 1098a26–b8). Consider, furthermore, the remarks in *Physics* Beta on the indemonstrable being there of the beings of nature and the attitude of receptivity required to take in the *fact that* they are (193a3–9).

53. Aristotle, *Metaphysics*, 1006a8–9.

54. *Nicomachean Ethics* Zeta, 1142a27 and 1143b1.

55. Here and consistently in his work, when reading Aristotle, Heidegger conflates *logos* and *nous*, unquestioningly following the Scholastic fusion of *ratio* and *intellectus* or *intuitus*. I have examined this problematic interpretation of *nous* in various contexts. Here it may suffice to mention, specifically concerning Heidegger, the essay "On Heidegger, the Greeks, and Us," 162–69.

56. I address this and related issues in *Aristotle's Ethics as First Philosophy*, passim and especially 220–59, and in "The Condition of First Philosophy," 8–29.

57. Heidegger, "Ende der Philosophie," 61.

58. This line of thinking by no means implies a reduction of noetic perception to sensation and sensory perception. However, as is clear especially in the *vexata quaestio* of induction (*epagôgê*), the relation between sensibility and noetic intuition, as well as the undeniable role of sensation in the constitution of universals and principles, remains an open field of investigation. In this regard, I refer again to my *Aristotle's Ethics as First Philosophy*.

59. This stands contrary to Levinas, who emphasizes the disruptive character of sensibility vis-à-vis the aspiration to systematic construction (*Totalité et infini*, 53).

60. Heidegger, "Ende der Philosophie," 80.

61. Heidegger, "Ende der Philosophie," 80.

62. Heidegger, "Ende der Philosophie," 80.

63. Again, it can only be barely mentioned here that, understood in ancient terms, sensibility (*aisthêsis*), far from merely providing undifferentiated perceptual data to be subjected to the ordering work of the concept, in and of itself displays order and determinacy. Sensing is already a discerning, *krinein*.

Bibliography

Agamben, Giorgio. *Infanzia e storia. Distruzione dell'esperienza e origine della storia*. Torino: Einaudi, 1978.

Aristotle. *Metaphysics*. Edited by Werner Jaeger. Oxford: Oxford University Press, 1957.

Baracchi, Claudia. *Aristotle's Ethics as First Philosophy*. Cambridge: Cambridge University Press, 2008.

——. "The Condition of First Philosophy." In *Sources of Desire: Essays on Aristotle's Theoretical Works*, edited by James Oldfield, 8–29. Newcastle upon Tyne: Cambridge Scholars Publishing, 2012.

——. "On Heidegger, the Greeks, and Us: Once More on the Relation of *Praxis* and *Theôria*." *Philosophy Today* 50 (Supplement 2006): 162–69.

——. "A Vibrant Silence: Heidegger and the End of Philosophy." In *Being Shaken: Ontology and the Event*, edited by Michael Marder and Santiago Zabala, 92–121. New York: Palgrave Macmillan, 2014.

Benjamin, Walter. "Erfahrung und Armut." In *Illuminationen. Ausgewählte Schriften 1*, 313–18. Frankfurt am Main: Suhrkamp, 1961.

Chantraine, Pierre. *Dictionnaire étymologique de la langue grecque*. Paris: Klincksieck, 1968.

Goethe, Johann W. von. *Die Schriften zur Naturwissenschaft*. Vol. 4, 2nd ed. Edited by K. Lothar Wolf and Wilhelm Troll. Weimar: Böhlaus, 1957.

Heidegger, Martin. "Einleitung in die Phänomenologie der Religion." In *Phänomenologie des religiösen Lebens*, GA 60. Frankfurt am Main: Klostermann, 1995.

——. "Das Ende der Philosophie und die Aufgabe des Denkens." In *Zur Sache des Denkens*, 61–80. Tübingen: Niemeyer, 1969.

——. "The End of Philosophy and the Task of Thinking." In *Basic Writings*, edited by David Farrell Krell, 431–49. New York: HarperCollins, 1993.

——. *Die Grundbegriffe der Metaphysik. Welt—Endlichkeit—Einsamkeit*, GA 29-30. Frankfurt am Main: Klostermann, 1983.

——. Interview with Martin Heidegger. By Richard Wisser. Broadcast by channel ZDF, September 24, 1969.

——. Interview with Martin Heidegger. By Bhikkhu Maha Mani. Broadcast by channel SWR, 1963.

——. "Platons Lehre von der Wahrheit." In *Wegmarken*, GA 9, 203–38. Frankfurt am Main: Klostermann, 1976.

——. *Plato's Sophist*. Translated by Richard Rojcewicz and André Schuwer. Bloomington: Indiana University Press, 1997.

——. "Spiegel-Gespräch mit Martin Heidegger." In *Rede und andere Zeugnisse eines Lebensweges*, GA 16, 652–83. Frankfurt am Main: Klostermann, 2000.

——. "Die Sprache im Gedicht. Eine Erörterung von Georg Trakls Gedicht." In *Unterwegs zur Sprache*, GA 12, 31–78. Frankfurt am Main: Klostermann, 1985. Originally published as "Georg Trakl. Eine Erörterung seines Gedichtes," in *Merkur* 61 (1953): 226–58.

——. *Was heißt Denken?* Tübingen: Niemeyer, 1954.

Lacan, Jacques. "Fonction et champ de la parole et du langage en psychanalyse." In *Ecrits I*, 111–209. Paris: Seuil, 1966.

Levinas, Emmanuel. *Totalité et infini. Essai sur l'extériorité*. La Haye: M. Nijhoff, 1971.

CLAUDIA BARACCHI is Professor of Moral Philosophy at the University of Milano-Bicocca. She is author of *Aristotle's Ethics as First Philosophy* and, most recently, of *Amicizia*.

8 Thinking at the First Beginning

Heidegger's Interpretation of the Early Greek Physis

Damir Barbarić

Translated by Guang Yang

For Heidegger, φύσις is "the inceptive and, therefore, pervasive determination of Being in the whole history of Occidental philosophy."[1] If this is so, φύσις determines Being itself rather than a domain or realm of entities. To understand the place Heidegger grants to φύσις in his philosophy, it is essential to spell out the consequences of this idea; φύσις does not refer to the domain of the natural in contrast to the domain of spirit or of culture; nor does φύσις refer to the empirical world (standing under the law of causality) in contrast to the domain of human history shaped by human freedom. If we take serious Heidegger's claim, then φύσις also does not extend to the realm of the sensible in contrast to the intelligible: the spiritual, the historical, and the intelligible, no less than their opposites, belong to φύσις. As the Being of beings, φύσις inheres in everything that, in some way or other, *is*. It encompasses, in Heidegger's words, "both sky and earth, both the stone and the plant, both the animal and the human being, and human history as the work of humans and gods; and finally and first of all it means the gods who themselves stand under destiny."[2] It also encompasses, Heidegger holds, both "becoming" and "Being" in the narrower sense of fixed subsistence.[3]

1.

What are the implications of this fundamental word? Translating φύσις as *nature* is reductive, restrictive, and misleading, and the same holds true of the Latin *natura*, from which the English word derives. Although *to be born* (the English translation of the Latin verb *nasco*) brings an essential moment of φύσις to light, it does not even come close to rendering its sense in full. To translate this "perhaps untranslatable word φύσις" into the German language, Heidegger chooses the substantivized verb *emergence* (*das Aufgehen*).[4] φύσις is "what emerges from itself"; it is "the unfolding that opens itself up."[5] Such emergence does not continue indefinitely or infinitely; rather, emergence simultaneously closes itself off, withdrawing into itself. In such a way, φύσις, in the process of its emergence, comes to a certain standstill. This is the second essential moment in Heidegger's notion of φύσις: "In emerging and as emergence, [φύσις] does not elude self-enclosing, but lays claim to it as that which grants emergence, as that which is the only and constant guarantee of emergence."[6] The movement of emergence is thus at the same time a holding-fast, an abiding in that place opened by φύσις itself.[7] Heidegger uses the term *standing* (*das Stehen*) for this simultaneity of emergence and self-withholding: all that is in accordance with φύσις stands in itself and is steady or "stable."[8] And the same holds true for φύσις as for Being in an even more originary sense: "φύσις is the emerging sway, the standing-there-in-itself, the constancy."[9] Hence it is quite appropriate when Heidegger also describes φύσις as a "standing-forth" (*Ent-stehen*).

There is a third essential characteristic. To understand what φύσις is for Heidegger, it is decisive not to consider the standing in itself and the constancy of the constant independently, cut from the process of coming into standing. What has become stable doesn't simply persist but continues to exist as standing forth, as it has been brought forth and continues to stand forth from the concealed. φύσις, Heidegger writes, means an "arising from the concealed and thus enabling the concealed to take its stand for the first time."[10] That the stability of φύσις comes forth from concealment is another essential moment, along with the arising self-opening and the moment of self-closure. Only as "the rising-up which goes-back-into-itself" is φύσις properly understood, in its genuine sense: "φύσις is an emerging and an arising, a self-opening, which, while rising, at the same time turns back into what has emerged, and so shrouds within itself that which on each occasion gives presence to what is present."[11]

We can gather from this last phrase that Heidegger calls the constancy proper to φύσις a "presencing" (*Anwesung*); presencing is the duality of emergence and self-closure. Heidegger insists on the gerund, on the verbal expression in contrast to "presence" (*Anwesenheit*), because that may prevent the misunderstanding that what is presencing has the stability and permanence (*Beständigkeit*) of the extant or occurrent (*das Vorhandene*). Rendering φύσις as *presencing* attempts to bring into view the "coming forth into the unhidden, [and the] placing itself into the open."[12] For Heidegger, this is something different from mere subsistence, from mere duration in time. "For the Greeks," Heidegger explains, "Being means: *presencing into the unhidden*. What is decisive is not the duration and extent of the presencing but rather whether the presencing is dispensed into the unhidden and simple, and thus withdrawn into the hidden and inexhaustible."[13] It is no doubt difficult to grasp the peculiar form of movement, what Heidegger calls the "movedness" (*Bewegtheit*), that inheres in the standing of φύσις and of all that is through φύσις; standing (or steadiness) seems but an absence of movement, mere rest. Yet what appears to be at rest while standing is rather the gathering concentration of strongest movedness; it is this trait of dynamic rest that allows Heidegger to establish φύσις "as a mode of being." Heidegger distinguishes sharply this movedness from spatial movement: it is not motion in the sense of a change of place within a given spatial order. For Heidegger, the form of movement, the movedness experienced by the Greeks as φύσις, is deeper and more originary: it is both arrival and withdrawal; it is outburst and simultaneous departure, or, in Heidegger's words, "the character of emerging into presencing."[14] If one were to compare the movedness of φύσις to geometrical figures, one could say that the form of its movement cannot be seen as a line or a surface. If images such as these are appropriate here at all, the movement of φύσις instead arises from the dimension of depth.

2.

Recall that the "standing in itself" is a peculiar movedness. In its tense rest, the opposition between the coming into appearance and the departure from presencing is held together. For Heidegger, the nature of manifestation, of appearance, is precisely this back-and-forth of emerging and self-closing. In such a way, φύσις is the genuine form of all appearance, revealing another constitutive moment. For the Greeks, Heidegger believes, Being is φύσις, and as such, it is manifestation: "The emerging-abiding sway is in itself at the same time the appearing that seems. The roots *phu-* and *pha-* name the same thing. *Phuein*, the emerging that reposes in itself, is *phainesthai*, lighting-up, self-showing, appearing."[15] This semantic connection makes Heidegger aware that emerging, light, and shining are all "[rooted] in one and the same essence of what neither any inceptual Greek thinker nor any later system of thought has ever captured in the unity of its essential richness."[16]

This idea enriches Heidegger's idiom of φύσις with yet another register: φύσις, understood as self-unfolding and "rising into the open," is also light, "the transparency of brightness," granting manifestation.[17] As self-enclosing pure presencing, φύσις sets itself into its genuine outline (*Umriss*), giving to the process of manifestation a specific figure, a *Gestalt*; it is "arising into pure presencing."[18] Assuming its figure, shape, and outline, what is each time present shows itself "as this or that."[19] Arising and turning back into the concealed, the presencing of φύσις is the source of both light and shadow. According to Heidegger, this luminous standing is called δόξα in Greek, and it belongs essentially to Being in terms of φύσις.[20] And the verb δοκέω, Heidegger holds, does not imply a deceitful and misleading appearance but only means "I show myself, I appear, I step into the light."²¹ Δόξα, thus understood, essentially belongs to φύσις, giving it the meaning of brilliance, luster, and radiance: "Emerging out of itself and yet remaining with itself—continuously radiating out from itself and yet nothing given away or lost. Gleaming—shining not only away from itself and an emergence, but also beckoning back into something dark, concealed, inaccessible. *Shining—the radiance of the self-concealing*."²²

Shining, appearing, gleaming, and radiating—all of these belong to the basic traits of Being qua φύσις. If this is so, then the Greek's sensibility for light, vision, and the visible, as well as their preference for sight over the other senses, is hardly surprising. The hierarchy of the senses doesn't arise from a purported optical instinct of the Greeks but follows from their assumption that Being has the sense of emerging, standing in itself in the self-given outline, in a shape wrested from the concealed; this is the genuine reason for their indisputable liking for the optical. Yet to speak of the so-called optical is already misleading because seeing was not restricted to eyes and visual sense for the Greeks; gleaming and shining confront the Greeks in the realm of the audible no less than in the visible, above all as glory and fame (κλέος). According to Heidegger at least, the Greeks' receptivity and almost devastating passion for the appearing and for what appears often verged on helpless dazzlement: "The Greeks are those human beings who lived immediately in the openness of phenomena—through the expressly ek-static capacity of letting the phenomena speak to them. . . . No one has ever again reached the heights of the Greek experience of a being as phenomenon."²³

Heidegger further points to the elemental making most manifest the nature of φύσις: rather than being illuminated by a source of light independent from and separate from darkness, the manifestation of φύσις appears like fire, as fire not only is bright but also is a self-consuming and extinguishing "blaze."²⁴ With open approval, Heidegger emphasizes "the φύσις-character of fire and also the fire-character of φύσις"²⁵ conceived by Heraclitus. Heidegger's marvelous characterization of the essence of fire deserves to be cited in its entirety:

> In "fire," the aspects of lighting, glowing, blazing, and the formation of an expanse are essential, but also those of consuming, of smashing and sinking in itself, of closing and extinguishing. The fire flames and, in its inflaming [*Entflammen*], is the separation between the light and the dark; the inflaming joins the light and the dark to and into and against one another. In inflaming, what occurs is what we grasp in the blink of an eye; the momentary and unique happens that, in separating and forcing its decision, dividing the light from the dark. The moment of inflammation opens up the free-play of appearing against the domain of disappearing. Inflammation lights up the realm of all showing and revealing for but a moment; but it also reveals what is without way and without steering, being completely non-transparent.²⁶

3.

The essence of φύσις as jointure of manifestation can hardly be grasped better than by the example of fire. It also captures the greatness Heidegger ascribed to the first beginning of philosophy, which we, in the wake of Nietzsche, should call tragic. For the first time in history, the Being of beings appears in φύσις; its light reveals the overabundance and excess of presencing, bringing forth the question of Being: "In the Greek climate, the human is so overwhelmed by the presencing of what presences, that he is compelled to the question concerning what presences *as* what presences."[27] This question is not the question *why* there is such manifestation; that question arises from a calculating urge to explain and, as it were, attack what presences, trying to get to terms with it at any cost. The Greeks asked a different, dignifying question with which thinking makes the attempt to abide and withdraw from what presences in order to let it manifest itself, to let it be in all its unfamiliarity and disconcertment.

The Greeks called such restrained dignifying θαυμάζειν (*wonder*). Heidegger finds in this word the fundamental attunement expressed, "within which the Greek philosophers were granted correspondence to the Being of being."[28] It was this attunement that informed and determined every act, every thought, and every wish in primordial Greek existence, or so Heidegger imagines. If this is true, it defines our task: to access this fundamental attunement, even if it may be difficult to approach and only may be intimated from afar. As Heidegger describes it, the state of wonder repeats the dynamic of φύσις: the human, awe-struck, retreats from what is present and, in this retreating and self-restraining, is at the same time drawn to and, as it were, held fast by that from which one retreats.[29] In wonder, the uncanny and enigmatic unusualness of the most ordinary announces itself. Again, one may, with Heidegger, express this in figural terms: what is closest becomes inaccessible and furthest remote; yet what is most remote appears pressing and frighteningly close. Wonder dwells in the "between" (*Zwischen*) of these extremes: "Not knowing the way out or the way in, wonder dwells in a *between*, between the most usual, beings, and their unusualness, their '*is*' . . . Wonder does not divert itself from the usual but on the contrary adverts to it, precisely as what is the most unusual of everything and in everything."[30]

One should be clear about the importance Heidegger thus attributes to wonder: the dignifying self-restraint in such abysmal *between* is the genuine way for human *Dasein* to respond to φύσις. Standing in this between is something simple, yet it holds inexhaustible wealth. As one accepts the simplicity of wonder, φύσις grants an intimate experience of inner overabundance. It is from such overabundance that philosophy sprang in the first beginning, as an "answer of a humanity that has been struck by the excess of presence—an answer which is itself excessive."[31]

4.

Yet the presencing of φύσις, although it marked the inception of philosophy, did not sustain its inceptiveness. The luminous overabundance became gradually weaker, poorer, until it finally withdrew altogether: "presencing recedes as things become present."[32] Heidegger here draws from the dual nature of φύσις as presencing (*Anwesen*) on the one hand and presence (*Anwesenheit*) and what is present (*das Anwesende*) on the other; presencing recedes because presence longs to extend its duration as long as possible and into eternity. The presence of the present, craving duration, transforms itself into constant, always existent stability. In the language of the beginnings of philosophy: φύσις became οὐσία.

Δόξα underwent a comparable change. Φύσις as form of manifestation became ἰδέα, and this transformation began the fatal process of a progressive subjectification in the history of metaphysics. For ἰδέα, the fundamental word of Plato's philosophy, means that which "is seen in the visible, the view that something offers."[33] Yet what is thus seen is no longer the radiating gleam and dignity of φύσις but only "a determination of the constant, insofar as, and only insofar as, it stands opposed to a seeing."[34] As ἰδέα became the guiding thread for human thinking and our relation to Being as a whole, the presencing of φύσις became exterior and superficial. The whole of φύσις was absorbed into the aspect, offering itself to contemplative gaze. Manifestation thus lost its abysmal depth, revealing only its surface: "The aspect, offered by the thing, and no longer the thing itself, now becomes what is decisive."[35]

This transformation has had immeasurable consequences with regard to the Being of humans. Being was no longer manifest for them as φύσις but only as ἰδέα, as the look of things that met their gaze. But those looks now longed for an explanation, and the obtrusive and aggressive *why* question became the means of such explanation. There was no longer any mere stepping back from what appears in the attempt to let it be; the fundamental attunement of wonder vanished. What came into view was no longer dignified in its unfathomable strangeness but taken in advance as something that could be explainable. Having lost its unfamiliarity, φύσις was seen in general categories already familiar and all too common: "The incipient wonder is overpowered by the growing familiarity of beings, it makes way for this familiarity and thus abandons itself and coalesces with the mere amazement about what is astonishing."[36] When Aristotle at the beginning of his *Metaphysics* declared wonder as the origin of philosophy, it had already become only the curiosity of mere surprise. Yet this deteriorated form of wonder has been regarded as the origin of thinking in subsequent philosophy, so as to constitute its beginning.

One must raise the question: Where does this transformation, fatal in every respect, have its origin? Whence the collapse of φύσις? The following may begin to answer that question: φύσις, from the outset, is marked by deep ambiguity. Manifestation is both "the self-gathering event of bringing-itself-to-stand and thus standing in gatheredness" and "something already standing there, to offer a foreground, a surface, a look as offering to be looked at."³⁷ This is the ambiguous nature of φύσις. Manifestation means "the unique essence of [an] arrangement"³⁸ of φύσις and concealment. It is not difficult to see that the collapse of φύσις comes from severing both sides of this deep ambiguity: the overabundance and excess of φύσις, at once an emerging and withdrawing presence, like fire, is lost, and only stable presence and continuous endurance remain. The originary sense of manifestation, deeper and more true, is lost.

But why? Why was primordial presencing suppressed and covered up at once by presence? Why did stability take the place of the presencing of presence? If one were to open one's eyes to φύσις, the reverse would reveal itself, or so Heidegger supposes: "Unconcealment is more inceptive, but also more concealing and indeed itself more concealed than presencing. As emergence and withdrawal, presencing is more inceptive than presence. And presence is in turn more inceptive than stability."³⁹ So why did we come to think the very opposite?

The question begins a vicious game. What happened, no doubt, was an attempt to escape concealment for the sake of presence and of duration. But why is duration so attractive? One might come to think that all of this is a human wrongdoing, a human inclination for overcoming the brevity of our lives. Has there been a lack of will? Have we lacked the power to hold out and live in the abysmal between of primordial φύσις, as we should? Heidegger's answer is in the negative. For him, a preference for the enduring, for the present, and for the real is simply part of the meaning of φύσις and of Being: "The advancement of the present (of presencing and constancy) and with this the mania for 'preserving' and the will to 'eternity' in the sense of duration, and the preference of actuality and effectivity that is at the service of actuality"⁴⁰ originates with φύσις.

5.

This is Heidegger's most daring claim, forcing us to rethink what has been said. In order to make good on that claim, one would need to understand Heidegger's account of ἀλήθεια, for the history of truth has a beginning even more primordial than φύσις; ἀλήθεια precedes φύσις both historically and with regard to the inherent logic of manifestation. To understand why φύσις must transform into enduring, stable presence, we must understand the relation of the first to the other beginning. Only from this can we hope to glance back at the first beginning and interpret it in this light.

I shall leave this for another occasion, as both an inquiry into ἀλήθεια and into the first and other beginning are daunting tasks. I will conclude instead with more general remarks on early Greek philosophy and our relation to it: Heidegger is convinced that it is precisely the collapse of φύσις that makes the first beginning of philosophy an inevitable challenge for thinking today; he insists "that every reflection upon that which now is can take its rise and thrive only if, through a dialogue with the Greek thinkers and their language, it strikes root into the ground of our historical existence."[41] Heidegger then goes on to argue that such dialogue with early Greek thinking still lies ahead. Indeed, we are hardly prepared for it—and yet it remains, in turn, the condition of present thinking. Allowing early Greek thought to speak to us is also the precondition for entering into another essential dialogue, that with the East Asian world. Such dialogue must, from the outset, consider that what we call genuine "Greek philosophy," the philosophy of Plato and Aristotle, is in truth already the first completion of the Greek beginning of philosophy: "We surmount Greek philosophy as the inception of Western philosophy only if we also grasp this inception as its inceptive end; for it was solely and only the end that became the 'inception' for the subsequent age, in such a way that this inception also covers up the inceptive inception."[42]

Such inceptive inception announced itself once the fundamental word φύσις assumed its place in the poetizing thinking of the pre-Socratics, of the inceptive thinkers. What Heidegger anticipates as a leap into the other beginning, into the inceptive inception, is no mere renewal or repetition. Such beginning is something unique and quite distinctive to us. Our "new fundamental experience of Beyng" must be even "more originary than that of the Greeks articulated in the word and concept of φύσις."[43] So in turning to φύσις, we try to devote ourselves to the first beginning, precisely by questioning and thinking the first beginning. The retrieval of the first beginning, the attempt to begin questioning more originarily, is our only hope to open up "the solitary remoteness of the first beginning to everything that follows it historically."[44]

Notes

1. "Anfängliche und daher die ganze Geschichte der abendländischen Philosophie durchherrschende Bestimmung des Seins" in Heidegger, *Geschichte des Seyns*, 6. Translation by Guang Yang.
2. Heidegger, *Introduction to Metaphysics*, 16; Heidegger, *Einführung in die Metaphysik*, 17.
3. Heidegger, *Introduction to Metaphysics*, 16; Heidegger, *Einführung in die Metaphysik*, 17.
4. Heidegger, "On the Essence and Concept of Φύσις," 199. Heidegger, "Vom Wesen und Begriff der Φύσις," 259.
5. Heidegger, *Introduction to Metaphysics*, 15; Heidegger, *Einführung in die Metaphysik*, 16.
6. "Im Aufgehen und als Aufgehen entgeht dieses keineswegs dem Sichverschließen, sondern nimmt dieses für sich in den Anspruch als dasjenige, was das Aufgehen gewährt

und allein und stets die einzige Gewähr für das Aufgehen gönnt" (Heidegger, *Heraklit*, 133). Translation by Guang Yang.

7. Heidegger, *Introduction to Metaphysics*, 15; Heidegger, *Einführung in die Metaphysik*, 16.

8. Heidegger, "On the Essence and Concept of Φύσις," 188; Heidegger, "Vom Wesen und Begriff der Φύσις," 246.

9. Heidegger, *Introduction to Metaphysics*, 194; Heidegger, *Einführung in die Metaphysik*, 191.

10. Heidegger, *Introduction to Metaphysics*, 16; Heidegger, *Einführung in die Metaphysik*, 17.

11. Heidegger, *Elucidations of Hölderlin's Poetry*, 79. Heidegger, *Erläuterung zu Hölderlins Dichtung*, 56.

12. Heidegger, "On the Essence and Concept of Φύσις in Aristotle's *Physics* B, I," 208; Heidegger, "Vom Wesen und Begriff der Φύσις," 272.

13. Heidegger, "On the Essence and Concept of Φύσις in Aristotle's *Physics* B, I," 206; Heidegger, "Vom Wesen und Begriff der Φύσις," 270.

14. Heidegger, "On the Essence and Concept of Φύσις in Aristotle's *Physics* B, I," 191; Heidegger, "Vom Wesen und Begriff der Φύσις," 249.

15. Heidegger, *Introduction to Metaphysics*, 106; Heidegger, *Einführung in die Metaphysik*, 108.

16. "in einem und dem selben Wesen dessen [wurzeln], was weder die anfängliche Denker der Griechen noch gar je ein späteres Denken in der Einheit seines Wesensreichtums gedacht hat" (Heidegger, *Heraklit*, 17). Translation by Guang Yang.

17. Heidegger, *Elucidations of Hölderlin's Poetry*, 79; Heidegger, *Erläuterung zu Hölderlins Dichtung*, 56.

18. Heidegger, *Mindfulness*, 328; Heidegger, *Besinnung*, 369.

19. Heidegger, *Introduction to Metaphysics*, 196; Heidegger, *Einführung in die Metaphysik*, 192.

20. Heidegger, *Introduction to Metaphysics*, 108; Heidegger, *Einführung in die Metaphysik*, 110.

21. Heidegger, *Introduction to Metaphysics*, 109; Heidegger, *Einführung in die Metaphysik*, 111.

22. Heidegger, *Event*, 24; Heidegger, *Ereignis*, 32.

23. Heidegger, *Four Seminar*, 37; Heidegger, *Seminare*, 330.

24. Heidegger, *Elucidations of Hölderlin's Poetry*, 79; Heidegger, *Erläuterung zu Hölderlins Dichtung*, 57.

25. "der φύσις-Charakter des Feuers, aber auch der Feuercharakter der φύσις" (Heidegger, *Heraklit*, 162). Translation by Guang Yang.

26. "Im ‚Feuer' sind die Bezüge des Lichtenden, des Glühenden, des Lodernden und eine Weite Bildenden, aber auch des Verzehrenden, des in sich Zusammenschlagens und Zusammensinkens und Verschließens und Verlöschens wesentlich. Das Feuer flammt und ist im Entflammen die Scheidung zwischen dem Lichten und dem Dunklen; das Entflammen fügt das Lichte und das Dunkle gegen- und ineinander. Im Entflammen ereignet sich dasjenige, was das Auge in einem Blick faßt, das Augenblickliche, Einzige, das scheidend, entscheidend das Helle gegen das Dunkle abscheidet. Das Augenblickliche des Entflammens eröffnet den Spielraum des Erscheinens gegen den Bezirk des Verschwindens. Das Augenblickhafte des Entflammens lichtet zumal den Bereich alles Weisens und Zeigens, aber

auch in einem damit den des Weiselosen und Steuerlosen und schlechthin Undurchsichtigen" (Heidegger, *Heraklit*, 161–62). Translation by Guang Yang.

27. Heidegger, *Four Seminars*, 38; Heidegger, *Seminare*, 331.

28. "innerhalb derer der griechischen Philosophie das Entsprechen zum Sein des Seienden gewährt war" (Heidegger, *Identität und Differenz*, 23). Translation by Guang Yang.

29. See Heidegger, *Identität und Differenz*, 23. Translation by Guang Yang.

30. Heidegger, *Basic Questions of Philosophy*, 145; Heidegger, *Grundfragen der Philosophie*, 168.

31. Heidegger, *Four Seminars*, 38; Heidegger, *Seminare*, 331.

32. Heidegger, *Event*, 18; Heidegger, *Ereignis*, 25. Translation modified.

33. Heidegger, *Introduction to Metaphysics*, 192; Heidegger, *Einführung in die Metaphysik*, 189.

34. Heidegger, *Introduction to Metaphysics*, 194; Heidegger, *Einführung in die Metaphysik*, 191.

35. Heidegger, *Introduction to Metaphysics*, 195; Heidegger, *Einführung in die Metaphysik*, 192. Translation modified.

36. Heidegger, *Mindfulness*, 242; Heidegger, *Besinnung*, 273.

37. Heidegger, *Introduction to Metaphysics*, 194–95; Heidegger, *Einführung in die Metaphysik*, 191.

38. "das einige Wesen der Fügung" (Heidegger, *Heraklit*, 158). Translation by Guang Yang.

39. "Die Entbergung ist anfänglicher aber auch verbergender und deshalb verborgener als die Anwesung. Die Anwesung ist anfänglicher (als Aufgang und Rückgang) denn die Anwesenheit. Die Anwesenheit ist anfänglicher denn die Beständigkeit" (Heidegger, *Über den Anfang*, 63). Translation by Guang Yang.

40. Heidegger, *Mindfulness*, 71; Heidegger, *Besinnung*, 85.

41. Heidegger, *Question concerning Technology and Other Essays*, 157–58; Heidegger, "Wissenschaft und Besinnung," 43.

42. Heidegger, *Introduction to Metaphysics*, 191; Heidegger, *Einführung in die Metaphysik*, 188.

43. "neue Grunderfahrung des Seyns . . . ursprünglicher sein müssen [wird] als die der Griechen, die sich im Wort und Begriff der φύσις ausspricht" (Heidegger, *Hölderlins Hymnen »Germanien« und »Der Rhein,«* 196). Translation by Guang Yang.

44. Heidegger, *Contributions to Philosophy*, 396; Heidegger, *Beiträge zur Philosophie*, 504.

Bibliography

Heidegger, Martin. *Basic Questions of Philosophy: Selected "Problems" of "Logic."* Translated by Richard Rojcewicz and André Schuwer. Bloomington: Indiana University Press, 1994.
——. *Beiträge zur Philosophie (Vom Ereignis)*. GA 65. Frankfurt am Main: Klostermann, 1994.
——. *Besinnung*. GA 66. Frankfurt am Main: Klostermann, 1997.
——. *Contributions to Philosophy (of the Event)*. Translated by Richard Rojcewicz and Daniela Vallega-Neu. Bloomington: Indiana University Press, 2012.
——. *Einführung in die Metaphysik*. GA 40. Frankfurt am Main: Klostermann, 1983.

———. *Elucidations of Hölderlin's Poetry.* Translated by Keith Hoeller. Amherst, NY: Humanity Books, 2000.

———. *Das Ereignis.* GA 71. Frankfurt am Main: Klostermann, 2009.

———. *Erläuterung zu Hölderlins Dichtung.* GA 4. Frankfurt am Main: Klostermann, 1996.

———. *The Event.* Translated by Richard Rojcewicz. Bloomington: Indiana University Press, 2013.

———. *Four Seminars. Le Thor 1966, 1968, 1969, Zähringen 1973.* Translated by Andrew Mitchell and François Raffoul. Bloomington: Indiana University Press, 2003.

———. *Die Geschichte des Seyns. 1. Die Geschichte des Seyns. 2. Κοινόν. Aus der Geschichte des Seyns.* GA 69. Frankfurt am Main: Klostermann, 1998.

———. *Grundfragen der Philosophie. Ausgewählte »Probleme« der »Logik«.* GA 45. Frankfurt am Main: Klostermann, 1992.

———. *Heraklit. 1. Der Anfang des abendländischen Denkens. 2. Logik. Heraklits Lehre vom Logos.* GA 55. Frankfurt am Main: Klostermann, 1979.

———. *Hölderlins Hymnen »Germanien« und »Der Rhein.«* GA 39. Frankfurt am Main: Klostermann, 1999.

———. *Identität und Differenz.* GA 11. Frankfurt am Main: Klostermann, 2006.

———. *Introduction to Metaphysics.* Translated by Gregory Fried and Richard Polt. New Haven, CT: Yale University Press, 2000.

———. *Mindfulness.* Translated by Parvis Emad and Thomas Kalary. New York: Continuum, 2006.

———. "On the Essence and Concept of Φύσις in Aristotle's *Physics* B, I." In *Pathmarks*, 183–231. Translated by William McNeill. Cambridge: Cambridge University Press, 1998.

———. *The Question concerning Technology and Other Essays.* Translated by William Lovitt. New York: Harper and Row, 1977.

———. *Seminare.* GA 15. Frankfurt am Main: Klostermann, 2005.

———. *Über den Anfang.* GA 70. Frankfurt am Main: Klostermann, 2005.

———. "Vom Wesen und Begriff der Φύσις. Aristoteles, Physik B, 1." In *Wegmarken*, GA 9, 239–303. Frankfurt am Main: Klostermann, 1996.

———. "Wissenschaft und Besinnung." In *Vorträge und Aufsätze*, GA 7, 37–67. Frankfurt am Main: Klostermann, 2000.

DAMIR BARBARIĆ is Professor at the Institute of Philosophy in Zagreb. Barbarić's latest books in a foreign language: *Wiederholungen. Philosophiegeschichtliche Studien*, Tübingen, 2015; *Zum anderen Anfang. Studien zum Spätdenken Heideggers*, Freiburg/Munich, 2016.

III.

Phenomenology, the Thing, and the Fourfold

9 *Tautóphasis*

Heidegger and Parmenides

Günter Figal
Translated by Margot Wielgus

For A.M.E.S.—in the Same

1.

As often as Heidegger may have read Parmenides, only in his later years did Heidegger come nearest to him. *Nearest* means so close that Heidegger identified the "task of thinking" (which is, for him, singular) with what is to be read in Parmenides's fragments. Thus, the task of thinking—something he was already talking about in a lecture from the year 1964[1]—seems to have become a task of reading. As one might imagine, Heidegger thinks as a reader, which he has always done. In his later years, after a long phenomenological abstinence, the "task of thinking" again had to do with the meaning of phenomenology. Then, his primary text was Parmenides's didactic poetry. Of course, Heidegger understood the task of thinking as a task of hearing—and, indeed, a task of hearing of a very special kind. If one follows Heidegger, one must tune out the idea that thinking means abandoning listening. One must listen in order to receive what comes from another voice, like that of Parmenides, so that it can be understood and considered. What is heard is not valid in itself as a word [*ein Wort*] for which an antonym [*ein Gegenwort*], a response [*ein Antwort*], can be found. Rather, attentive listening gives up its independence when it takes up the "task of thinking." Now, the voice that is heard sounds only in listening and, indeed, is such that the voice sounds back from out of the listener. As soon as what is heard is articulated [*zu Wort kommt*], it is not the listener but, rather, the voice the listener heard that speaks. Thinking speaks, as Heidegger says, "in the echo of Parmenides."[2] Speaking takes place in every "hearing which opens itself to the word of Parmenides from out of our present age," and it happens in such a way that the "return to the beginning" of thinking is performed in the articulation of what has been heard.[3] This does not amount to a "question of returning *to* Parmenides."[4] There is no distance to overcome; no experience must be translated into understanding (as

Heidegger had still assumed in his lectures on Parmenides in the winter semester of 1942–43).[5] It is enough "to *turn towards* Parmenides," and, already, the reverberation of his voice is there in the saying.[6]

The statements quoted above come from a seminar that Heidegger held in his house in Freiburg-Zähringen with a small circle of friends and students in 1973. When one reads the records documenting the seminar, there is admittedly no voice to be heard. One can only read of voices and, so, of Heidegger's voice reading and clarifying a text he composed about Parmenides. "Heidegger reads slowly," remarks the minute taker.[7] One does not, oneself, however, hear Heidegger reading. Rather, one reads. "Here ends the lecture [*Lesung*]," one reads, but, since the voice never sounds, the voice does not fall silent.[8] Reading, one does not hear and one also does not echo the text. The text does not reverberate but, rather, stands opposite; one must understand it and also, on the other hand, interpret it. To read is to discern and, therefore, to critique; it is to compare, connect, and contend. Reading is not reverberation and, thus, initially does not offer true unison. In reading, the task of thinking poses itself differently and, thereby, anew.

2.

Heidegger's considerations, which he understood as echoes of Parmenides, revolve around a phrase from Parmenides's didactic poetry. It is a phrase that Heidegger lifts out of its context and takes simply by itself: ἔστι γὰρ εἶναι, "Being namely *is*" ["*Ist* nämlich Sein"], as Heidegger initially and roughly translates it.[9] The phrase, explains Heidegger, had long irritated him because, understood superficially, it reduces "being to the level of beings."[10] But this is not so. As Heidegger wants to show, the phrase brings being to language, and, indeed, that being comes to language as itself.

To show this, Heidegger first indicates that the word εἶναι, thought in a "Greek manner," means "to presence."[11] This way of reading is not new in Heidegger's thought. The idea that, "for the Greeks," being signifies presence can already be found in his lecture on Plato's *Sophist* from the winter semester of 1924–25.[12] Of course, as is already in Heidegger's considerations about the meaning of φύσις in the 1930s,[13] presence no longer operates as a state of being but, rather, as an occurrence, precisely as "to presence." Correspondingly, ἔστι γὰρ εἶναι means "presencing namely presences."[14] The neuter present participle, τὸ ἐόν, as for Parmenides, is to be understood in this sense. What is meant is "neither beings, nor simply being" but, rather, being as and in its presencing.[15] The corresponding translation should read: "presencing: presencing itself."[16]

Even before he translates the interpreted phrases, Heidegger introduces the key point of his lecture on Parmenides: to say that the present presences is "clearly a tautology"—it is, however, not a problematic tautology but "a genuine tautology."[17] It names "the Same only once" (*"nur einmal das Selbe"*),[18] and it names this "as itself."[19] This is more than a mere characterization of the Parmenidean phrase. Because reading the sentence should function as an echo, in which the voice of thinking reverberates in its beginning, the tautology must designate the essence of this thinking. In fact, Heidegger leaves no doubt as to whether the tautology should be the main feature of thinking, the feature of thinking with which he is concerned. He calls the thinking "here in question" "tautological thinking."[20] And as Heidegger succinctly adds, "this" (that is, to be sure, thinking) is the "primordial sense of phenomenology."[21]

These are neither matters of course nor matters that are evident. Is Parmenides's phrase tautological? Is it even "genuinely" tautological and, thereby, phenomenological? Its tautological character is in no way "obvious," because the duplicated verb could always be used in a different way. If one clarifies how the verb behaves in the phrase, the question of whether Parmenides's—genuine or alleged—tautology can amount to the "primordial sense of phenomenology" can be answered. Additionally, the translation Heidegger gives for εἶναι, "to presence," must, at least, be justified. But the factual question of whether phenomenology, in its "primordial sense," is tautological would not yet, thereby, be answered. In order to answer this question, one must clarify whether a tautological phenomenology is at all possible. If Heidegger wants to prove its possibility in his reading of Parmenides, the question concerning the possibility of tautological phenomenology leads, once again, back to Parmenides.

3.

To find out what Parmenides's phrase is primarily concerned with, it is helpful to pay attention to its relationship to the text (where it appears). One can then see, namely, that the phrase is contrastive and that its meaning can be understood from out of this contrast. "It is possible for [being] to be, but not possible for nothing to be" (ἔστι γὰρ εἶναι, μηδὲν δ' οὐκ ἔστιν).[22] Although it may seem to be, "nothing is not" is not a tautological phrase. Rather, it is the rejection of the possibility of speaking about something that is not. The assumption that it is possible to talk about a nonbeing, if one follows Parmenides's didactic poetry, designates the opinion of the "mortals," who do not consider the sense in which everything that can be spoken about also always must *be*. Whatever is absent is, nevertheless, in one's perception. Yet, in that it is perceived in thought, it is there in a definite way. The goddess in Parmenides's didactic poem says, "Regard what is absent in reason as a being that is definitely there" (λεῦσσε δ' ὅμως ἀπεόντα νόωι παρεόντα βεβαίως).[23] According to this, the negation is a deceiving language trick that does not correspond to anything in the world, and if one takes a closer look, one realizes that language itself refutes it. Additionally, as it says in an implicit explanation of Parmenides's phrase in Plato's *Sophist*, if one contests the existence of something, one is constrained to use *is*.[24] The *is* is always there, along with everything that is there for perception, for νοεῖν. Therefore, Parmenides can also say that perception and being are the same—τὸ γὰρ αὐτὸ νοεῖν ἐστίν τε καὶ εἶναι.[25] If one says, "*is* is," one does not treat it as a being but, rather, emphasizes its inevitability and unavoidability. ἔστιν γὰρ εἶναι is the inevitability of the enunciated emphasis of εἶναι, which also indicates that *is* is no mere word. Rather it is always perceptible and perceived, and, conversely, perception allows it to be what it is. In contrast to negation, it is not a deceiving language trick. On the other hand, it can only be said through the word whose inevitability is emphasized. This is because everything (that is not a mere word) *is*; *being is* means that one must first take the word *is* seriously.

Accordingly, it is as Heidegger says: Parmenides's phrase is tautological. But is it also "genuinely tautological" in Heidegger's sense? To be genuinely tautological, the phrase would have to be, in addition, phenomenological "in the primordial sense." It would have to name, as Heidegger's formulation shows, "the Same only once, and indeed as itself." In naming, the named must be there "as itself." Naming would, then, be nothing other than this being there of the named.

When Heidegger, commenting on Parmenides's phrase, says of the Greek language that it "speaks so much *more revealingly* and thus more precisely than we do," he also provides an explanation of the "genuine tautology."[26] This revealing does not name by pointing or identifying but, rather, such that, in naming, it immediately allows what is to be revealed to reveal itself. Translating the word σῆμα, Heidegger also speaks of "revealing" (*Zeignis*) and says that it "shows and lets be seen, in that it depicts what is to be seen."[27] In this depicting [*Zeichnung*], the self-revealing would be there because depicting would come forth as not depicting. Rather, depicting only allows what reveals *itself* to be seen. *The Same* would be like this. Heidegger determines phenomenology precisely in this manner in his Zähringen Seminar. Phenomenology is "a path that leads away to come before . . . and it lets that before which it is led show itself."[28]

Heidegger already emphasized phenomenology's revealing character in *Being and Time*. Phenomenology is precisely "letting something be seen by indicating it";[29] it lets "what shows itself in itself, the manifest," be seen.[30] This letting something be seen is only necessary because the manifest "is something that does *not* show itself initially and for the most part."[31] It must, thus, be indicated as the "meaning and ground" of what, first, initially, and for the most part does show itself.[32] In Heidegger's later thought, and also in his earlier determinations of phenomenology, what reveals itself is only there when it is revealed. But, as Heidegger understands it in *Being and Time*, revealing is *showing*, while, in his later thought, revealing is *naming*. Revealing, in the sense of *Being and Time*, has the character of λόγος, and, therein, it is clearly a creative power.[33] In opposition, naming, in the sense of his later thought, is simply achieved by the named, and it can be achieved by the named because naming is *the Same* as the named.

Since naming does not have the same character as λόγος, it is also noteworthy that, in the end, Heidegger dispenses with the word *tautology*. This happens in notes that he likely generated between 1973 and 1975 as the preliminary work to an unfinished introduction to his collected writings, lectures, and notes. Instead of using *tautology*, Heidegger speaks of *tautóphasis*, which he also translates as "saying-two-together" [*Selbander-sage*] and clarifies as "phenomenóphasis."[34] His notes are accompanied by self-critical annotations. In *Being and Time*, as Heidegger notes, "what is proper to phenomenó*phasis*" has not yet been glimpsed.[35] In *Being and Time*, it is clear that Heidegger had not yet adequately recognized the occurrence announced in the word φάσις (as in all Greek substantives ending in -σις).

Heidegger explains the word φάσις only by referring to "saying" and the "path-character of naming."[36] He had clearly not considered that the word φάσις is ambiguous. Said more precisely, it is composed of two words that sound equally. Of the two words, one can be traced back to the verb φημί, while the other is derived from φαίνω and can, accordingly, be translated as "to appear" [*Erscheinen*]. What Heidegger names with "saying" would then, also (and completely in the sense of the "genuine tautology"), be addressed as "to appear." Heidegger's word *phenomenóphasis*, understood in this way, would announce the appearing of appearances and, thus, phenomena. At the same time, this reading would clarify what Heidegger's tautophatic understanding of phenomenology is about: it is not about appearances but, rather, only appearing; it is not about those beings that are present, but only presencing. Phenomenóphasis is actually only *phasis*; it is tautóphasis, the saying of presencing alone. This occurs as such in that it is said. And insofar as it occurs, it allows saying to occur.

When one thinks of them in this way, saying and presencing, the two sides of φάσις, are indeed intertwined with each other, though they are, nevertheless, differentiated. One reads this in Heidegger's works. In his posthumous notes concerning phenomenology, he notes that "saying-two-together" is not the coincidence of the saying and the said; rather "each [should] indicate in its own way that it belongs together with the other."[37] Heidegger already, in his lecture on the "Principle of Identity," wanted to show that belonging together does not exclude Sameness. There, it says that what belongs together belongs "together in the Same and by virtue of this Same."[38] This comes just after the quoted passage from Parmenides on thinking (νοεῖν) and being (εἶναι), as cited above.[39] The Same of thinking and being would not, then, be understood as the Sameness of the two but, rather, as the Same that, as such, thinking as well as being is. Correspondingly, the ταυτόν in tautóphasis must not be understood as the identity of naming and presencing, of saying and appearing, but, rather, as the Same in which the two differentiated aspects belong. *As* this Sameness, both would come to bear in intertwined differentiatedness.

What is this Same? In the Zähringen Seminar it is referred to as unconcealment, ἀλήθεια. Unconcealment, Heidegger adds, is τὸ ἐόν and, thus, presencing itself understood as occurrence. It is "no empty opening, no motionless chasm" but, rather, "disclosure."[40] In the lecture titled *The End of Philosophy and the Task of Thinking*, as well as in the notes on phenomenology, Heidegger speaks of "opening" [*Lichtung*] in the same sense. There, "opening" is not essentially deemed an "empty opening" but is meant, rather, as the occurrence of the clearing.[41] Insofar as it names "the Same," tautóphasis occurs in disclosure, in which it belongs as tautóphasis.

4.

And Parmenides? Heidegger had already understood ἀλήθεια in the sense of disclosure as the center of Parmenidean thought in his lecture from the summer semester of 1926. In that lecture, one reads, "Through and in the one truth, the one Being; and only in Being, truth."[42] This passage nearly anticipates the intertwining of disclosure and presencing, as he later speaks of it in the Zähringen Seminar. Admittedly, in the 1926 lecture, "being" is not clarified as "presencing" but, rather, as "constant presence."[43] This is much fairer to Parmenides's didactic poetry than the tautological or tautophatic reading of Heidegger's later years. One may be permitted to hold that in the didactic poetry, ἐόν and εἶναι mean presence and not an occurring presencing. Otherwise, it could not be that which is "complete on all sides, like the bulk of a well-rounded ball."[44]

And phenomenology? In Parmenides's didactic poetry, there is evidence that presence, expressed by the word ἐόν, is to be understood as a phenomenon. If it were identical with the real existence of something, Parmenides could not also say that the absent, which is only there in memory, is. Therefore, Heidegger can rightly read Parmenidean thinking as an earlier version of phenomenology.[45] Nevertheless, Parmenides's thinking is not phenomenology in the sense of Heidegger's later considerations. Parmenides's thinking of being is tautological; it is not tautophatic. Parmenides's phrase, according to which thinking and being are the same, is not a saying of presence. If being, for Parmenides, means the same as the presence of phenomena, then the phrase indicates, moreover, that every correlate of thinking (understood as perception, νοεῖν) *is* and that, accordingly, without "being," nothing can be thought or perceived. On the other hand, the saying of presence, the occurrence of disclosure, reaches behind the presence of that which is present. This presence, rather than its becoming possible, is said. Its possibility cannot be in the same way as what is present presences, but is present only in presencing, in the saying of presence as such—in the processual and not the resultative sense of the participle.

The notion that presencing requires allowing presence itself to presence in the naming word is not found in Parmenides or any other thinker before Heidegger. It is the fundamental idea of Heidegger's later phenomenology, which, in the Zähringen Seminar, he calls "a phenomenology of the inapparent."⁴⁶ When conscious of the presencing of what is itself present, one is "in the domain of the inapparent."⁴⁷ In other words, one is in the "domain" of the appearance-less or the not phenomenal, one is at the site of inapparent "disclosure" because and in that the disclosure is the emergence of appearances or phenomena. Yet the inapparent is not hidden; it can cannot disappear with the emergence of phenomena, for it is precisely this emergence. Thus, presence [*Anwesenheit*] and its "disclosure" (which Heidegger also calls "clearing") may, indeed, remain "unheeded."⁴⁸ But it can also be articulated when presencing itself is named.

And phenomena? What does Heidegger's phenomenology of the inapparent have to do with phenomena that, in the end, owe their names to phenomenology? The naming of presencing is singularly what it is. It is and remains the naming of presencing, and it is not fulfilled by understanding things that are present. Therein, tautophatic thinking follows the program of the lecture *On Time and Being*, according to which it is essential to "think Being without beings."⁴⁹ Thinking being is, thus, no longer (as it is in *Being and Time*) the being of a distinctive being, namely Dasein. It is also no longer as in an "ontological difference" about beings in general, as Heidegger thought it in his lecture "The Basic Problems of Phenomenology," given during the summer semester of 1927.⁵⁰ Tautóphasis is nothing other than the fulfilled happening of saying. This saying cannot make anything comprehensible, for, as Heidegger says in the Zähringen Seminar, "in con-ceiving [*Be-greifen*], there is the gesture of taking possession," and presencing is not something one can possess.⁵¹

5.

Heidegger himself formulated the obvious objection against this rejection of conceiving. In *The End of Philosophy and the Task of Thinking*, he asks if the attempt to think the "clearing"—that is, the happening of the clearing—is not "ungrounded mysticism or even bad mythology, in any case a ruinous irrationalism, the denial of *ratio*."⁵² The objection is answered with countering questions that suggest that what "*ratio*, νοῦς, νοεῖν, *perceiving*" are called cannot be "sufficiently determined unless we experience Ἀλήθεια in a Greek manner as unconcealment and then, above and beyond the Greek, think it as the opening of self-concealing," as the presencing of the present in its inapparentness, as it is called in his later texts.⁵³

On the one hand, that should be clear. If *ratio* is essentially reason (that is, νοῦς), and if νοῦς, in turn, has its essence in νοεῖν (that is, in perception), then presencing cannot be perceived like something present. Moreover, perception must belong in the very openness that Heidegger tries to think as presencing.

Then why this openness eludes the grounding *ratio* is also clear. Openness cannot evince itself or be proven, for perception does not come back from behind it. For the sake of philosophical clarity, this should be accepted. It would be uneducated to seek proof where there can be no proof.[54]

Still, on the other hand, it is dubious that every conceptually conducted or accompanied understanding of the inapparent openness can, therefore, be ruled out. In the Zähringen Seminar, Heidegger himself says that "the Greek ὁρισμός," clearly a concept of a kind other than possessive, "firmly and delicately" surrounds "that which sight takes into view."[55] The seeing that is a thinking seeing, thus, requires something to surround that can be understood as the boundary of the thought-sight field, and perhaps also as its demarcation. Then the demarcations of this field would indicate how what is seen is to be understood.

Heidegger did not further pursue his considerations concerning ὁρισμός— how should they have conformed to the context of tautophatic thinking? He thus did not realize a possibility that the fundamental text for his considerations on tautóphasis offered him. Heidegger only grazed this possibility without understanding it as possibility; he virtually concealed by interpreting it tautophatically, so that it hardly comes into the reader's view.

It has to do with the sign (σήματα), about which one can read in Parmenides's didactic poetry. The sign's revealing does not dawn on Heidegger in a tautophatic naming, which he calls "letting-be-seen" [*Zeignis*]. It is different from the tautology, ἔστιν γὰρ εἶναι, but the two belong together. The saying of εἶναι or ἐόν—which, taken as itself, is a sheer naming—becomes a λόγος through the sign alone. It is, admittedly, λόγος as a tautologically marginal case of λόγος.

The signs—indications, distinctive marks, guiding symbols—that can be found along the way for thinking about being are marks of comprehensibility; they allocate possibilities for appearing that are, as such, comprehensible. They show being in a comprehensible way without making being itself as itself comprehensible. The signs are not predicates of being—as if this were something determinate, like a living creature or a thing to which characteristics can be attributed. The concepts that Parmenides enumerates—not becoming, imperishable, whole, simultaneous, immovable, complete—are determinations that cannot, as such, be attributed to being but, rather, only to beings. Only beings are determinable. But there are determinations of beings in which being, as it were, shows through. If one designates something as imperishable, whole, immovable, or complete, one, thereby, superficially shows the *is*; something imperishable is, it *is* in that it does not decay. But the *is* itself arises neither in imperishability nor in any other sign for it. Every sign indicates it differently, no sign exhausts it, and no sign makes it comprehensible. The understanding itself belongs in the play of being and its sign or, said in another way, in the play of an unsignifiable border concept and referential concept that designates appearances in their differentiatedness. Plato refines and develops what

Parmenides discovers in this way, what we call *dialectic*. Plato refines and develops it into a determination of relationships of pure relational possibilities, which are the forms of appearance. In this determination of relationships, concepts can also exemplarily account for nonreferential border concepts, one of which is *being*.

Heidegger explicitly repudiated the possibility of dialectic. At the end of the Zähringen Seminar, he recalls the identifying mark of dialectic as a "genuine philosophic embarrassment" of which Aristotle already had no understanding.[56] Heidegger maintains that "tautology is the only possibility for thinking what dialectic can only veil."[57] One may doubt that this is so and yet rely on Heidegger. In his later notes on phenomenology, there is evidence that it is not dialectic but tautological thinking that is an "embarrassment" and, thus, an ἀπορία.[58] Heidegger holds that the tension between "phenomenology" and ὁδός, considered "methodologically," is "the virtual destitution of saying since the 'Contributions.'"[59] He adds that "all possibilities of a 'system' up to aphorisms" are "dubious."[60] What, on the other hand, "the right determination of the path and the path-field [*Wegfeld*]" could be remains open.[61] In a provisional sense, dialectic would be, conversely, a path in the "path-field" of λόγοι, which, although Heidegger thinks otherwise, was not first treaded by Heraclitus but, rather, by Parmenides.[62] Heidegger's reluctance to go along this path does not change the fact that it is a path.

Notes

1. Heidegger, "End of Philosophy," 55–73.
2. Heidegger, "Seminar in Zähringen 1973," 77.
3. Heidegger, "Seminar in Zähringen," 77.
4. Heidegger, "Seminar in Zähringen," 77.
5. Heidegger, *Parmenides*, 12–13. Cf. Figal, "Seinserfahrung und Übersetzung," 173–84.
6. Heidegger, "Seminar in Zähringen," 77.
7. Heidegger, "Seminar in Zähringen," 78.
8. Heidegger, "Seminar in Zähringen," 80.
9. Heidegger, "Seminar in Zähringen," 79.
10. Heidegger, "Seminar in Zähringen," 79.
11. Heidegger, "Seminar in Zähringen," 79.
12. Heidegger, *Plato's Sophist*, 23.
13. Cf. Heidegger, *Introduction to Metaphysics*, 15. Cf. also Figal, "Heidegger als Aristoteliker," 55–81, 74–81.
14. Heidegger, "Seminar in Zähringen," 79.
15. Heidegger, "Seminar in Zähringen," 79.
16. Heidegger, "Seminar in Zähringen," 79.
17. Heidegger, "Seminar in Zähringen," 79.
18. Translator's note: In subsequent instances in this piece, I have translated *das Selbe* as *Same* (with a capital *S*) in order to denote instances of its special nominal usage.

19. Heidegger, "Seminar in Zähringen," 79.
20. Heidegger, "Seminar in Zähringen," 80.
21. Heidegger, "Seminar in Zähringen," 80.
22. Parmenides, "Fragments," 153.
23. Parmenides, "Fragments," 152.
24. Plato, "Sophist," 252c.
25. Parmenides, "Fragments," 152.
26. Heidegger, "Seminar in Zähringen," 79.
27. Heidegger, "Seminar in Zähringen," 79.
28. Heidegger, "Seminar in Zähringen," 80.
29. Heidegger, *Being and Time*, 31.
30. Heidegger, *Being and Time*, 27.
31. Heidegger, *Being and Time*, 33. Translator's note: Here, the words *show* and *showing* are translations of *zeigen* and *zeigend*, which I have elsewhere translated as *reveal* and *revealing* for the sake of consistency.
32. Heidegger, *Being and Time*, 33.
33. Cf. Heidegger, *Being and Time*, 32: "λόγος as discourse really means δῆλουν, to make manifest."
34. Heidegger, "Auszüge zur Phänomenologie," 70, 62, 89.
35. Heidegger, "Auszüge zur Phänomenologie," 89.
36. Heidegger, "Auszüge zur Phänomenologie," 89.
37. Heidegger, "Auszüge zur Phänomenologie," 62.
38. Heidegger, "Principle of Identity," 27.
39. Parmenides, "Fragments," 152.
40. Heidegger, "Seminar in Zähringen," 80.
41. Heidegger, "End of Philosophy," 65; Heidegger, "Auszüge zur Phänomenologie," 62.
42. Heidegger, *Basic Concepts of Ancient Philosophy*, 53.
43. Heidegger, *Basic Concepts of Ancient Philosophy*, 57.
44. Parmenides, "Fragments," 154.
45. Cf. Heidegger, "Auszüge zur Phänomenologie."
46. Heidegger, "Seminar in Zähringen," 80.
47. Heidegger, "Seminar in Zähringen," 79.
48. Heidegger, "End of Philosophy," 71.
49. Heidegger, "Time and Being," 2.
50. Cf. Heidegger, *Basic Problems of Phenomenology*, 319.
51. Heidegger, "Seminar in Zähringen," 80–81.
52. Heidegger, "End of Philosophy," 71.
53. Heidegger, "End of Philosophy," 71.
54. Heidegger, "End of Philosophy," 72.
55. Heidegger, "Seminar in Zähringen," 81.
56. Heidegger, "Seminar in Zähringen," 81.
57. Heidegger, "Seminar in Zähringen," 81.
58. In *Being and Time* Heidegger translates ἀπορία as *embarrassment* (*Verlegenheit*) and, thus, suggests understanding the "genuine embarrassment" of dialectic as aporia. Cf. Heidegger, *Being and Time*, 22.
59. Heidegger, "Auszüge zur Phänomenologie," 91.

60. Heidegger, "Auszüge zur Phänomenologie," 91.
61. Heidegger, "Auszüge zur Phänomenologie," 91.
62. Heidegger, "Seminar in Zähringen," 81.

Bibliography

Figal, Günter. "Heidegger als Aristoteliker." In *Zu Heidegger. Antworten und Fragen*, 55–81. Frankfurt am Main: Vittorio Klostermann, 2009.

———. "Seinserfahrung und Übersetzung. Hermeneutische Überlegungen zu Heidegger." In *Zu Heidegger. Antworten und Fragen*, 173–84. Frankfurt am Main: Vittorio Klostermann, 2009.

Heidegger, Martin. "Auszüge zur Phänomenologie." In *Vermächtnis der Seinsfrage*, Jahresgabe of the Martin-Heidegger-Gesellschaft 2011–12, Germany, 2012.

———. *Basic Concepts of Ancient Philosophy*. Translated by Richard Rojcewicz. Bloomington: Indiana University Press, 2007.

———. *The Basic Problems of Phenomenology*. Translated by Albert Hofstadter. Bloomington: Indiana University Press, 1982.

———. *Being and Time*. Translated by Joan Stambaugh. Albany: State University of New York Press, 2010.

———. "The End of Philosophy and the Task of Thinking." In *On Time and Being*. Translated by Joan Stambaugh. Chicago: University of Chicago Press, 1972.

———. *Introduction to Metaphysics*. Translated by Gregory Fried and Richard Polt. New Haven, CT: Yale University Press, 2014.

———. *Parmenides*. Translated by André Schuwer and Richard Rojcewicz. Bloomington: Indiana University Press, 1992.

———. *Plato's Sophist*. Translated by Richard Rojcewicz and André Schuwer. Bloomington: Indiana University Press, 1997.

———. "The Principle of Identity." In *Identity and Difference*, 23–41. Translated by Joan Stambaugh. Chicago: University of Chicago Press, 1969.

———. "Seminar in Zähringen 1973." In *Four Seminars*. Translated by Andrew Mitchell and François Raffoul. Bloomington: Indiana University Press, 2003.

———. "Time and Being." In *On Time and Being*. Translated by Joan Stambaugh. Chicago: University of Chicago Press, 1972.

Parmenides. "Fragments." In *Philosophy Before Socrates*, 145–73. Translated by Richard D. McKirahan Jr. Indianapolis: Hackett, 1994.

Plato. "Sophist." Translated by Nicholas P. White. In *Plato: Complete Works*, edited by John M. Cooper. Indianapolis: Hackett, 1997.

GÜNTER FIGAL was until his retirement Professor of Philosophy at the University of Freiburg im Breisgau. He is author of *Objectivity, Aesthetics as Phenomenology*, and many other works both in German and English.

10 Radical Contextuality in Heidegger's Postmetaphysics

The Singularity of Being and the Fourfold

Jussi Backman

1. Being: From Ontotheological Universality to Transitional Singularity

In his *Postmetaphysical Thinking* (1988), Jürgen Habermas describes "radical con-textualism" as the defining mark of "postmodern" thought and as a "manifesta-tion of the spirit of the times."[1] Indeed, the theme of the radical contextuality of meaning is common to a wide variety of contemporary philosophical orien-tations, from hermeneutics, structuralism, poststructuralism, and deconstruc-tion to the ordinary language philosophy rooted in the later Wittgenstein. As opposed to the classical Platonic and Aristotelian model of the ideality and per-manence of the meanings expressed and communicated through material lan-guage, the many variants of the radical contextual approach typically hold that linguistic and discursive meaning is itself context-sensitive and generated in the dynamic and holistic frameworks of different historical languages, cultures, and discursive practices.

In what follows, it will be argued that a certain type of radical contextuality is a key topic of Heidegger's thinking.[2] Heidegger's "contextualism," it must be added, is of a particular kind. It concerns being as such, in the broad phenomeno-logical sense of the intelligible or meaningful givenness of things corresponding to human openness or receptivity to this givenness.[3] In keeping with Heidegger's historical self-interpretation, his position can indeed be designated as "postmeta-physical" in the sense that it calls into question some of the most fundamental presuppositions of the Western metaphysical tradition, the paradigmatic struc-ture of which Heidegger discovers in Aristotle's *Metaphysics*.

For the Aristotelian metaphysical approach, the fundamental problem inherent in the term *being* (*to on, ens*) is its extreme universality. In scholastic terminology, being is a "transcendental" notion, that is, one that transcends the most general kinds of things but is not itself a definable kind or genus.[4] Being pertains to particular instances of *to be* in different senses that are irreducible to any common definition. For Aristotle, however, this does not make *to be* a merely equivocal expression. Everything that is said to *be*, in one sense or another, does share a common point of reference, which eventually turns out to be an *exemplary* sense of *to be*: *ousia*, substantiality or Entity, that is, the being-ness of a determinate particular entity.[5] As opposed to particular material and spatiotemporally situated entities involved in the potentiality and contingency of matter, the supreme and perfect entity that serves as an ideal reference point for all others is a completely actualized, simple, and constant being: the metaphysical divinity (*theos*), whose being, Aristotle argues, consists in the absolutely self-sufficient activity of pure intuitive self-awareness, thought thinking itself (*noēsis noēseōs*).[6] The greatest part of Aristotle's *Metaphysics* thus turns out to be a preparation for the conclusion that the pursued science of being qua being (ontology) is, in fact, achievable only in the form of theology, of the study of the supreme *kind* of entity.[7]

Settling the question of being by referring to a supreme instance of *to be* is what the later Heidegger designates as the "ontotheological" constitution of Aristotelian metaphysics. This he finds at work already in Plato's account of the Idea of the Good as the supreme Idea.[8] In Heidegger's historical narrative, the hierarchical ontotheological model has fundamentally dominated Western metaphysics through medieval Aristotelianism and the modern, post-Cartesian metaphysics of the subject, which shifted the metaphysical Archimedean point from the transcendence of divine self-awareness into the immanent self-awareness of the thinking ego. For Heidegger, the proper culmination of modern metaphysics is Nietzsche. In thinking subjectivity as life and as will to power, that is, as a nonteleological and self-referential movement of self-enhancement in which subjectivity imposes temporary and instrumental "values" upon an inherently valueless and meaningless reality, Nietzsche produced an "inverted Platonism," a "negative ontotheology" that unfolded the final implicit possibilities of the metaphysical tradition and thus exhausted its basic conceptual resources.[9] This exhaustion makes possible the radical reconsideration of the pre-Socratic "first inception" (*der erste Anfang*) of metaphysical thought—a reconsideration that Heidegger, in his later thought, describes as an emerging "transition" (*Übergang*) from the end of metaphysics into "the other inception" (*der andere Anfang*) of Western thought.[10]

This transition is most comprehensively traced out in Heidegger's *Contributions to Philosophy*, written between 1936 and 1938. The transition is, of course, an immensely multifaceted process that Heidegger never exhaustively systematized. Heidegger is mostly content with tentatively pointing out individual aspects of the transition. We will see that a central aspect of this process is the move from the Aristotelian-scholastic understanding of the transcendental universality of being to a postmetaphysical perspective on the singularity of being, or rather on being as singularization—as a spatiotemporal instantiation that is never "the same" in two different instants but rather renders every instance of being intelligible as a unique constellation of meaningful presence.

2. Being as Singularization: Heidegger's "Last Word"

As Reiner Schürmann puts it, the singular event of being, which Heidegger thought in correlation with the singular *there* (*Da*) of openness, is the "other" of the ontological tradition. The singular, Schürmann concludes, is Heidegger's "penultimate" word, and his *last* word is, accordingly, "singularization."[11] The fact that this "last word" has attracted relatively little attention in Heidegger scholarship is at least partly due to the experimental and tentative character of Heidegger's relevant formulations.[12] The uniqueness (*Einzigkeit*) and singularity (*Einmaligkeit*) of being are perhaps most clearly indicated in the following passages from *Contributions* and the subsequent treatise *Mindfulness*:

> Within the realm of the leading question [that is, the Aristotelian metaphysical question concerning being qua being], . . . the essentiality of essence [*Wesen*] consists in the greatest possible generality. . . . By contrast, when beyng [*Seyn*] is grasped as event [*Ereignis*], essentiality is determined in terms of the primordiality and uniqueness [*Einzigkeit*] of beyng itself. The essence is not the general but, rather, precisely the abidance [*Wesung*] of uniqueness in each instant.[13]

> The uniqueness and singularity [*Einmaligkeit*] of beyng are not properties attributed to beyng or even deduced determinations. . . . Rather, beyng itself is uniqueness, is singularity.[14]

Even though the singularity of being does not explicitly emerge as a theme in Heidegger's work until the mid-1930s, formulations foreshadowing this topic can be found in texts from the very outset of his philosophical career. In a 1915 trial lecture on the concept of time in the science of history, echoing the Baden Neo-Kantians, Wilhelm Windelband and Heinrich Rickert, Heidegger calls for a radically "individualizing" historical science, the goal of which would be to "depict the context of the effects and development of the objectifications of human life in the uniqueness [*Einzigartigkeit*] and singularity [*Einmaligkeit*] of these objectifications."[15] In Heidegger's early work, however, the problem of giving an account of the historical situatedness of singular lived situations is not addressed simply as a problem for the methodology of historical science. It is already meant as a challenge to the entire philosophical tradition. In 1923, Heidegger announced the task of elaborating a radicalized ontology—a new approach to the question of being as such—by way of a "hermeneutics of facticity," that is, a radically interpretive phenomenology of concrete lived experience in its context-specific and situated character.[16] This task of elaborating a new fundamental ontology of situatedness set the course for *Being and Time*. In a structural analogy with

Aristotle's metaphysics, fundamental ontology was to articulate the meaning or sense (*Sinn*) of being as such, that is, the basic structural precondition for meaningfulness in general, by way of an analysis of an "exemplary being," an outstanding instance of being.[17] The exemplary being of fundamental ontology is, however, fundamentally different from the Aristotelian God. It is precisely the mortal and finite human *Dasein* that is "exemplary" simply in the sense that it is characterized by an understanding openness to meaning, thus providing the receptive *there* for any meaningful being-there.[18]

The first stage of fundamental ontology, the analytic of Dasein, aims at disclosing temporal situatedness—Dasein's temporality or "timeliness" (*Zeitlichkeit*)—as the basic structure of Dasein's "caring," that is, purpose- and meaning-oriented, existence. After a preparatory analysis of the different categories or modes of existence, the existentials, these existentials are referred back to three temporal ecstases, that is, three dynamic aspects or vectors of Dasein's unitary temporal happening ("temporalization," *Zeitigung*) as contextual and situated.[19] In terms of the ecstasis of futurity or "forthcoming" (*Zukunft*), Dasein "comes forth to itself" from its open futural possibilities by grasping the fact that it has always already come to be in a specific situation (the ecstasis of "already having been," *Gewesenheit*) in terms of the finite possibilities orienting this precise situation.[20] On the basis of this initial temporal contextuality, Dasein is receptive to the concerns of the present (*Gegenwart*), the ecstasis through which the things of the world are primordially given as meaningful in a practical world context (readiness-to-hand or availability, *Zuhandenheit*). Things are available within a temporally multidimensional network of references to practical possibilities and existing practices. Contrary to the "vulgar" linear representation of time as a succession of *now*-points, the three ecstases in their reciprocal interplay are essentially "contemporaneous" (*gleichzeitig*), in the sense that they form a unitary, although complex, process of contextual meaning generation. As Heidegger puts it in his 1936 Schelling lectures, this "at once" (*Zumal*) of the three ecstases is "the singular uniqueness [*einmalige Einzigkeit*] of the inexhaustible fullness of timeliness [*Zeitlichkeit*] itself."[21]

The most "authentic" or "proper" (*eigentlich*), that is, ontologically most primordial, mode of temporal existence is the primarily future-oriented *resoluteness* (*Entschlossenheit*) in which Dasein is released from its ordinarily exclusive immersion in present concerns to experience the full temporal dimensionality of its own being.[22] The ecstasis of the present is thereby singularized into an *instant* (*Augenblick*),[23] an instantaneous "glance of the eye" into the unique context specificity of one's singular situation and into the situated, processual identity of Da-sein as "in each instance mine" (*je meines*).[24] In brief, in the instant, Dasein grasps a singular constellation of meaningfulness in its temporally constituted singularity and its own receptivity to such singularity. As Heidegger puts it in his 1924–25 lecture course, the instant is "*catching sight of the just-this-once [Diesmaligen]*, of the concrete singularity [*Diesmaligkeit*] of the instantaneous situation [*augen-blicklichen Lage*]."²⁵ In the 1929–30 lectures, the instant is described as what "properly makes *Dasein* possible. . . . This instant is the look of the resoluteness of *Dasein* for being-the-there [*Da-sein*], the being-the-there that, in each instance [*je*], is in such a way that it exists in the situation it has unreservedly seized upon, an existing which is in each instance singular [*einmalige*] and unique [*einzige*]."²⁶

Fundamental ontology seeks a path from Dasein's timeliness to the tempo-rality (*Temporalität*) of being as such—that is, to the contextual singularity of the givenness of meaningful presence. Heidegger's potentially misleading character-izations of the disclosure of being as a "transcendental cognition" and of being as the "*transcendens* pure and simple" are modified by the following remark: "The transcendence of the being of *Dasein* is a distinctive one since in it lies the pos-sibility and necessity of the most radical *individuation*."²⁷ Being is "transcen-dental," no longer in the scholastic sense of that which is most universal and transcends all limited determinations, but rather in the sense of the contextualiz-ing horizon that transcends simple and immediate presence and, in its structural correlation with Dasein's temporally contextual receptivity to meaning, "gives" meaningful presence as singular.²⁸

The completion of fundamental ontology would ultimately have required a turnabout or reversal (*Kehre*) of its initial approach, a turning back to reconsider Dasein on the basis of the temporal sense of being, in order to render visible the reciprocity of the structural correlation between being and Dasein.²⁹ Already in *Being and Time*, Heidegger points out that Dasein is the point from which fun-damental ontology sets out and to which it must again revert (*zurückschlagen*).³⁰ Furthermore, in 1928 Heidegger explicitly announces that after the completion of the temporal analytic, fundamental ontology is to undergo a conversion into a "metontology" or "metaphysical ontic," that is, a "post-ontology" or "reverse ontology" in which beings are to be approached again in terms of an explica-tion of the sense of being.³¹ This turn or conversion was to be accomplished in the missing Division I.3 of *Being and Time*, "Time and Being." It turned out, however, to be unfeasible within the conceptual framework of fundamental ontology, which Heidegger eventually deemed to be too deeply anchored in tra-ditional terminology.³² During the early 1930s, Heidegger therefore concentrates his efforts on developing his discourse with the help of "reversed" expressions. Most conspicuously, fundamental ontology's vocabulary of going outside and beyond—*existence, ecstasis,* and *transcendence,* terms that could still be con-strued as implying an outset in a self-immanent subjectivity that is only subse-quently exceeded—is replaced by a vocabulary of entering and remaining within. The seemingly converse turn from designating Dasein's mode of being as "exis-tence" (*Existenz,* literally, "standing out") to "insistency" (*Inständigkeit,* literally, "standing in") in the "there" shifts the emphasis to the fact that the singular and situated disclosure of being in specific beings is "entered" *from* a preceding, sin-gularizing background context and not vice versa.[33]

An "instant" of meaningful presence is thus literally a "standing within" (Latin: *in-stans*) a specific meaning context. On the other hand, Heidegger now reconsiders the development of the metaphysical tradition in the light of a deepened perspective on the historicity of being itself. The various epochs in the metaphysical tradition are now regarded as articulations of the respective experiences of being in its historically situated configurations. The transitional experience of being as singularization is not presented as a genial insight into some underlying suprahistorical truth that was there all along. This experi-ence is, rather, a new instant—Heidegger presents it, at this point, as a pure possibility—in which the entire tradition from which it has emerged would gain a transformed meaning.[34]

The fruit of these reconsiderations is *Contributions to Philosophy*, which looks at the postmetaphysical transitional situation with a view to an emerging possibility of thinking, namely, articulating being postmetaphysically as event (*Ereignis*). As its parenthesized subtitle, *Vom Ereignis*—literally *of* or *from* the event—emphasizes, being is no longer approached by way of the exemplary recep-tive being, Dasein. Rather, the point of departure is the event of being itself, in the sense of the reciprocal correlation between the contextual givenness of mean-ing and Dasein, which is no longer simply identified with human being as such but rather understood as a determinate possibility of human being.[35] Heidegger's textual strategy in *Contributions* is to emphasize the difference between the tran-sitional approach to being as singularization and the traditional metaphysical notion of being as extreme universality by designating the former with the obso-lete German orthography *Seyn*, translated into English as "beyng" or "beying," and the latter with *Sein*.[36] *Ereignis*, the title for the basic dynamic character of *Seyn*, is the event or the "taking place" of historical singularity in which meaningful presence "finds its place"—in other words, is contextualized and situated within the "instantaneous site" (*Augenblicksstätte*) of spatiotemporal situatedness (*Zeit-Raum*) furnished by Dasein. As a situated site of the event of meaningful pres-ence, Dasein "corresponds to the uniqueness of beyng as event [*Ereignis*]."[37] As Heidegger later notes, he uses the word *Ereignis* as a *singulare tantum*, a noun (like *wine* or *sugar*) singular by definition: *Ereignis* is not a general term compre-hending a multiplicity of single events but rather refers to the singularization of the singular as such.[38]

3. The Fourfold Contextuality of Singular Presence

The topics of radical contextuality and singularization are particularly relevant for understanding the purpose of one of the most important and most enigmatic figures of Heidegger's later thought: the *fourfold*, first introduced in its definitive form in the 1949 Bremen lecture on "The Thing" and reappearing in texts of the 1950s.[39] The fourfold is a model consisting of two pairs—sky (*Himmel*) and earth (*Erde*), divinities (*die Göttlichen*) and mortals (*die Sterblichen*)—intersecting in a "onefold of four," in the complicated unity of a singular thing. This can be seen as Heidegger's most ambitious articulation of being as the event of the contextual singularization of the meaningful presence of things to the human being.[40] As Graham Harman points out, the primary weakness of the fourfold is the fact that Heidegger never adequately links it to the rest of his project; it rather "seems to drop magically from the clouds."[41] Heidegger did, however, apparently incubate the figure for a long time, only to leave it more or less embryonic. An early diagram of the fourfold can be found already in *Contributions*.[42] In the lectures of the same period, notably the 1934–35 Hölderlin course,[43] *Introduction to Metaphysics* (1935),[44] and "The Origin of the Work of Art" (1935–36),[45] Heidegger develops related models.[46] It appears that at this point Heidegger had begun to consider the three-dimensional ecstatic temporal model of *Being and Time* an insufficient account of the contextuality involved in a singular meaningful situation.

Jean-François Mattéi has interestingly suggested a structural analogy between Heidegger's fourfold and the Aristotelian doctrine of the four causes.[47] This approach is all the more compelling since Heidegger, in "On the Essence of Ground" (1929), explicitly connects the three temporal ecstases, as three modes of providing "grounds" for a meaningful situation, to the traditional metaphysical question concerning the fundamental kinds of reasons or causes. In this text, Heidegger also points to the lack of unity and ultimate justification of the four Aristotelian causes. He adds, however, that there is "an unmistakable orientation toward illuminating ground in general in an originary manner" in Aristotle, who "was not content merely to list the 'four causes' alongside one another, but was concerned with understanding their interconnection and the grounding of this fourfold division."[48] The Aristotelian causes articulate different factors that account for the presence of a particular material entity, making it warranted and comprehensible; they are different types of answer to the question, "Why [this, rather than something else]?"[49] For Heidegger, the fourfold clearly has an analogous function: it articulates the basic structure of the multidimensional context that individuates and singularizes a thing as a situated instance of meaningful presence.

This should not, of course, mask the profound differences between the two fourfold models. For Aristotle, a thing is an ontologically independent and (relatively) self-sufficient entity; its "causes" are either aspects of its intrinsic ontological structure (form and matter) or other entities (its originator, such as its producer, and the final cause, ultimately divine perfection) to which it stands in an extrinsic relationship.[50] In the 1949 Bremen lectures and the associated 1953 lecture, "The

Question concerning Technology," Heidegger maintains that the Aristotelian doctrine of the four causes is fundamentally related to the process of *production* (*poiēsis*), which, he insists, provides the basic ontological model for Platonic and Aristotelian metaphysics. In his view, Plato and Aristotle basically articulate entities as *products*, that is, as particular implementations of an ideal prototype.[51] By contrast, as is clear already from *Being and Time*, the Heideggerian model first and foremost applies to things as they are encountered in the context of concernful dealings, of *use* and *employment*. In this model, a thing as a singular focal point of meaningfulness is *nothing but* a "onefold of four," in other words, a temporary intersection of four dimensions involved in a *practical* situation.[52] These dimensions are not things or entities in their own right.[53] They are merely evoked and referred to and thereby "employed," in the literal meaning of the German *dingen* ("to hire," "to employ"): engaged, gathered, enfolded in and by the thing, and thus "present" only indirectly *as* references or orientations, *in* and *through* their "employment."[54] The focal point of a practice and the practical context it focalizes are not two separate relata of an extrinsic relation. Rather, they presuppose each other and are intelligible only in terms of their reciprocal interplay.

The basic phenomenological function of the fourfold can be illustrated with the help of a simple and concrete example. The fundamental Platonic orientation of philosophical inquiry toward the realm of ideas is motivated by the insight that any concrete and particular spatiotemporal thing is, to a certain extent, in each instant singular.[55] My desk, for example, is never *exactly* identical in two different instants. What does persist as identical is its specific whatness, that is, its ideal desk-ness; its numerical self-identity (its being *this* desk and no other) is dependent upon its species-identity (its being a *desk*). Aristotle concludes, with Plato, that the primary (but not exclusive) aspect of the entity-ness of entities is their conceptual determinacy, that is, their universal form.[56] It is an ontological deficiency of concrete particulars that they are not simply equivalent to their form but require spatiotemporal instantiation in matter in order to be actualized as being "there," as a "this-here-now."

In the transitional perspective outlined by Heidegger, the determinate and persistent conceptual self-identity of my desk in each instance would, however, no longer be seen as the primary and predominant feature of its being there. Account would rather be taken of the full context-specificity that makes my desk singularly meaningful to me in each concrete practical situation: it is now a storeroom for my books, now a support for my computer, now a surface on which to place my cup of coffee, now a concrete example to be used in my work, and so on. The whatness of the desk is, of course, there as a constitutive element of permanent identity in each instant of the desk's presence. If at any moment I ask myself *what* this thing before me is, I already distance myself from my current practical involvement with it, and the answer will almost inevitably be that it is a *desk*. But as Plato himself shows in the *Republic*, the "Idea" that guarantees the applicability of the name is, first and foremost, a certain kind of function.[57] The applicability of the name *desk* obviously depends on whether or not the thing at hand can function as a desk. The desk can be painted red, and it will still be a desk, but if its legs are cut off, it is no longer truly worthy of the name *desk*, at least in its usual sense.

Plato, however, does not take the analysis further. He focuses on just one of altogether four relevant factors at play here.

1. For Plato, the primary factor involved in the ideal conceptual identity of a thing is, as we saw, its *functionality*. However, this functionality has now turned out to be dependent on three other factors.

2. Another aspect of the meaningful functional presence of my desk is clearly its sheer *materiality*. This materiality is defined by the desk's material makeup, its implementation, and its current material condition (for example, its being worn down and cluttered with books and papers). This materiality delimits its capacity to fulfill its function as my desk. This factor was, to a certain extent, recognized already in ancient metaphysics. Plato himself implicitly acknowledges that an understanding of what a thing *is* involves an understanding of what kind of material implementation can fulfill its determining function. Aristotle's basic critique of Plato is that the conceptual forms of concrete things, as universal and common to many instances, are not substances, that is, not *there* in their own right, but only insofar as they are materially instantiated.[58]

3. On a further level, it can be argued that I can encounter my desk as a functioning desk only in the context of a *purposive* project involving a desk, such as writing an article or organizing my papers. Moreover, such projects are arguably meaningful only with regard to more and more comprehensive projects, such as philosophical study and academic scholarship, professionalism and intellectual work in general, and so on. The purposes of such projects are ultimately dependent upon the comprehensive "purposes of life" that orient me as a member of a specific community—in other words, the ultimate ends and aims, if any, orienting all particular projects within a given cultural context.

4. Immediately connected to the previous factor is the historically specific *cultural and communal* dimension that delimits in advance the kinds of projects I am likely to be involved in. It is within a particular historical community that certain overarching purposes (such as academic scholarship) are shared and certain individual projects (such as writing academic papers) make sense. Arguably, something can function as a desk—and consequently be subsumed under the concept *desk*—only in a certain kind of culture that allows certain practices, projects, and ends. Nonliterate cultures do not have desks because they have no use for them, lacking the relevant practices.

Beyond the dimension that the Platonic-Aristotelian tradition has perceived as alone or primarily constitutive of the beingness of my desk—namely, related to the first factor, its whatness—three interrelated dimensions of functional meaningfulness can thus be distinguished: its particular materiality, the practical context of ends and purposes to which it belongs, and the historical, cultural, and communal context within which such practices and projects, as well as their ends, are shared.

The point of distinguishing these four dimensions is to suggest the following preliminary interpretation of the fourfold:

1. *Sky* can be understood as the realm of shared and visible openness, of articulated appearing and appearance. As the dimension of visibility and articulation, its function is analogous to that of the "formal cause" or conceptual form (*eidos, logos*) in Aristotelian metaphysics. Heidegger's sky is, however, clearly not the Platonic "heaven"[59] of eternally stable Ideas or forms but rather a dynamic historical and cultural sphere of appearing that is constituted only in an interaction with the other dimensions.[60] An indication of this can be found in Heidegger's 1957 essay on the poet Johann Friedrich Hebel, in which the "sky" in Hebel's work is interpreted as standing for non-sensuous "sense" (*Sinn*) or "spirit" (*Geist*). "Sky" intertwines with "earth," the symbol for the "sensuous" (*das Sinnliche*), to form the "sensuous sense" of (linguistic) meaning.[61]

2. The *earth*, as the counterpart of sky, is the opaque dimension of inarticulate materiality, the "ground" or "soil" that grants here-and-now-ness to things. Its function is analogous to the Aristotelian "material cause." Aristotle, however, subordinates matter (*hylē*) to form as the ontological "residue" in things that are not simply identical with their form but that require spatio-temporal instantiation in order to be actualized. Conversely, Heidegger, in "The Origin of the Work of Art," characterizes the relation between earth and "world" (the historical realm of relational meaning comprising aspects of the "sky," "mortals," and "divinities") as "strife" (*Streit*).[62] This emphasizes that materiality and articulation are equally primordial and irreducibly interdependent aspects.[63]

3. The *divinities* or *gods* are the orienting dimension of ideals, aims, norms, final purposes, or "values." As the plural form emphasizes, in spite of the analogy they do not simply correspond to the Aristotelian God as an absolute "final cause" for all things.[64] The Heideggerian gods are the gods of a specific people, that is to say, historically and culturally situated ideals and ends.

4. The *mortals*, that is, finite and situated humanity, are the dimension of culture and community, of historical and cultural facticity, and of communal and linguistic receptivity to shared experience with regard for shared ideals and norms.[65] This dimension is parallel to the Aristotelian "efficient cause," which Aristotle generally associates with the human being as an initiating

agent, but first and foremost in the role of a "producer," as the initiator of a process of production or implementation.

4. Conclusion: Singularity and the History of Being

We have argued that the theme of the radical contextuality of being—of the embeddedness of each instance of meaningful presence in a multidimensional context of references that makes it meaningful in a unique and singular way—runs through Heidegger's work, from his fundamental ontology to his mature thinking of *Ereignis*. We also presented a tentative reading of Heidegger's fourfold (*Geviert*) as his most developed articulation of this contextuality, building on the incomplete account of the temporal sense of being in *Being and Time*. The remaining step is to consider the implications of this fourfold contextuality for the postmetaphysical approach to being as singular and historically configured.

When each instance of being is regarded as constituted by *all* of the four dimensions of the fourfold described above, none of which has any independent subsistence but is irreducibly intertwined with the other three, it becomes evident that no two instances can be simply equivalent to each other in the sense of manifesting some homogeneous universal form. Each situation is rather a heterogeneous and complicated configuration of multiple dimensions. This singularity of particular constellations of the fourfold is indicated by Heidegger's words: "Each thing arrests [*verweilt*] the fourfold into an instance of the resting [*in ein je Weiliges*] of the onefold of the world. . . . Only what is compliantly conjoined [*gering*] from a world becomes a thing once [*einmal*]."[66]

What, then, becomes of the persistent identity of meanings that their ideality was supposed to guarantee? Here, close attention must be paid to Heidegger's distinction between two senses of "identity" or "sameness": *das Gleiche*, "alike," "equal," or "equivalent," and *das Selbe*, "identical" in the sense of "one and the same" or "selfsame." The former designates a homogeneous unity, a lack of distinction; it "constantly moves toward the indifferent [*Unterschiedslose*]," dispersing differences into "the bleak unity of what is one in a merely uniform manner [*einförmig*]."[67] The latter, by contrast, is a heterogeneous and complex unity, a "belonging-together of the diverse," a Heraclitean harmony of the discordant that "gathers what is distinct into a primordial unison [*Einigkeit*]."[68] This distinction offers a new point of view on the difference between Aristotelian metaphysics and Heideggerian postmetaphysics. It is precisely a hallmark of Aristotle's question concerning being qua being to look for a common denominator, something equal and equivalent in all particular beings, some "indifferent oneness." "Being as such" (*to on*) is shown by Aristotle not to be such a principle; the only common feature that can be discovered in all instances of *to be* is their membership in the *hierarchy* of being, which entails a ubiquitous reference to the universally valid, constantly intelligible, and accessible supreme entity as an ideal of *perfect* being. Heidegger's thinking of being, however, is not a quest for a universally equivalent principle. What is "identical" in Heidegger's sense of "selfsame" in each instance of being, in each meaningful situation, is simply the *singular situatedness* in a meaningful context that differentiates situations. Being is not something that precedes individual situations or instants in order to be instantiated in them. Being is, rather, this *event of instantiation as such*, the "employment" of the fourfold context into the onefold-ness of a singular thing. As Heidegger puts it in *Contributions*: "The eternal is not the incessant; rather, it is that which can withdraw in the instant so as to return once more. That which can return, not as the *equal* [*das Gleiche*] but as what transforms ever anew, the one-unique [*Eine-Einzige*], beyng [*Seyn*], such that in this manifestness it is at first not recognized as the selfsame [*das Selbe*]!"[69]

The contextual singularity of being does not mean that each instant flashes forth once and then vanishes into the past without a trace. Nor is it simply retained in the form of a past present. Each instant rather dynamically transforms and modifies the "already having been," the factical background of subsequent instants from which their respective futural prospects emerge. It remains as an aspect of the tradition that admits of being "repeated," in Heidegger's emphatic sense of *retrieval* (*Wiederholung*) as a transformative reappropriation of a situation that has already been, not as mere reproduction of something past.[70] To retrieve an instant is to experience it anew in the context of another instant, in which it will, however, always have a transformed meaning. "*Only the singular* [*das Einmalige*] *can be re-trieved*."[71] It is precisely because of its singularity that being can "have" a "history" (*Geschichte*) in the sense of the series of transformative reappropriations of the first, Greek inception of the Western philosophical engagement with being and of the different encounters with being made possible by these transformations—a series that constitutes the unfolding of Western metaphysics.[72] Or rather, "the history of being is being itself and only that"[73]: being *is* the historical unfolding of meaningfulness in singular situations that are never mutually equivalent but nevertheless constitute a continuous tradition of retrieval and inheritance. "The unity and cohesiveness of history [*Geschichte*] is determined in terms of the uniqueness of beyng. *In* uniqueness every single thing is in each instance unique and only *thus* belongs to the One. The essential relations to history are grounded not in that which is general in a multiplicity . . . but in the uniqueness of the simple."[74]

Notes

For extremely helpful comments on earlier versions of this essay, I thank Brendan Mahoney and Andrew Mitchell, as well as the editors of this volume. For an in-depth discussion of these topics, see Backman, *Complicated Presence*.

1. Habermas, *Nachmetaphysisches Denken*, 58–59, 153–55, 179; *Postmetaphysical Thinking*, 49–50, 115–17, 139. On historical singularization as a specifically "postmodern" topos, see Magnússon, "Singularization of History."

2. Brent Slife ("Information and Time," 533–50) mentions Heidegger's "radical contextuality and holism."

3. As Thomas Sheehan concisely puts it: "As a phenomenologist, Heidegger understands *Sein* in all its historical incarnations as the *meaningful presence* (*Anwesen*) of things to human beings—that is, as the changing *significance* of things within various contexts of human interests and concerns" (*Making Sense of Heidegger*, xii). The question of being thus also inherently involves a question of the *correlation* between encountered things and the corresponding human concerns and intentions.

4. The term *(nomina) transcendentia* is used by Thomas Aquinas (*Summa theologiae* 1.30.3; 1.39.3; 1.93.3) of being (*ens*), unity (*unum*), truth (*verum*), and goodness (*bonum*). The form *transcendentalia* was introduced in the seventeenth century.

5. Aristotle, *Metaphysics* 4.2.1003a33–b16; 7.1.1028a13–b7; Cf. Owens, *Doctrine of Being*, 265. I borrow the translation of *ousia* as "Entity/entity" from Owens (137–54).

6. Aristotle, *Metaphysics* 12.6.1071b2–7.1073a13; 12.9.1074b15–1075a10.

7. See Aristotle, *Metaphysics* 6.1.1026a18–32. Cf. Owens, *Doctrine of Being*, 300, 453–54.

8. On ontotheology, see, for example, Heidegger, *Wegmarken*, 235–36, 378–79; *Pathmarks*, 180–81, 287–88; *Nietzsche*, vol. 2, 311–15; *Nietzsche*, vol. 4, *Nihilism*, 207–10; *Identität und Differenz*, 31–67; *Identity and Difference*, 42–74.

9. See, for example, Heidegger, *Nietzsche*, vol. 1, 415–32; *Nietzsche*, vol. 2, *Eternal Recurrence*, 198–208; *Nietzsche*, vol. 2, 1–22, 177–229, 231–361; *Nietzsche*, vol. 3, *Will to Power*, 161–251; *Nietzsche*, vol. 4, *Nihilism*, 147–250.

10. See, for example, Heidegger, *Beiträge zur Philosophie*, 4–6; *Contributions to Philosophy*, 6–8. Cf. *Nietzsche*, vol. 2, 21; *Nietzsche*, vol. 3, *Will to Power*, 182.

11. Schürmann, *Des hégémonies brisées*, 718, 733; *Broken Hegemonies*, 581, 594. Cf. Schürmann, *Heidegger on Being and Acting*, 12–13, 219; "Ultimate Double Binds," 243–46. See also White, *Logic and Ontology in Heidegger*, 194–95; Nancy, *L'expérience de la liberté*, 91–93; *Experience of Freedom*, 66–68; *La communauté désœuvrée*, 191–92; *Inoperative Community*, 103–5; Greisch, "La parole d'origine," 204; Ruin, *Enigmatic Origins*, 206; Narbonne, *Hénologie, ontologie et Ereignis*, 204, 211–12, 244–82; Beistegui, *Truth and Genesis*, 147; Malpas, *Heidegger's Topology*, 16, 86, 173, 244, 313; Ziarek, *Language after Heidegger*, 33–41.

12. Heidegger also seems to speak of the uniqueness (*Einzigkeit*) of being in a wider and more indeterminate sense in which it encompasses even the traditional metaphysical notion of being as the unique "one over many" (*Einführung in die Metaphysik*, 60; *Introduction to Metaphysics*, 83; *Grundbegriffe*, 51–54; *Basic Concepts*, 43–46).

13. Heidegger, *Beiträge zur Philosophie*, 66; *Contributions to Philosophy*, 53; translation modified.

14. Heidegger, *Besinnung*, 128; *Mindfulness*, 108; translation modified.

15. Heidegger, *Frühe Schriften*, 427; *Supplements*, 56; translation modified. Here, Heidegger is picking up Wilhelm Windelband's famous distinction between the "nomothetic" explanatory generalization characteristic of natural sciences and the "idiographic" descriptive study of individual historical phenomena that is particular to the humanities (Windelband, *Präludien*, 136–60; "History and Natural Science"). This distinction became a central theme in the Southwest or Baden School of Neo-Kantianism,

which had an unmistakable influence on the young Heidegger. Cf. Barash, *Martin Heidegger and the Problem of Historical Meaning*, 20–63.

16. Heidegger, *Ontologie*, 1–3; *Ontology*, 1–3.

17. This structural analogy between fundamental ontology and Aristotelian metaphysics is emphasized by Heidegger (*Geschichte der Philosophie von Thomas von Aquin bis Kant*, 60; *Grundprobleme der Phänomenologie*, 26; *Basic Problems of Phenomenology*, 19–20; *Metaphysische Anfangsgründe der Logik*, 201–2; *Metaphysical Foundations of Logic*, 158).

18. Heidegger, *Sein und Zeit*, 6–7; *Being and Time*, 5–6; cf. Heidegger, *Sein und Zeit*, 439n7[c]; *Being and Time*, 6n§.

19. Heidegger, *Sein und Zeit*, 323–31; *Being and Time*, 309–16. For the characterization of the ecstases as "vectors" of the unitary movement of temporalization, see Protevi, *Time and Exteriority*, 126.

20. I borrow the apt rendering of *Zukunft* as "forthcoming" from Chernyakov, *Ontology of Time*, 192.

21. Heidegger, *Schellings Abhandlung*, 136; *Schelling's Treatise*, 113–14; translation modified. Cf. Heidegger, "Unbenutzte Vorarbeiten zur Vorlesung vom Wintersemester 1929/30," 11; *Zur Sache des Denkens*, 14–16; *On Time and Being*, 14–16. See also Pöggeler, *Der Denkweg Martin Heideggers*, 251; *Martin Heidegger's Path of Thinking*, 203.

22. On resoluteness, see Heidegger, *Sein und Zeit*, 295–310, 325–30, 338–39, 382–87; *Being and Time*, 282–88, 311–15, 323–24, 364–68.

23. Heidegger, *Sein und Zeit*, 328, 338; *Being and Time*, 313, 323.

24. Heidegger, *Sein und Zeit*, 41; *Being and Time*, 41.

25. Heidegger, *Platon: Sophistes*, 163–64; *Plato's Sophist*, 112; translation modified.

26. Heidegger, *Die Grundbegriffe der Metaphysik*, 251; *Fundamental Concepts of Metaphysics*, 169; translation modified. As William McNeill (*The Glance of the Eye*) has shown, the instant (*Augenblick*) is Heidegger's reappropriation of the kind of intuitive apprehending of a singular situation that Aristotle attributes to practical insight or prudence (*phronēsis*). Designating the instant as Dasein's most primordial mode of receptivity inverts the Aristotelian subordination of *phronēsis* to comprehensive understanding or wisdom (*sophia*), which is characterized by an intuitive apprehending of the supremely *universal* determinations. Cf. Aristotle, *Nicomachean Ethics* 6.7.1141a16–b16; 6.8.1142a23–30, 6.11.1143a32–b5.

27. Heidegger, *Sein und Zeit*, 38; *Being and Time*, 36. Cf. Heidegger, *Sein und Zeit*, 3; *Being and Time*, 2.

28. Cf. Heidegger, *Sein und Zeit*, 440n38[a]; *Being and Time*, 36n*. See also Slife, "Information and Time," 542.

29. Cf. Heidegger, *Zur Sache des Denkens*, 34; *On Time and Being*, 31; Preface to *Heidegger: Through Phenomenology to Thought*, XVII–XXII. See also von Herrmann, *Die Selbstinterpretation Martin Heideggers*, 264–78; *Wege ins Ereignis*, 67–68; Gadamer, *Gesammelte Werke*, vol. 3, 191; *Heidegger's Ways*, 20–21; Sheehan, *Making Sense of Heidegger*, 231–45; Backman, *Complicated Presence*, 121–53.

30. Heidegger, *Sein und Zeit*, 38, 436; *Being and Time*, 36, 413.

31. Heidegger, *Metaphysische Anfangsgründe der Logik*, 199–202; *Metaphysical Foundations of Logic*, 156–59.

32. Heidegger, *Wegmarken*, 327–28; *Pathmarks*, 249–50.

33. Heidegger, *Beiträge zur Philosophie*, 319, 467; *Contributions to Philosophy*, 253, 368; *Besinnung*, 144–45; *Mindfulness*, 123; *Die Metaphysik des deutschen Idealismus*, 54;

Wegmarken, 325–26; *Pathmarks*, 247–49. Cf. Heidegger, *Beiträge zur Philosophie*, 322; *Contributions to Philosophy*, 255.

34. Cf. Heidegger, *Zur Sache des Denkens*, 44, 53–58; *On Time and Being*, 41, 49–54.

35. Heidegger, *Beiträge zur Philosophie*, 319; *Contributions to Philosophy*, 252.

36. I adopt here the established English rendering of *Seyn* as *beyng*. The use of this obsolete eighteenth-century German orthography is supposedly meant to stress the "anteriority" of being as *Ereignis* in relation to the metaphysical perspective on being; the early modern English variant *beyng* (used in sixteenth-century texts interchangeably with *beynge* and *being*) thus performs roughly the same function. Heidegger adopts the use of *Seyn* in his first lecture course on Hölderlin (*Hölderlins Hymnen "Germanien" und "Der Rhein"*; *Hölderlin's Hymns "Germania" and "The Rhine"*), and it can thus be taken also as a reference to Hölderlin as the postmetaphysical poet. It should be noted that Heidegger later drops even this spelling, noting that it is improper to use any cognate of *Sein* for postmetaphysical purposes (*Holzwege*, 364n[d]; *Off the Beaten Track*, 275n[a]).

37. Heidegger, *Beiträge zur Philosophie*, 375; *Contributions to Philosophy*, 296. Cf. Heidegger, *Beiträge zur Philosophie*, 323, 384; *Contributions to Philosophy*, 255–56, 303–4. See also Ruin, *Enigmatic Origins*, 200–201; Beistegui, *Truth and Genesis*, 147.

38. Heidegger, *Identität und Differenz*, 25; *Identity and Difference*, 36.

39. Heidegger, *Bremer und Freiburger Vorträge*, 11–12, 17–21; *Bremen and Freiburg Lectures*, 10–12, 16–19; *Vorträge und Aufsätze*, 164–66, 170–75; *Poetry, Language, Thought*, 170–72, 175–80. Cf. *Erläuterungen zu Hölderlins Dichtung*, 152–81; *Elucidations of Hölderlin's Poetry*, 175–208; *Vorträge und Aufsätze*, 139–56; *Poetry, Language, Thought*, 143–59; *Unterwegs zur Sprache*, 9–33, 157–216; *Poetry, Language, Thought*, 187–208; *On the Way to Language*, 57–110.

40. Polt (*Emergency of Being*, 74n97) and Mitchell (*Fourfold*, 3–4) point out Heidegger's (perhaps exaggerated) statement, in a 1964 letter to Dieter Sinn (cited in Sinn, *Ereignis und Nirwana*, 172), according to which the "thing lecture" was thus far his only published attempt to present his thinking directly "on its own terms," rather than relating it to the tradition.

41. Harman, "Dwelling with the Fourfold," 294. This is without doubt the reason for the "tragic mistake," noted by Harman, that "no major concept of Heidegger's career has received less detailed treatment than the fourfold" (292). For a more extensive discussion of my reading of the fourfold, see Backman, *Complicated Presence*, 135–53, 165–69, 180, 190–202. Andrew Mitchell's recent outstanding work *The Fourfold: Reading the Late Heidegger* is one of the only book-length studies on the topic. Among other major contributions toward a concrete interpretation are those of Jean-François Mattéi ("Le chiasme heideggérien"; "Heideggerian Chiasmus"; "L'étoile et le sillon"; "Le quadruple fondement"; *Heidegger et Hölderlin*; "La quadruple énigme de l'être"), James C. Edwards (*Plain Sense of Things*, 165–94), Karsten Harries (*Ethical Function of Architecture*, 158–62), and Graham Harman (*Tool-Being*, 190–204; *Heidegger Explained*, 131–35; "Dwelling with the Fourfold").

42. Heidegger, *Beiträge zur Philosophie*, 310; *Contributions to Philosophy*, 246.

43. Heidegger, *Hölderlins Hymnen "Germanien" und "Der Rhein,"* 245; *Hölderlin's Hymns "Germania" and "The Rhine,"* 222–23.

44. Heidegger, *Einführung in die Metaphysik*, 149; *Introduction to Metaphysics*, 209.

45. Heidegger, *Holzwege*, 1–74; *Off the Beaten Track*, 1–56.

46. For a discussion of the "prehistory" of the fourfold in Heidegger's work of the 1930s, see Backman, *Complicated Presence*, 135–53.

47. Mattéi, "L'étoile et le sillon"; "Le quadruple fondement"; *Heidegger et Hölderlin*, 33–85, 189–271; "Le quadruple énigme de l'être," 136–37. It should be noted, however, that Mattéi's way of construing the analogy differs from the model suggested here: Mattéi associates the sky with the efficient cause, earth with final cause, divinities with formal cause, and mortals with material cause ("L'étoile et le sillon," 61–65; *Heidegger et Hölderlin*, 201).

48. Heidegger, *Wegmarken*, 124; *Pathmarks*, 98.

49. Aristotle, *Physics* 2.1.194b16–195a26; *Metaphysics* 5.2.1013a24–b28.

50. Heidegger notes Aristotle's failure to distinguish between "ontical" causes (other entities) and transcendental causes (ontological structures) (*Wegmarken*, 170–71; *Pathmarks*, 131).

51. Heidegger, *Bremer und Freiburger Vorträge*, 6–7; *Bremen and Freiburg Lectures*, 6–7; *Vorträge und Aufsätze*, 11–17, 160–61; *Basic Writings*, 313–19; *Poetry, Language, Thought*, 166–67.

52. For an elegant articulation of Heidegger's thing as a "focus" or "focal point" of a practice, see Borgmann, *Technology and the Character of Contemporary Life*, 196–99; cf. Roesner, *Metaphysica ludens*, 237.

53. Heidegger, *Erläuterungen zu Hölderlins Dichtung*, 170; *Elucidations of Hölderlin's Poetry*, 194–95.

54. Heidegger, *Bremer und Freiburger Vorträge*, 13; *Bremen and Freiburg Lectures*, 12; *Vorträge und Aufsätze*, 166; *Poetry, Language, Thought*, 171–72. On the etymologies of *Ding*, *thing*, and *employing*, see Grimm and Grimm, *Deutsches Wörterbuch*, 1169–72; Klein, *Comprehensive Etymological Dictionary*, 516, 1607.

55. See, e.g., Plato, *Cratylus* 432d4–440d2.

56. Aristotle, *Metaphysics* 7.17.1041a6–b33.

57. Plato, *Republic* 10.596b12–608b10.

58. See, e.g., Aristotle, *Metaphysics* 7.8.1033a24–1034a8.

59. In the *Phaedrus*, Plato famously situates the ideas in a "place beyond the heavens" (*hyperouranios topos*) (247c3).

60. James C. Edwards interprets *sky* as standing for the "ongoing social practices . . . within which things come to presence as the things they are," as the "illuminating linguistic and behavioral practices that constitute us and our common world" (*Plain Sense of Things*, 170). For Andrew Mitchell, the sky is the "wide expanse of appearance" and the "space of the earth's irruption" that is "nothing inert or stable, but constantly aflutter with the streaming of . . . relations" (*Fourfold*, 116, 307); Mitchell also emphasizes the "natural" association between the sky and time (145–62).

61. Heidegger, *Aus der Erfahrung des Denkens 1910–1976*, 150; "Hebel," 100.

62. Heidegger, *Holzwege*, 35–36; *Off the Beaten Track*, 26–27.

63. Cf. Haar, *Le chant de la terre*, 122–33; *Song of the Earth*, 57–64; Edwards, *Plain Sense of Things*, 169–70; Dreyfus, "Heidegger's Ontology of Art," 411–13; Mitchell, *Fourfold*, 71–115.

64. Aristotle, *Metaphysics* 12.7.1072a21–27.

65. Cf. Edwards: "To know oneself to be mortal . . . is to know that . . . *everything* . . . is contingent upon a constellation of circumstances that will someday no longer hold together" (*Plain Sense of Things*, 173).

66. Heidegger, *Bremer und Freiburger Vorträge*, 20, 21; *Bremen and Freiburg Lectures*, 19, 20; *Vorträge und Aufsätze*, 173, 175; *Poetry, Language, Thought*, 178, 180; translation modified. On the meaning of the more or less artificial verb *geringen*, see Gadamer, *Gesammelte Werke*, vol. 3, 283; *Heidegger's Ways*, 135–36; cf. Mitchell, *Fourfold*, 269–78.

67. Heidegger, *Vorträge und Aufsätze*, 187; *Poetry, Language, Thought*, 216–17.
68. Heidegger, *Vorträge und Aufsätze*, 187; *Poetry, Language, Thought*, 216–17; translation modified. Cf. Heidegger, *Der Satz vom Grund*, 152; *Principle of Reason*, 89–90. See also Vattimo, *End of Modernity*, 154–55; *Adventure of Difference*, 168.
69. Heidegger, *Beiträge zur Philosophie*, 371; *Contributions to Philosophy*, 293; translation modified.
70. On retrieval (*Wiederholung*), see Heidegger, *Sein und Zeit*, 385–86; *Being and Time*, 367–68.
71. Heidegger, *Beiträge zur Philosophie*, 55; *Contributions to Philosophy*, 45; translation modified. Cf. Heidegger, *Hölderlins Hymnen "Germanien" und "Der Rhein,"* 144–45; *Hölderlin's Hymns "Germania" and "The Rhine,"* 127.
72. On the history of being (*Geschichte des Seins*) as metaphysics, see *Nietzsche*, vol. 2, 363–448; *End of Philosophy*, 1–83.
73. Heidegger, *Nietzsche*, vol. 2, 447; *End of Philosophy*, 82; translation modified.
74. Heidegger, *Über den Anfang*, 44. Cf. Vail, *Heidegger and Ontological Difference*, 45; Ruin, *Enigmatic Origins*, 206; Beistegui, *Truth and Genesis*, 147; Polt, *Emergency of Being*, 86.

Bibliography

Aristotle. *Metaphysics*. 2 vols. Edited by David Ross. Oxford: Clarendon, 1924.
———. *Nicomachean Ethics* (*Ethica Nicomachea*). Edited by Ingram Bywater. Oxford: Clarendon, 1894.
———. *Physics*. Edited by David Ross. Oxford: Clarendon, 1936.
Backman, Jussi. *Complicated Presence: Heidegger and the Postmetaphysical Unity of Being*. Albany: State University of New York Press, 2015.
Barash, Jeffrey Andrew. *Martin Heidegger and the Problem of Historical Meaning*. Dordrecht: Nijhoff, 1988.
Beistegui, Miguel de. *Truth and Genesis: Philosophy as Differential Ontology*. Bloomington: Indiana University Press, 2004.
Borgmann, Albert. *Technology and the Character of Contemporary Life: A Philosophical Inquiry*. Chicago: University of Chicago Press, 1987.
Chernyakov, Alexei. *The Ontology of Time: Being and Time in the Philosophies of Aristotle, Husserl and Heidegger*. Dordrecht: Kluwer, 2002.
Dreyfus, Hubert L. "Heidegger's Ontology of Art." In *A Companion to Heidegger*, edited by Hubert L. Dreyfus and Mark A. Wrathall, 407–19. Malden, MA: Blackwell, 2005.
Edwards, James C. *The Plain Sense of Things: The Fate of Religion in an Age of Normal Nihilism*. University Park: Pennsylvania State University Press, 1997.
Gadamer, Hans-Georg. *Gesammelte Werke*. Vol. 1, *Hegel-Husserl-Heidegger*. Tübingen: Mohr, 1987.
———. *Gesammelte Werke*. Vol. 3, *Neuere Philosophie*. Tübingen: Mohr, 1987.
———. *Heidegger's Ways*. Translated by John W. Stanley. Albany: State University of New York Press, 1994.
Greisch, Jean. "La parole d'origine, l'origine de la parole: logique et sigétique dans les *Beiträge zur Philosophie* de Martin Heidegger." *Rue Descartes* 1 (1991): 191–224.

Grimm, Jacob, and Wilhelm Grimm. *Deutsches Wörterbuch.* Vol. 2, *Biermörder–D.* Leipzig: Hirsel, 1860.

Haar, Michel. *Le chant de la terre: Heidegger et les assises de l'histoire de l'être.* Paris: L'Herne, 1987. Translated by Reginald Lilly as *The Song of the Earth: Heidegger and the Grounds of the History of Being.* Bloomington: Indiana University Press, 1993.

Habermas, Jürgen. *Nachmetaphysisches Denken: Philosophische Aufsätze.* Frankfurt am Main: Suhrkamp, 1988. Translated by William Mark Hohengarten as *Postmetaphysical Thinking: Philosophical Essays.* Cambridge: Polity, 1992.

Harman, Graham. "Dwelling with the Fourfold." *Space and Culture* 12 (2009): 292–302.

———. *Heidegger Explained: From Phenomenon to Thing.* Chicago: Open Court, 2007.

———. *Tool-Being: Heidegger and the Metaphysics of Objects.* Chicago: Open Court, 2002.

Harries, Karsten. *The Ethical Function of Architecture.* Cambridge: MIT Press, 1997.

Heidegger, Martin. *Aus der Erfahrung des Denkens 1910–1976.* GA 13. Edited by Hermann Heidegger. Frankfurt am Main: Klostermann, 2002.

———. *Basic Writings: From* Being and Time *(1927) to* The Task of Thinking *(1964).* Edited by David Farrell Krell. 2nd ed. San Francisco: HarperSanFrancisco, 1993.

———. *Beiträge zur Philosophie (Vom Ereignis).* GA 65. 1936–38. Edited by Friedrich-Wilhelm von Herrmann. Frankfurt am Main: Klostermann, 1989. Translated by Richard Rojcewicz and Daniela Vallega-Neu as *Contributions to Philosophy (Of the Event).* Bloomington: Indiana University Press, 2012.

———. *Besinnung.* GA 66. 1938–39. Edited by Friedrich-Wilhelm von Herrmann. Frankfurt am Main: Klostermann, 1997. Translated by Parvis Emad and Thomas Kalary as *Mindfulness.* London: Continuum, 2006.

———. *Bremer und Freiburger Vorträge.* GA 79. 1949–57. Edited by Petra Jaeger. Frankfurt am Main: Klostermann, 1994. Translated by Andrew Mitchell as *Bremen and Freiburg Lectures.* Bloomington: Indiana University Press, 2012.

———. *Einführung in die Metaphysik.* 1935/1953. 6th ed. Tübingen: Niemeyer, 1998. Translated by Gregory Fried and Richard Polt as *Introduction to Metaphysics.* New Haven, CT: Yale University Press, 2000.

———. *The End of Philosophy.* Translated by Joan Stambaugh. Chicago: University of Chicago Press, 2003.

———. *Erläuterungen zu Hölderlins Dichtung.* 1936–68. Edited by Friedrich-Wilhelm von Herrmann. 6th ed. Frankfurt am Main: Klostermann, 1996. Translated by Keith Hoeller as *Elucidations of Hölderlin's Poetry.* Amherst, NY: Humanity Books, 2000.

———. *Frühe Schriften.* GA 1. 1912–16. Edited by Friedrich-Wilhelm von Herrmann. Frankfurt am Main: Klostermann, 1978.

———. *Geschichte der Philosophie von Thomas von Aquin bis Kant.* GA 23. 1926–27. Edited by Helmuth Vetter. Frankfurt am Main: Klostermann, 2006.

———. *Grundbegriffe.* GA 51. 1941. Edited by Petra Jaeger. 2nd ed. Frankfurt am Main: Klostermann, 1991. Translated by Gary E. Aylesworth as *Basic Concepts.* Bloomington: Indiana University Press, 1998.

———. *Die Grundbegriffe der Metaphysik: Welt—Endlichkeit—Einsamkeit.* GA 29–30. 1929–30. Edited by Friedrich-Wilhelm von Herrmann. Frankfurt am Main: Klostermann, 1983. Translated by William McNeill and Nicholas Walker as *The Fundamental Concepts of Metaphysics: World, Finitude, Solitude.* Bloomington: Indiana University Press, 1995.

———. *Die Grundprobleme der Phänomenologie*. GA 24. 1927. Edited by Friedrich-Wilhelm von Herrmann. 3rd ed. Frankfurt am Main: Klostermann, 1997. Translated by Albert Hofstadter as *The Basic Problems of Phenomenology*. Revised ed. Bloomington: Indiana University Press, 1988.

———. "Hebel: Friend of the House." Translated by Michael Heim and Bruce Foltz. In *Contemporary German Philosophy*, vol. 3, edited by Darrel E. Christensen et al., 89–101. University Park: Pennsylvania State University Press, 1983.

———. *Hölderlins Hymnen "Germanien" und "Der Rhein."* GA 39. 1934–35. Edited by Susanne Ziegler. Frankfurt am Main: Klostermann, 1980. Translated by William McNeill and Julia Ireland as *Hölderlin's Hymns "Germania" and "The Rhine."* Bloomington: Indiana University Press, 2014.

———. *Holzwege*. 1935–46. Edited by Friedrich-Wilhelm von Herrmann. 8th ed. Frankfurt am Main: Klostermann, 2003. Translated by Julian Young and Kenneth Heynes as *Off the Beaten Track*. Cambridge: Cambridge University Press, 2002.

———. *Identität und Differenz*. 1957. 12th ed. Stuttgart: Klett-Cotta, 2002. Translated by Joan Stambaugh as *Identity and Difference*. Chicago: University of Chicago Press, 2002.

———. *Die Metaphysik des deutschen Idealismus*. GA 49. 1941. Edited by Günter Seubold. Frankfurt am Main: Klostermann, 1991.

———. *Metaphysische Anfangsgründe der Logik im Ausgang von Leibniz*. GA 26. 1928. Edited by Klaus Held. 2nd ed. Frankfurt am Main: Klostermann, 1990. Translated by Michael Heim as *The Metaphysical Foundations of Logic*. Bloomington: Indiana University Press, 1992.

———. *Nietzsche*. Vol. 1. 1936–39. 6th ed. Stuttgart: Neske, 1998.

———. *Nietzsche*. Vol. 2. 1939–46. 6th ed. Stuttgart: Neske, 1998.

———. *Nietzsche*. Vol. 2, *The Eternal Recurrence of the Same*. Edited and translated by David Farrell Krell. San Francisco: HarperSanFrancisco, 1991.

———. *Nietzsche*. Vol. 3, *The Will to Power as Knowledge and as Metaphysics*. Edited by David Farrell Krell. Translated by Joan Stambaugh, David Farrell Krell, and Frank A. Capuzzi. San Francisco: HarperSanFrancisco, 1991.

———. *Nietzsche*. Vol. 4, *Nihilism*. Edited by David F. Krell. Translated by Frank A. Capuzzi. San Francisco: HarperSanFrancisco, 1991.

———. *On the Way to Language*. Translated by Peter D. Hertz. San Francisco: Harper and Row, 1982.

———. *Ontologie (Hermeneutik der Faktizität)*. GA 63. 1923. Edited by Käte Bröcker-Oltmanns. 2nd ed. Frankfurt am Main: Klostermann, 1995. Translated by John van Buren as *Ontology: The Hermeneutics of Facticity*. Bloomington: Indiana University Press, 1999.

———. *Platon: Sophistes*. GA 19. 1924–25. Edited by Ingeborg Schüßler. Frankfurt am Main: Klostermann, 1992. Translated by Richard Rojcewicz and André Schuwer as *Plato's Sophist*. Bloomington: Indiana University Press, 1997.

———. *Poetry, Language, Thought*. Translated by Albert Hofstadter. New York: Harper and Collins, 2001.

———. Preface to *Heidegger: Through Phenomenology to Thought*. 1963. By William J. Richardson, VIII–XXIII. 4th ed. New York: Fordham University Press, 2003.

———. *Der Satz vom Grund*. 1955–56. 8th ed. Stuttgart: Neske, 1997. Translated by Reginald Lilly as *The Principle of Reason*. Bloomington: Indiana University Press, 1996.

———. *Schellings Abhandlung über das Wesen der menschlichen Freiheit (1809)*. 1936. Edited by Hildegard Feick. 2nd ed. Tübingen: Niemeyer, 1995. Translated by Joan Stambaugh as *Schelling's Treatise on the Essence of Human Freedom*. Athens: Ohio University Press, 1985.

———. *Sein und Zeit*. 1927. 18th ed. Tübingen: Niemeyer, 2001. Translated by Joan Stambaugh as *Being and Time*. Translation revised by Dennis Schmidt. Albany: State University of New York Press, 2010.

———. *Supplements: From the Earliest Essays to* Being and Time *and Beyond*. Edited by John van Buren. Albany: State University of New York Press, 2002.

———. *Über den Anfang*. GA 70. 1941. Edited by Paola-Ludovika Coriando. Frankfurt am Main: Klostermann, 2005.

———. "Unbenutzte Vorarbeiten zur Vorlesung vom Wintersemester 1929/30: 'Die Grundbegriffe der Metaphysik: Welt-Endlichkeit-Einsamkeit.'" *Heidegger Studies* 7 (1991): 6–12.

———. *Unterwegs zur Sprache*. 1950–59. 13th ed. Stuttgart: Klett-Cotta, 2003.

———. *Vorträge und Aufsätze*. 1936–53. 9th ed. Stuttgart: Neske, 2000.

———. *Wegmarken*. 1919–61. Edited by Friedrich-Wilhelm von Herrmann. 3rd ed. Frankfurt am Main: Klostermann, 1996. Translated by William McNeill et al. as *Pathmarks*. Edited by William McNeill. Cambridge: Cambridge University Press, 1998.

———. *Zur Sache des Denkens*. 1962–64. 4th ed. Tübingen: Niemeyer, 2000. Translated by Joan Stambaugh as *On Time and Being*. Chicago: University of Chicago Press, 2002.

Klein, Ernest. *A Comprehensive Etymological Dictionary of the English Language*. Amsterdam: Elsevier, 1971.

Magnússon, Sigurdur Gylfi. "The Singularization of History: Social History and Microhistory within the Postmodern State of Knowledge." *Journal of Social History* 36 (2003): 701–35.

Malpas, Jeff. *Heidegger's Topology: Being, Place, World*. Cambridge: MIT Press, 2006.

Mattéi, Jean-François. "Le chiasme heideggérien ou la mise à l'*écart* de la philosophie." In *La métaphysique à la limite: cinq études sur Heidegger*, by Dominique Janicaud and Jean-François Mattéi, 49–162. Paris: Presses Universitaires de France, 1983. Translated by Michael Gendre as "The Heideggerian Chiasmus or the *Setting Apart* of Philosophy." In *Heidegger: From Metaphysics to Thought*, by Dominique Janicaud and Jean-François Mattéi, 39–150. Albany: State University of New York Press, 1995.

———. "L'étoile et le sillon: l'interprétation heideggerienne de l'être et de la nature chez Platon et Aristote." In *Heidegger et l'idée de la phénoménologie*, by Franco Volpi et al., 43–66. Dordrecht: Kluwer, 1988.

———. *Heidegger et Hölderlin: le Quadriparti*. Paris: Presses Universitaires de France, 2001.

———. "La quadruple énigme de l'être." In *Heidegger: l'énigme de l'être*, edited by Jean-François Mattéi, 131–57. Paris: Presses Universitaires de France, 2004.

———. "Le quadruple fondement de la métaphysique: Heidegger, Aristote, Platon et Hésiode." In *La métaphysique: son histoire, sa critique, ses enjeux*, edited by Jean-Marc Narbonne and Luc Langlois, 203–28. Paris: Vrin, 1999.

McNeill, William. *The Glance of the Eye: Heidegger, Aristotle, and the Ends of Theory*. Albany: State University of New York Press, 1999.

Mitchell, Andrew. *The Fourfold: Reading the Late Heidegger*. Evanston, IL: Northwestern University Press, 2015.

Nancy, Jean-Luc. *La communauté désœuvrée*. Paris: Bourgois, 1990. Translated by Peter
    Connor et al. as *The Inoperative Community*. Edited by Peter Connor. Minneapolis:
    University of Minnesota Press, 1991.
———. *L'expérience de la liberté*. Paris: Galilée, 1988. Translated by Bridget McDonald as *The
    Experience of Freedom*. Stanford, CA: Stanford University Press, 1993.
Narbonne, Jean-Marc. *Hénologie, ontologie et Ereignis: Plotin—Proclus—Heidegger*. Paris: Les
    Belles Lettres, 2001.
Owens, Joseph. *The Doctrine of Being in the Aristotelian "Metaphysics": A Study in the
    Greek Background of Mediaeval Thought*. 1951. 2nd ed. Toronto: Pontifical Institute of
    Mediaeval Studies, 1963.
Plato. *Platonis opera*. Vol. 1. Edited by E. A. Duke et al. Oxford: Clarendon, 1995.
———. *Platonis opera*. Vol. 2. Edited by John Burnet. Oxford: Clarendon, 1901.
———. *Platonis opera*. Vol. 4. Edited by John Burnet. Oxford: Clarendon, 1902.
Pöggeler, Otto. *Der Denkweg Martin Heideggers*. Pfüllingen: Neske, 1963. Translated by
    Daniel Magurshak and Sigmund Barber as *Martin Heidegger's Path of Thinking*.
    Atlantic Highlands, NJ: Humanities Press International, 1987.
Polt, Richard. *The Emergency of Being: On Heidegger's Contributions to Philosophy*. Ithaca,
    NY: Cornell University Press, 2006.
Protevi, John. *Time and Exteriority: Aristotle, Heidegger, Derrida*. Lewisburg, PA: Bucknell
    University Press, 1994.
Roesner, Martina. *Metaphysica ludens: Das Spiel als phänomenologische Grundfigur im
    Denken Martin Heideggers*. Dordrecht: Kluwer, 2003.
Ruin, Hans. *Enigmatic Origins: Tracing the Theme of Historicity through Heidegger's Works*.
    Stockholm: Almqvist & Wiksell, 1994.
Schürmann, Reiner. *Des hégémonies brisées*. Mauvezin: Trans-Europ-Repress, 1996.
    Translated by Reginald Lilly as *Broken Hegemonies*. Bloomington: Indiana University
    Press, 2003.
———. *Heidegger on Being and Acting: From Principles to Anarchy*. Translated and expanded
    into English by Christine-Marie Gros and Reiner Schürmann. Bloomington: Indiana
    University Press, 1990.
———. "Ultimate Double Binds." In *Heidegger Toward the Turn: Essays on the Work of the
    1930s*, edited by James Risser, 243–46. Translated by Kathleen Blamey. Albany: State
    University of New York Press, 1999.
Sheehan, Thomas. *Making Sense of Heidegger: A Paradigm Shift*. London: Rowman and
    Littlefield, 2015.
Sinn, Dieter. *Ereignis und Nirwana: Heidegger, Buddhismus, Mythos, Mystik: Zur Archäotypik
    des Denkens*. Bonn: Bouvier, 1991.
Slife, Brent D. "Information and Time." *Theory & Psychology* 5 (1995): 533–50.
Thomas Aquinas. *Summa theologiae: cum textu ex recensione Leonine*, 1, 1:2. Edited by Pietro
    Caramello. Turin: Marietti, 1963.
Vail, Loy M. *Heidegger and Ontological Difference*. University Park: Pennsylvania State
    University Press, 1972.
Vattimo, Gianni. *The Adventure of Difference: Philosophy after Nietzsche and Heidegger*.
    Translated by Cyprian Blamires and Thomas Harrison. Cambridge: Polity, 1993.
———. *The End of Modernity: Nihilism and Hermeneutics in Post-Modern Culture*. Translated
    by Jon R. Snyder. Cambridge: Polity, 1988.

von Herrmann, Friedrich-Wilhelm. *Die Selbstinterpretation Martin Heideggers.* Meisenheim am Glan: Hain, 1964.
———. *Wege ins Ereignis: Zu Heideggers "Beiträgen zur Philosophie."* Frankfurt am Main: Klostermann, 1994.
White, David A. *Logic and Ontology in Heidegger.* Columbus: Ohio State University Press, 1985.
Windelband, Wilhelm. "History and Natural Science." Translated by Guy Oakes. *History and Theory* 19 (1980): 169–85.
———. *Präludien: Aufsätze und Reden zur Philosophie und ihrer Geschichte.* Vol. 2. 9th ed. Tübingen: Mohr, 1924.
Ziarek, Krzysztof. *Language after Heidegger.* Bloomington: Indiana University Press, 2013.

JUSSI BACKMAN is Academy of Finland Research Fellow at the University of Jyväskylä, Finland. He is author of *Omaisuus ja elämä: Heidegger ja Aristoteles kreikkalaisen filosofian rajalla* and *Complicated Presence: Heidegger and the Postmetaphysical Unity of Being* as well as the Finnish translator of Heidegger's *Introduction to Metaphysics.*

11 The Phenomenon of Shining

Nikola Mirković

Heidegger has become a classic in modern philosophy. The controversies about his political ideas and actions confirm this rather than calling it into question. If he had no influence on contemporary philosophy, his temporary commitment to National Socialism would attract much less attention; Heidegger's influence on contemporary philosophy is not marginal, and it is quite diverse. In order to understand Heidegger's philosophy, one has to take into account this complex reception of his thought. Different strands of interpretation inevitably shape the expectations of later readers and subtly influence the process of reading an author like Heidegger; occasionally, they obscure the understanding of the text. But such prejudices may also enhance our understanding of a particular argument. Generally speaking, the principle of *Wirkungsgeschichte*—as Gadamer calls it—provides an important access to a particular author. Yet one has to read and reread the original texts to separate what is convincing in an interpretation from what is not. In this chapter, I will take *All Things Shining* by Hubert Dreyfus and Sean D. Kelly as a point of departure in a search for the phenomenon the later Heidegger addresses when he writes about *shining* (*Schein/scheinen*). Only then will I turn to Heidegger's texts, and by emphasizing his background in phenomenology, I will argue for an understanding of *shining* in Heidegger that goes beyond the one Dreyfus and Kelly propose.

1. Dreyfus and Kelly on Shining

All Things Shining is not a book about Heidegger, but it is representative of a worldview that is based in large part on a reading of Heidegger's philosophy. Hubert Dreyfus and Sean Kelly define our age by its secular character and the threat of nihilism.[1] This is generally in accord with Heidegger's critical stance toward modernity and his understanding of the history of metaphysics. In this perspective, modern life appears to be threatened by a loss of meaning that is based on a delusive understanding of being. Heidegger famously argued that this threat is rooted in the nature of human existence: everyday life prevents us from experiencing situations that provide a deepened understanding of our existence. Heidegger shows in *Being and Time* that self-understanding cannot be achieved without authentic decisions and that these decisions are made difficult by our linguistic repertoire and the norms of our actions widely coinciding with unquestioned social conventions.[2] In order to find meaning in life, one does not necessarily have to overcome these conventions. Yet one has to see them for what they are and take this knowledge into account when choosing between different options. Dreyfus and Kelly point out that the challenge of experiencing life as meaningful becomes even more complicated when we face the excess of options that is characteristic of highly developed modern societies. Instead of making authentic choices or acting intuitively in a successful way, one might get stuck in futile self-reflection.[3]

The idea of nihilism certainly has shaped important aspects of modern and contemporary culture.[4] Still, whether the threat of nihilism should be acknowledged as *the* defining character of the present age is an entirely different question. It is striking that Dreyfus and Kelly provide no philosophical arguments for this view.[5] Instead of locating nihilism in a philosophical interpretation of history, they draw on the work of David Foster Wallace to describe the cultural manifestation of nihilism more closely.[6] In consequence, *All Things Shining* seems to primarily address those readers who already share the view that it can be difficult to find meaning in life in the contemporary world. This presupposition, however, should not be left unchallenged. If one wants to distinguish philosophy from the expression of a worldview,[7] an understanding of the age we live in, the presupposition should, at least, remain open to debate. Furthermore, one might argue that the complexity of modern societies makes it impossible to describe their current state without acknowledging fundamental differences between the groups and communities that constitute societies and hold diverging convictions. Instead of developing one big narrative, we should emphasize the plurality of sources modern identities are built on.[8]

This said, Dreyfus and Kelly succeed in showing that the classics of literature provide rich material for a diagnosis of the times we live in. They interpret the writings of Homer, Aeschylus, Dante, Melville, and others in order to highlight paradigms of successful coping with life. In their view, success can be measured by the extent to which one meets or exceeds one's own expectations and those of other people. In this context, the participation in shared practices counts as much as individual actions in extraordinary situations. Dreyfus and Kelly give a broad range of examples. When interpreting the *Iliad*, they point out the role of Helen. When she betrays her husband with Paris, her behavior can be criticized on the basis of the social expectations that are connected to the idea of marriage. Still, Homer presents her passion as praiseworthy: "What makes Helen great in Homer's world is her ability to live a life that is constantly responsive to golden Aphrodite, the shining example of the sacred erotic dimension of existence."[9]

In their comments on Homer, Dreyfus and Kelly draw on an understanding of Greek gods as forces that can manifest themselves momentarily in the lives of humans. Thus gods and humans are related to each other by their very nature. More specifically, the notion of the divine is bound to an interpretation of lived experience. In this context, the gods are referred to as radiant or shining. This understanding of the Greek gods can be found in Heidegger's interpretation of Sophocles's Oedipus as well: "Oedipus, who at the beginning is the savior and the lord of the state, in the brilliance [Schein] of glory and the grace of the gods, is hurled out of this seeming [Schein]. This seeming is not just Oedipus' subjective view [Ansicht] of himself, but that within which the appearing [Erscheinen] of his Dasein happens."[10] The moments of life that are characterized by their presence stand out:

> Perhaps this is a lesson about the sacred that we [should] appreciate [today]: when things are going at their best, when we are the most excellent version of ourselves that we can be, when we are, for instance, working together with others as one, then our activity seems to be drawn out of us by an external force. These are shining moments in life, wondrous moments that require our gratitude. In those episodes of excellence, no matter the domain, Odysseus's voice should ring through our heads: "Be silent; curb your thoughts; do not ask questions. This is the work of the Olympians."[11]

This praise of a polytheistic attitude toward life does not prevent Dreyfus and Kelly from presenting Jesus as a "shining example of a new background understanding of what it is to be a human being."[12] By interpreting the notion of ἀγαπή as a call for entering a certain mood in which one relates to other people and the world—a *Grundstimmung* in Heidegger's sense—Dreyfus and Kelly try to integrate Christian ideas into a pluralist framework. Ishmael, the narrator from Melville's *Moby Dick*, in turn, is interpreted as a "shining example" of a man who resists the temptation to search for a "single, universal truth" and successfully copes with the plurality of meaningful perspectives in a secular world.[13] Dreyfus and Kelly identify this postmetaphysical standpoint as the best way of confronting the danger of nihilism in the present age. If there is no single, universal truth, there is no reasonable claim to absoluteness in any domain of society. This standpoint has the advantage of supporting an enlightened and liberal approach to social and political issues. Yet it is difficult to defend this kind of pluralism philosophically. Isn't the pluralist perspective itself, insofar as it has to confront metaphysical standpoints, in danger of turning into a theory that makes a universal claim, namely the claim that there is no universal truth? In *All Things Shining*, this question is not addressed.

Another difficulty concerns the meaning of the word *shining*. Dreyfus and Kelly repeatedly refer to "shining examples," "shining moments," or "shining things" in life,[14] yet they do not explain what they mean exactly by *shining*. From the use of the word, it is possible to infer that the authors are thinking of something that stands outs, something that exceeds the ordinary, something that is loved and cherished by those who come across it. In addition, it is likely that the frequent employment of the metaphor of radiance and shining has been informed by Heidegger's philosophy of art. Though the topic of shining (*Schein/ scheinen*) seems to be rather a marginal aspect in Heidegger's work, a close reading of the passages where Heidegger describes actual works of art shows that he is constantly associating the beauty of art with the phenomenon of shining. The way Dreyfus and Kelly locate the phenomenon of shining, it seems to depend on the background practices of our culture. In this sense, they provide a *pragmatist account* of the phenomenon of shining. Dreyfus and Kelly focus on the sense of shining within a cultural community. But in order to fully understand the notion of shining, one has to account for its phenomenological meaning as well. For this task, Heidegger's later work provides valuable insights.

2. Beauty and Shining

For Heidegger, shining is primarily a matter of beauty.[15] There are very few passages where Heidegger explicitly talks about beauty, and as we will see, these passages are often linked to the Platonic notion of the beautiful (ἐκφανέστατον).[16] One of these passages can be found in the afterword to "The Origin of the Work or Art," where Heidegger points out that beauty is inherent to truth. More precisely, he states that the radiance associated with beauty is an aspect of the truth of art: "It appears when truth sets itself into the work. This appearing (as this being of truth in the work and as the work) is beauty."[17]

In what follows, Heidegger distances himself from Kant's aesthetics, according to which the beautiful exists only in the relation of the subject to an aesthetic object.[18] In Heidegger's view, this approach leads to a separation of art and truth that is incapable of doing justice to the historical impact of art and aesthetic experience. Art is more than a matter of taste because it can provide standards for the self-understanding of a community; when this happens, art also acquires a political significance. This is why Heidegger avoids the separation of the theoretical from the practical and returns to an understanding of beauty by connecting beauty to truth on an ontological level. In an earlier passage from the text, he gives a hint of how such an understanding of beauty can be developed. Heidegger points out how works of art may appear as beautiful: "The more simply and essentially the shoe-equipment is absorbed in its essence, the more plainly and purely the fountain is absorbed in essence, the more immediately and engagingly do all beings become, along with them, more in being. In this way self-concealing being becomes illuminated. Light of this kind sets its shining into the work. The shining that is set into the work is the beautiful. *Beauty is one way in which truth as unconcealment comes to presence.*"[19]

Three aspects of this passage are remarkable. First, Heidegger puts emphasis on the simplicity, purity, and immediacy of the art he is interested in. Second, the constant use of comparative adjectives in this passage indicates that a work of art can be perceived as a thing that has an intensified presence. Third, and most important, Heidegger specifies the way in which truth sets itself to work in art. In the work of art, truth illuminates the "clearing" as an unconcealment of truth, and at the same time, it makes visible the necessary self-concealment of being.[20] This is why the ontological function of the work of art is described through the metaphorical use of the notions of light, illumination, and shining. Heidegger does not explain why he employs this language, but it is clear that the potential of illumination is thought to distinguish the work of art from other things. The work of art is perceived as beautiful because it is shining. And this specific form of shining is not delusive but connected to the experience of truth. In addition, the phenomenon of shining is addressed as the origin of sensuous qualities the beholder may observe. This becomes evident in Heidegger's description of the materiality of the work of art: "The rock comes to bear and to rest and so first becomes rock; the metal comes to glitter and shimmer, the colors to shine, the sounds to ring, the word to speak. This comes forth as the work sets itself back into the massiveness and heaviness of the stone, into the firmness and flexibility of the wood, into the hardness and gleam of the ore, into the lightening and darkening of color, into the ringing of sound, and the naming power of the word."[21]

This radiance is part of the phenomenal presence of the materiality of art, and it has to be distinguished from an immediate form of the beauty of nature. The shining comes forth only when the earth is incorporated into works of art. Thus, the beauty of artworks is related to their materiality. Heidegger did not draw this conclusion in "The Origin of the Work of Art," but if one wants to understand the implicit concept of beauty inherent in his understanding of art, the connection between shining and materiality has to be taken into account.

In Heidegger's later work, we can find further proof for this connection. In his first lecture course on Nietzsche, *The Will to Power as Art*, which Heidegger delivered just one year after he wrote the essay "The Origin of the Work of Art," he examines and criticizes Nietzsche's aesthetics. In Heidegger's interpretation, the "will to power" is the most important teaching of Nietzsche's philosophy, and he identifies it as the historical culmination of metaphysics. In Heidegger's view, by claiming that everything is governed by the will to power, Nietzsche reduces being to a subjective principle. In this context, art is understood as the "supreme configuration [*höchste* Gestalt] of will to power."[22] Art can turn truth into mere appearance and mere appearance into truth. The lines between what is true and what is not are blurred by art, in favor of a perspective that enhances human life.

This relativist understanding of reality, however, has problematic consequences. A question presents itself: How can we know that art actually enhances life if it negates the difference between true and false? If we realize that art enhances life, then the opposite has to be wrong. Yet this conclusion cannot be reconciled with a relativist understanding of truth. Heidegger himself was aware of this philosophical problem and its consequences for Nietzsche's understanding of art. In his lecture course, Heidegger quotes a biographical statement by Nietzsche, which was published posthumously: "Very early in my life I took the question of the relation of *art* to *truth* seriously: and even now I stand in holy dread in the face of this discordance."[23]

Heidegger associates this statement with Nietzsche's intention of overturning Platonism. Famously, Plato was critical of the role of poets and artists in the state, but, at the same time, he developed a concept of beauty connecting aesthetic experience to the truth of being. Plato's understanding of beauty as ἐκφανέστατον, as that which is most radiant, describes the sensuous presence of an intelligible idea. When we recognize the idea of a thing, our perception of its sensible qualities can change. In the *Symposium*, Plato describes this moment as a transfiguration that creates a longing for something that truly exists.[24] If the beautiful awakens the love of truth, it can lead someone to engage in philosophy, which may improve one's life in an ethically relevant manner.

Insofar as Nietzsche—at least in Heidegger's reading—subordinates the difference between mere appearance and truth to the principle of the will to power, the beautiful in Nietzsche's understanding cannot have the effect Plato described. According to Nietzsche, the beautiful is supposed to become an antidote against nihilism, yet it is conceived as an illusion that ultimately does not lead beyond the finite world and the danger of an existential loss of meaning. It thus remains an open question how Nietzsche's relativist stance about truth can be reconciled with the idea that life not only appears to be enhanced by art but really is enhanced by it. In other words, the idea of turning life itself into a work of art does not provide a standard that could be used to measure the success of an aesthetic transformation of the self. Furthermore, it is unclear to what extent the ideal of an artistic life can be informed by philosophy. When Heidegger criticizes Nietzsche's philosophy of art, he is aware of the conflicting presuppositions inherent in it. Still, Heidegger's criticism of Nietzsche's aesthetics is based on a very selective reading; one might even argue that it is more illuminating for understanding Heidegger's own position than Nietzsche's. As mentioned above, Heidegger repeatedly links the experience of beauty to an understanding of truth as unconcealment or "clearing" (*Lichtung*) of being. In addition, Heidegger associates this process with the phenomenon of shining. Both are true for the Platonic tradition of thinking about beauty as well. This raises the question of whether Heidegger's philosophy of art is able to include Plato's idea of the beautiful.

Interestingly, Heidegger introduces a number of neologisms and quite original expressions in the passages in his lecture course where he interprets central passages on beauty from Plato's dialogues. He writes, for example, that the beautiful is "what is most luminous and what thereby most draws us on and liberates us."[25] The experience of beauty is presented as liberating in this passage because it can inspire one to see things as they truly are. The beautiful has the potential to turn the soul toward a philosophical life. Even if Heidegger does not address this potential explicitly, it can be integrated into his understanding of art. When art "sets up a world," it also has to make room for philosophical thinking.[26] The work of art may provide intuitive access to the basic concepts constitutive of philosophy. While interpreting Plato in his lecture course on Nietzsche, Heidegger, in a way, translates Plato's understanding of beauty into his own thought.

Yet some crucial differences between Heidegger's understanding of beauty and the Platonic concept of the beautiful still remain. Whereas Plato attributes the shining to the presence of an idea in the realm of the sensible, Heidegger tries to avoid the classical distinction between the sensible and the intelligible. He attempts to avoid reiterating the metaphysical tradition that has made it increasingly difficult in modern philosophy to grasp being as a whole. This is why he associates the phenomenon of the shining with the materiality of the work of art and its connection to the earth. The earth includes everything sensible yet does not define it in opposition to the intelligible. It is conceived as meaningful and, at the same time, as evading the restrictions of conceptual knowledge. And Heidegger does not present the earth in itself as radiant. Rather, it becomes radiant through its interplay with art and its integration into actual works of art. Heidegger also marks the difference between traditional concepts of beauty and his own understanding of beauty to point out the difference between ancient and modern conceptions. In *Contributions to Philosophy (Of the Event)*, Heidegger characterizes his own time as the "abandonment by being," which brings with it the withdrawal of the divine as well as the lack of genuine art.[27] Yet Heidegger does not rule out the possibility of an "other beginning," where art contributes to a new foundation of being. When he describes the transition to the other beginning, he again alludes to the beauty and radiance of art: "Art, however, will be for the future the putting into work of truth (or it will be nothing), i.e., it will be one essential grounding of the essence of truth. According to this highest standard, anything that would present itself as art must be measured as a way of letting truth come into being in these beings, which, as works, enchantingly transport man into the intimacy of Being while imposing on him the luminosity of the unconcealed and disposing him and determining him to be the custodian of the truth of Being."[28]

According to this passage, the experience of beauty through art bears the potential to change the relation of man and being. The unconcealed becomes luminous through art, and this event provides insight into the essence of the need of preservation. The same reservations regarding a uniform, secular picture of the contemporary world mentioned above also concern Heidegger's understanding of modernity as a time abandoned by being. Heidegger did not intend to create a comprehensive picture of the modern world, yet this happens in his description of the ways in which modernity is supposedly lacking being or has to be characterized as being "abandoned by being." He gives a one-sided account of modernity that ignores the plurality of stances and interests of different groups. Even if Heidegger's criticism of metaphysics and his philosophy of technology have been very influential in twentieth-century thought, this does not mean that they provide a comprehensive understanding of modern conditions of human existence. Furthermore, it is noteworthy that there is a certain shift in Heidegger's understanding of history between his work in the 1930s and his work after the war. This shift affects his understanding of art as well. To put if briefly, after the Second World War, Heidegger is less interested in thinking about fundamental changes and the transition to the other beginning. He begins paying more attention to ephemeral and marginal phenomena. He also becomes increasingly interested in the experience of the beautiful.

3. Shining in the Staiger Correspondence

From the end of 1950 until early 1951, Heidegger corresponded with the literary scholar and critic Emil Staiger. The correspondence began after Staiger delivered a lecture on Eduard Mörike's poem *On a Lamp (Auf eine Lampe)* at the University of Freiburg. The English translation of the poem reads:

> Yet not displaced, o fair lamp,
> hanging here delicately on light chains,
> you adorn the ceiling of this now almost forgotten love chamber.
> Upon your white tray of marble, whose rim
> is ringed by a wreath of ivy made of gold-green bronze,
> a band of children happily hold hands in a circle dance.
> How adorable it all is! it smiles, and yet a gentle spirit
> of solemnity pervades the entire formation
> —an artistic creation of the genuine kind. Who notices it?
> No matter; what is fair seems to find joy [is shining forth joyfully, *selig scheint es*] in itself."[29]

According to Staiger's understanding of Mörike's poem, the last line of the English translation should read "seems to find joy," whereas Heidegger suggests that the translation "shining forth joyfully" would be the correct rendering. This difference is due to the fact that the German word *scheinen* has two separate meanings: (1) "to shine," "to appear"; and (2) "to merely appear as something." In the case of Mörike's poem, the meaning of *es scheint* can be determined only by way of interpretation. Heidegger argues that the lamp in Mörike's poem has to be understood as a work of art and that Mörike was thinking of it as beautiful in the sense of Hegel's concept of beauty: "As 'an artistic [creation] of a genuine kind,' the lamp, 'what is glowing,' is the σύβολον of the work of art as such—'of the ideal,' in Hegel's language. The lamp, the aesthetic composition ('Oh, beautiful lamp'), joins [two things] together into one: the physical shining and the shining of the idea as the essence of the work of art. As a linguistic aesthetic composition, the poem itself is the symbol, reposing in language, of the work of art in general."[30]

With this reading, Heidegger challenges Staiger's interpretation of Mörike's work, but the literary scholar defends his view with the help of historical arguments, which, in turn, spur Heidegger's motivation to explain his interpretation in more detail. At the end of the remarkable correspondence, Staiger puts forward a compromise: since it is possible that the last line of the poem was meant to be ambivalent, both readings of the poem can be considered as legitimate. Following this, it seems pointless to evaluate which interpretation is more likely to be true to the poet's original intention. More important, however, is the fact that Heidegger felt the urge to defend his interpretation. If Mörike's poem did not matter to him, he would not have written a letter to Staiger.

Therefore, it is likely that he considered the poem to be a work of art that does not simply belong to the past but still speaks to his readers today. Consequently, the claim that modernity lacks genuine art cannot be defended, if only because art from previous centuries is still accessible to a modern audience. Metaphorically speaking, Heidegger assumes that the lamp in Mörike's poem is still shining, that it remains beautiful today. It can be read as a poem that shows the beauty of an artistic creation and the sensuous qualities of its presence. The poem evokes the picture of a lamp inspiring the imagination of the beholder and motivating the beholder to look closer to perceive the details and the physical presence of this particular object.[31] The poem points to the "white tray of marble," the "wreath of ivy made of gold-green bronze," and a "band of children happily hold[ing] hands in a circle dance." These are details that might be overlooked in everyday life but that draw attention to themselves when this particular object is acknowledged as a work of art. This phenomenological potential of art is meaningful beyond the time of the poem's creation. In order to describe it more precisely, one would have to turn to the phenomenology of perception rather than a speculative philosophy of history.

Nevertheless, Heidegger associates Mörike's poem with the hermeneutical situation of its author and claims that the poem opens up a world: "the ivy garland and the group of children belong to the aesthetic composition of the beautiful lamp insofar as this [lamp], lighting, grants the world of the love cham-ber."[32] The particular historical and social context of a nineteenth-century "love chamber" may be something past, yet this context is made accessible through the poem. Thus, the very fact that Heidegger, here, employs the concept of *world* in the way he used it in "The Origin of the Work of Art" can be taken as another indication of his implicit assumption that Mörike's work remains a valid example for art in general and may even have existential meaning for a modern reader.

On the other hand, Heidegger also associates Mörike's poetry with Hegel's aesthetics. In his reading, the lamp is a symbol for the work of art in Hegel's sense as described in *Lectures on Aesthetics*. Heidegger, however, explicitly dismissed Hegel's definition. Yet, if Heidegger wanted to reduce the poem to an exchange-able example for Hegel's aesthetical standpoint, there would be no reason for him to insist on his reading against Staiger's. The continuous radiance he attributes to the lamp is obviously opposed to Hegel's judgment that art has become "a thing of the past."

In the 1950s, Heidegger's understanding of art shifts toward a point where the difference between present and past seems to be less important for him than it was in "The Origin of the Work of Art." The revolutionary pathos and the nation-alist agenda are replaced by a more pluralist attitude toward art. This entails a new focus on ephemeral and marginal things as well as a heightened attention to the sensuous presence of everything that is shining. The work of art is shining not only because of its meaning in a social context but because of the sensuous qualities that draw our attention to it and inspire our imagination. Thus, the pragmatist account for the quality of shining has to be complemented by a phe-nomenological account.[33]

4. Conclusions

If one adopts a pluralist attitude toward different artworks from the same as well as different time periods, the question becomes, what place is there for history in the philosophy of art? Both Heidegger's criticism of modernity and Dreyfus and Kelly's attempt to define the present age as a secular age that is threatened by nihilism obviously overestimate the difference between historical periods and the difference between the works of art that belong to them. The very fact that authors like Kelly and Dreyfus can find something meaningful in the classics from virtually all major epochs of Western history shows that history is orga-nized much more by continuity and mutually overlapping elements of meaning than by crisis, radical change, and loss.

Heidegger's insistence on his interpretation of Mörike's poem *On a Lamp* is another proof for this continuity. Nonetheless, insofar as art has to be understood as a "cultural practice," it is always connected with the social norms of a particular historical period.[34] By investigating the relations between art and society, we can achieve a better understanding of why a particular work of art *mattered*, why it was considered meaningful by a particular audience. Yet to understand why a work of art *matters* in the present—regardless of its provenance—encompasses a phenomenological account of its beauty. Such an account consists in a description of the ways in which a work of art is "shining." As an account of the beauty of artworks, it will include a description of the sensuous presence that makes it stand out in an environment and that inspires the imagination of the beholder.

When Heidegger stresses the importance of the materiality of a work of art, this can be interpreted as a *phenomenological account* of shining. Art allows us to see materials in a way that we cannot experience when they are used for purely practical reasons. A poem about a lamp might change the way we perceive artificial light and the room that is illuminated by it. In this case, a work of literature draws the attention to a thing that harbors the potential to appear as beautiful within itself.

But the phenomenon of shining is not restricted to the domain of art. Dreyfus and Kelly have convincingly shown that human actions and habitual practices can shine forth in certain situations in the same way traits of literary characters do—and when they do, they appear as beautiful. The connection between the ethical and aesthetic, which too could be traced back to Plato, is constitutive of the phenomenon of shining.

Notes

1. See Dreyfus and Kelly, *All Things Shining*, 12–21.
2. "The kind of movement of plunging into and within the groundlessness of inauthentic being in the they constantly tears understanding away from projecting authentic possibilities, and drags it into the tranquillized supposition of possessing or attaining everything" (Heidegger, *Being and Time*, 172; *Sein und Zeit*, 178).
3. See Dreyfus and Kelly, *All Things Shining*, 3–5.
4. For an endorsement of nihilism as a "speculative opportunity" that refrains from the modern philosophical tradition of "re-establishing the meaningfulness of existence," see Brassier, *Nihil Unbound*, 239.
5. This might be due to the fact that the book is targeting a broader audience than strictly academic publications do. In an academic context, the authors would probably support their diagnosis of modern times with a reading of Charles Taylor, *A Secular Age*.
6. See Dreyfus and Kelly, *All Things Shining*, 22–57.
7. A distinction that was very important for Heidegger's early work. See Heidegger, *Towards a Definition of Philosophy*, 3–12.
8. Every attempt of characterizing "our age" by a single threat has to face the general disbelief toward an encompassing diagnosis of the times, which Lyotard called the "postmodern incredulity towards metanarratives." See Lyotard, *Postmodern Condition*, xxiv.

9. Dreyfus and Kelly, *All Things Shining*, 62.

10. Heidegger, *Introduction to Metaphysics*, 112; *Einführung in die Metaphysik*, 114.

11. Dreyfus and Kelly, *All Things Shining*, 81.

12. Dreyfus and Kelly, *All Things Shining*, 106.

13. Dreyfus and Kelly, *All Things Shining*, 168.

14. See Dreyfus and Kelly, *All Things Shining*, 89, 104–5, 192–94, 201, 206, 214, 220–24.

15. Notable exceptions are Heidegger's understanding of the "holy" (*das Heilige*) and the ancient Greek account of appearance (*Erscheinung*). The essence of being is encompassing appearance, which is interpreted as the process of coming forth or shining forth (*zum Vorschein kommen*). See Heidegger, *Einführung in die Metaphysik*, 110.

16. For a comprehensive account of Heidegger's notion of beauty, see Poltrum, *Schönheit und Sein bei Heidegger*.

17. Heidegger, "Origin of the Work of Art," 52. The original text reads: "Die Wahrheit ist die Wahrheit des Seins. Die Schönheit kommt nicht neben dieser Wahrheit vor. Wenn die Wahrheit sich in das Werk setzt, erscheint sie. Das Erscheinen ist—als dieses Sein der Wahrheit im Werk und als Werk—die Schönheit. So gehört das Schöne in das Sichereignen der Wahrheit. Es ist nicht nur relativ auf das Gefallen und lediglich als dessen Gegenstand" (Heidegger, "Der Ursprung des Kunstwerkes," 69).

18. Kant understands the beautiful as the object of a "satisfaction" that is experienced through a "free play of imagination and understanding." This process has no determinate rule. Consequently, art—which is defined by beauty—cannot provide any kind of knowledge that would be significant beyond the aesthetical realm. See Kant, *Critique of the Power of Judgment*, 89–127.

19. Heidegger, "Origin of the Work of Art," 32. The original text reads: "Je einfacher und wesentlicher nur das Schuhzeug, je ungeschmückter und reiner nur der Brunnen in ihrem Wesen aufgehen, um so unmittelbarer und einnehmender wird mit ihnen alles Seiende seiender. Dergestalt ist das sichverbergende Sein gelichtet. Das so geartete Licht fügt sein Scheinen ins Werk. Das ins Werk gefügte Scheinen ist das Schöne. *Schönheit ist eine Weise, wie Wahrheit als Unverborgenheit west.*" Heidegger, "Der Ursprung des Kunstwerkes," 43.

20. The self-concealment of being is thought to be necessary by Heidegger, insofar as particular beings by their actual appearing impede the understanding of the possibility of appearing as such. See Heidegger, "Origin of the Work of Art," 36; Heidegger; "Der Ursprung des Kunstwerkes," 48.

21. Heidegger, "Origin of the Work of Art," 24. The original text reads: "Der Fels kommt zum Tragen und Ruhen und wird so erst Fels; die Metalle kommen zum Blitzen und Schimmern, die Farben zum Leuchten, der Ton zum Klingen, das Wort zum Sagen. All dieses kommt hervor, indem das Werk sich zurückstellt in das Massige und Schwere des Steins, in das Feste und Biegsame des Holzes, in die Härte und den Glanz des Erzes, in das Leuchten und Dunkeln der Farbe, in den Klang des Tones und in die Nennkraft des Wortes" (Heidegger, "Der Ursprung des Kunstwerkes," 32).

22. Heidegger, *Nietzsche*, 72; *Nietzsche: Der Wille zur Macht als Kunst*, 85.

23. Heidegger, *Nietzsche*, 74. The original text reads: "Über das Verhältnis der *Kunst* zur *Wahrheit* bin ich am frühesten ernst geworden: und noch jetzt stehe ich mit einem heiligen Entsetzen vor diesem Zwiespalt." *Nietzsche: Der Wille zur Macht als Kunst*, 87.

24. Plato, *Symposium*, 210e5–212a7.

25. Heidegger, *Nietzsche*, 197. The original text reads: "[Das Schöne] ist das Leuchtendste und als dieses das Fortziehendste und Entrückendste." *Nietzsche: Der Wille zur Macht als Kunst*, 243. The combination of three adjectives in the superlative form in the original German text is quite peculiar. Instead of distancing himself from Plato's sentence, Heidegger chooses an emphatic and highly individual style of writing for his translation. This indicates that—at least in this passage of the lecture course—Plato's idea becomes a part of his own language and thinking.

26. In the essay "On the Origin of the Work of Art," Heidegger describes the creation of art as an event that "sets up a [new] world." See Heidegger, "Origin of the Work of Art," 22–23; "Der Ursprung des Kunstwerkes," 30–31. This means that, according to Heidegger, an original work of art is supposed to contribute in a decisive way to the historical, social, political, and religious emergence and self-understanding of a community.

27. See Heidegger, *Contributions to Philosophy*, 92–94; *Beiträge zur Philosophie*, 116–19.

28. Heidegger, *Basic Questions of Philosophy*, 164. The original text reads: "Die Kunst aber ist künftig—oder sie ist gar nicht mehr—das Ins-Werk-setzen der Wahrheit—*eine* wesentliche Gründung des Wesens der Wahrheit. Nach diesem höchsten Maß ist Jegliches zu messen, was als Kunst auftreten möchte—als der Weg, die Wahrheit seiend werden zu lassen in jenem Seienden, das als *Werk* den Menschen in die Innigkeit des Seyns entzückt, indem es ihn aus der Leuchte des Unverhüllten berückt und so zum Wächter der Wahrheit des Seyns stimmt und bestimmt" (Heidegger, *Grundfragen der Philosophie*, 190).

29. See Heidegger, *Staiger-Heidegger Correspondence*, 294. The original poem reads:

> Noch unverrückt, o schöne Lampe, schmückest du,
> An leichten Ketten zierlich aufgehangen hier,
> Die Decke des nun fast vergessnen Lustgemachs.
> Auf deiner weißen Marmorschale, deren Rand
> Der Efeukranz von goldengrünem Erz umflicht,
> Schlingt fröhlich eine Kinderschar den Ringelreihn.
> Wie reizend alles! lachend, und ein sanfter Geist
> Des Ernstes doch ergossen um die ganze Form—
> Ein Kunstgebild der echten Art. Wer achtet sein?
> Was aber schön ist,
> selig scheint es in ihm selbst.

See Heidegger, *Aus der Erfahrung des Denkens*, 93.

30. Heidegger, *Staiger-Heidegger Correspondence*, 294. The original text reads: "Die Lampe, 'das Leuchtende' ist als *ein Kunstgebild echter Art* das σύμβολον des Kunstwerkes als solchen—in Hegels Sprache 'des Ideals.' Die Lampe, das Kunstgebild (*o schöne Lampe*), bringt in eines zusammen: das sinnliche Scheinen und das Scheinen der Idee als Wesen des Kunstwerkes. Das Gedicht selbst ist als sprachliches Kunstgebilde das in der Sprache ruhende Symbol des Kunstwerkes überhaupt" (Heidegger, *Aus der Erfahrung des Denkens*, 95).

31. For the importance of the imagination for the understanding of art, see Sallis, *Force of Imagination*, 215–30.

32. Heidegger, *Staiger-Heidegger Correspondence*, 301. The original reads: "Efeukranz und Kinderschar gehören zum Kunstgebilde der schönen Lampe, insofern diese die Welt des Lustgemachs lichtend einräumt" (Heidegger, *Aus der Erfahrung des Denkens*, 104).

33. A phenomenological account of the beauty of art that is much more indebted to Kantian aesthetics than Heidegger's philosophy of art has been given in Figal, *Aesthetics as Phenomenology*. Figal, however, does not take the pragmatist interpretation of *shining* into consideration. Thus, the social and ethical potential of art remains marginal for Figal's understanding of aesthetics.

34. For an understanding of art as a cultural practice that is characterized by its reflective potential, see Bertram, *Kunst als menschliche Praxis*, 15.

Bibliography

Bertram, Georg. W. *Kunst als menschliche Praxis*. Berlin: Suhrkamp, 2014.

Brassier, Ray. *Nihil Unbound: Enlightenment and Extinction*. London: Palgrave Macmillan, 2007.

Dreyfus, Hubert, and Sean D. Kelly. *All Things Shining: Reading the Western Classics to Find Meaning in a Secular Age*. New York: Free Press, 2011.

Figal, Günter. *Aesthetics as Phenomenology: The Appearance of Things*. Translated by Jerome Veith. Bloomington: Indiana University Press, 2015.

Heidegger, Martin. *Aus der Erfahrung des Denkens, 1910–1976*. GA 13. Edited by Hermann Heidegger. Frankfurt am Main: Klostermann, 1983.

———. *Basic Questions of Philosophy, Selected "Problems" of "Logic."* Translated by Richard Rojcewich and André Schuwer. Bloomington: Indiana University Press, 1994.

———. *Being and Time*. Translated by Joan Stambaugh. Revised and with a foreword by Dennis J. Schmidt. Albany: State University of New York Press, 2010.

———. *Beiträge zur Philosophie (Vom Ereignis)*. GA 65. Edited by Friedrich-Wilhelm von Herrmann. Frankfurt am Main: Klostermann, 1989.

———. *Contributions to Philosophy (Of the Event)*. Translated by Richard Rojcewicz and Daniela Vallega-Neu. Bloomington: Indiana University Press, 2012.

———. *Einführung in die Metaphysik*. GA 40. Edited by Petra Jäger. Frankfurt am Main: Klostermann, 1983.

———. *Grundfragen der Philosophie, Ausgewählte "Probleme" der "Logik."* GA 45. Edited by Friedrich-Wilhelm von Herrmann. Frankfurt am Main: Klostermann, 1984.

———. *Introduction to Metaphysics*. 2nd edition. Translated by Gregory Fried and Richard Polt. New Haven, CT: Yale University Press, 2014.

———. *Nietzsche*. Translated by David Farrell Krell. San Francisco: Harper and Row, 1979.

———. *Nietzsche: Der Wille zur Macht als Kunst*. GA 43. Edited by Bernd Heimbüchel. Frankfurt am Main: Klostermann, 1985.

———. "The Origin of the Work of Art (1935–36)." In *Off the Beaten Track*, edited and translated by Julian Young and Kenneth Haynes. Cambridge: Cambridge University Press, 2002.

———. *Sein und Zeit*. GA 2. Edited by Friedrich-Wilhelm von Herrmann. Frankfurt am Main: Klostermann, 1977.

———. "The Staiger-Heidegger Correspondence." Translated by Arthur A. Grugan. *Man and World* 14, no. 3 (1981): 291–307.

———. *Towards a Definition of Philosophy*. Translated by Ted Sadler. London: Continuum, 2008.

———. "Der Ursprung des Kunstwerkes (1935/36)." In *Holzwege*, GA 5, edited by Friedrich-Wilhelm von Herrmann, 1–74. Frankfurt am Main: Klostermann, 1977.

Kant, Immanuel. *Critique of the Power of Judgment.* Edited and translated by Paul Guyer and Eric Matthews. Cambridge: Cambridge University Press, 2000.

Lyotard, Jean-François. *The Postmodern Condition.* Translated by Geoff Bennington and Brian Massumi. Minneapolis: University of Minnesota Press, 1984.

Plato. *Symposium.* In *Platonis Opera*, vol. 2, edited by Jon Burnet, 172–223. Oxford: Clarendon, 1901.

Poltrum, Martin. *Schönheit und Sein bei Heidegger.* Wien: Passagen, 2005.

Sallis, John. *The Force of Imagination.* Bloomington: Indiana University Press, 2000.

Taylor, Charles. *A Secular Age.* Cambridge, MA: Harvard University Press, 2007.

NIKOLA MIRKOVIĆ is Post-Doctoral Research Fellow of Philosophy and Education at the University of Koblenz-Landau. He has published articles in phenomenology, hermeneutics, aesthetics, and philosophy of music. Most recently, he coedited the volume *Heideggers* Schwarze Hefte *im Kontext. Geschichte, Politik, Ideologie.*

12 A Brief History of Things

Heidegger and the Tradition

Andrew J. Mitchell

HEIDEGGER'S POSTWAR THINKING radicalizes the phenomenological call for a return to the things themselves. Indeed, the lecture "The Thing" marks Heidegger's first public speaking engagement after the war. The importance of this lecture and the problem of the thing as the cornerstone of Heidegger's later thinking should not be underestimated. In a 1964 letter reflecting on his path of thought hitherto, Heidegger observes: *"Apart from the thing lecture, I have never once presented my own thinking purely on its own terms in publications,* however far it has come in the meantime, but rather have always only presented it in such a way that, provisionally, I wanted to make my thinking *understandable in terms of the tradition."*[1] While Heidegger singles out "The Thing" as voicing his own thought, he does so in tandem with letting that thought speak "in terms of the tradition." Looking at Heidegger's critique of the traditional approach to things across the history of philosophy should provide us unique access to his own thinking of things as well. Rather than address his own thinking directly, then—where the thing is a matter of the "fourfold" (the belonging together of earth, sky, divinities, and mortals)—something I have done at length elsewhere, I would like to reconstruct this Heideggerian history of things.[2]

The history of the thing that Heidegger provides runs through the ancient Greeks, the Romans, the medievals, and the moderns. I will add to this account consideration of Husserl's lecture course *Thing and Space* (1907), perhaps the canonical phenomenological treatment of things as such, as well as Heidegger's own *Being and Time* (1927), arguing that *Being and Time* itself ultimately participates in the historical neglect of the thing endemic to the metaphysical tradition. Exploring this history of the thing reveals a fundamental tension between what we might call an "objectification" or "encapsulation" of the thing and a thinking of the thing as embedded in a network of relations, as relational, a tension central to Heidegger's thinking of the fourfold as well.

Beginning with the ancients, the Greeks understood the thing as anything but self-contained, as Heidegger's treatments of Aristotle show. Rather, the thing for them bore an ineradicable relation to what lies outside it, and this in at least two ways. First, the thing is related to its place, which for Aristotle is assigned to bodies as their nature. In *The Question concerning the Thing*, Heidegger addresses this relationship through a reading of Aristotle's *De Caelo* on the natural body. Second, the thing is related to what lies outside it in regard to its "causes." Heidegger explores this in his reading of Aristotle's *Physics* at the opening of "The Question concerning Technology." In each of these cases, the sense of thing that emerges is one inherently disposed to relationality.

For the Greeks, the natural body is a body that is in motion. In Heidegger's translation of *De Caelo* 268 b14, "the bodies which belong to 'nature' and constitute this [*ta physika sômata*] are, by themselves [*kath auta*], movable in regard to place."³ These bodies, however, are not simply movable but moved of themselves (*gemäß ihnen selbst*). Heidegger explains that "the movement of the body is *kath auta*, by itself; that means: How a body moves about, i.e. how it relates to its place and to which place it relates—all this has its basis in the body itself."⁴ The body determines its relation to space. An earthly body will move downward, toward the center (*Mitte*), toward the earth, a fiery one, upward and away. "*To each its place according to its* kind—every body has a place towards which it also strives."⁵ The thing seeks the space that is appropriate for it. Indeed, it can only be what it is when situated within that medium. Contravention of these natural movements is understood as violence, as when a stone is shot in the air by a slingshot.⁶ Greek "things" are inherently spatial; they seek the medium that belongs to them. But here we still might imagine a separate body suspended in an indifferent space. The privilege accorded to circular motion puts such suspicions to rest.

In circular motion the place of the body could be said to have merged with its motion; "it contains, so to speak, its place in itself."⁷ It is perfectly where it is, ending where it begins. "In circular motion the body has its place in the motion itself, for which reason this motion is also the ever-enduring, properly extant [*die eigentlich seiende ist*]."⁸ Thus for the Greeks there is a thinking of the thing, the body, as belonging to a proper place and as tied to its surroundings: "How a body moves about depends on its kind and the place to which it belongs. The *where* determines the *how* of being."⁹

When we say that the thing is essentially tied to its surroundings, we mean by this that the thing is *dependent* upon those surroundings to be what it is. The thing is nothing encapsulated or self-enclosed, but rather a relational greeting of world. Things exceed themselves to enter into relations with other things, with us, with whatever they encounter in the world. The thing needs the medium that supports these relations in order to be the thing that it is: the relational thing. The thing is *indebted* to the medium for what it is. Heidegger reads the treatment of the four causes in Aristotle's *Physics* to address just this kind of "dependence" or "indebtedness." The *aitiai* are not "causes" in the sense of actuating forces taking effect upon reality but instead ways in which the thing owes itself to something beyond it; "the four causes are ways of indebtedness [*Weisen des Verschuldens*]."[10]

In Heidegger's analysis of these four ways of indebtedness—to the material of which the thing consists, to the appearance it takes, to the context that delimits the thing as its "end," and to the gathering power of the *logos* of the artisan that decides whether and how to bring the other three to appearance—each is shown to participate in a common endeavor. Together they serve to bring something into the world: "The four ways of indebtedness bring something into appearance. They let it come forth into presence [*das An-wesen*]. They let it loose there and thus let it in [*lassen . . . an*], namely into its completed arrival. The basic trait of indebtedness [*Verschulden*] is this letting-in to arrival [*An-lassens in die Ankunft*]. In the sense of such a letting-in, indebtedness is an occasioning [*Ver-an-lassen*]."[11]

The four causes are thus named "the four ways of occasioning," an occasioning that Heidegger wants to distinguish from the notion of a "secondary cause."[12] Instead, the four modes of indebtedness are understood as ways of allowing (*lassen*) something to come to (*an*) appearance and to presence there (*an-wesen*). The four relationships so described thus concern an arriving (*An-kunft*). The thing could not arrive into presencing without the support of these occasioning *aitiai*, but none of them alone is capable of bringing this about. Each is "co-responsible" for bringing this about.[13] The emergence of the thing is only possible through a gathering of these co-relations. In both of these ways, then, in regard to its place and in regard to its occasioning, the Greek sense of the thing is one of relational connectivity.

The Romans present a somewhat ambiguous moment in this history, at least as it is cursorily sketched in the lecture "The Thing." On the one hand, there is an understanding of the thing, the *res*, as "what concernfully approaches [*das Angehende*]."[14] As Heidegger explains, for the Romans "*res publica* does not mean 'the state,' but rather that which openly concerns [*angeht*] every one of the people and therefore is negotiated publicly."[15] Not only does this thing concern us (*geht uns an*), but in so doing it also approaches us, "goes" to us (*geht uns an*). The thing thus is not defined by an encapsulated body, but it issues to us as a concern: "The Roman word *res* names that which concernfully approaches the human, the affair [*Angelegenheit*], the disputed matter, the case [*Fall*]."[16] From this sense of *res* emerges the Latin term *causa*: "In no way does this authentically and primarily mean 'cause'; *causa* means 'the case' and for this reason also 'that which is the case,' that something comes to pass and becomes due [*fällig wird*]."[17] It is this sense of a matter that addresses us, that reaches us and claims us, that falls to us, that informs subsequent Latinate understandings of the thing: "From this word of the Roman language, with its inner correspondence to the word *res*, from the word *causa* in the meaning of case and affair, there arose in the Romance languages *la cosa* and the French *la chose*; we say: *das Ding* [the thing]."[18]

On the other hand, despite this conception of things as *res*, the Romans fail to think through the concernful approach that is essential to the *res* and instead adopt an understanding of being from the Greeks, which ultimately ends up reifying their own experience of the thing. They come to understand the thing now as *ens,* a static entity:

> The *realitas* of the *res* was experienced by the Romans as what concernfully approached. But the Romans have never properly thought what they thus experienced in its essence. Much more, through the adoption of late Greek philosophy, the Roman *realitas* of the *res* was conceived in the sense of the Greek *on*; now *on*, Latin *ens*, means what presences in the sense of what stands here. The *res* becomes *ens*, that which presences in the sense of what is produced and represented. The characteristic *realitas* of the originally Roman experienced *res,* the concernful approach, remains buried as the essence of what presences.[19]

For Heidegger this same ambiguity, between an understanding of the thing as something that approaches us and concerns us, or as something of a relational node, on the one hand, and a conception of the thing as an encapsulated body, or as an object, on the other, can be traced through the Middle Ages. Here Heidegger turns to the Old High German language (c. 500–1050) to show the connection with the Roman understanding of the thing as *res*. In fact, "the Old High German word *thing* and *dinc*, with its meaning of gathering, namely for the negotiation of an affair, is thus appropriate like no other for fittingly translating the Roman word *res*, that which concernfully approaches."[20] The Old High German *thing* or *dinc* is understood in terms of a gathering (*Versammeln*), which has to do with the concernful approach of the thing. The thing approaches us and "gathers" us to it as we enter into a relationship with it and negotiate the bounds and obligations of that relation. This is the affair of the thing. We are gathered together with the thing, as well as with others, in this discussion: "The Old High German word *thing* means gathering and indeed a gathering for the negotiation of an affair under discussion, a disputed case. Consequently the Old High German words *thing* and *dinc* become the name for an affair; they name what concernfully approaches the human in some way, what accordingly is under discussion."[21]

From here, Heidegger argues that the relational notion of *res* is completely overshadowed in favor of the more generic *ens*, explaining that, "in subsequent times, particularly the Middle Ages, the name *res* serves to indicate every *ens qua ens*, i.e. everything that is somehow presencing, even if it only stands here in representation and presences like the *ens rationis*. The same thing that happens with the word *res* happens with the name corresponding to *res, dinc*; for *dinc* means every single thing that somehow is."²² This is observable in the work of Meister Eckhart (c. 1260–c. 1327), in whose German sermons (delivered in Middle High German) the term *dinc* is used as "the careful and unassuming name for anything that is at all."²³ In this, *dinc* is like the generic *ens*.

But Eckhart also reveals another side of the thing. Heidegger does not make this explicit, but the citations from Eckhart that appear in the first and the last of the Bremen lectures present a sense of the thing quite distinct from this generic determination. In "The Thing," for example, Heidegger cites Eckhart as saying, "Love is of such a nature that it changes man into the things [*dink*] he loves," and in "The Turn" he cites Eckhart's claim that "those who are not of great essence, whatever work they effect, nothing will come of it."²⁴ In the first, the thing is nothing that is standing over and against us but instead something that is engaged with us in the most intimate of ways. My love is invested in the thing, and we (the thing and I) are both transformed through this relationship. In the second, the same idea is presented again, now in terms of an individual's work. What is brought about by a person is nothing alien or independent of that person; rather its success is precisely tied to the greatness of the producer. In these citations, Eckhart escapes the generic and empty universal sense of thing through a latent thinking of relationality.

With the advent of modernity, the earlier relational sense of the thing is swept away in favor of complete objectification as represented to a subject. This is accomplished through a "mathematization" of entities. The mathematization in question is not simply the application of numerical quantities in our dealings with beings. Rather, Heidegger evokes the Greek sense of the term, where *ta mathêmata* names the things insofar as they are "learnable," understanding this sense of learning as a "taking notice." As Heidegger states, "Precisely this 'taking notice' is the authentic essence of learning, of *mathêsis*. The *mathêmata* are the things insofar as we take notice of them, as that which is taken notice of, as which we authentically know them already in advance."²⁵ In this learning we only ever learn what we already know. Heidegger uses the number three as an example. We could not learn that there are three chairs here if we were not already aware of, and did not already somehow know, this number three. We bring this number three to bear on our experience in advance: "When we bring this [our previous knowledge of three] properly and in a definite way to our notice [i.e., in regard to the three chairs], then we take notice of something which we actually already have."²⁶ On this account, learning thus becomes a *"giving to oneself."*²⁷ Applying this conception of the mathematical to things, then, results in "a projection [*Entwurf*] of thinghood which, as it were, leaps out over the things. The projection first opens a play-space wherein the things, i.e., the facts, show themselves."²⁸ The mathematical is a "fundamental position toward things" and "the fundamental presupposition of the knowledge of things."²⁹

Nowhere is this more evident than in Newton's first law of motion: "Every body perseveres in its state of being at rest or of moving uniformly straight forward, except insofar as it is compelled to change its state by forces impressed."[30] Concerning such a body, which Heidegger glosses as one "left to itself" (*corpus quod a viribus impressis non cogitur*), he asks, "Where do we find it? There is no such body."[31] This point shows a seeming contradiction in one of the prized distinctions between modern and medieval science, that the former would be tied to the facts and experiential, but nowhere do we experience the body in such abstraction: "Now, in distinction from the mere conceptual poetizing of medieval scholasticism and science, modern science is supposed to be grounded upon experience. Instead of this, such a basic principle stands at its pinnacle. It speaks of a thing that does not exist. It requires a basic conception of things that contradicts the usual."[32] As such, modern science is at root mathematical in the sense outlined above: "The mathematical is based upon such a claim, i.e., the application of a determination of the thing, which is not experientially created out of the thing and yet lies at the base of every determination of the things, making them possible and making room for them."[33]

The determinative projection of things as cast by Newton is one that holds for "every body." As Heidegger notes, "with the onset of the first basic principle of motion, all the essential alterations are set into place along with it."[34] Heidegger itemizes a number of these alterations, ways in which the understanding of being in modern science is homogenized against the variability of the Greek experience. For the moderns, for Newton, "the natural bodies are all essentially equivalent."[35] The distinction between the heavenly and earthly bodies falls away; "the upper realm is not a superior one."[36] In regard to motion, both the Greek privileging of circular motion over rectilinear and their distinguishing between natural and violent motions are abandoned by the modern understanding. With the homogenization of the body, Heidegger notes, "the distinguishing of determinate places also disappears. Every body can in principle be at any place. The concept of place itself is changed. Place is no longer the place to which a thing belongs in accordance with its inner nature, but rather only a position [*Lage*]."[37] The result of the mathematical project thrown over the world is a homogenized body in an indifferent space, a situation amenable to mathematization in the narrow sense. The thing becomes the "object."

Heidegger pursues this conception of the mathematical in *The Question concerning the Thing* as propaedeutic to a consideration of Kant. But with Kant we also find an opening onto Heidegger's own view. The ambiguity of the thing that we have seen across Heidegger's historical account resurfaces in the modern era between Newton and Kant. Kant, too, shares the modernist mathematical framework. His thinking is devoted to an understanding of the a priori, of that which precedes experience. Heidegger's focus in the lecture course is on the section of

The Critique of Pure Reason dealing with the principles of the understanding. Here Kant details how the understanding bears on the material of intuition so as to yield a representation of the object. For Heidegger, in these pages "the meaning of the center of the whole work [*The Critique of Pure Reason*] first becomes visible."[38] Kant reviews the ways in which the categories are concretely applied in the constitution of the object. For Heidegger, this is the core of the critique; it is a rendering of things: "The essential delimitation of the thing is no arbitrary byproduct to Kant's philosophy, *the determination of the thinghood of the thing is its metaphysical center*."[39] For this reason, the Kantian critique of pure reason is really a critique of mere reason, stale reason, reason devoid of this transcendental effectiveness. What needs to be thought is the constitution of the thing, an act that implicates both subject and object. According to Heidegger, Kant transforms our understanding of the subject by introducing intuition into the heart of thinking. Without this there is only "mere" reason, the "pure" reason that stands in need of critique. Fulfilled reason is transcendentally active reason, at grips with the object. For such an object (*Gegenstand*), intuition yields the *Gegen*, the object's position across or over against the subject, and thinking produces the *Stand*, the persistence of what stands over against the subject. *The Critique of Pure Reason*, "this title says nothing other than the question concerning the thing—but as question."[40]

The Kantian thinking of the a priori, the development of a transcendental philosophy itself, culminates the mathematical project of modernity. Kant overlooks the things closest to him in favor of their "transcendental conditions of possibility," knowable a priori. "From the outset, Kant does not pose the question concerning the thinghood of the things around us."[41] Instead, "from the very outset and like the tradition before and after him, Kant leaped over that realm of things in which we know ourselves to be immediately at home."[42] The Kantian mathematical projection operates a priori, specifying in advance the constitution of the object. Simply put, "the *a priori* is the title for the essence of things."[43] In concerning himself with this, Kant neglects "to question and determine what is manifest [*das Offenbare*] in terms of its own essence, that which encounters us before its objectification into an object of experience."[44] In fact, for Kant, the principles of understanding are literally mathematizing; as Heidegger explains, "the pure concept of the understanding—here the category of quality—determines the appearances in advance in regard to *what* is to be encountered in them; that as a result of this quality of the appearances a quantity—in the sense of an intensity—is possible and the application of number, of mathematics, is guaranteed."[45] This is why Kant refers to his first two principles, the axioms of intuition and the anticipations of perception, as the "mathematical principles."[46] As Heidegger sums up, in the Western philosophical tradition, up to and even after Kant, "the mathematical basic character is decisive: the recourse to axioms in every determination of beings. *Kant remains in this tradition*."[47]

And yet the same opening of the transcendental realm that would situate Kant amid the mathematical projectors of modernity also gestures toward something different. What Kant addresses here is a dimension of existence that is neither that of the subject nor that of the object alone. How we understand things is determinative for how we understand ourselves. As Heidegger notes in the course conclusion, "the question: What is a thing? is the question: Who is the human?"[48] The transcendental cannot be located within a subject-object dualism. Rather, as Heidegger states in the course's closing lines, "in Kant's question concerning the thing a dimension is opened that lies between the thing and the human, one that reaches out beyond the things and back behind the human."[49] Neither thing nor human is the source of this; it encompasses both of them; they are *in* it. The name for this dimension is "the between."[50] In regard to this between, Heidegger singles out three points for emphasis:

1. that we must always move about in the between, between human and thing;
2. that this between is only in that we move ourselves therein;
3. that this between does not stretch like a cord from thing to human, but rather this between as an anticipation [*Vor-griff*] about the thing reaches out ahead of us and likewise back behind us.[51]

The between is not something from which we can take an outside perspective. We cannot get behind it, for it has already encompassed us. To enter this dimension is to enter into relation with the manifestness of the things themselves, to see these things as themselves and as always already involved with us. The transcendental dimension of experience culminates the mathematical trajectory of modernity while simultaneously revealing the inherently relational nature of existence in the between. The thing exhibits this ambiguity.

To this brief sketch of a philosophical history of the thing in Heidegger's works, we could add a further stage that does not appear there, Husserl's phenomenological account of the thing in *Thing and Space* (1907). Without entering into the wealth of detail and distinction that this text provides for understanding and articulating perceptual experience, we again see here the same basic tension between what we are terming a thinking of relationality and a metaphysics of presence.

To begin with, we should note that Husserl's engagement with things, like Kant's, largely occurs at a transcendental level. Husserl is quite comfortable speaking about a "pre-phenomenal or transcendental temporality," the "pre-phenomenal extension of the appearance," or the "pre-empirical color" and "pre-empirical filling" of appearances.[52] Against this, Heidegger will later propose that the thing is only found in concrete instantiation, as upon the earth and under the sky. What ameliorates this situation to a certain extent is Husserl's emphasis on the importance of the "Body" (*Leib*, the "bearer of the Ego")[53] in the concretizing of perception. This "Ego-Body," as he terms it, "stands there as the ever-abiding point of reference, to which all spatial relations seem to be attached."[54] This Body orients us in the world and thereby participates in the constitution of the objective world of things around us. For Husserl, "the constitution of the Objective location and of Objective spatiality is essentially mediated by the movement of the Body or, in phenomenological terms, by the kinaesthetic sensations."[55] As such, Husserl's concern is with "the intertwining, in a remarkable correlation, of the constitution of the physical thing with the constitution of an Ego-Body."[56] We should note, though, that the concern here is for the co-constitution of the Ego-Body, not of the Ego itself.

Perception is to be understood as an expression of this Ego-Body; it is a movement out toward the world. Thus Husserl will speak of it in terms of rays moving from the subject to its object, "*perception* is, as I also express it, a complex of full and empty intentions (rays of apprehension)," or as a beam of intentionality, "the living intention is a beam which sends its implicated rays through all these pieces and points."[57] The idea that it would be the subject that bestows meaning upon the world is one that Heidegger will reject, and it seems fully operative in Husserl's account of the transcendental constitution of the things of experience: "As to the intentional rays that penetrate the actually given images, in this way they connect, in a consciousness of unity, the corresponding points of the images that continually pass over into one another, and they thereby constitute the same objective moment that always comes to proper appearance."[58] The intentional activity of the subject (ego) bestows unity and thus meaning on the world.

For Husserl, it is not simply the sheer reality or actuality of the thing that is constituted but its inherent possibilities as well. Indeed, "every phase of apprehension, in its very essence, contains the relation to all the possibilities."[59] One does not see what one sees; one sees beyond it, around it, behind it. One sees things in relation to others, to other possible positionings of the thing whereby it could be given. Along the same line, "it pertains to the essence of this givenness to leave open infinitely many possibilities of new givenness in a determinate way as motivated possibilities."[60] Having established this perception of the possible, Husserl can provocatively claim that "a line of actual givenness (most proper perception) is bathed in a halo of *quasi*-intentions,"[61] where these quasi-intentions pursue the possibilities of the thing.

But Husserl's considerations ultimately reiterate the metaphysical privilege of presence by construing this potentially liberating possibility solely in terms of presence and actuality, as the actual to come. According to Husserl, "every real possibility is a possibility under the association of an actuality, which means, here, under the association of the present actuality of these or those appearances."[62] Indeed, Husserl concludes the lecture course as a whole on this very point: "We have to do everywhere in this domain with these sorts of dependent possibilities, which are not . . . mere possibilities in general, but which are instead possibilities that are dependent on posited actualities, motivated by them, and which pass over into motivated actualities by the assumptive actualization of supplementary circumstances. This is what is meant by placing real existence in relation to a system of perceptual possibilities."[63] Because possibility is always a modification of the actual, within actuality, Husserl's thinking remains grounded in presence.

Despite these areas of contention, we can nonetheless read in Husserl's course a proto-thinking of relationality. We could begin by noting that the actuality of the given is never itself completely given: "Things, and everything pertaining to the sphere of things in general, are never given conclusively and never can be. They come to givenness only in an infinite progression of experience."[64] While this infinite ideal governs the whole process, it nevertheless likewise entails that what appears is never *actually* (or, in Husserl's term, "properly") a whole. Indeed, as Husserl points out, "if the task lies in the production of absolutely complete givenness, then it is a priori unsolvable; it is an unreasonably posited task."[65] The actual is never complete in this way.

This incompletion of the thing could be said to open the thing to its surroundings as well. The constituted thing is nothing encapsulated: "While it stands there as a thing, it has, in terms of the apprehension, a relation to all [i.e., to all possible continuities of apprehending the appearance]."[66] These continuities are not without effect; they form what Husserl terms a "nexus," and in so doing they join with one another and compound their effect, and this is true for every perception: "a kind of perceptual nexus belongs to the essence of every perception."[67] This nexus intertwines our perceptions of one thing to the others; it weaves the continuity of experience as such. The compounding of experience lends resilience to that nexus: "Every perception, already while it endures, integrates its force [the force of experience], and in the perceptual nexus every perception is augmented by every other one, corresponding to all the series of fulfillments which interweave into a manifold braid, unitarily and harmoniously, the various sides and rays of the perceptions."[68] Because of this, we live lives of meaning in a world of things.

By virtue of this halo around the perceived thing, we do not perceive simply it alone but likewise the way it relates beyond itself, the way it relates to world: "What is at any time properly seen is not all that is there for our 'seeing'; just as the back side of the Object is not properly seen and yet is co-apprehended and co-posited, so likewise is the unseen environment of the Object as well. The presented field of Objects is a field of Objects in a 'world.'"[69] Consequently, toward the close of the course, Husserl can claim that "an absolute necessity can be demonstrated for the fact that there must be a world, *nota bene* a real world as a world of things."[70] Perception is worldly. And because this world is the creation of experience, gaining resilience (or being) through its own experiential confirmation in corroborating fulfilled intentions, it is not a world that is given beforehand but instead one that must be founded in experience itself. For Husserl, this is a long-held belief and the sole option: "The existence of a world in which not only do individual realities come together in general, but to which ultimately each and every occurring datum makes its contribution, is the only rational possibility, one which is indeed not pregiven *a priori* but founded *a posteriori*."[71]

Despite the transcendentalism, the subjectivism, and the presentism, Husserl's relentless and provocative conceptualization of the thing and its constitution ultimately liberates the thing from the bounds of objective encapsulation, perhaps more so than elsewhere in the history of philosophy heretofore.

At this point, however, one might object that a thinking of things is nothing completely novel for Heidegger. Undoubtedly one of the major breakthroughs of *Being and Time* (1927) was its reconsideration of the beings around us and the discernment of a distinction within their mode of existence, as either present at hand or ready to hand. The theoretico-scientific approach to beings, predominant across the history of philosophy, presents itself as an unprejudiced regard for the entity, "when concern holds back from any kind of producing, manipulating, and the like."[72] In comporting toward beings in this way, the being is understood in terms of presence at hand (*Vorhandenheit*). But this presumed objectivity of beings is itself founded upon a more primordial pragmatic relationship, in which we are already engaged with these beings, in which they are themselves matters of our concern (*pragmata*).[73] Such beings are defined as equipment—"We shall call those entities which we encounter in concern 'equipment,'"—whereas "the kind of being which equipment possesses—in which it manifests itself in its own right—we call 'readiness-to-hand [*Zuhandenheit*].'"[74] This fundamental mode of existence is nothing substantial, but it is located within an underlying context of use and application through which Dasein as a being in the world preconceptually organizes and evaluates beings in the service of its always ongoing projects. Dasein is always in a world, always ahead of itself, always engaged in projects, and always comporting to beings within an equipmental context of its concerns, whereby these beings are useful to it. This pragmatic basis underlies any objective regard for a present-at-hand object. In other words, the objection would go, beings—or "things"—indeed appear in *Being and Time* and do so in terms of either presence or utility.

Further, if we were to respond to this objection by insisting on the term *thing* (*Ding*) as distinct from the present at hand or the ready to hand, to claim that Heidegger does not think "things" in *Being and Time*, our interlocutor could simply point to the text—to wit, Heidegger's analysis of the worldhood of the world. This investigation begins from a conception of the "world of everyday Dasein," the environment: "We shall seek the worldhood of the environment (environmentality) by going through an ontological interpretation of those entities within-the-environment which we encounter as closest to us."[75] Heidegger wonders what sort of entities these may be (entities that will grant us access to Dasein's understanding of being as displayed in its concernful dealings). His response tells us all we need to know about the role of "things" in *Being and Time*:

> One may answer: "Things." But with this obvious answer we have perhaps already missed the pre-phenomenal basis we are seeking. For in addressing these entities as "Things" (*res*), we have tacitly anticipated their ontological character. When analysis starts with such entities and goes on to inquire about being, what it meets is thinghood and reality. Being as substantiality, material-ity, extendedness, side-by-side-ness, and so forth. But even pre-ontologically, in such being as this, the entities which we encounter in concern are proxi-mally hidden. When one designates things as the entities that are "proximally given," one goes ontologically astray, even though ontically one has something else in mind. What one really has in mind remains undetermined.[76]

Being and Time would thus already think the particular beings of the world and rebut any attempt to simply cast these beings as "things" as itself overlooking their fundamental status as ready to hand.

But it is precisely for this reason that we cannot speak of any "things" in *Being and Time* at all—not in the sense that Heidegger will develop the thing in his later work. A thing is no simple presence, nothing that can be understood as an inde-pendent and relationless unit of objective presence. Things concern us and appeal to us; we care for them and live with them. We leave our marks upon them, even wear them out, and they leave their marks upon us. They are nodes of a relation, not inert and dumb objects. Yet when *Being and Time* recognizes this and offers the ready to hand as an alternative to such objective presence, it changes nothing. To think of things in terms of tools is only to subordinate them to the purposes of a user. They serve as means to an external end. But things do not serve; they *are*. Heidegger's reflections through the 1930s lead to an understanding of the history of philosophy as a history of the will (as a 1945 dialogue expresses it, "with the word 'will' I do not in fact mean a faculty of the soul, but rather that wherein the essence of the soul, mind, reason, love, and life is based, according to a unani-mous yet hardly thought through doctrine of occidental thinkers").[77] Approach-ing the world in terms of use and utility, in terms of tools, is part and parcel of this metaphysical world of the will. It culminates in Nietzsche, or more precisely in that last avatar of Nietzsche, Ernst Jünger, who understands all of reality in terms of the worker (*Der Arbeiter*). The worker makes the world an unworld, a "workshop landscape."[78] In such a workshop, there is no place for things, only for tools that serve purposes outside of themselves and that are utterly replaceable in an endless mobilization.

For all its transformation of our conceptions of "subjectivity," *Being and Time* remains wedded to an inadequate conception of "objectivity," or thing-hood. To change our understanding of the subject, it is not enough to rethink human existence as Dasein. Humans do not exist alone, as no one knew better than Heidegger; they exist in a world, one replete with things. To transform the human through a thought of being in the world is to likewise transform the world, and so long as the hard philosophical work of transforming the conception of the thing in that world remains outstanding, nothing changes at all. To change the "subject" while retaining the "object" is to change nothing. The project of *Being and Time* demands more. The thinking of the fourfold provides this rethinking of thing and world and in this regard arguably could be read as the consummation of *Being and Time's* effort to think being in the world. But from another perspective, *Being and Time* could be said to participate in the general ignorance of things endemic to the history of philosophy itself. Heidegger's later thought corrects for this.

The thinking that Heidegger claims as his own is a thinking of things. In his publications, this thinking of things becomes understandable in terms of the philosophical tradition. Examining his views on that tradition, and his own formation within it, we can discern a few recurrent motifs that will come to fruition in his later thinking of things in his own terms.

1. The thing is nothing contained. Time and again things have been misunderstood as finished and encapsulated pieces of furniture. This trapping of the thing is one of the main trends of the traditional ways of conceiving them.
2. The thing is relational. Against this metaphysical confinement, Heidegger is able to detect another sense of things eluding that completion, a relational sense whereby things surpass themselves and enter into meaningful relations with the world around them, ourselves included.
3. These two conceptions, confinement and relationality, form a tension in the thinking of the thing. Heidegger's subsequent thinking of the fourfold does not alleviate this tension but exacerbates it, by breaking with the very notion of confinement as objectification in the name of a technological commodification and making-replaceable of the thing. Strikingly enough, we are not faced with a mere opposition, because it is this threatening replaceability that makes for the very singularity of things. Heidegger's history of things prepares us for this move and this new tension of thought endemic to his thinking of the fourfold.

Notes

1. Letter to Dieter Sinn of August 24, 1964, cited in Sinn, *Ereignis und Nirwana*, 172–73, emphasis modified.
2. See Mitchell, *Fourfold*.
3. Heidegger, *Die Frage Nach Dem Ding*, 83; *What Is a Thing?*, 83. Translation mine.

4. Heidegger, *Die Frage Nach Dem Ding*, 84; *What Is a Thing?*, 83. Translation mine.

5. Heidegger, *Die Frage Nach Dem Ding*, 84; *What Is a Thing?*, 83. Translation mine.

6. All natural motion is understood in terms of the earth, as either up or down in regard to it, or even as circling around it, as is the case with the vaulting sky. These are the same kinesthetic movements that Husserl discerns to be the bare minimum required for a three-dimensional world. Cf. Husserl, *Ding Und Raum*, 255; *Thing and Space*, 216.

7. Heidegger, *Die Frage Nach Dem Ding*, 85; *What Is a Thing?*, 84. Translation mine.

8. Heidegger, *Die Frage Nach Dem Ding*, 85; *What Is a Thing?*, 84. Translation mine.

9. Heidegger, *Die Frage Nach Dem Ding*, 85; *What Is a Thing?*, 84. Translation mine.

10. Heidegger, "Die Frage Nach Der Technik," 10; "Question concerning Technology," 7. Translation mine.

11. Heidegger, "Die Frage Nach Der Technik," 12; "Question concerning Technology," 9. Translation mine.

12. Heidegger, "Die Frage Nach Der Technik," 12; "Question concerning Technology," 10. Translation mine.

13. Heidegger says *mitschuld* and *mitverschuldet*, "co-indebted." Heidegger, "Die Frage Nach Der Technik," 10; "Question concerning Technology," 7; Heidegger, "Die Frage Nach Der Technik," 11; "Question concerning Technology," 8. Translation mine.

14. Heidegger, "Das Ding," 14; "Thing," 13.

15. Heidegger, "Das Ding," 13; "Thing," 12.

16. Heidegger, "Das Ding," 14; "Thing," 13.

17. Heidegger, "Das Ding," 14; "Thing," 13.

18. Heidegger, "Das Ding," 14; "Thing," 13.

19. Heidegger, "Das Ding," 15; "Thing," 14.

20. Heidegger, "Das Ding," 14; "Thing," 13.

21. Heidegger, "Das Ding," 13; "Thing," 12.

22. Heidegger, "Das Ding," 15; "Thing," 14.

23. Heidegger, "Das Ding," 15; "Thing," 14.

24. Heidegger, "Das Ding," 15; "Thing," 15; Heidegger, "Die Kehre," 70; "The Turning," 66.

25. Heidegger, *Die Frage Nach Dem Ding*, 73; *What Is a Thing?*, 72–73.

26. Heidegger, *Die Frage Nach Dem Ding*, 73; *What Is a Thing?*, 72. Translation mine.

27. Heidegger, *Die Frage Nach Dem Ding*, 73; *What Is a Thing?*, 73. Translation mine.

28. Heidegger, *Die Frage Nach Dem Ding*, 92; *What Is a Thing?*, 92. Translation mine.

29. Heidegger, *Die Frage Nach Dem Ding*, 76; *What Is a Thing?*, 75. Translation mine.

30. Newton, *Principia*, 416.

31. Heidegger, *Die Frage Nach Dem Ding*, 89; *What Is a Thing?*, 89.

32. Heidegger, *Die Frage Nach Dem Ding*, 89–90; *What Is a Thing?*, 89. Translation mine.

33. Heidegger, *Die Frage Nach Dem Ding*, 90; *What Is a Thing?*, 89.

34. Heidegger, *Die Frage Nach Dem Ding*, 89; *What Is a Thing?*, 88.

35. Heidegger, *Die Frage Nach Dem Ding*, 87; *What Is a Thing?*, 86. Translation mine.

36. Heidegger, *Die Frage Nach Dem Ding*, 87; *What Is a Thing?*, 86.

37. Heidegger, *Die Frage Nach Dem Ding*, 87; *What Is a Thing?*, 86. Translation mine.

38. Heidegger, *Die Frage Nach Dem Ding*, 173; *What Is a Thing?*, 169.

39. Heidegger, *Die Frage Nach Dem Ding*, 55; *What Is a Thing?*, 55. Translation mine.

40. Heidegger, *Die Frage Nach Dem Ding*, 61; *What Is a Thing?*, 62. Translation mine.

41. Heidegger, *Die Frage Nach Dem Ding*, 131; *What Is a Thing?*, 128. Translation mine.

42. Heidegger, *Die Frage Nach Dem Ding*, 214; *What Is a Thing?*, 211. Translation mine.

43. Heidegger, *Die Frage Nach Dem Ding*, 170; *What Is a Thing?*, 166.
44. Heidegger, *Die Frage Nach Dem Ding*, 144; *What Is a Thing?*, 141. Translation mine.
45. Heidegger, *Die Frage Nach Dem Ding*, 220; *What Is a Thing?*, 218. Translation mine.
46. Kant, *Critique of Pure Reason*, A160, B199.
47. Heidegger, *Die Frage Nach Dem Ding*, 188; *What Is a Thing?*, 184. Translation mine.
48. Heidegger, *Die Frage Nach Dem Ding*, 246; *What Is a Thing?*, 244. Translation mine.
49. Heidegger, *Die Frage Nach Dem Ding*, 246; *What Is a Thing?*, 244. Translation mine.
50. Heidegger, *Die Frage Nach Dem Ding*, 244; *What Is a Thing?*, 242.
51. Heidegger, *Die Frage Nach Dem Ding*, 245; *What Is a Thing?*, 242. Translation mine.
52. Husserl, *Ding Und Raum*, 62, 63, 72; *Thing and Space*, 52, 53, 60.
53. Husserl, *Ding Und Raum*, 162; *Thing and Space*, 137.
54. Husserl, *Ding Und Raum*, 80; *Thing and Space*, 66. Husserl later specifies that "this relational point is not the entire body but is set within an unseen part of the body. It resides somewhere in the head, in the eye or behind the eye" (Husserl, *Ding Und Raum*, 227–28; *Thing and Space*, 193).
55. Husserl, *Ding Und Raum*, 176; *Thing and Space*, 148.
56. Husserl, *Ding Und Raum*, 162; *Thing and Space*, 137.
57. Husserl, *Ding Und Raum*, 57, 193; *Thing and Space*, 48, 162.
58. Husserl, *Ding Und Raum*, 191; *Thing and Space*, 161.
59. Husserl, *Ding Und Raum*, 188; *Thing and Space*, 158.
60. Husserl, *Ding Und Raum*, 189; *Thing and Space*, 159.
61. Husserl, *Ding Und Raum*, 189; *Thing and Space*, 159.
62. Husserl, *Ding Und Raum*, 292; *Thing and Space*, 252–53.
63. Husserl, *Ding Und Raum*, 293; *Thing and Space*, 253.
64. Husserl, *Ding Und Raum*, 138; *Thing and Space*, 114.
65. Husserl, *Ding Und Raum*, 138; *Thing and Space*, 114–15.
66. Husserl, *Ding Und Raum*, 189; *Thing and Space*, 159.
67. Husserl, *Ding Und Raum*, 61; *Thing and Space*, 52.
68. Husserl, *Ding Und Raum*, 290; *Thing and Space*, 251.
69. Husserl, *Ding Und Raum*, 209; *Thing and Space*, 177. It is noteworthy that for Husserl this world or field is nothing homogeneous: "the field that is given to us phenomenologically is inhomogeneous" (Husserl, *Ding Und Raum*, 192; *Thing and Space*, 162).
70. Husserl, *Ding Und Raum*, 288; *Thing and Space*, 249.
71. Husserl, *Ding Und Raum*, 290; *Thing and Space*, 250–51.
72. Heidegger, *Sein Und Zeit*, 82; *SZ*, 61.
73. Cf. Heidegger, *Sein Und Zeit*, 92; *SZ*, 68.
74. Heidegger, *Sein Und Zeit*, 92, 93; *SZ*, 68, 69.
75. Heidegger, *Sein Und Zeit*, 89; *SZ*, 66.
76. Heidegger, *Sein Und Zeit*, 91; *SZ*, 67–68.
77. Heidegger, *Feldweg-Gespräche*, 78; *Country Path Conversations*, 49.
78. "Werkstättenlandschaft" (Jünger, *Essays*, 224).

Bibliography

Heidegger, Martin. *Country Path Conversations*. Translated by Bret Davis. Bloomington: Indiana University Press, 2010.

———. "Das Ding." In *Bremer und Freiburger Vorträge*, GA 79, edited by Petra Jaeger, 5–23. Frankfurt am Main: Klostermann, 1994.

———. *Feldweg-Gespräche*. GA 77. Edited by Ingrid Schüßler. Frankfurt am Main: Klostermann, 1995.

———. *Die Frage Nach Dem Ding. Kants Lehre von Den Transzendentalen Grundsätzen*. GA 41. Edited by Petra Jaeger. Frankfurt am Main: Klostermann, 1984.

———. "Die Frage Nach Der Technik." In *Vorträge Und Aufsätze*, GA 7, edited by Friedrich-Wilhelm von Herrmann, 5–36. Frankfurt am Main: Klostermann, 2000.

———. "Die Kehre." In *Bremer Und Freiburger Vorträge*, GA 79, edited by Petra Jaeger, 68–78. Frankfurt am Main: Klostermann, 1994.

———. "The Question Concerning Technology." In *The Question Concerning Technology, and Other Essays*. Translated and with an introduction by William Lovit, 3–34. New York: Harper and Row, 1977.

———. *Sein Und Zeit*. 18th ed. Tübingen: Niemeyer, 2001.

———. *Sein Und Zeit*. GA 2. Edited by Friedrich-Wilhelm von Herrmann. Frankfurt am Main: Klostermann, 1977.

———. "The Thing." In *Bremen and Freiburg Lectures: Insight into That Which Is and Basic Principles of Thinking*. Translated by Andrew J. Mitchell, 5–22. Studies in Continental Thought. Bloomington: Indiana University Press, 2012.

———. "The Turning." In *Bremen and Freiburg Lectures: Insight into That Which Is and Basic Principles of Thinking*. Translated by Andrew J. Mitchell, 64–76. Studies in Continental Thought. Bloomington: Indiana University Press, 2012.

———. *What Is a Thing?* Translated by W. B. Barton Jr. and Vera Deutsch. Chicago: H. Regnery, 1968.

Husserl, Edmund. *Ding Und Raum. Vorlesungen 1907*. Vol. Husserliana 16. Edited by Ulrich Claesges. The Hague: Martinus Nijhoff, 1973.

———. *Thing and Space: Lectures of 1907*. Translated by Richard Rojcewicz. Dordrecht: Kluwer Academic, 1997.

Jünger, Ernst. *Essays*. Vol. SW 8. Werke. Stuttgart: Klett, 1963.

Kant, Immanuel. *The Critique of Pure Reason*. Translated by Paul Guyer and Allen W. Wood. Cambridge: Cambridge University Press, 1998.

Mitchell, Andrew J. *The Fourfold: Reading the Late Heidegger*. Evanston, IL: Northwestern University Press, 2015.

Newton, Isaac. *The Principia: Mathematical Principles of Natural Philosophy*. Translated by I. Bernhard Cohen and Anne Whitman. Berkeley: University of California Press, 1999.

Sinn, Dieter. *Ereignis und Nirwana: Heidegger, Buddhismus, Mythos, Mystik; zur Archäotypik des Denkens*. Abhandlungen zur Philosophie, Psychologie und Pädagogik. Bonn: Bouvier, 1991.

ANDREW J. MITCHELL is Winship Distinguished Research Professor of Philosophy at Emory University. He focuses on nineteenth- and twentieth-century German philosophy. He is author of *The Fourfold: Reading the Late Heidegger* and *Heidegger among the Sculptors: Body, Space, and the Art of Dwelling*.

IV.
Ground, Non-ground, and Abyss

13 Heidegger, Leibniz, and the Abyss of Reason

Hans Ruin

1.

Heidegger's first systematic and most detailed confrontation with the work of Leibniz is a lecture course he gives in the academic year 1928. The result comprises the volume *Metaphysische Anfangsgründe der Logik im Ausgang von Leibniz*[1] and also the separate lecture "On the Essence of Ground" ("Vom Wesen des Grundes").[2] In the winter semester of 1935–36, he returns again to Leibniz in a series on "Leibniz' concept of world and German idealism (Monadology)." The context here is his extensive project during this time to come to terms with German idealism, its philosophical roots and legacy.[3] The lecture notes from this course were released in 2013. Some of the sessions were devoted to the problem of reason/ground. However, because of the brevity and incompleteness of both Heidegger's lectures and the preserved student's notes in this volume, it is a material that does not really permit a systematic interpretation. In the context of his work on Nietzsche during the period 1936–42, Heidegger also discusses Leibniz and his position within the history of modern philosophy, but here the topic is not that of ground.[4] The final and philosophically most decisive stage of his encounter with Leibniz takes place in 1955–56 when he gives the lecture series *The Principle of Reason* (*Der Satz vom Grund*) and also presents a separate talk under the same heading, which was published in the same volume.[5] In what follows I will concentrate on the first and last stage of this lifelong philosophical confrontation (*Auseinandersetzung*).

The first series of lectures on Leibniz and the problem of ground is given in the year following the publication of *Being and Time*. Heidegger refers to his own book throughout the course, and its basic notions are deployed as a theoretical framework for the interpretation. This is true also of the subsequent essay "On the Essence of Ground," which I will here treat as part of the same material. At this time, he still sustains the ambition of performing a "destruction" (*Destruktion*) of the history of ontology with the project of reopening the question of being through an existential analytic—in other words, the program that had been outlined in *Being and Time*. The interpretation of Leibniz presented there could well have been fit into one of its remaining projected but unpublished parts.

The starting point for the lectures is the question of logic, its historical development and significance. Heidegger's overall ambition is to show how the ordinary and present-day understanding of logic is in need of a deeper foundation. More specifically, he wants to demonstrate how this foundation could and must be achieved through an ontological interpretation. It is within this framework that Leibniz's thought is presented as a paradigmatic case of a philosophy often taken to emanate exclusively from logical considerations. At the outset Heidegger presents the famous Leibniz-scholar Louis Couturat's reading and that of Bertrand Russell as examples of work along this line of interpretation.[6] In contrast with this thinking, he argues that the goal of a contemporary critical understanding should instead be to lay bare the foundations that were neither seen nor reflected on by Leibniz himself. A certain "violence" must therefore be committed to the original text, with the risk of losing sight of what could be called "Leibniz's original intention," which is a risk that he also acknowledges.[7]

Heidegger's hermeneutic disloyalty becomes especially clear in the case of the principle of sufficient reason/ground. In the end, he refuses to accept the principle as such and also to take it at its face value, as a "principium," as what comes *first*. Instead he raises the question of what being must be like in order for the quest for a reason or foundation—for a *Grund*—to appear in the first place. The principle of an ultimate foundation is thus itself questioned with regard to its ultimate foundation. From one perspective Heidegger's approach could appear circular. But he is seeking to turn Leibniz's system inside out, rearranging the parts while still leaving something of the totality intact. This rearrangement is performed with the help of three fundamental concepts—truth, world, and *Dasein*—in ways that I will briefly recapitulate.

When discussing Leibniz's understanding of truth, Heidegger refers to it as a "theory of inclusion."[8] If the complete concept of an entity implies all its predicates, then the true judgment is simply a parallel coupling of properties, and truth itself becomes such a "coupling" or "connection." Truth for Leibniz is a relation of *inesse*, in both a logical and an ontic sense. This means that truth is present and actual even when not expressed in a human judgment, and the original substance in its self-identity is a permanent truth in the eye of God. Heidegger writes: "The original truth, the totality of all true knowledge, is absolute, and is found in the *scientia Dei*. . . . The basic problems of modern philosophy remain completely closed to one who has no acquaintance with and understanding of these connections."[9]

It is through the mediation of the eye of God that this identity of the truth and objectivity can be sustained, as an identity that is achieved through

perception and that exists as a unified manifold in and of itself. Given this identity, perception, thought, and existence are the same in God, and the individual
human being is seen as ultimately oriented toward the same ideal. Truth is identity, and identity characterizes existence as such on the ultimate level. This idea
is also what guarantees the foundational role of the principle of sufficient reason
in Leibniz's system. Heidegger writes: "The principle of reason holds first rank,
albeit unclearly, among the principles. A connection emerges between reason, or
ground, and truth and being, with reference to identity."[10]

The notion of a basic metaphysical identity that unifies a manifold both
implies and is implied by the structure of the monad. Consequently, the first part
of the lectures deals extensively with this part of Leibniz's metaphysics, which
in Heidegger's eyes both incorporates and anticipates some of the basic tenets
of modern thinking. For the present purpose, however, it suffices to see how a
deeper understanding of the principle must be extracted from within the constellation of reason/ground, truth, and being.

The next step is therefore to question the notion of truth that more or less
explicitly guides Leibniz's reasoning. At this point of the argument, Heidegger
activates the critical understanding of truth that he had developed in *Being and
Time* the year before. In the second part of the lectures, he recapitulates at length
the analysis of truth as disclosure (*Erschlossenheit*) and discoveredness or unconcealment (*Unverborgenheit*). By turning the focus away from truth as the equivalent of being and toward truth as manifestation and appearance, and thus to the
existential conditions of disclosure, he transforms the question of truth into what
we could call a "transcendental" concern: the condition of the possibility of truth
(in the ordinary correspondence-theory version). At the same time, the concept
of "the transcendental" also needs to be understood in a somewhat different way
from what we are used to from Kant and Husserl. It is not a stable extra-empirical
ground or condition but rather an inherent structure of *transcendence*, of a constant going beyond "in the direction of which."

This takes him to the next two concepts mentioned above, namely *world* and
Dasein. Dasein is a being that transcends, by going beyond the purely factual in
establishing a reciprocal relation to a world and also to itself. The world is not
something that simply subsists, waiting for Dasein to enter into a relation with
it. In the schema that Heidegger outlines, *world* becomes available only through
the transcending movement of Dasein. *World* is a horizon from within which
singular beings and states of affairs can emerge and take on importance. It is
what encompasses every single being, and yet it should not be understood as
a substantial manifold: "'World' as a concept of the being of beings designates
the wholeness of beings in the totality of their possibilities, a wholeness which
is itself, however, essentially related to human existence, and human existence
taken in its final goal."[11]

The disclosive opening up of a world within which beings can come to presence is an "event" or "happening" (*Geschehen*) in which Dasein is involved as both active and passive. It is a "transcending" event of projection toward a world, to which it also abandons itself. Transcendence is described as a "for the sake of" (*Umwillen*) along the same line as "care" (*Sorge*) in *Being and Time*. It is also given a temporal interpretation and described as the basic movement of temporalization. "I maintain that the intrinsic possibility of transcendence is time, as primordial temporality!"[12]

With regard to the more fundamental level of original temporality and temporalization, Heidegger thus claims to have established the basis he needs for interpreting the Leibnizian principle of ground/reason. In the concluding part of the lecture series, he returns to give the principle a fuller treatment. His central idea is that the whole question of an ultimate reason or ground leads back toward itself as a question. It leads back to that which is in need of such a foundation, and also to that which is capable of providing it. More specifically, it points to the *freedom* of human existence as transcendence and "for the sake of," and ultimately to the problem of time and temporality. The origin of ground/reason, Heidegger writes, "lies in freedom as the freedom for ground."[13] Through this move he does not wish to diminish the issue of ultimate foundations by portraying them as simply a meaning projection issuing from human existence, or in other words, as something purely "subjective." Instead he wants to maintain the two aspects or dimensions of the problem, where being is understood as containing its own transcendental foundation in the form of human transcendence and freedom. The whole issue of ground is thereby pushed back toward the grounding as an aspect of the ontology of human existence and thus as an aspect of being as such. Only in the context of this reflexively understood ontology can the principle of sufficient reason be adequately interpreted and understood.

This interpretation of the problem of ground may at first seem entirely out of touch with Leibniz's original problem and its articulation. Replacing the problem of explicability with that of human transcendence and freedom could seem to amount precisely to a subjectification of the basic principle of causal explanation. But through a closer examination of the argument, the apparent disparity is transformed into a more complex and multifaceted philosophical relation.

The first question to ask is then on what specific point Heidegger reproaches Leibniz in his use and understanding of the principle of sufficient reason. Mainly, he refers to the fact that Leibniz seems to take its applicability for granted. Why can he take it for granted? Because Leibniz's notion of truth as identity guarantees that there is always an ultimate reason to be given for every phenomenal truth. Heidegger's point would then be that this takes something else for granted, something that rests on an unarticulated foundation. We cannot, according to his view, develop metaphysics simply by using a principle without bringing that very principle in question. The move is similar to that which we find at the outset of *Being and Time*, where the question of being is accessed through an investigation of the being of the questioner itself—Dasein. Such a hermeneutic, reflexive, and perhaps critical turn of the argument would seem entirely foreign to Leibniz. In other words, this very move would seem to take us away from what is at stake in his thinking. At the same time, we should consider the fact that the hermeneutic question emphasizes the need to rethink the relation between the subject and object in the act of knowledge. One of Heidegger's fundamental claims is to have shown how this subject-object dichotomy collapses on a deeper level of analysis, where it could be seen as emanating from within the more basic ontological existential category of Being in the world. When we look closer at Leibniz's system, we can sense a similar trajectory. Leibniz too seeks to escape the fundamental separation between subject and object. At the deepest metaphysical level of his system, this distinction is replaced by the monad, which in itself and through its own existence seems to encompass the world as a web of internal relations. At the monadological level, there is no longer any distinction between subject and object because both converge in the perception that constitutes, so to speak, the "life" of this manifold unity.[14]

It is true that Leibniz lacked the conceptual tools and the inclination to question the notion of objectivity and, thus, the concept of substance, just as he was unable to articulate a convincing path leading from natural experience to that of metaphysical description. All of these factors give his system a somewhat alien and even arcane character from the perspective of modern, post-Kantian philosophy. This impression nevertheless changes when it is interpreted in the direction of its more far-reaching implications. In the case of the principle of sufficient reason, its applicability is said to rest on a notion of truth as identity, which then results in the fact *that there is always a reason to be given*. But another way of stating the same point is to say that *everything is in principle knowable*. The principle would then be seen as a principle of universal intelligibility. This necessity implies the existence of someone who understands and is potentially open to being and to what is potentially there to be revealed.

Questions nevertheless remain: How can Leibniz be certain that there is always something to be known, and how can he be certain concerning the ultimate rationality of being? This last question leads to God, as the ultimate guarantee not only of the fact of being but also of its rationality, its *intelligibility*. God is the guarantee and the giver of light, a light that from God's perspective is always present but that is and must be concealed in its plenitude to finite beings. Truth in Leibniz can thus be said to be rooted in a spiritual openness to being, namely to that of God. Truth and light, as metaphors of intelligibility, are somehow secured from the start, and their failure to shine forth is only the result of the contingent finitude of man.

In Heidegger's view, this openness to being can only be understood from the point of view of where it actually takes place (viz., in the temporalizing existence of finite Dasein). Its finitude and its freedom—in other words, its transcendence—cannot be separated since they are ultimately rooted in temporality as finite meaning projections. For Leibniz, there is always a reason to be articulated and given, since the existence of such a reason belongs to being itself through God. For Heidegger, there is rather always a *question* about reason to be raised since it is part of the being of Dasein to be projected toward the world. From this sketchy comparison, we can sense how the ultimate discrepancy between the two partially hinges on the issue of the finitude of subjectivity and on the question of whether we can legitimately assume the existence of a positive infinity.

A somewhat simplistic way of summarizing Heidegger's first attempt to confront Leibniz's metaphysics of ground and truth would be to say that, whereas Leibniz upholds an "objectivist" or "naturalist" position, Heidegger tries to show how the objective conception of ground and truth ultimately recoils back to the meaning projections of finite Dasein. For Heidegger, the overall project during this period was the attempt to articulate the free and transcending finitude of Dasein as a nonfoundational foundation and to show that the infinite is only comprehensible from this finite perspective. In the debate with Cassirer in Davos the following year, this is the key issue, where Heidegger defends the idea that the infinite can only be understood on the basis of a finite existence. In contrast to this position, we have Cassirer's more Kantian, and perhaps also Leibnizian, premise, according to which Heidegger's insistence on finitude inevitably results in a subjectification of truth and a neglect of the necessity of positing the infinite as horizon in order even to speak of the finite.[15]

Even though Heidegger will never recognize that the existential analytic of *Being and Time* amounted to a "subjectification" of truth and being, his subsequent writings display an attempt to more clearly distance himself from such implications. After his "turning" (*die Kehre*), roughly around 1930, human Dasein is increasingly seen as itself the effect or outcome of being rather than as a finite ground of being's appearing. In my reading of the second stage of Heidegger's discussion of the principle of reason, this tendency is also clearly visible in his continued encounter with Leibniz.

2.

In a passage from the 1928 lecture "On the Essence of Ground" ("Vom Wesen des Grundes"), Heidegger gathers some of the elements from his extensive interpretation in the lecture course in a dense and poetic formulation: "Only if, amid beings in their totality, beings come to be 'more in being' in the manner of the temporalizing of Dasein are there the hours and days of beings' entry into world."[16]

In the accompanying notes, which were taken from Heidegger's own copy of the text and added by the editor to the *Gesamtausgabe* edition, Heidegger reacts strongly to this particular passage, and for two reasons. The first concerns the way in which it anticipates what is to come later, and the second, that it does so in a confused and only tentative way. He writes: "Here the preparation of the quite other commencement; everything still mixed and confused; contorted into phenomenological-existential . . . 'research.'"[17] The remark refers to the afore-mentioned "turning" in his own thinking, from the existential ontology of Das-ein to the thinking of the truth and event of being. The implications of this new approach are most systematically explored and developed in the *Contributions to Philosophy (of the Event)*, from the years 1936–38, but it was initiated some years earlier. By the time Heidegger returns to Leibniz and the problem of ground/rea-son in the early to middle 1950s, this reorientation is part of a completed journey. When looking back on his 1928 course, he concludes that it was correct insofar as it saw Leibniz's principle of sufficient reason/ground as not saying anything about reason/ground itself. For this reason he thought it justified to interpret it as speaking about beings rather than about being. Still, the earlier interpretation is said to have ignored the next step, which is to truly *listen* to what the prin-ciple says about being on a deeper level.[18] The main goal of the later lectures thus amounts to demonstrating how the principle can be *heard* in such a different key.

Heidegger begins his analysis by pointing out how the human being is guided by the principle of sufficient reason in its daily life and activities, as it always attempts to give a reason for its judgments and convictions. It is a desire to provide rational foundations for what it encounters, a "quest for reasons," as he phrases it.[19] This desire is rooted in a certain understanding of being as that which stands before the rationally grounding subject and as that which is in need of a foundation. The very activity of providing a reason is located within an implicit subject-object dichotomy in which knowledge is equated with representation.[20] Heidegger writes that it is precisely this sense of the principle that is brought out by Leibniz when the latter speaks of it as a principle of "giving grounds," *rationis reddendae*. It is a principle that speaks of and regulates knowing, as a relation between the knower and the known, where the known is the represented or that which is "placed in front of," as *vorgestellt*.

As a guiding principle for knowledge acquisition, the principle constitutes what he calls a "power region," a *Machtbereich*. It is within this region that we find the principle of causation. The idea that everything should have a cause is guided by the desire to secure a foundation for everything that occurs. Heidegger stresses the Latin root of *ratio* as having to do with accounting and calculation.[21] The imperative to provide a reason is thus equated with giving an account or providing an encompassing calculation: "The principle of ground is the principle of rational thought in the sense of a calculation that certifies."[22]

These formulations point to the dominant, and perhaps most familiar, aspects of these lectures: their critique of a modern, technological, calculating administrative culture. This critique is not as explicit in the earlier lectures, even though it can be detected there as well. According to Heidegger's reading, the form of knowledge that is guided by the principle, as heard in this first key, reaches its culmination in the modern era of technology. He refers to it as the "atomic age," as the "information age," and as the epoch where the human domination of the earth has reached its peak: "As the global epoch of humanity, the atomic age is distinguished by the fact that the power of the mighty Principle, of the *principium reddendae rationis*, displays itself (if not completely unleashed) in a strange manner in the normative domain of human existence."[23]

This aspect of the interpretation is an important incentive for the lecture series as a whole, and as such it realigns the later readings of Leibniz to the central topics of his later writings on technology, *Gestell*, and modernity as dominated by a metaphysical will to power.

In his continued exploration of the principle, Heidegger moves along two different trajectories. One has to do with how the principle itself is linguistically formulated, and the second issues from more general considerations. For the first, Heidegger focuses on the expression *nihil est sine ratione*, "nothing is without ground/reason." This can be heard first as a statement about things and events in the world, namely saying that none of them lacks a reason or ground. When heard in this way, the principle calls on one to find the reason or produce the appropriate account. The very same statement can also be heard in another tonality. This happens if one shifts the stress from the *nihil* to the *est*. Then it reads "*nothing* is without reason/ground" (*nichts* ist ohne Grund).[24] In this reading it points instead to the intimate connection between being as nothingness and reason/ground; in Heidegger's words, it indicates that "to being there belongs something like ground/reason. Being is akin to grounds, it is ground-like."[25] As long as the principle is applied to beings, it always points to that which lies beyond being. Yet when it is heard as a statement about being itself, it no longer speaks of what is to be found but rather *of that which in itself is a foundation*, or which is or prevails in a foundational way.

This conclusion leads us to the second approach. As long as the principle is heard in the first sense, it articulates a "why?" In other words, it directs the eye and the mind toward beings with a question concerning the reason for their existence. The statement "nothing is without reason/ground" can then be understood as saying that "nothing is without why." But when heard in the second key or tonality, this "why" disappears in favor of a sort of resting upheaval of the questioning mode itself. Heidegger quotes two lines from a poem by a contemporary of Leibniz, the Catholic priest and poet Angelus Silesius: "The rose is without why: it blooms because it blooms / It pays no attention to itself, asks not whether it is seen."[26] The German title of the two lines is "Ohne warum." The important move in these lines—which occupy a significant place within the lectures—is precisely the transition from the *warum* (why) to the *weil* (because). The translation of the *weil* becomes decisive here, since it partly carries the weight of Heidegger's critical interpretation. In most instances *weil* would be rendered as "because." But here this translation would eradicate the point he wants to make. The line articulates a perspective on being where there is no longer the question of giving a reason; it is not *because* it flowers that the rose flowers, which would make the line nonsensical. It flowers *in that it* flowers, and in this process it is without why. When heard in this key, the line speaks against the principle as formulated above, "Nothing is without why," since it says, "The rose is without why."

Such a reading of the line requires what Heidegger, with a Kierkegaardian formulation, speaks of as a "leap of thinking," a *Sprung des Denkens*.[27] The principle itself, when heard in this second tonality, is such a leap in and toward being. Playing on the double meaning of *Satz* in German, as both sentence and leap, Heidegger writes: "The principle of reason is a leap into being qua being, that is, qua ground/reason."[28] Being has no reason or ground; being is groundless, or in other words, an abyss, *Ab-grund*.[29] When the flowering of the flower is seen in this perspective, it ceases to point toward anything beyond itself. The flowering has its ground in itself, and as such it is what Heidegger calls a pure *Aufgehen*, a dawning or arising, a term he also used in his interpretations of the pre-Socratic *physis*.[30] Behind this move we can trace a polemical historical strategy; the first sense of the principle has already been said to regulate what is today conceived of as "physics" and its offspring, such as atomic power plants. Now the second sense is presented as a recovering of a supposedly more original sense of the physical, namely the Greek conception of nature as incessant abyssal arising.

If we compare these reflections with the formulations in the lectures from twenty-five years earlier, one aspect immediately stands out: the absence of an explicit discussion of human existence. In the earlier analysis, the focus was on the role of transcendence as a movement ultimately identical with Dasein's freedom, projecting it toward the world so as to let the world appear in a reciprocal constitution of subject and object. The change in the later interpretative encounter with Leibniz is both marginal and radical, depending on which perspective one chooses. In the later stage, Heidegger apparently no longer feels the need to take the detour over the analysis of Dasein as transcendence and freedom. This preparatory move is now substituted by an exhortation to listen and to leap into a state of responsive reverence with regard to being as such.

The principal feature, nevertheless, remains in that it is the aim of the analysis to extract a description of the transcendental and abyssal unity of being. In the early lectures, the aim was to see the foundation "occur" as an opening up of a "transcendental" space of meaning where beings can emerge, namely the temporality of Dasein. Here in the later analysis, this occurrence is described as a "happening" or "sending" of being itself, which is defined as "the proffering of the lighting and clearing that furnishes a domain for the appearing of beings."[31] Despite the change of focus and formulation, the issue nevertheless remains the relation between human existence and being as articulated through the principle of sufficient reason/ground, and the main point is to give an account of this ultimately abyssal domain of coming to be.

To summarize this schematic interpretation, we can distinguish two parallel movements that illustrate the relative change of scope. First, there is the movement from freedom to address (*Zuspruch*), as a means to convey Dasein's standing in regard to being. After first having been characterized as the transcending being, Dasein is now seen as the one being spoken to and called to respond. Second, there is a move from temporalization to event, from *Zeitigung* to *Ereignis*. In the early lectures, the original event was the temporality of human existence, from within whose transcending ecstatic movement being in the world is disclosed. In the later lectures, the original event is seen as emerging from within being itself, as a "sending of being," as an opening or "spacing" within which things and events can take place. In the 1962 lecture "On Time and Being" ("Zeit und Sein"), he will even speak of it as a "gift of being."[32]

3.

We have seen how the confrontation with Leibniz and the problem of ground/ reason holds a central place in the trajectory of Heidegger's path of thinking as a whole. It is in the attempt to interpret, make sense of, and ultimately locate the nature and meaning of this basic principle of logic and science that he elaborates some of his most far-reaching arguments. In the 1928 lectures on the metaphysical foundations of logic, he makes an effort to illuminate Leibniz's thinking from within itself and thus to generate a genuine confrontation, an *Auseinandersetzung*, with his work. In the 1955 course, Leibniz has been reduced more to the role of symbol or philosophical representative for an attitude toward thinking and philosophizing that is entirely guided by the principle of sufficient reason/ground, as heard in the first and conventional mode, where it implies total intelligibility.

It is also in relation to this attempt that the inner development of Heidegger's work, over and across the "turning," becomes visible in an exemplary way. For Heidegger, the confrontation with Leibniz is not just an attempt to come to terms with a central figure in the history of philosophy and a key predecessor to German idealism. Leibniz is also the symbol of a certain understanding of thinking that Heidegger will ultimately identify with "calculating" rationality, in explicit contrast to what he, from the late 1930s onward, will refer to as "reflexive" or "meditative" thinking (*Besinnung*).[33] In this concluding section, I want to indicate a few different ways in which his somewhat overly essentializing contrast of the two comportments can and should be problematized.

When introducing the lines by Silesius, Heidegger also quotes a letter where Leibniz speaks favorably of this somewhat older contemporary poet. After noting the interesting fact that not only Leibniz but also later Hegel held Silesius in high esteem, he nevertheless goes on to distinguish from the rationalism of Leibniz what he takes to be a poetic mode of thinking found in the contemplative tradition to which Silesius belongs.

In noting Leibniz's fascination for this "other" tradition, Heidegger has nevertheless opened a perspective on European rationalism that became the topic of several studies in more recent decades: its close connection to mystical and also Kabbalistic traditions. Allison Coudert speaks of it as the "important ways in which mystical and occult thinking contributed to the development of science and the emergence of toleration."[34] The kind of rationality that Leibniz represents is not simply the "other" of a supposedly more genuine "mystical" thinking. He could even be seen as someone who not only anticipates an age of expanded scientific-technological domination of the earth but also points toward a way of thinking the rationality of reason from within its own abyssal ground. The point was already made in Renato Cristin's 1990 dissertation in Italian, which also critically analyses Heidegger's dichotomous reading of Leibniz and the legacy of European rationalism.[35]

Leibniz repeatedly recognizes that the ultimate reason for the world cannot be given from within the world itself but must instead be sought in something extramundane. For him, this extramundane ground or reason for the world is God as creator. Such a solution would of course seem both unsatisfactory and disturbing to Heidegger, since it robs the world of its transcendent and abyssal character, transforming it into some kind of higher-order product or artifact. Heidegger therefore never recognizes that Leibniz's theological reflections or solutions could have any other sense than that of a hidden continuation of a metaphysics of human subjectivity and as ontotheology. Still, there is a similarity between their forms of reasoning when Leibniz speaks of God and Heidegger speaks of being. God is the uncaused cause, the unmoved mover, and the groundless ground. He is the abyssal presence and, as such, the giver of grace and enactor of miracles. Seen from this perspective, Heidegger's ontology could be read as a transformation of a Leibnizian God, dismantled of its ontotheological characteristics, returning again as the ultimate ungrounded ground. In the thinking of the event, we would then trace the problem of creation, as the incalculable happening of being. This is not meant to say that Leibniz' philosophical theology and Heidegger's ontology are "the same." Simply equating the two amounts to a superficial eradication of difference. The point here is that we need to question and learn to move across the strict borders that Heidegger creates in his own somewhat Manichean conception of the tradition. Leibniz is a particularly good case in point since his work is so much more complex and multifaceted than it ultimately appears in Heidegger's later writings on the problem of ground.

In Heidegger's view, the modern attitude toward knowledge and being not only presupposes a metaphysics but is actually seen as emanating from a particular metaphysical articulation of being, for which Leibniz, with his principle of reason, becomes an ultimate representative. He traces this notion of being not only to its early modern European roots, but also to its Greek heritage, and to Platonism in particular. Throughout his later writings, he seeks support from alternatives, notably in the poetry of Hölderlin and in pre-Socratic thinking, but also in sources, such as Eckhart, Hamann and Silesius, that are often labeled as belonging to a "mystical" and esoteric tradition. But in order to see the complex interpenetrations of traditions here, we need to question also the meaning of "the mystical."

Despite his profound interest in these sources, Heidegger was in fact quite skeptical vis-à-vis *mysticism* as a name for a doctrine and philosophical tradition. This is clearly the case in his outline for a course on mysticism that he had already designed in 1919 but never presented.[36] In the end, Heidegger never tries to come to terms with this tradition in its own right; instead he chooses to insert bits and pieces from it in his readings of others, as in the exemplary case of his Leibniz interpretations, where the particular quotation from Silesius obtains a decisive role for the whole argument.[37] This somewhat peculiar situation of reverence and lack of genuine philosophical confrontation should not, however, be taken to mean that Heidegger uncritically embraced Christian mysticism as a secret source for his own work. He makes it very clear on several occasions that he wants to maintain a distance from this tradition, as when in the Nietzsche lectures he remarks that many people try in vain to take refuge in mysticism. In the few explicit remarks on Eckhart that we find in his work, Heidegger even suggests, in a somewhat uncritical affirmation of will and reason, that Eckhart himself never escaped the confines of Christian metaphysics. In sum, we do not find in Heidegger's work a clear and positive endorsement of the "mystical."

An important reason for this is his insistence that we should refrain from becoming trapped in the dichotomous contrast between rationality and mysticism. Translated back to the discussion about the principle of ground, it means that what we seek in the critical, poetical listening to the principle of ground is not an alternative, separate, and different type of rationality. Instead it is the ability to listen to and from within reason itself, for its own hidden other. Then the critical potential is not primarily agonistic, as it was sometimes indicated and often portrayed. Rather it is emancipatory, in the sense that it listens for the binding compulsion to give grounds, as something that itself is ultimately ungrounded. In this way, and despite Heidegger's reluctance to speak of the problem of freedom in the later writings, it opens for a liberating comportment vis-à-vis the inner demand of rationality. In any case, the great merit of Heidegger's reading of the principle of reason is to have permitted this idea to resonate in a key where reason is becoming free for itself and for the opening "toward the secret," of which the later essay on *Gelassenheit* so beautifully speaks.[38] Whether or not this strategy marks a decisive step away from the confines of Leibniz's metaphysics seems to me a question that cannot be definitively answered. But through his creative appropriation and sounding displacement of the principle of reason/ground, Heidegger pointed the way toward a new and different appropriation of the legacy of European rationalism.

Notes

1. Heidegger, *Metaphysical Foundations of Logic*.

2. The lectures are published in German as GA 26, and the lecture was included in Heidegger, *Wegmarken*, 123–75.

3. Published as Heidegger, GA 84.1.

4. The lectures on Nietzsche were published in an edited form as his *Nietzsche I* and *Nietzsche II*, and then separately in six volumes of the *Gesamtausgabe* (GA 43, 44, 46, 47, 48, and 50). The excursus on Leibniz is found in Heidegger, *Nietzsche II*, 397–416.

5. Heidegger, *Der Satz Vom Grund*.

6. Heidegger pays particular tribute to the work of Louis Couturat, from which he obviously profited a great deal, especially for specific references to quotations from Leibniz. In the parallel lecture "Vom Wesen des Grundes," Couturat is mentioned in somewhat more critical terms. Here Heidegger states that he is in agreement neither with Couturat's overall interpretation of Leibniz nor with his understanding of logic. Cf. Heidegger, *Wegmarken*, 128.

7. For his remarks on interpretative methods, cf. Heidegger, *Metaphysische Anfangsgründe der Logik*, 88; 135–36.

8. Heidegger, *Metaphysical Foundations of Logic*, 29. ("Inklusionstheorie." Heidegger, *Metaphysische Anfangsgründe der Logik*, 57.)

9. Heidegger, *Metaphysical Foundations of Logic*, 43. Original text: "Die ursprüngliche Wahrheit, d.h. die Allheit aller wahren Erkenntnis, ist absolut, und zwar in der scientia Dei . . . Ohne Kenntnis und Verständnis dieser Zusammenhänge bleiben die Grundprobleme der neuen Philosophie völlig verschlossen" (Heidegger, *Metaphysische Anfangsgründe der Logik*, 54).

10. Heidegger, *Metaphysical Foundations of Logic*, 55. Original text: "Unter den Grundsätzen hat der Satz vom Grunde, obzwar undeutlich, den Vorrang. Es zeigt sich ein Zusammenhang von Grund und Wahrheit und Sein, im Hinblick auf Identität" (Heidegger, *Metaphysische Anfangsgründe der Logik*, 68).

11. Heidegger, *Metaphysical Foundations of Logic*, 180. Original text: "Welt' als Begriff des Seins des Seienden kennzeichnet die Ganzheit des Seienden in der Totalität seiner

Möglichkeiten, diese selbst aber ist wesenhaft bezogen auf menschliche Existenz, und diese genommen in ihrem Endzweck" (Heidegger, *Metaphysische Anfangsgründe der Logik*, 231).

12. Heidegger, *Metaphysical Foundations of Logic*, 195. Original text: "Die innere Möglichkeit der Transzendenz, so behaupte ich, ist die Zeit als ursprüngliche Zeitlichkeit!" (Heidegger, *Metaphysische Anfangsgründe der Logik*, 252.)

13. Heidegger, *Metaphysical Foundations of Logic*, 218. Original text: "liegt in der Freiheit als der Freiheit zum Grunde" (Heidegger, *Metaphysische Anfangsgründe der Logik*, 282).

14. Heidegger never tries to read the *Monadology* and the monadological model in this direction. Still, it would be a worthwhile task to try to develop it, and to see to what extent Leibniz, just like Kant in Heidegger's reading, could be brought closer to an existential-analytical interpretation. In such an attempt, one should also take note of the fact that in his later work, notably in the fifth *Cartesian Meditation*, speaks of transcendental intersubjectivity in terms of monadology.

15. For a more detailed reading of the Heidegger-Cassirer debate, see Ruin, "Technology and Destiny in Heidegger and Cassirer."

16. Heidegger, *Pathmarks*, 123. Original text: "Nur wenn in der Allheit von Seiendem das Seiende 'seiender' wird in der Weise der Zeitigung von Dasein, ist Stunde des Welteingangs von Seiendem. Und nur wenn diese Urgeschichte, die Transzendenz, geschieht, d.h. wenn Seiendes vom Charakter des In-der-Welt-Seins in das Seiende einbricht, besteht die Möglichkeit, daß Seiendes sich offenbart" (Heidegger, "Vom Wesen des Grundes," 159). This whole passage and the problem of world-entry has become the subject of heated discussions among the more analytical Heideggerians. See in particular David R. Cerbone's essay "World, World-Entry, and Realism in Early Heidegger," which was followed up in Taylor Carman's book *Heidegger's Analytic*.

17. Heidegger, *Pathmarks*, 123. Original text: "Hier: die Vorbereitung des ganz anderen Anfangs; alles noch gemischt und verworren; verzwungen in phänomenologisch-existenzialer . . . Forschung" (Heidegger, "Vom Wesen des Grundes," 159).

18. Heidegger, *Der Satz Vom Grund*, 84–85.

19. Heidegger, *Principle of Reason*, 3. "Trachten nach Gründen" (Heidegger, *Der Satz Vom Grund*, 13.)

20. Heidegger, *Der Satz Vom Grund*, 45.

21. Heidegger, *Der Satz Vom Grund*, 166–67.

22. Heidegger, "Principle of Ground," 212. Original text: "Der Satz vom Grund ist der Grundsatz des vernünftigen Vorstellens im Sinne des sicherstellenden Rechnens" (Heidegger, *Der Satz Vom Grund*, 197).

23. Heidegger, *Principle of Reason*, 30. Original text: "Das Atomzeitalter ist als planetarische Epoche der Menschheit dadurch ausgezeichnet, daß sich die Macht des großmächtigen Prinzips, des principium reddendae rationis auf eine unheimliche Weise im maßgebenden Bereich des Daseins des Menschen entfaltet, wenn nicht gar entfesselt" (Heidegger, *Der Satz Vom Grund*, 60).

24. Heidegger, *Der Satz Vom Grund*, 86.

25. Heidegger, *Principle of Reason*, 49. Original text: "Zum Sein gehört dergleichen wie Grund. Das Sein ist grundartig, grundhaft" (Heidegger, *Der Satz Vom Grund*, 90).

26. Silesius, *Cherubinic Wanderer*, 54. The quoted poem, entitled "Ohne Warum," is no. 289 in the first book of Silesius's *Cherubinischer Wandersmann* and is quoted in *Der Satz Vom Grund*, 68. ("Die Ros ist ohne warum: sie blühet, weil sie blühet, sie achtet nicht ihrer selbst, fragt nicht, ob man sie siehet.")

27. Heidegger, *Der Satz Vom Grund*, 95.

28. Heidegger, *Principle of Reason*, 53. Original text: "Der Satz vom Grund ist ein Satz in das Sein *als* Sein, d.h. als Grund" (Heidegger, *Der Satz Vom Grund*, 96).

29. Heidegger, *Der Satz Vom Grund*, 93. The reversal of *Grund* into *Abgrund* is first articulated in relation to Schelling, who himself makes use of this formulation. For Heidegger's interpretation of Schelling, see Heidegger, *Vom Wesen der menschlichen Freiheit*.

30. In the lectures he makes this explicit connection between being as pure "aus-sich-Aufgehen und Scheinen" and *physis* (Heidegger, *Der Satz Vom Grund*, 102). For his reading of the pre-Socratic understanding of *physis*, see, e.g., the 1943 lectures on Heraclitus fragment 123, on how "*physis* loves to hide," in Heidegger, *Heraklit*, 109–27. See also my review of Heidegger, *Heraclitus* in *The Classical Review*.

31. Heidegger, *Principle of Reason*, 88. Original text: "Sichzuschicken der lichtenden Einräumung des Bereiches für ein Erscheinen des Seienden" (Heidegger, *Der Satz Vom Grund*, 150).

32. In the volume *Zur Sache Des Denkens*, 1–26.

33. For a more extensive analysis of the concept of *Besinnung* in Heidegger, see Ruin, "Prudence, Passion, and Freedom."

34. The quotation is from her book *Leibniz and the Kabbalah*, 1, where she argues for the importance for Leibniz's mature monistic metaphysics. See also her subsequent coedited volume *Leibniz, Mysticism, and Religion*. A similar thesis had been presented by Susan Edel, who argued for the significance of Kabbalah and Christian mysticism in Leibniz. See her *Die individuelle Substanz bei Böhme und Leibniz*. Edel also emphasizes the importance of van Helmont, as well as Isaac Luria. The framework for her thesis is the need she sees to reinvestigate the mystical elements of rationalism generally.

35. See the English translation by Gerald Parks, *Heidegger and Leibniz*. Apart from Cristin's work, Heidegger's reading of Leibniz has generated surprisingly little philosophical commentary. One exception is Daniel J. Selcer's essay "Heidegger's Leibniz and Abyssal Identity," which argues in a more Deleuzian vein for a critical reappraisal of Heidegger's understanding of the principle of identity and of the concept of truth in Leibniz, who is credited with having conceived of "an abyssal method . . . that dispenses with the presupposition of a thinking subject" (Selcer, "Heidegger's Leibniz and Abyssal Identity," 320).

36. Eventually it was published as an appendix to his lecture course on phenomenology of religious life a few years later. Heidegger, *Phänomenologie des religiösen Lebens*, esp. 303–37. There he approaches "mysticism" as a "position of consciousness and knowledge" in a tradition of a philosophy of subjectivity with its root in antiquity.

37. For a pioneering study that sought to trace the mystic influence on Heidegger's thinking, see John Caputo's *The Mystical Element in Heidegger's Thought*. In the introduction Caputo points out how, in the Habilitation dissertation, Heidegger had already spoken of the need to transcend the dichotomy of the rational and the mystical. See also my "The Inversion of Mysticism."

38. For a more elaborated reading of the problem of *Gelassenheit* in relation to technology, see Ruin, "Ge-Stell."

Bibliography

Caputo, John D. *The Mystical Element in Heidegger's Thought*. Rev. reprint. New York: Fordham University Press, 1986.

Carman, Taylor. *Heidegger's Analytic: Interpretation, Discourse, and Authenticity in "Being and Time."* Cambridge: Cambridge University Press, 2003.

Cerbone, David R. "World, World-Entry, and Realism in Early Heidegger." *Inquiry* 38, no. 4 (December 1995): 401–21. doi:10.1080/00201749508602397.

Coudert, Allison. *Leibniz and the Kabbalah.* Archives Internationales D'histoire Des idées [International Archives of the History of Ideas] 142. Dordrecht: Kluwer Academic, 1995.

Coudert, Allison, Richard H. Popkin, and Gordon M. Weiner, eds. *Leibniz, Mysticism, and Religion.* Dordrecht: Kluwer Academic, 1998.

Cristin, Renato. *Heidegger and Leibniz: Reason and the Path.* Translated by Gerald Parks. Vol. 35 of Contributions to Phenomenology. Boston: Kluwer Academic, 1998.

Edel, Susanne. *Die individuelle Substanz bei Böhme und Leibniz: die Kabbala als tertium comparationis für eine rezeptionsgeschichtliche Untersuchung.* Sonderband 23. Studia leibnitiana. Stuttgart: F. Steiner, 1995.

Heidegger, Martin. *Heraklit.* GA 44. Edited by Manfred S. Frings. Frankfurt am Main: Klostermann, 1994.

———. *The Metaphysical Foundations of Logic.* Translated by Michael Heim. Bloomington: Indiana University Press, 1984.

———. *Metaphysische Anfangsgründe der Logik im Ausgang von Leibniz.* GA 26. Edited by Klaus Held. Frankfurt am Main: Klostermann, 1978.

———. *Nietzsche. Der Europäische Nihilismus.* GA 48. Edited by Petra Jaeger. Frankfurt am Main: Klostermann, 1986.

———. *Nietzsche: Der Wille Zur Macht Als Kunst. Freiburger Vorlesung WS 1936/37.* GA 43. Edited by Bernd Heimbüchel. Frankfurt am Main: Klostermann, 1985.

———. *Nietzsche I.* Vol. 1. Pfullingen: G. Neske, 1961.

———. *Nietzsche II.* Vol. 2. Pfullingen: G. Neske, 1961.

———. *Nietzsches Lehre Vom Willen Zur Macht Als Erkenntnis.* GA 47. Edited by Eberhard Hanser. Frankfurt am Main: Klostermann, 1989.

———. *Nietzsches Metaphysische Grundstellung Im Abendländischen Denken.* GA 44. Edited by Marion Heinz. Frankfurt am Main: Klostermann, 1986.

———. *Pathmarks.* Edited by William MacNeill. Cambridge: Cambridge University Press, 1998.

———. *Phänomenologie des religiösen Lebens.* GA 60. Edited by Matthias Jung, Thomas Regehly, and Claudius Stube. Frankfurt am Main: Klostermann, 2011.

———. "The Principle of Ground." *Man and World* 7, no. 3 (August 1, 1974): 207–22. doi:10.1007/BF01248755.

———. *The Principle of Reason.* Translated by Reginald Lilly. Indiana University Press, 1991.

———. *Der Satz Vom Grund.* Pfullingen: G. Neske, 1957.

———. *Seminare Kant—Leibniz—Schiller.* GA 84.1. Edited by Günther Neumann. Frankfurt am Main: Klostermann, 2013.

———. *Vom Wesen der menschlichen Freiheit. Einleitung in die Philosophie.* GA 31. Edited by Hartmut Tietjen. Frankfurt am Main: Klostermann, 1982.

———. "Vom Wesen des Grundes." In *Wegmarken,* GA9, edited by Friedrich-Wilhelm von Herrmann, 123–75. Frankfurt am Main: Klostermann, 1976.

———. *Vorlesungen 1919–1944. Nietzsches Metaphysik. Einleitung in Die Philosophie.* GA 50. Edited by Petra Jaeger. Frankfurt am Main: Klostermann, 1990.

———. *Wegmarken.* GA 9. Edited by Friedrich-Wilhelm von Herrmann. Frankfurt am Main: Klostermann, 1976.

———. *Zur Auslegung von Nietzsches II. Unzeitgemässer Betrachtung: Vom Nutzen Und Nachteil Der Historie Für Das Leben.* GA 46. Edited by Hans-Joachim Friedrich. Frankfurt am Main: Klostermann, 2003.

———. *Zur Sache Des Denkens.* Pfullingen: G. Neske, 1969.

Ruin, Hans. "Ge-Stell: Enframing as the Essence of Technology." In *Martin Heidegger Key Concepts*, 183–94. Durham, UK: Acumen, 2010.

———. "The Inversion of Mysticism: *Gelassenheit* and the Secret of the Open in Heidegger." *Religions* 10, no. 1 (2019): 15. doi: 10.3390/rel10010015.

———. "Leibniz and Heidegger on Sufficient Reason." *Studia Leibnitiana* 30, no. 1 (January 1, 1998): 49–67. http://www.jstor.org/stable/40694334.

———. "Prudence, Passion, and Freedom: On Heidegger's Ideal of *Besinnung*." *Giornale Di Metafisica* 28, no. 1 (2006): 29–52.

———. Review of *Heraclitus: The Inception of Occidental Thinking and Logic: Heraclitus's Doctrine of the Logos*, by Martin Heidegger, trans. Julia Goesser Assaiante and S. Montgomery Ewegen. *Classical Review*, 1–3 (2019). doi: 10.1017/S0009840X19001483.

———. "Technology and Destiny in Heidegger and Cassirer." In *Ernst Cassirer on Form and Technology: Contemporary Readings*, 133–56. Houndmills, UK: Palgrave Macmillan, 2012.

Selcer, Daniel J. "Heidegger's Leibniz and Abyssal Identity." *Continental Philosophy Review* 36, no. 3 (July 1, 2003): 303–24. doi:10.1023/B:MAWO.0000003973.40566.b7.

Silesius, Angelus. *The Cherubinic Wanderer.* Translated by Shrady Maria. New York: Paulist, 1986.

———. "Ohne Warum." In *Cherubinischer Wandersmann*, vol. 3 of Sämtliche Poetische Werke, 39. München: Hanser, 1949.

HANS RUIN is Professor of Philosophy at Södertörn University (Stockholm). He is author of *Freedom, Finitude, Historicity: Essays on Heidegger* (Ersatz, 2012, in Swedish) and *Being with the Dead: Burial, Ancestral Politics, and the Roots of Historical Consciousness* (Stanford University Press, 2018).

14 Ground, Abyss, and Primordial Ground

Heidegger in the Wake of Schelling

Sylvaine Gourdain

Translated by Christopher Merwin

ALTHOUGH HEIDEGGER USES the verb *to ground* (*gründen*) in a quasi-inflationary manner in *Being and Time* and in the *Basic Problems of Phenomenology*, the very same concept of *Grund* does not become the subject of a specific investigation as part of the metaphysics of *Dasein* before the 1928 text *On the Essence of Ground*. We notice that the term is used by Heidegger to oppose and redefine the classical figure of the metaphysical ground (*Grund*); from a critical perspective, it is applied to the question of the origin of the possibility of all thinking of being. However, the inquiry into the conditions of possibility is already what first characterizes the project of fundamental ontology as it is laid out in *Being and Time*. Fundamental ontology indeed puts in place a transcendental-critical approach, not in order to define a priori conditions of possibility and then develop downstream ontology, but rather to go up—upstream—to the origin of what makes possible any ontology. However, the project of fundamental ontology is problematic in that it does not clearly expose its own conditions of possibility, and, while attempting to get away from the metaphysical requirement of absolute self-foundation, it seems to eventually treat Dasein as an avatar of the classic conception of ground to the extent that it is described as a rigid and closed existential structure, going out of itself only to come back better.[1]

If fundamental ontology has the merit of highlighting the necessarily hermeneutic dimension of ontology (being is only accessible to us as a "meaning"), it proves to be still too transcendental in a Kantian sense (the structure of Dasein defines the conditions of possibility on preestablished, and therefore too rigid, terms). Fundamental ontology is thus not fundamental enough in a Heideggerian sense, which is to say, mobile and open. It is the metaphysics of Dasein that will provide an initial destabilization of the closed structure of Dasein because it

uncovers, through a metontology (*Metontologie*), the fundaments of the fundamental ontology itself. Indeed, metontology searches for the conditions of possibility, not of the sense of being, but of the understanding of being that takes
place in Dasein.[2] It demonstrates that this understanding of being is originally
based on the "temporalization of temporality" (*Zeitigung der Zeitlichkeit*),[3] from
now on to be conceived as an "ecstatic oscillation" (*ekstatische Schwingung*) that
comes to open, at its very foundation, the structure of Dasein. Therefore, the
freedom of Dasein, which determines the understanding's access to being, is
affected by an originary powerlessness, and it can be deployed as a projection
(*Entwurf*) of Dasein unto its possibilities only by binding or attaching itself (*sich
binden*) to the world, a world facing Dasein and resisting it in its beingness. Freedom is thus defined as the "ground of ground" (*Grund des Grundes*)[4] and as such
is neither an intensification nor a fortification of the ground but "the abyssal
ground [*Ab-grund*] of Dasein";[5] the projection (*Entwurf*) of possibilities presupposes a withdrawal (*Entzug*) of other possibilities. In the texts of the metaphysics
of Dasein, the inquiry into the ultimate origin of the understanding of being,
and therefore of any ontology, results in the idea of a "transcendental neediness"
(*transzendentale Bedürftigkeit*).[6]

It thus appears that the concept of ground, immediately associated with the
abyssal ground (*Ab-grund*), serves primarily to call into question some form of
self-stability, which remains attached to a transcendental dimension, even when
the transcendental is no longer subjective, as Heidegger wanted in *Being and
Time*. But the discovery of the transcendental powerlessness of Dasein, understood as abyssal ground, is only a first step toward the definitive abandonment
of the transcendental. For this abandonment will receive a decisive impulse
through a confrontation with the thought of Schelling and notably with what
Schelling too calls "ground," or, more specifically, "ground of existence" (*Grund
von Existenz*). The purpose of the present discussion is precisely to study the displacement in Heidegger's thought beginning in the mid-1930s, more precisely
between 1936 and 1938, that allows him to break free from the transcendental
without surrendering the concept of ground. I would like to show the central
role his reading of Schelling's *Philosophical Investigations into the Essence of
Human Freedom* plays with regard to this displacement. After having pointed to
an important aspect of Heidegger's interpretation of the "ground of existence"
in the Schelling lecture course of 1936 (i.e., the idea of ground as what closes and
withdraws in on itself), I will show resonances to Schelling's notion of *Grund* in
Heidegger's concept of earth (*Erde*) in "The Origin of the Work of Art" (1936).
I will then devote myself more extensively to the novel concept of *foundation*
(*Gründung*), which Heidegger makes use of in the *Contributions to Philosophy (of
the Event)* (1936–38) and which combines discoveries made in both the Schelling
course and "The Origin of the Work of Art."

Heidegger's Interpretation of the "Ground of Existence" as the "Self Closing Off" (*das Sichverschließende*)

Although Heidegger's interest in Schelling begins in 1927–28 when he gives a seminar "for advanced students" on *Philosophical Investigations into the Essence of Human Freedom*, from 1809, it is with a lecture course in the summer semester of 1936, delivered at Freiburg, that he deepens his understanding of the freedom essay. I highlighted previously that the most original foundation, for Heidegger, is tied closely to the freedom of Dasein, and it is thus no coincidence that during this time Heidegger takes an interest precisely in the 1809 treatise, two of the central concepts of which are human freedom and ground. Focusing more closely on the relationship between Heidegger and Schelling, one realizes that it is always at key moments of his thought that Heidegger turns to what many researchers tend to consider, with good reason, as his "incognito contemporary" (*Zeitgenosse inkognito*).[7] I now show how Heidegger articulates in his Schelling commentary his own self-interpretation, including how his reading of Schelling's *Seynsfuge* (as Heidegger calls Schelling's distinction between "being, in so far as it exists" and "being, in so far as it is merely the ground of existence"[8]) allows him to accomplish decisive progress in his thinking about ground and leads to the thinking of *Ereignis*. Note in this respect that the term (*Seynsfuge*) used by Heidegger to designate Schelling's disjunction between the two principles within the same being (*Wesen*) overlaps the way he describes his own conception of *Ereignis* in *Contributions*, namely as *Fuge des Seyns*.[9]

If Heidegger in his 1936 lecture course develops particular interest in Schelling's distinction between ground and the existent (*l'existant*), it is because he sees all too clearly that the Schellingian concept of ground shakes the metaphysical conceptions of foundation. Indeed, Heidegger describes with great rigor the *Grund* in Schelling as "under-lying, substratum, 'basis,' [*Grund-lage, Unterlage, 'Basis'*]—ὑποκείμενον."[10] Schellingian ground is not foundation in the sense of *ratio*, neither the motive nor the reason for this or that, but, on the contrary, "the non-rational" (*das Nicht-Rationale*), which, as Heidegger himself remarks, should not, however, be simply identified with "the irrational" (*das Irrationale*).[11] As such, this ground is rather a soil that withdraws, an abyssal base for every being or existence, a ground—but one that does not ground. In contrast, "Ex-sistenz" is aptly characterized by Heidegger as "*what emerges from itself* and in *emerging reveals itself.*"[12]

Heidegger underscores that the difference between the ground and the existent, which is within and part of creation, is no simple conceptual distinction but rather a real conflict of forces. From there, he succeeds brilliantly in showing that this strife between the ground and the existent should rather be understood as a description of the dynamics proper to phenomenality, dynamics that can unfold only as a struggle between a force that withdraws on itself and a force of clearing (*Lichtung*). Taking up the comparison, made by Schelling himself, between, on the one hand, the ground and gravity and, on the other, the existent and light, Heidegger writes: "Gravity is what burdens and pulls, contracts and in this connection what withdraws and flees. But light is always the 'clearing,' what opens and spreads, what develops. What is light is always the clearing of what is intertwined and entangled, what is veiled and obscure."[13]

Gravity as a force of weightiness and of contraction, attracting everything toward a dark ground and withdrawing, opposes the light as the luminous, as that which is rendered clearer, lighter, and that which unfolds and diffuses around itself. But the luminous is not radically distinct and separated from the dark; it is, on the contrary, the clearing of what retreats and withdraws. The darkness and the clearing are bound together both by an essential co-belonging and a relentless struggle, as Heidegger emphasizes in the following comment: "Light opens up darkness. But since darkness is longing willing itself, what is illuminated is now really aroused to strive back to itself and thus to strive toward the opening. This means that the separation as illumination in the ground brings it about that the ground strives more and more fundamentally toward the ground and as the ground individuating itself separates itself."[14]

We see here that the clearing only occurs as conflict between light (*das Licht*) and darkness (*das Dunkel*). As soon as the light tries to illuminate the ground, the latter folds into itself, attempting to remain in darkness, so that the clearing is always the result of an ongoing struggle between darkness and light. *Grund*, in Schelling, is this force of resistance and refusal struggling against the movement toward existence, to stand in its way, fleeing and sinking into the darkness to hide from the light. Yet the ground only withdraws on itself because it is cleared; the more the light clears, the more the ground attempts to sink into the darkness.

Schelling's conception of a distinction between the ground and the existent thus serves as a fundamental impulse in Heidegger's own thinking of phenomenality as strife between the clearing and what resists it. Yet let us recall that in Schelling, the two opposing forces are united in their antagonism to form one *Wesen* (being). It is not insignificant that Heidegger translates, in his own terminology, the Schellingian concept of *Wesen* with recourse finally to *Seyn*![15] The struggle between opening and closing appears, therefore, as a way of thinking the dynamics intrinsic to *Seyn*, which will soon take, in Heidegger, the name *Ereignis*. We also note that it is in the course of his investigations into Schelling that Heidegger uses for the first time the archaic *Seyn* spelling (which I translate as "beyng"), without, however, entirely replacing the concept of *Sein*. In the context of the 1936 lecture course, the two terms (*Seyn* and *Sein*) coexist, so we can assume that Heidegger does not merely reproduce the spelling used by Schelling but that he indeed intends a specific meaning for each. This change in spelling indicates a significant evolution in the thinking of being as we see it develop at this time.

Nevertheless, it is surprising that Heidegger is not more interested in Schelling's notion of "non-ground" (*Ungrund*), which he only points to once during the 1936 lecture course.[16] Indeed, since Heidegger stresses that it is the co-belonging of the two principles, the ground and the existent, that alone makes possible "the happening of the scission [*das Geschehnis der Scheidung*],"[17] he could have referred to the *Ungrund*, which for Schelling means the most originary grounding, grounding even this very difference itself. It is indeed not only by *Grund*, as closing force, but also by *Ungrund*, as the immemorial and unprethinkable origin of any *Wesen* (the origin of any beyng!), that Schelling exceeds the metaphysical conception of ground and avoids a dualism torn apart between opposing forces. However, we know that *Ungrund*, for Schelling, is also a way to indicate God before God, that is to say, the diving being in its origin, before even the scission between the principles, this unity allowing him to safeguard the internal unity of God. It is therefore very likely that Heidegger could find only some theological legitimation for the Schellingian non-ground, which would explain why he considered that the non-ground simply had no place in a strictly ontological framework. Besides, at this time Heidegger was mainly interested in the movement and tension of Schelling's *Seynsfuge*, and it is likely that in his view, the non-ground could smooth out the internal dynamics of beyng.

Anyway, if Heidegger seems to have found the concept of struggle (*Kampf, Krieg,* πόλεμος) in Heraclitus,[18] and the idea of light and clearing in both Plato and a verse of Schiller,[19] it is especially thanks to Schelling that he manages to link these two dimensions, to develop the specific configuration of the clearing as tension and conflict between, on the one hand, a movement of opening and unconcealing, attempting to illuminate what remains obscure, and, on the other, a dynamics of withdrawal that folds on itself and eludes clearing. It is notably the idea of a withdrawal constitutive of phenomenality, associated in Schelling with the figure of ground in creation, that will allow him to definitively abandon any transcendental dimension understood as a *condition* of possibility. *Grund* is for Schelling that which renders *impossible* any prior condition, because it refuses and eludes incessantly. Ground frustrates any transcendental approach because it indicates that the ground of beyng is an irreducible dimension of nontransparency, "an irreducible remainder" (*nie aufgehender Rest*),[20] which no transcendental gesture could ever recover.

The Opposition between Ground and the Existent and the Conflict between Earth and World

It is possible to see a first resonance of the conflict between ground and the existent, which Heidegger analyzed in Schelling, in the idea of a "strife between the world and earth,"[21] developed in Heidegger's "The Origin of the Work of Art." The third version of this text, published in volume five of the *Gesamtausgabe*, and dating from 1936, is from the same year as the lecture on Schelling.[22] Heidegger here insists that the quarrel between world and earth is not congruent with the conflict between concealing (*Verbergung*) and the clearing (*Lichtung*). Heidegger says explicitly: "But world is not simply the open which corresponds to the clearing, earth is not simply the closed that corresponds to concealment."[23] The world is thus not identified purely and simply with the clearing, and the earth is not synonymous with concealing, but it is "that which rises up in self-closing."[24] In other words, the earth indicates a dimension achieving phenomenality in that it withdraws itself. As such, it is precisely in this way that it can be brought close to Schelling's *Grund*, which Heidegger, in his course on Schelling, also called "the self closing off (*das Sichverschließende*)."[25] Heidegger, thus, has recourse to a number of common qualifiers to designate Schelling's earth and ground, and notably, he repeatedly uses the term *Grund* to designate earth: it is "the home-land ground" (*der heimatliche Grund*)[26] but also the "self-closing ground" (*der sich verschließende Grund*) or the "ground that bears" (*der tragende Grund*).[27] It seems then that Schelling's *Grund* and Heidegger's *Erde* represent a type of concealment that is an inherent part of any movement of phenomenalization; they both indicate a remainder that abides, an elusive soil that withdraws into the abyss.

More precisely, *Grund* for Schelling and *Erde* for Heidegger each signal the withdrawal and resistance of materiality, which never exhausts itself within a definitive meaning. The earth is thus "coming-forth-concealing" as "material," as are, for example "the stone," "the rock," "the metal," "the colors," or "the sound."[28] In the manufacture of equipment, the materiality of the stone is stripped away in its usage, and the equipment works even better when its materiality can blend in with its use. In the work of art, on the other hand, materiality grants access to the process of its manifestation as such, revealing its dimension of withdrawal and resistance without, of course, disappearing altogether. It remains "in the background," as "the irreducible remainder" and "the incomprehensible base of reality"[29] that was *Grund* for Schelling. Heidegger focuses on the example of the stone in particular, which allows us to even better highlight the parallel with ground in Schelling: "The stone presses downwards and manifests its heaviness. But while this heaviness weighs down on us, at the same time, it denies us any penetration into it."[30] The stone presses, it has weight,[31] and just in this way it recedes from all transparency. Even if we try to smash it, it never opens itself entirely to us; each of its shattered pieces continue to impose on us its mass by closing off any access. Even if we could place the stone on a scale to measure its mass, the number indicated would never allow us to access the entirety of the stone. This idea of mass, of weight (*Schwere*), obviously recalls the idea of gravity and of heaviness (*Schwerkraft*) that Schelling associated with *Grund*.

But the earth denies itself only insofar as it is also illuminated; it does not designate the nonphenomenal in opposition to the phenomenal, but on the contrary, precisely as withdrawal and resistance, it is a constitutive part of phenomenality: "The earth is openly illuminated as itself only where it is apprehended and preserved as the essentially undisclosable, as that which withdraws from every disclosure, in other words, keeps itself constantly closed up."[32] The earth thus indicates a dimension that escapes us but that is precisely illuminated, lit (*gelichtet*) as what escapes us. The earth shows itself, but as that which is not exhausted in the visible, as that which evades sense and rationality, in the same way that ground for Schelling represents the "non-rational" but not necessarily the "irrational."[33] *Grund* is the without-rule, "that which with the greatest exertion cannot be resolved in understanding";[34] exactly like the earth "it shows itself only when it remains undisclosed and unexplained."[35] The earth and the ground are inexplicable, unintelligible, undecipherable materiality—yet as we transfer earth and ground into the realm of meaning, try to force their sense into a concept, this sense proves even more elusive.

This is why between the earth and the world, between material and meaning, Heidegger sees not only tension but a real conflict, an incessant strife. In this strife, world and earth are constantly sent back to each other; the continuation of the conflict shows that they are both completely separate and fundamentally inseparable: "In the earth, however, as the essentially self-closing, the openness of the open encounters the highest form of resistance and through this finds the site of its steady stand in which the figure must be fixed in place."[36] It is in its withdrawal that the earth becomes a soil for the world. It is because the earth finds in the world its opposite that it can rely on it to make itself intelligible: "Earth is that in which the arising of everything that arises is brought back—as, indeed, the very thing that it is—and sheltered. In the things that arise the earth presences as the protecting one."[37] The earth, as *Grund*, designates what irritates phenomenality, the obscure point that abides in appearing and thereby exhibits that manifestation is never mere transparency. It is therefore because they do not exhaust themselves in their visible bearing of a uniform and univocal meaning but resist it that the earth and Schelling's *Grund von Existenz* make possible and preserve phenomenality as phenomenality. By letting any thought of an immediate and entire giving (*donation*) fail in grasping it, the conception of a withdrawal of the earth or of the ground saves phenomenality from any reduction to naive realism.

But when the strife between world and earth is preserved as strife, then the disclosure of the truth of being can occur, which for Heidegger is none other than the "ur-strife between clearing and concealment."[38] The truth of being can therefore be "fought out" (*erstritten*)[39] in the work of art, through "fighting the fight between world and earth,"[40] which, without becoming identical to it, preserves the original strife of concealing and unconcealing.[41] Indeed, the earth, in its opposition to the world, also shows that any unconcealing is rendered possible only by a more originary concealing. In this sense, Heidegger defines "the work-being of the work"[42] as but one of the modes in which truth occurs. The work of art allows us to see and hear the oscillation opening meaning unto out-of-meaning, the shadow of nonmeaning that comes to irritate meaning because, instead of trying to annihilate any resistance, instead of reducing materiality to any utility, the work of art brings nonmeaning out in the open as resistance, allowing what withdraws to withdraw. Yet, if any event unfolds on the basis of an irreducible withdrawal, which also indicates that the clearing is always only partial, then any transcendental perspective becomes impossible. The *condition* of appearing is rather an allowing to be (*le laisser-être*) of a resistance, of that on which any grasping fails. So because of the darkness that lies at the very *foundation* of any unconcealing, because of this shadow inherent to the open, Heidegger must renounce any transcendental dimension. What constitutes being in the most original sense will withdraw rather than appear as such; it is not so much the understanding of being but that which does not allow for itself to be controlled by meaning:

The Grounding (*Gründung*) of the Human Being in Da-sein and the Fathoming (*Ergründung*) of the Truth of Beyng

The *Contributions to Philosophy (of the Event)*, written between 1936 and 1938, also contain echoes of Schelling's thought. We here find the philosopheme of *Grund* and the particular figure of grounding (*Gründung*), as well as the idea that the strife of world and earth testifies to the conflict between concealing (*Verbergung*) and clearing (*Lichtung*). While his commentary on the *Investigations* seemed to invalidate a transcendental approach, Heidegger does not abandon any requirement of grounding. On the contrary, grounding corresponds to one of the junctures (*Fügungen*) of the conjuncture of beyng (*Fuge des Seyns*). However, a careful reading of the *Contributions* shows a reversal of the classic transcendental gesture. Not only is the transcendental no longer subjective, as we know, if not from the time of *Being and Time*, then at least from the period of the metaphysics of Dasein; not only is the transcendental negated by the intrinsic dimension of withdrawal in phenomenality, what Heidegger described in detail in his reading of Schelling—but it is now the human being that must itself be grounded (*gegründet*). Heidegger calls this ground of the human-being *Da-sein*, hyphenating the term familiar from *Being and Time*. The hyphen is of importance because it highlights that this ground of the human being (*Da-sein*) is not the human itself. "Da-*sein* is not the mode of actuality of just any being; instead, it is itself the being of the 'there.'"[43] Far from indicating a "human character" (*Charakter des Menschen)*, *Da-sein* is a ground for the human being, and "through this ground (and its grounding), the human being is transformed from the ground up."[44] Thus, if *Da-sein* is a ground, it is a ground still to come; it grounds what is not yet, "being-human" *(Menschsein)*. Put differently, the human being is not yet what it has to be, and this to be will have to be related to *Da-sein*: "Nevertheless, Da-sein and human being are essentially related, inasmuch as Da-sein signifies the ground of the possibility of future human being, and humans *are* futural by accepting to be the 'there,' provided they understand themselves as the stewards of the truth of beyng."[45] If *Da-sein* is a ground to come, it is because it is "a ground of possibility *(Grund der Möglichkeit)*"; *Da-sein* grounds the possibility of the human being but does not ensure its realization. Heidegger gives even more detail: "'Ground of possibility' is still a metaphysical *expression*, but it is *thought* out of the abyssal and steadfast *belongingness*."[46] Thus, *Da-sein* is a soil, a place, a space of possibility rather than a ground in the sense of an effecting metaphysical cause. It cannot ground in the classical sense, since it itself can only be thought from the abyss *(Abgrund)* preceding it.

The grounding of the human being in *Da-sein*, or what Heidegger also calls "Da-sein in mortals" *(Da-sein im Menschen)* refers to "the coming to pass of that grounding,"[47] and this event is based, in turn, on an essential abyss, an *Abgrund*. Even more originary than *Da-sein* is the truth of beyng: "The original grounding of the ground is the essential occurrence of the truth of being; truth is a *ground* in the original sense."[48] The most originally grounding, then, is that of the truth of beyng in its unfolding, in its essential occurrence *(Wesung)*. Yet, in order to describe the unfolding of the truth of beyng, Heidegger has recourse to the concepts of clearing *(Lichtung)* and concealing *(Verbergung)*, but instead of considering them as two separate principles, he conceives of the truth of beyng as an indissoluble unity of clearing *and* self-concealing, as "not simply clearing but precisely clearing for self-concealing."[49] "Truth is never merely clearing; it essentially occurs as concealment just as originarily and intimately along with the clearing. These, clearing and concealment, are not two; instead, they constitute the essential occurrence of the one truth itself."[50] Not only does the manifestation of beyng inherently include a concealment, an irreducible withdrawal, but the truth of beyng unfolds itself equally as clearing and as self-concealment, equally as *Lichtung* and as *Verbergung*. Because in revealing certain possibilities of being it covers over many others, the unconcealing *(Unverborgenheit)* that is the truth of beyng is at the same time a concealing. Consequently, the truth of beyng can no longer be a stable foundation and absolute certainty; it is a ground that collapses into itself. Ground *(Grund)* is abyssal ground *(Ab-grund)*.

Let us pause a moment on the self-concealing that Heidegger insists originates in the unfolding of the event *(Ereignis)* and the truth of beyng. It is only because of concealment that there may be clearing. Heidegger, therefore, also calls the "clearing of beyng" (*Lichtung des Seyns*) "the openness of what is self-concealing" (*Offenheit des Sichverbergenden*).⁵¹ "Self-concealing is an essential character of *beyng*."⁵² Yet this concealment can be abyss (*Abgrund*) or distorted ground (*Ungrund*). The abyss (*Abgrund*) has absolutely nothing negative or incomplete; it only corresponds to the mode of appearing of beyng insofar as it rests on an abyss. Heidegger writes: "The abyss is not a 'no' to every ground in the manner of groundlessness; it is rather a 'yes' to the ground in the concealed breadth and remoteness of that ground."⁵³ Speaking of the abyss (*Abgrund*) thus implies that concealment inhabits phenomenality as its first soil, its very root. Heidegger thus writes: "Ground: self-concealing in a protruding that bears."⁵⁴ The ground (*Grund*) that hides is the very same one that bears phenomenality as phenomenality, that crosses and pierces simultaneously, and by which the truth of beyng becomes abyss. This concealment can be manifested through the movement of withdrawal (*Entzug*), and it is precisely this notion that Heidegger will henceforth bring to the fore: withdrawal means a concealment that can become "bestowal" (*Schenkung*) the moment it is perceived as an essential moment of phenomenality.⁵⁵ But concealment can also be merely and simply ignored, or it can sink into oblivion. In this case, it is no longer abyss (*Abgrund*) but is distorted ground or non-ground (*Ungrund*). Heidegger thus finally makes use of the term *Ungrund* but gives it a meaning different from the one it has in Schelling: the non-ground is a deficient mode of grounding; it is the grounding that is no longer entrusted to its abysmal character but is, rather, flawed and distorted from the very beginning. We understand now a posteriori why Heidegger, in his lectures of 1936, avoids this concept as it is used by Schelling: in his view, the non-ground, as a distorted ground, is necessarily flawed and incomplete. In this vein, Heidegger relates the distorted ground (*Ungrund*) to "the origin of errancy" (*Ursprung der Irre*), "the power and possibility of the abandonment by being" (*Macht und Möglichkeit der Seinsverlassenheit*),⁵⁶ "the dissemblance" (*Verstellung*), or again, "the decomposition" (*Verwesung*).⁵⁷

Yet distorted ground (*Ungrund*) and abyss (*Abgrund*) are actually two modes of the very same ground (*Grund*), as Heidegger clearly states: "The grounded ground is at once abyss for the fissure of beyng and distorted ground for the abandonment of beings by being."⁵⁸ What differs in these two cases, and what makes ground (*Grund*) either a distorted ground (*Ungrund*) or an abyss (*Abgrund*), is the relation of the human being to this concealing grounding. If, indeed, the human being is no longer the transcendental subject, it nevertheless receives a central role in the grounding of the truth of the beyng and the appropriation (*Ereignung*) of the event (*Ereignis*): it must signal and preserve the concealing inherent in the unconcealing that constitutes the truth of beyng. The human being must therefore be wary about pretending to reach a transparency without rupture; it has to wrest the primordial concealing from being forgotten. Such "sheltering" (*Bergung*) of the truth of beyng can happen precisely through the "playing out of the strife" (*Bestreitung des Streites*) of world and earth, to which the human being can contribute. If the human being maintains, as such, the primordial "self-concealing" (*das Sichverbergen*), then its grounding in *Da-sein* can occur. In order to do this, the human being cannot stand aside but must rather run all the risks of what comes through the "steadfastness" (*Inständigkeit*) in *Da-sein*. Therefore, "steadfastness" is "the domain of the human being who is grounded in Da-sein."[59] No longer is the human being the one who constitutes and guarantees truth, but it is the truth of beyng that makes it possible for humans to take root in *Da-sein*. But if the human being cannot engender its own grounding, it has the task of responding to this primordial event, which requires and requests it in its grounding. The human being is, therefore, "needed by beyng for the sake of withstanding the essential occurrence of the truth of beyng" but "only inasmuch as [it is] grounded in Da-sein."[60]

This idea amounts to a genuine undermining of the transcendental because now it is the event (*Ereignis*), beyng itself, that grounds the human being and transforms it "from the ground up."[61] The human being who steps into the heart of the event (*Ereignis*) and lets itself be called by the event, "the human being on *this* ground of Da-sein," is now said to be "the seeker of beyng (event)" (*Sucher des Seyns*), "the preserver of the truth of being" (*Wahrer der Wahrheit des Seins*), "the steward of the stillness of the passing by of the last god" (*Wächter der Stille des Vorbeigangs des letzten Gottes*).[62] Human beings must expose themselves to the clearing, precisely insofar as the clearing is closely linked to concealment; it is this co-belonging that the human must preserve from oblivion: "The steadfast enduring of the clearing of self-concealing is taken up in the seeking, preserving, and stewardship carried out by that human being who has self-knowledge as one appropriated to being and belonging to the event qua the essential occurrence of beyng."[63]

The term *Da-sein* thus denotes that situation out of which the human being assumes responsibility for the truth of being as the clearing of an originary concealment. This is why it is opposed to "being-away" (*Weg-sein*), which characterizes the position of the human being as fleeing responsibilities and ignoring the call of the event: "Da-*sein*: withstanding the openness of self-concealing. Being-away: pressing on with *the closedness of the mystery and of being*; forgottenness of being."[64] When the human is resolutely engaged in *Da-sein*, it becomes "the ground and abyss of the historical human being";[65] the human being thus engaged must be "dislodged" (*ver-rückt*)[66] in order to become the one it has to be.

This letting-be of the primordial grounding of the truth of being, which is not passivity because it assumes instead that the human being is exposed to the abyss from *Da-sein*, corresponds to what Heidegger calls "fathoming the ground" (*Er-gründung*):

Fathoming the ground:

a) to let the ground *essentially occur* as grounding;
b) to *build* on it as the ground, to bring something to the ground.
    The original grounding of the ground . . . is the essential occurrence of the
truth of beyng; truth is a *ground* in the original sense.⁶⁷

The origin is therefore the truth of being as abyssal ground (*Ab-grund*), a ground that withdraws and does not let itself be stabilized. This truth is the concealing clearing that opens the space of "oscillation" (*Schwingung*)⁶⁸ of the event. Because of its mediating role, the human being must take care not to be fooled by the illusion of transparency but rather call into question the crystallizations and the figments of univocal systems of meaning in order to recover the primordial trembling of the event. If the abyssal ground that is the truth of being, that is to say the oscillation of the event, is allowed in its dynamics, fathoming (*Ergründung*) takes place. Now *Da-sein* can become ground (*Grund*) in the sense of a soil for the truth in that it is itself founded and made possible by this truth. The event, which thus occurs from out of the abyssally grounding truth, is none other than the primordial ground.⁶⁹ "The primordial ground opens itself, as what is self-concealing, only in the abyssal ground. . . . The primordial ground, the one that grounds, is beyng, but in each case as essentially occurring in its truth."⁷⁰ The primordial ground (*Ur-grund*) is thus cleared as what is concealed only in the abyssal ground (*Ab-grund*), and it is in this sense that the truth of beyng requires the human being in its occurring and is in need of the human. It is clear that Heidegger now has fully renounced transcendental subjectivity, because now the human being is no longer identified as *Da-sein* but must take root in it. Yet *Da-sein* is itself grounded by the truth of being, which cannot be grounding in a metaphysical sense because it no longer dictates a fixed, single standard of presence. The grounding of the truth of beyng, in contrast, is rather a grounding of the ungroundable. Thus, the joining (*Fügung*) of the grounding takes place in a threefold perspective that is really but a single movement: the grounding (*Gründung*) of the human being as *Da-sein*, the fathoming (*Ergründung*) of the truth of beyng, and the letting-be of the ground(ing) (*Grund*) that is the primordial ground (*Ur-grund*) of the event (*Ereignis*).

From this, a parallel to Schelling's conception of truth from the *Investigations* can be sketched, although we should still remain cautious. Indeed, what Heidegger called *ground* in the *Contributions* does not correspond directly and unequivocally to what Schelling called *ground* in *Investigations*: ground (*Grund*), according to Heidegger's *Contributions*, is either abyssal ground (*Ab-grund*) or distorted ground (*Un-grund*), and these two concepts denote two modes of possible relation of the human being to the primordial concealing, or in other words to the self-concealing (*das Sichverbergen*). Such double possibility, however, can be found in Schelling, not in the same figure of ground (*Grund*), but in the relationship that the human being has to the ground. If the human being attributes to itself its origin and comports itself as if it could be self-grounding, or, put differently, if it tries to deny any concealment and any withdrawal, then a constellation resembling what Heidegger calls the distorted ground (*Ungrund*) can be discerned—yet this ground in no way resembles Schelling's *Ungrund*, as I explained above. If the human being knows it is preceded and grounded by what exceeds it, and if it takes up its central role within creation by preserving the bond of principles, that is to say, by supporting "the playing out of the strife" (*Bestreitung des Streites*), then we approach what Heidegger calls the abyss (*Abgrund*).

In other words, Heidegger and Schelling come together in the idea of a withdrawal required for the truth of being to happen. In Schelling, this withdrawal takes the form of a subordination of the ground to the existent, which for Heidegger corresponds to a letting-be of the ground. It is important here to note the difference in the language used while recalling the close convergence that unifies the two conceptions of the truth of beyng: Schelling also discusses a specific "letting" of the ground, a "letting-actualize of the ground" (*Wirkenlassen des Grundes*),[71] which suggests a letting-be of the ground but in an opposite sense to that given to it by Heidegger. In Schelling's conception, the letting-be of the ground in humans means a reversal and a perversion of the truth. Ground now takes the place of the existent, which leads to falsehood and, even worse, evil and therefore untruth. The letting-be is permitted only in God, in whom the principles are inseparable, such that the ground can never become evil; but in human beings, this letting-be of the ground represents, par excellence, that which is prohibited and the very potentiality of evil. Beyond this difference in terminology, however, there remains a close parallel nonetheless between the accounts of the relationship that human beings must maintain vis-à-vis the withdrawal. In Schelling and in Heidegger, the task of human beings is to take heed of this withdrawal, to remain alert to all the figments of meaning, and to preserve the trembling that constitutes the proper opening of the truth of beyng.

Conclusion

I have shown the central importance of Heidegger's confrontation in the *Investigations* of Schelling from 1936, that is to say, precisely when Heidegger attempts to move away from a notion of ground (*Grund*) to that of abyssal ground (*Ab-grund*). Heidegger was indeed strongly inspired by the Schellingian idea of an abyssal ground that is at the same origin of any beyng, inspired by the idea of a ground that is rather an unstable soil, a ground that withdraws, suggesting that phenomenality can only emerge from a primordial concealment. It is thus particularly through his reading of Schelling that Heidegger understands that concealing and veiling are inherent in beyng and that we should not try to suppress such primordial concealing and rather attempt to preserve it. We also find echoes of Schelling's ground in the figure of earth, as described in "The Origin of the Work of Art" in particular. Schelling here plays a crucial role in the evolution of Heidegger's thought because he allows him to get out of a transcendental approach that would seek to determine a priori conditions of possibility; Schelling allows Heidegger to redefine rather than abandon the very concept of ground. The fathoming (*Ergründung*) of the *Contributions* is, in fact, not a process of constituting the conditions of possibilities but rather the letting-be of a grounding that precedes it and always already exceeds it—that is the primordial ground that is beyng itself. Furthermore, this conception of beyng as abyssal ground (*Ab-grund*) will become central to a course that Heidegger will hold almost twenty years later, in 1955–56, namely *The Principle of Reason*, making manifest an important development from the 1928 text "On the Essence of Ground." However, *The Principle of Reason* is a continuation of what Heidegger already described in the *Contributions* and what he seems to have taken from his course on Schelling: the idea that beyng unfolds (*west*) itself in existence or in phenomenality from an abysmal ground. Thus when Heidegger writes, "the principle of reason says: *to being there belongs something like ground/reason. Being is akin to grounds, it is ground-like*" and then adds, "'Being is ground-like' . . . in no way means 'being has a ground'; rather, it says: *being in itself essentially comes to be as grounding*,"[72]—has he not become again even more Schellingian?

Notes

1. Death as the "possibility of the *im*possibility of existence" (Heidegger, *Being and Time*, 293; *Sein und Zeit*, 306) is no more a possible opening, much less a break, of the structure since it must always be recovered and be taken on oneself in resoluteness (*Entschlossenheit*) and anticipation (*Vorlaufen*).

2. On the metaphysics of Dasein, see particularly François Jaran, *La métaphysique du Dasein.*

3. Heidegger, *Metaphysical Foundations of Logic*, 208–9; *Metaphysische Anfangsgründe der Logik*, 270.

4. Heidegger, *Pathmarks*, 134; *Wegmarken*, 174.

5. Heidegger, *Pathmarks*, 134; *Wegmarken*, 174. Translation modified.

6. Heidegger, *Kant and the Problem of Metaphysics*, 165; *Kant und das Problem der Metaphysik*, 236.

7. Scheier, "Die Zeit der Seynsfuge," 29.

8. Schelling, *Philosophical Investigations*, 27.

9. Heidegger, *Contributions to Philosophy*, 16, 180; *Beiträge zur Philosophie*, 18, 228.

10. Heidegger, *Schelling's Treatise*, 107; *Schelling*, 187.

11. Heidegger, *Schelling's Treatise*, 107; *Schelling*, 187.

12. Heidegger, *Schelling's Treatise*, 107; *Schelling*, 187.

13. Heidegger, *Schelling's Treatise*, 114; *Schelling*, 199.

14. Heidegger, *Schelling's Treatise*, 132; *Schelling*, 229.

15. Thus, he names the distinction that Schelling makes between "being, in so far as it exists" and "being, in so far as it is merely the ground of existence" (Schelling, *Philosophical Investigations*, 27) the *Seynsfuge* (and not *Wesensfuge*).

16. Heidegger, *Schelling's Treatise*, 122; *Schelling*, 213.

17. Heidegger, *Schelling's Treatise*, 105; *Schelling*, 183. Translation modified.

18. See, notably, "On the Essence of Truth": "The Saying of Heraclitus: Struggle as the essence of beings" (72–76; *Sein und Wahrheit*, 89–95).

19. See his interpretation of the Allegory of the Cave, during the winter semester of 1931–32, repeated again in winter semester 1933–34 (with some alterations), and the citation from Schiller: "The night is lit up bright as day" (Heidegger, *Essence of Truth*, 44; *Vom Wesen der Wahrheit*, 59). See also "On the Essence of Truth," 124. Note, however, that here it is the transformation of the darkness into light—that is to say, the passage from one to another—that is described, and the notion of conflict is absent.

20. Schelling, *Philosophical Investigations*, 29.

21. Heidegger, "Origin of the Work of Art," 27; "Der Ursprung des Kunstwerkes," 36.

22. Note that a year earlier, in a passage from the course *Introduction to Metaphysics*, held in the summer semester of 1935, Heidegger had already described the unconcealing taking place within the "work" (*Werk*) as a struggle against the concealing: "The striving for the unconcealment of beings and thus of Being in the work, this striving for the unconcealment of beings, which in itself already happens only as constant antagonism, is always at the same time the strife against concealment, covering-up, against seeming" (Heidegger, *Introduction to Metaphysics*, 205; *Einführung in die Metaphysik*, 205).

23. Heidegger, "Origin of the Work of Art," 31; "Der Ursprung des Kunstwerkes," 42.

24. Heidegger, "Origin of the Work of Art," 31; "Der Ursprung des Kunstwerkes," 42.

25. Heidegger, *Schelling's Treatise*, 137; *Schelling*, 236. Translation modified.

26. Heidegger, "Origin of the Work of Art," 21; "Der Ursprung des Kunstwerkes," 28.

27. Heidegger, "Origin of the Work of Art," 47; "Der Ursprung des Kunstwerkes," 63.

28. Heidegger, "Origin of the Work of Art," 24; "Der Ursprung des Kunstwerkes," 32.

29. Schelling, *Philosophical Investigations*, 29.

30. Heidegger, "Origin of the Work of Art," 24; "Der Ursprung des Kunstwerkes," 33.

31. I note that the same idea of "weigh" (*lasten*), which Heidegger attributes here to the stone (Heidegger, "Origin of the Work of Art," 24; "Der Ursprung des Kunstwerkes," 33), was used to describe Schelling's *Grund* in the 1936 lecture course. See Heidegger, *Schelling's Treatise*, 114; *Schelling*, 199.

32. Heidegger, "Origin of the Work of Art," 25; "Der Ursprung des Kunstwerkes," 33.

33. Heidegger, *Schelling's Treatise*, 107; *Schelling*, 187.

34. Schelling, *Philosophical Investigations*, 29.

35. Heidegger, "Origin of the Work of Art," 25; "Der Ursprung des Kunstwerkes," 33.

36. Heidegger, "Origin of the Work of Art," 42; "Der Ursprung des Kunstwerkes," 57.

37. Heidegger, "Origin of the Work of Art," 21; "Der Ursprung des Kunstwerkes," 28.

38. Heidegger, "Origin of the Work of Art," 32; "Der Ursprung des Kunstwerkes," 42.

39. Heidegger, "Origin of the Work of Art," 32; "Der Ursprung des Kunstwerkes," 42.

40. Heidegger, "Origin of the Work of Art," 27; "Der Ursprung des Kunstwerkes," 36.

41. Presumably Heidegger sees equally represented in the *Investigations* the originary conflict between unconcealment and concealment, when he interprets the conflict between the ground and the existent as strife between *Sehnsucht* and *Verstand* (in God), a strife that engenders the manifestation of logos as unity in itself split between a disclosing clearing or a clearing concealing. We should note that he thus defines understanding (*Verstand*) as "the faculty of clearing" clarifying "what is confused and obscure" (Heidegger, *Schelling's Treatise*, 119; *Schelling*, 207). I cannot develop this idea further here, but two levels seem to be at work in the Heideggerian interpretation of the Schellingian opposition between ground and the existent. On the one hand, Heidegger interprets it as the opposition between the open and that which it resists, which also corresponds to the strife between earth and world. On the other hand, the distinction between ground and the existent could equally be understood as the originary conflict between concealment and unconcealment—strife that is none other than the unfolding of the truth of beyng itself and that renders the emergence of phenomenality possible.

42. Heidegger, "Origin of the Work of Art," 26; "Der Ursprung des Kunstwerkes," 36.

43. Heidegger, *Contributions to Philosophy*, 234; *Beiträge zur Philosophie*, 296.

44. Heidegger, *Contributions to Philosophy*, 232; *Beiträge zur Philosophie*, 294.

45. Heidegger, *Contributions to Philosophy*, 234; *Beiträge zur Philosophie*, 297.

46. Heidegger, *Contributions to Philosophy*, 234; *Beiträge zur Philosophie*, 297.

47. Heidegger, *Contributions to Philosophy*, 237; *Beiträge zur Philosophie*, 301.

48. Heidegger, *Contributions to Philosophy*, 243; *Beiträge zur Philosophie*, 307.

49. Heidegger, *Contributions to Philosophy*, 273; *Beiträge zur Philosophie*, 346.

50. Heidegger, *Contributions to Philosophy*, 276; *Beiträge zur Philosophie*, 349.

51. Heidegger, *Contributions to Philosophy*, 235; *Beiträge zur Philosophie*, 297.

52. Heidegger, *Contributions to Philosophy*, 262; *Beiträge zur Philosophie*, 330.

53. Heidegger, *Contributions to Philosophy*, 306; *Beiträge zur Philosophie*, 387.

54. Heidegger, *Contributions to Philosophy*, 300; *Beiträge zur Philosophie*, 379.

55. See Heidegger, *Contributions to Philosophy*, 231; *Beiträge zur Philosophie*, 293: "Yet how abyssally cleared must the clearing for self-concealing be, such that the withdrawal might not appear superficially as mere nullity but might reign as bestowal."

56. Heidegger, *Contributions to Philosophy*, 277; *Beiträge zur Philosophie*, 351.

57. Heidegger, *Contributions to Philosophy*, 244; *Beiträge zur Philosophie*, 308.

58. Heidegger, *Contributions to Philosophy*, 27; *Beiträge zur Philosophie*, 31.

59. Heidegger, *Contributions to Philosophy*, 235; *Beiträge zur Philosophie*, 298.

60. Heidegger, *Contributions to Philosophy*, 252; *Beiträge zur Philosophie*, 318.

61. Heidegger, *Contributions to Philosophy*, 232; *Beiträge zur Philosophie*, 294.

62. Heidegger, *Contributions to Philosophy*, 232; *Beiträge zur Philosophie*, 294.

63. Heidegger, *Contributions to Philosophy*, 235; *Beiträge zur Philosophie*, 298.

64. Heidegger, *Contributions to Philosophy*, 238; *Beiträge zur Philosophie*, 301.

65. Heidegger, *Contributions to Philosophy*, 251; *Beiträge zur Philosophie*, 317.

66. Heidegger, *Contributions to Philosophy*, 251; *Beiträge zur Philosophie*, 317.

67. Heidegger, *Contributions to Philosophy*, 243; *Beiträge zur Philosophie*, 307.

68. See, for example, Heidegger, *Contributions to Philosophy*, 303; *Beiträge zur Philosophie*, 383.

69. Heidegger, *Contributions to Philosophy*, 300; *Beiträge zur Philosophie*, 380.

70. Heidegger, *Contributions to Philosophy*, 300; *Beiträge zur Philosophie*, 380.

71. Schelling, *Philosophical Investigations*, 42. Translation modified.
72. Heidegger, *Principle of Reason*, 49; *Der Satz vom Grund*, 73.

Bibliography

Heidegger, Martin. *Being and Time*. Translated by Joan Stambaugh. New York: State University of New York Press, 2010.
——. *Beiträge zur Philosophie (Vom Ereignis)*. GA 65. Edited by Friedrich-Wilhelm von Herrmann. Frankfurt am Main: Klostermann, 1989.
——. *Contributions to Philosophy (of the Event)*. Translated by Richard Rojcewicz and Daniela Vallega-Neu. Bloomington: Indiana University Press, 2012.
——. *Einführung in die Metaphysik*. GA 40. Edited by Petra Jaeger. Frankfurt am Main: Klostermann, 1983.
——. *The Essence of Truth: On Plato's Cave Allegory and Theaetetus*. Translated by Ted Sadler. London: Continuum, 2002.
——. *Introduction to Metaphysics*. Translated by Gregory Fried and Richard Polt. New Haven, CT: Yale University Press, 2000.
——. *Kant and the Problem of Metaphysics*. Edited and translated by Richard Taft. Bloomington: Indiana University Press, 1997.
——. *Kant und das Problem der Metaphysik*. GA 3. Edited by Friedrich-Wilhelm von Herrmann. Frankfurt am Main: Klostermann, 1991.
——. *The Metaphysical Foundations of Logic*. Translated by Michael Heim. Bloomington: Indiana University Press, 1992.
——. *Metaphysische Anfangsgründe der Logik im Ausgang von Leibniz*. GA 26. Edited by Klaus Held. Frankfurt am Main: Klostermann, 1978.
——. "On the Essence of Truth." In *Being and Truth*. Translated by Gregory Fried and Richard Polt, 67–201. Bloomington: Indiana University Press, 2011.
——. "The Origin of the Work of Art." In *Off the Beaten Track*, Edited and translated by Julian Young and Kenneth Haynes, 1–56. Cambridge: Cambridge University Press, 2002.
——. *Pathmarks*. Translated by William McNeill. Cambridge: Cambridge University Press, 1998.
——. *The Principle of Reason*. Translated by Reginald Lilly. Indianapolis: Indiana University Press, 1991.
——. *Der Satz vom Grund*. GA 10. Edited by Petra Jaeger. Frankfurt am Main: Klostermann, 1997.
——. *Schelling's Treatise on the Essence of Human Freedom*. Translated by Joan Stambaugh. Athens: Ohio University Press, 1984.
——. *Schelling: Vom Wesen der menschlichen Freiheit (1809)*. GA 42. Edited by Ingeborg Schüßler. Frankfurt am Main: Klostermann, 1988.
——. *Sein und Zeit*. Tübingen: Max Niemeyer, 1957.
——. "Der Ursprung des Kunstwerkes (1935/36)." In *Holzwege*, GA 5, edited by Friedrich-Wilhelm von Herrmann. Frankfurt am Main: Klostermann, 1977.
——. "Vom Wesen der Wahrheit." In *Sein und Wahrheit*, GA 36–37, edited by Hartmut Tietjen, 83–264. Frankfurt am Main: Klostermann, 2001.

———. *Vom Wesen der Wahrheit. Zu Platons Höhlengleichnis und Theätet.* GA 34. Edited by Hermann Mörchen. Frankfurt am Main: Klostermann, 1988.

———. *Wegmarken.* GA 9. Edited by Friedrich-Wilhelm von Herrmann. Frankfurt am Main: Klostermann, 1976.

Jaran, François. *La métaphysique du Dasein. Heidegger et la possibilité de la métaphysique (1927–1930).* Bucharest: Zeta, 2010.

Scheier, Claus-Artur. "Die Zeit der Seynsfuge. Zu Heideggers Interesse an Schellings Freiheitschrift." In *Schellings Weg zur Freiheitsschrift. Akten der Fachtagung der Internationalen Schelling-Gesellschaft vom 14.-17. Oktober 1992,* edited by Hans Michael Baumgartner and Wilhelm G. Jacobs. Stuttgart: Frommann-Holzboog, 1996.

Schelling, Friedrich Wilhelm Joseph von. *Philosophical Investigations into the Essence of Human Freedom.* Translated and with an introduction by Jeff Love and JohannesSchmidt. Albany: State University of New York Press, 2006.

SYLVAINE GOURDAIN is Doctor in Philosophy (Albert-Ludwigs-Universität Freiburg) and Doctor in German Studies (Université Paris-Sorbonne). Currently, she is Feodor-Lynen-fellow of the Alexander-von-Humboldt-Stiftung at the Bergische Universität Wuppertal. She is the author of two books on Heidegger and Schelling in French, *L'Ethos de l'im-possible: Dans le sillage de Heidegger et Schelling* and of *Sortir du transcendental: Heidegger et sa lecture de Schelling.*

15 *Erklüftung*

Heidegger's Thinking of Projection in Contributions to Philosophy

Tobias Keiling

IF PHILOSOPHICAL LANGUAGE cannot avoid turning to imagery, it will always, at least to some degree or in some respect, be metaphorical. Linguistic images that have no conceptual substitute are what Hans Blumenberg calls "absolute metaphors," "'translations' that resist being converted . . . into authenticality and logicality"—in other words, into a form of philosophical language that, as Descartes envisaged, would be fully transparent, with concepts clearly and distinctly delimiting what is to be understood, to be seen through them.[1] Accepting that linguistic images are "*foundational elements*" of philosophical language and rejecting the "Cartesian teleology of logicization," as Blumenberg thinks we should, enlarges both the freedom and the responsibility of the philosopher.[2] Philosophers become aware that they are, at least in principle, at liberty to reject a certain philosophical image they find themselves using and turn to another. If the philosopher is a phenomenologist, the criteria for such choice of metaphors will have to do with the fittingness of the image to the "things themselves," its appropriateness for the phenomenon they want to "let be seen" in such a way as to reveal its essential traits. Conceived in this way, studying the logic inherent to its metaphors is no alternative to phenomenology but its hermeneutical or metaphorological supplement. It allows one to understand the implications a certain choice of metaphors has for philosophical theory.

Although his case is complicated in this respect as in many others, studying the "absolute metaphors" at play in Heidegger's philosophy is rewarding. As has often been remarked, Heidegger's mastery of philosophy has much to do with his skill in using the expressive capacities of the German language, and his success in the formation of new philosophical terms and images is particularly striking. For instance, by introducing a notion such as *die Lichtung, the clearing,* into philosophical discourse, Heidegger was able to coin a new philosophical term. The metaphoric association of light and truth has a long history, to be sure, to which both Blumenberg and Derrida have pointed.[3] Presenting *the clearing* as image for the manifestation of truth and the condition of phenomenal presence, Heidegger has not simply continued this tradition but brought into circulation a new philosophical image. However, this introduction of the image of the clearing into philosophy has a history of its own. Heidegger's image for the site of truth and presence is not the product of a simple, conscious choice. Rather, in the course of his writings, Heidegger has tested, as it were, and eventually discarded a number of alternative images. The logic behind this development can be thought of as a kind of phenomenological thought experiment guided by the question of how plausible a description is, if I describe a phenomenon in light of different philosophical metaphors.

One of the alternatives in such experiment is indicated by the term *Erklüftung*, another German word Heidegger has discovered for philosophy.[4] That *Erklüftung* is much less prominent in both Heidegger's works and in the literature devoted to it, however, is no coincidence. My aim in the following is to show why the image it suggests is inherently contradictory and why Heidegger turned away from it for good reason. To show this, I will first turn to the term itself and develop the meaning of the German word, in particular reference to Goethe's writings. In the second and third section, I will reconstruct Heidegger's thinking of projection (*Entwurf*) in *Being and Time* in order to situate the notion of *Erklüftung* in reference to it. I will follow the connection of projection and ground (*Grund*), which Heidegger develops most explicitly in a passage from "The Origin of the Work of Art." I then turn to Heidegger's *Contributions to Philosophy* and address the role that the image of *Erklüftung* plays in this text. Although I reconstruct the implications this notion has for Heidegger, in a fifth section, I ask why *Erklüftung* eventually fails to accomplish the philosophical aims to which Heidegger attempts to submit the word. The image of the clearing, first at play in parallel to his other metaphors, eventually replaces the other options in Heidegger's experiment: the metaphor of Dasein as projection, the metaphor of Dasein as ground, and the metaphor of *Erklüftung* as attempted fusing of the two. Although reference to the word and the image of *Erklüftung* addresses the problems resulting from Heidegger's earlier choice of metaphors, it does not resolve its inherent contradiction. To describe the site of truth and the condition of manifestation, *the clearing* is simply the much better image.

The Meaning of *Erklüftung*

To find out what a German word means, especially an extremely rare word such as *Erklüftung*, there is a simple step to take: looking into the dictionary compiled by the Brothers Grimm. There one finds two entries:

> ERKLÜFTEN, *findere*, zerklüften.
> ERKLÜFTUNG, *f. fissura, rima*: diese masse, von jenen erklüftungen wenig erleidend. GÖTHE 51, 74.[5]

Erklüften, we learn, has the meaning of Latin *findere*, of which *fissus* is the past participle from which the German loanword *Fissur* is derived, as is the English *fissure*. Then, the Brothers Grimm explain, *erklüften* is a synonym for *zerklüften*. In the entry for the substantive *Erklüftung*, one finds a complementary reference to the Latin nouns *fissura* and *rima* as well as a single reference to the word *Erklüftung* in German literature. The reader consulting the Grimm dictionary should be surprised by this: that an entry features only a single reference is very rare in view of the abundance of examples from German literature that the dictionary typically contains.

In distinction to *erklüften*, *zerklüften* is determined as a transitive verb with the basic meaning "to cleave wide, to divide with gaping cuts [*breit zerspalten, mit klaffenden einschnitten zertheilen*]." *Zerklüften*, "in its authentic meaning," is used "mostly as adjective and participle [i.e., *zerklüftet*] of rocky mountains, blocks of stone or the coast of a land [*im eig. sinne, zumeist nur als adj. partic., von felsgebirgen, gesteinsblöcken oder der küste eines landes*]." Secondly, *zerklüften* also means "to divide up into groups or to be divided by groups and the like [*in oder durch parteien spalten u. ä.*]." In this entry one also finds the addition that *zerklüften* has another "authentic" meaning, namely "to cleave wood [*eig. schlieszlich noch holz z[erklüften]*]," or as one may say more frequently in English, to "split wood." In "extremely rare" cases, there is also an intransitive meaning of *zerklüften*.[6] A reference for this is given in a passage from Adalbert Stifter, where Stifter writes: "The wood split and fell down in pieces [*das holz zerklüftete und fiel in stücken herab*]."[7]

The single reference given for *erklüften* is also about such an intransitive meaning of the verb. It can be found—as the only occurrence of *durchklüften* the Brothers Grimm note[8]—in Goethe's scientific writings. More precisely, it is found in a text entitled *The Formation of Mountains in the Whole and in the Particular* (*Gebirgsgestaltung im Ganzen und Einzelnen*, printed 1824). In this text, Goethe is interested in the "macro-micromegic process of Nature [*makro-mikromegische Verfahren der Natur*]," which "does nothing on the bigger scale that it would not also do in the smaller [*im Großen nichts [tut], was sie nicht auch im Kleinen thaete*]," and also does "nothing concealed what it would not also show to the day of light [*nichts im Verborgenen [bewirkt,] was sie nicht auch am Tagslicht offenbarte*]."[9] Given this premise of his philosophy of nature, fundamental insights in geology may be gained from single examples such as the importance of the so-called "solidification [*Solidescenz*]" in the emergence and formation of mountains: "Solidification is the last stage of becoming, the liquid being led through the soft to the solid, presenting the becoming in enclosed form [*Solidescenz ist der letzte Act des Werdens, aus dem Flüssigen durch's Weiche zum Festen hingeführt, das Gewordene abgeschlossen darstellend*]."[10] *Erklüftungen* occur in such a process of the becoming of mountains, in the transition from potentiality (*potentia*) to reality (*actus*), which Goethe calls the "originary grating [*Urdurch-gitterung*]" of stone.[11] Yet an *Erklüften* is part of the gradual solidification of stone only because of a phenomenon that, Goethe says, "does not let go of us because of its inscrutability: *solidification is associated with tremor*. This phenomenon, because of its delicacy, is decisively recognized only very rarely [*uns bei seiner Unerforschlichkeit nicht losläßt: Solidescenz ist mit Erschütterung verbunden. Nur selten kommt dieses Phänomen, seiner Zartheit wegen, zur unmittelbaren entsch-iedenen Anerkennung*]."[12] The cleavages, the cracks and fissures in stone, its *Erklüftungen*, are thus produced through a shock interrupting the solidification of the liquid rock.

A remarkable example for this, Goethe notes, is the "Florentine ruin marble we all know [*allbekannte Florentinische Ruinenmarmor*]." The marble, so Goethe imagines, "was just in the process of layering . . . when some twitching cut through the fine layers with little vertical cleaves, significantly displacing the horizontal lines . . . such that we now see before our eyes the shape of a breached wall [*sich bandartig zu bilden im Begriff . . ., als ein gewisses Zucken die zarten Streifen mit verticalen Klüftchen durchschnitt und die horizontalen Linien bedeutend verrückte . . . wodurch uns dann die Gestalt einer lückenhaften Mauer vor Augen tritt*]." The marble is indeed, as the reference quoted in the Grimm dictionary reads, "suffering very little from these *Erklüftungen* [*von diesen Erk-lüftungen wenig erleidend*]"; despite the cracks in its structure, the stone can be worked in many ways; it may be cut, polished, and even painted. The cracks in particular account for the beauty of the marble: the "fine stripes [*zarten Strei-fen*]" and the "little vertical splits [*verticalen Klüftchen*]" in cut and polished tab-lets" may appear "as sky above a landscape, if one is willing to take them for it [*bei geschnittenen und polirten Tafeln über der Landschaft als Bewölkung, wer es dafür will gelten lassen*]."[13] Goethe owned about twenty of such marble plates, and when we look at them, it becomes indeed apparent what must have been so fascinating to him about these stones.

Erklüftungen, according to Goethe's use of the word, are thus the result of a sudden interruption in the process of solidification. Astonishingly, though, this interruption joins in with the hidden formation of stone in a harmonious way, for the marble does not break open. Rather, the solidity of the stone encloses the cracks, halting the process of splitting so only the inside splits remain. These *Erk-lüftungen* of the marble, although they are created by a spontaneous interruption in the process of solidification, therefore essentially occur in concealment and do not expose the transformative process that created them. Only those pieces broken out of the stone and the "cut and polished tablets" attest to them. None-theless, his samples of such stone move Goethe to describe the event causing *Erklüftungen*, and the solidly conjoined fractures provide an occasion to imagine the concealed origin of rocks and mountains.

The Temporality of Projection

At first sight, Heidegger's thinking of projection has little to do with hidden cracks in stone. It is rather marked by a somewhat forced determination of that which is projected: beings as a whole, the whole of experience, of the open and of what can be understood—*Dasein*. This philosophical appreciation of the image of projection results from Heidegger's use in discussing the understanding (*Verstehen*) grasping everything in human existence, even Being itself: all understanding has the same structure as projection, so that everything understood is as such projected.[14]

What provides a justification for Heidegger to make this transference, the explicative identification of Dasein, projection, and understanding, is the modality of *potentiality* or *possibility* (*Möglichkeit*). Dasein is a being of possibility, and it understands itself in this potential being by projecting. In Heidegger's words: "Dasein as understanding projects its being upon possibilities."[15] Only the "projecting character of understanding" makes "the there as there of a potential being" accessible to Dasein. But, Heidegger emphasizes, this projecting "has nothing to do with being related to a plan thought out in advance, according to which Dasein arranges its being"; rather, because Dasein is an essentially projecting entity, it has "always already projected itself, and it is, as long as it is, projecting." The fact that "Dasein has always understood itself and will understand itself from out of possibilities [*aus Möglichkeiten*]" is grasped by the idea that "understanding as projecting is the mode of being of Dasein in which it *is* its possibilities as possibilities."[16]

These conceptual operations are comprehensible in the context of *Being and Time* and may be further explicated from this context. Choosing the language of *Entwerfen*, however, Heidegger apparently wishes to draw from its descriptive potential to provide an intuitive confirmation of his ideas. Yet this association of understanding, potentiality, and projection only corresponds to a very limited degree to what is commonly understood by *etwas entwerfen*. To have a specific project, to *project* something, rather seems to be precisely what Heidegger excludes as the "being related to a plan thought out in advance." In the process of *Entwerfen*, a plan is made and tested in view of its possible realization, transforming mere potentiality as such into a certain delimited project and a concrete possibility. In idiomatic German, *Entwerfen* is what architects and designers do.[17] *Projecting* in this sense then may indeed naturally be described as an understanding of possibilities, as the human capacity to determine possibilities, to explore them and even reject them without having to realize and exhaust them, drawing from an imagination of their reality for such decision. For projection to operate in such a way, however, it is decisive that it be integrated into a larger process of understanding, of planning, and of realization that exceeds the stage of *entwerfen* and that will eventually produce an objective result in one way or another, be it in the form of a sketch, an outline, or some other form of draft, a preliminary model, something akin to a first entelechy. It is only because an *Entwerfen* leads to an *Entwurf*, *projecting* to a determinate *project*, that it may disclose specific potentialities of being.

However, this is not the way in which Heidegger uses projection as an image for Dasein's understanding of its potential being. The idea that projecting, the description of a project or the making of a model, relates to the possible in contrast to the actual is one-sided because the actual context of the project or the actual properties of the material needed are disregarded. Nonetheless, it is plausible enough to give primacy to the possible over the actual in describing the essential trait of projection. One may further accept that Heidegger disregards the fact that *Entwerfen* as an activity is bound to creating particular sketches, drafts, proposals, or outlines. But there is another, much more ambitious claim that follows from his identification of projecting and understanding: projecting is to be thought of as essentially reflexive.[18] Thus, for Heidegger, to be able to be (*Seinkönnen*) is to project one's potential being, and this means to project *oneself* (*Sichentwerfen*). That the object and the subject of projection are the same, however, lies well outside the common meaning of *Entwerfen*. As a consequence, it becomes questionable whether projecting provides an image apt to the illustration of fundamental ontology.

Rather than dismissing this image, however, Heidegger reacts to the semantic resistance of the word by superimposing yet another layer of philosophical terminology: projecting is to be understood as an eminently *temporal* experience, such that Dasein's *temporality* provides a foundation for the self-referential and self-sustaining character of projecting. Heidegger determines a complex structure of the experience of time in past, present, and future, rated as either authentic or inauthentic, in order to describe the temporality of Dasein. In this setup, the aspect of time specific for projecting is the *future*: "the self-projecting grounded in the future [*das in der Zukunft gründende Sichentwerfen*]" belongs to "the essential character of existence," and because Dasein as a whole projects itself in its existence, the "*primary meaning* [*primärer Sinn*]" of existing is "*the future*."[19] Yet Heidegger is not interested in the fact that planning or projecting something implies that the project one has in mind can be realized at a later time; this is not what it means for Dasein to be "grounded" in the future. Rather, because of its temporal and futural being, Dasein does not seem to know any concrete projects or have any determinate projections of itself that it could realize in the future. Heidegger is instead led by another consideration: if projecting is the understanding of possibilities, disclosing Dasein in its being possible, then it relates to the indeterminate and indefinite potential that an open and undecided future offers. For Dasein to project itself into the future means for it to sever itself from any determination through its past or present.

Heidegger expresses this idea with yet another twist in the register of *entwerfen*: to project something *upon* something (*etwas auf etwas entwerfen*), or, in the case of Dasein, to project *oneself* upon something (*sich auf etwas (hin) entwerfen*). If *to project* may indeed mean to disclose the indefinite, indeterminate and undecided openness of the future, then there is a sense in which one may speak of a projecting *upon* the indeterminate and *into* the future. It is in this sense that one has to understand the formulation that Dasein projects *itself* upon its possibilities. Yet if this is its genuine philosophical import, *entwerfen* in *Being and Time* has severed completely any connection with its idiomatic meaning, to form a particular project or to produce a draft, a sketch, or a model embodying the possible before it is realized. Rather, it is oriented toward nothing but itself; it is a projecting onto "the always already projected being possible [*immer entworfene Seinkönnen*],"[20] in other words, upon the projecting, a projecting continuously reaffirming itself. In the peculiar understanding of *Entwerfen* as *Sichentwerfen* Heidegger develops, then, there is no way back from the "transcendental" disclosure of the indeterminate future as the mere possibility of projection to specific, albeit provisional, "empirical" projects. Thus projection, in the overdetermination to which Heidegger submits the notion, generates its own meaning. In contrast to the usual semantics of *entwerfen*, it needs nothing outside itself, nothing that it makes use of or upon which its realization would depend. As anticipating disclosure of potentiality, projecting never takes a specific shape and never discloses concrete possibilities as particular projects do. It only discloses its own future as wholly indeterminate potentiality in Being. If Heidegger turned to the language of *entwerfen* in order to provide an image for fundamental ontology, the result is quite the opposite: overdetermined and distorted, the illustration of Dasein as *Entwurf* can no longer give an intuitive confirmation of the philosophical theory put forth in *Being and Time*.

Ground and Projection

Heidegger's reaction to this problem, however, is not to let go of the metaphor of *Entwurf* but rather to fuse it with another. Despite all the vehemence with which Heidegger attempts to demonstrate the primacy of the future for Dasein, Heidegger is well aware that it would not be plausible to describe Dasein as nothing but a wholly indeterminate, future potential being. Some structure and limitation must be given to the self-referential indeterminacy Heidegger has associated with projection. Rather than returning to the common meaning of *entwerfen*, however, he introduces another image representing Dasein, a sort of counterimage aiming to balance, as it were, the idea that Dasein is a self-referential process of projection: not only is Dasein projected and projecting at once but it is also said to be the *ground (Grund)* of its own projection. Although there is another idea limiting projecting, namely the idea of "thrownness into the there [*Geworfenheit in das Da*]"[21] and the recurring phrase of a "thrown projection [*geworfener Entwurf*],"[22] these formulations lack the necessary force. For even if Dasein "as thrown [is] thrown into the mode of being of projecting [*in die Seinsart des Entwerfens geworfen*],"[23] this means nothing more than that it is forced, being thrown, to project itself (onto itself) at all. Thrownness does not give structure to or establish a limitation of projection but only reaffirms the necessity and primacy of the activity of projecting. Only with the identification of Dasein as *ground* does Heidegger give a more forceful and, as it were, material limitation to the metaphor of projection.

Yet the images of projection and ground are quite distinct, if not outright contradictory in their semantic and metaphorical implications. How can something be closed off and fixed as well as open and indeterminate? How can we think about ourselves as both an abiding ground and a continuous projection into an open future? Heidegger's answer is the idea that Dasein, although it is itself the "ground of its potential being," has "*not itself* laid this ground." Although, qua projecting, it should anticipate and run ahead into its future, Dasein "rests in its heaviness [*ruht in seiner Schwere*]," too. Paradoxically, it is only out of such heaviness, Heidegger says, that Dasein may project itself "upon those possibilities . . . into which it is thrown." Although attempting to control its own ground, Dasein can "fundamentally *never* possess [*von Grund auf nie mächtig werden*]" it.[24] This negativity of the ground, carrying but uncontrollable, provides an intuitively accessible counterimage to the self-disclosure of Dasein as the being of projecting potentiality—or so Heidegger's text calls on us to imagine. The idea that Dasein is *both* projection and ground may be pronounced in a few words, but it is difficult to integrate both aspects coherently and to see before the mind's eye, as it were, both images as one. Pointing to this difficulty is another way of describing the failure of *Being and Time*: in using such distinct metaphors for Dasein, Heidegger draws from semantic fields that lie too far apart for the conflicting ideas of fundamental ontology to be intelligible in the philosophical use of the imagination.[25]

It is plausible to conjecture that Heidegger must, in some way, have taken notice of the competition of philosophical images in *Being and Time*. One reaction to their incongruence can be found in "The Origin of the Work of Art," where both projection and ground are associated with *die Erde, the earth*: in his discussion of the establishing (*Stiften*) of history in the third part of the artwork essay, Heidegger distinguishes giving (*Schenken*), grounding (*Gründen*), and beginning (*Anfangen*) as different aspects of the way a work of art can be understood as a historical event. These three aspects of the historical character of the work of art take up past, present, and future as the different directions of the temporal ecstasies discussed in *Being and Time*. Significantly, however, projection is discussed, not in terms of the relation of art to the future, but in view of its relation to the past. To provide a succinct image for its withdrawal and inaccessibility, Dasein's past is in turn associated with the earth. Rather than as relation to the open future, projection is now to be understood as the

> opening up of that wherein Dasein has already been thrown as historical being. This is the earth, and for a historical people their earth, the self-concealing ground upon which they rest with all that it, though maybe still hidden to itself, already is. . . . This is why everything already given to humans must still be extracted from the closed ground and set upon it. In such a way the ground is founded as a carrying ground. [*Eröffnung von Jenem, worein das Dasein als geschichtliches schon geworfen ist. Dies ist die Erde und für ein geschichtliches Volk seine Erde, der sich verschließende Grund, dem es aufruht mit all dem, was es, sich selbst noch verborgen, schon ist. [. . .] Deshalb muß alles dem Menschen Mitgegebene im Entwurf aus dem verschlossenen Grund heraufgeholt und eigens auf diesen gesetzt werden. So wird er als der tragende Grund erst gegründet.*][26]

This reorientation toward the earth makes the limitation of projection most concrete. Albeit still somewhat enigmatic, *earth* can be coherently construed as a philosophical notion.[27] As a consequence of situating the notion in this context, Heidegger now also argues that projection, if it is geared toward the past, is not disclosing the wholly indeterminate, retracting his earlier claim.[28] Heidegger thus corrects two ideas from *Being and Time*: projection is directed not *toward* the indeterminate but *into* the ground, and its temporal orientation is not *toward* the future but *into* the past. These conceptual shifts, however, do not change the fact that ground and projection remain incongruent philosophical images. Yet how is one to imagine a projection going on *within* the earth? The image of *Erklüftung* is Heidegger's answer to that question and his attempt to present a unified image for the identity of ground and projection.

Recall the ruin marble. It shows that there are processes that resemble human creativity (projecting) but are not caused by any human, allowing one to imagine that there is a projecting taking place in the earth itself (in the ground). If one accepts Goethe's choice of words and returns to his example, the ruin marble can *show* how ground and projection can be one.

Erklüftung in *Contributions to Philosophy*

The word *Erklüftung* occurs in the fifth part of *Contributions*, entitled *The Grounding* (*Die Gründung*), in a section entitled *Of Da-sein*. This is the section where, for the first time in Heidegger's *oeuvre*, he sketches the structure of the *fourfold* (*das Geviert*), or a structure at least very much resembling the later so-called fourfold, positioned originally on the extreme lower right corner of the manuscript page, much less prominent than in print. The section aims to speak of Dasein "by way of grounding [*gründend*]." This is inherently related to the second metaphor of Dasein, for it can only be done "in a rightly understood projection [*im rechtverstandenen Entwurf*]." Being both their own ground and essentially projecting, human beings are "*broken out* into the open [*ausgebrochen . . . ins Offene*]."[29] Heidegger thus defines the ecstatic constitution of Dasein, not as anticipation of the future, or in temporal terms, but as the dual movement of opening (qua projection) and of closure (qua grounding). This movement takes the form of the event (*Ereignis*) relating world and earth, humans and gods, all at once. From the little sketch with its centripetal arrows, so Heidegger thinks, "it can already be seen which unitarily formed force of projection is required [*einheitlich gefügte Entwurfskraft*]"[30]—that is, the unitary force of projection the event is said to hold, limited by the self-enclosing nature of the ground.

Heidegger begins his discourse on *Erklüftung* in the attempt to describe such a pluridirectional force of projection: the "event [*Geschehnis*] of *Erklüftung*" is the "appropriation [*Er-eignung*]" of the four dimensions that Heidegger identifies. Through *Erklüftung*, "historical man" finds himself and experiences the "nearing and distancing [*Nahung und Fernung*]" of the gods. The word further designates the dynamic spatiality of this "nearing and distancing" that is further said to be "the origin of time-space [*Zeit-Raum*]" and the "realm of the strife"[31] between world and earth. In astonishing similarity to Goethe's use of the word, *Erklüftung* is to be regarded, according to Heidegger, as the reshaping of the ground through the projective force, which does not come from the subject but which has the form of an event. It occurs out of its proper force, without human manipulation and outside human viewing.

The two other passages of *Contributions* where Heidegger speaks of *Erklüftung* confirm this understanding. In the first passage, the role of humans in the event of *Erklüftung* is determined and related to the analytic of Dasein. Authentic "selfhood [*Selbstheit*]," as Heidegger says, develops from the strife of this splitting sundering, given that one accepts the need "to stand into and to stand through [*ausstehen*]"[32] this event. Authentic existence is thus the acceptance of the event of *Erklüftung*, of a hidden fracturing both in the self and in the world. But this event is no longer structured, formatted, or filtered, as it were, by the three ecstasies of time, and Dasein can no longer be closed by an anticipation of the future, which ends in one's own death. Rather, the four dimensions of the fourfold, as well as time and space, are instead to be thought from the idea of a sundering that is both concealing and opening, shaping in such a way the manifestation of particular local contexts of meaning, of what Heidegger calls *Zeit-Räume,* *time-spaces.* In an "inceptual consideration of time-space," the image of the centrifugal movement is taken up and varied accordingly: time-space is the "appropriated sundering of the turning paths of the event [*ereignete Erklüftung der Kehrungsbahnen des Ereignisses*]." This dynamic is not to be understood "as in the usual conceptions of time and space," nor from the three-dimensionality of a threefold ecstatic structure of time he had described in *Being and Time.* Rather, one is to see the "concealed appearance of time-space" in "nearness and distance, emptiness and giving, momentum and hesitation [*Nähe und Ferne, Leere und Schenkung, Schwung und Zögerung*]."³³ *Erklüftung,* one may paraphrase, designates an ungraspable disclosing of time and space through the force of events, concealed as if it were hidden in stone itself.

These ideas are paralleled in Heidegger's use of *Zerklüftung.* By this term, Heidegger understands the "unfolding of the intimacy of Being remaining in itself [*in sich bleibende Entfaltung der Innigkeit des Seyns*]." Being essentially split, Being is thus both open and closed; it remains in itself while expanding and unfolding. Making use of the "'metaphysical' modalities," one can think of *Zerklüftung* only as an essential paradox, as the "highest reality of the highest possible as possible and therefore as first necessity [*höchste Wirklichkeit des höchsten Möglichen als des Möglichen und damit die erste Notwendigkeit*]."³⁴ Because of this, it should be possible, Heidegger claims, to reinterpret the ontological modalities in view of the manifestation of the event, although it remains unclear how this could be done. And although projecting, according to *Being and Time,* at least, discloses the possible as possible in understanding, the rutted and indented *Being* of the form of projection Heidegger calls *Zerklüftung* cannot be understood as mere potentiality. With respect to the analytic of Dasein and the primacy of potentiality as the ultimate positive determination of Dasein developed in *Being and Time,* this is a radical rehabilitation of reality and necessity, linked here with those phenomena Heidegger describes as the remaining-in-itself (*In-sich-bleiben*). As *zerklüftet,* Being is not mere potentiality but is itself the conditioned necessary condition of the possibility of beings, or, in paradox terms, the "first necessity" and also the "highest possibility."³⁵

The second passage can be found on the page of *Contributions* in which the word *Erklüftung* appears four times. It is the longest such passage Heidegger highlights in the entire volume. In this passage, the above considerations are gathered in one of the most enigmatic formulations: Dasein is the "event of *Erklüftung* of the midst of the turning of the event [*Geschehnis der Erklüftung der Wendungsmitte der Kehre des Ereignisses*]."³⁶ Interpreting this cascade of genitives, one can say that Dasein takes place in the field structured by the dimensions of the fourfold and in the interplay of time and space that Heidegger calls the time-space, preceding all determinate spatiotemporal orders. In this taking-place, Dasein does not project itself into the future but sunders itself as the ground that it also is. Sundered in and by its own being, Dasein is exposed to the resonance of events that are not mere possibilities of human manipulation or reducible to a manifestation of any other of the four dimensions of the fourfold.[37] In such a way, Heidegger believes, the being of Dasein is revealed as the event, as the turning in the center of the field structured by the different determinations Heidegger gives—world, earth, humans, gods, time, space. This revelation, however, is not to be seen. We turn to the image of sundering because the interplay of these determining factors in the process of manifestation withdraws from thinking. To be Dasein, then, means to be in the "turning midst" of these events, even if this midst must be *within* the concealed ground.

If we take these passages together, it is difficult to see how this abundance of determinations could be gathered in a single philosophical concept or even a single metaphor. Although there may be a unitary image associated with *Erklüftung*, like the one the ruin marble provides, Heidegger's overdetermination of the term, similar to the overdetermination of *Entwerfen* in *Being and Time*, calls into question the value of this metaphor as intuitive confirmation of a philosophical theory. The fusion of ground and projection proclaimed in *Being and Time* inspires Heidegger to think of the accessibility of beings not just as a dynamic event but also as an event taking place in what is concealed—not *on* the earth but *in* the earth. It is the image of *Erklüftung* that is supposed to bring it into view nonetheless.

Clearing, Place, and the Void

To find a name for the problem inherent in this conception, one might say that it is *speculative* rather than *descriptive*. One way to understand what *speculate* can mean here is to say that *Erklüftung* functions as a philosophical mirror, as it were, where the two conflicting images of projection and ground are reflected back and forth in our use of the imagination. That may well be true, and it explains how we can entertain the thought *that* these images are *contradictory* at all, for it is not evident what it should mean for images to be contradictory: the logic of imagination does indeed allow us to think of the two images as contradicting each other.[38] Referring to a literal meaning of *speculative*, one may say that *Erklüftung* is a speculative notion in this sense. This meaning of *speculative*, however, does not yet yield a contrast with *descriptive*. This contrast emerges, however, once one understands that, in thus being reflected back and forth, these images cease to be disclosing: in their reciprocal mirroring, they no longer let anything be seen. A contradictory image like that of *Erklüftung* ceases to be phenomenological in the sense that it can no longer be integrated into descriptions of something determinate. It breaks with the essential insight of phenomenology that any experience, including one made possible by metaphors as nonconceptual descriptions, must be *of something.*

It speaks for his phenomenological ethos, then, that Heidegger seems not content with the imagining set free by *Erklüftung* and the incoherent descriptions it implies. If the above discussion of the inherent logic of philosophical imagination is correct, it is for this reason that Heidegger, in a later passage of *Contributions*, gives the reader another philosophical image for Dasein: Dasein is the *clearing.* Expressed in the logic of his metaphors, what is decisive for this turn toward the clearing is that there must already be an open space even for something self-concealing to appear as such, as concealing. Much later, Heidegger will make this point explicitly, pointing to what is specific about the image of the clearing: "something absent can only be as such if it is present in the *free open of the clearing.*"[39] In the same vein, one will have to say of the philosophical images of projecting and ground that they require at least an openness for speculative imagination to relate, some leeway, as it were, for them to hover in the imagination.

In a passage from *Contributions* where he explicitly relates the imagination with the metaphor of the clearing, Heidegger indeed argues that, precisely in order to be manifest as the "grounding of the openness of self-concealing [*Gründung der Offenheit des Sichverbergens*]," Dasein must be conceived as clearing, which in turn means to speak of the clearing of the "imagination" (*Einbildung*). Heidegger indeed grants primacy to the imagination over both ground and projection when he says that, precisely as "projecting-thrown grounding [*entwerfend-geworfene Gründung*]," Dasein would have to be determined as the "highest reality in the domain of imagination [*höchste Wirklichkeit im Bereich der Einbildung*]." For even concealed ground to be present means that it "becomes shining in the clearing, in the there [*zum Scheinen gebracht werde in die Lichtung, in das Da*]."[40] If this is so, in the logic of these metaphors, the clearing or *das Da*, the there, as the space of Dasein is not first created by the interplay of ground and projection. Rather, this interplay can only take place within the prior openness of Dasein.

Looking at it with a fresh pair of eyes, we confirm this by our example. It is the astonishing trait of the ruin marble that it has been shaped as if it were made by humans even before human hands had touched it and that it thus appears to hold a spontaneous and natural creativity; nature forms its own images.[41] That this is the case becomes manifest only when the stone comes to light, yet this does not happen as the stone sunders, splits itself (*sich erklüftet*), but only when it breaks open or is smashed. These images can only be described when they come into the clearing, into an openness of a different origin from the cracks and rifts inside a stone. Before, one may at best speculate. If this is a proper discussion of the implications of Heidegger's metaphors, allowing the competing philosophical images to unfold their own logic and proper sense, then it is no surprise that the image of the clearing becomes determinative for what Heidegger attempts to think.

That Heidegger abandons the identification of projection with ground and the idea of a concealing-opening fracturing is confirmed by two related passages from later texts. Heidegger here further determines the image of the clearing and connects it with the notions of *place* (*Ort*) and *void* (*Leere*). That there is such a thing as a stable, delimited *place* or an indeterminate void is constitutively excluded in the logic of *Erklüftung*, which implies that the space of manifestation is both compact and unrelentingly dynamic. Yet these two notions now appear to be essential for the phenomenology of projecting. In such a way, projecting itself is put in a more limited but also much more plausible position, and one can begin to describe, following Heidegger but beyond the logic of *Erklüftung*, how projecting operates in the clearing and on a ground with which it is not identical—namely, in the creation of places and as formation of the void.

The first passage is a marginal note in "The Origin of the Work of Art," which Heidegger must have written after 1960. Next to the word *projecting*, Heidegger notes that it is "not the clearing as such" that is projected, "because only in the clearing is a project placed [*denn in [der Lichtung] erst ist der Entwurf geortet*]."[42] Thus, even if projecting creates places, it does not create them out of nothing. That would be the explicitly excluded self-disclosure of projecting according to which the clearing would be created by some form of projection, be it the temporal projection of *Being and Time* or the sundering of Being from *Contributions*. Heidegger's self-criticism points to a particular weakness of the idea of *Erklüftung*: it does not become clear how, from out of the event of the sundering taking place in the compact solidity of the earth, places can come into being. The claim that *Erklüftung* is the origin of time-space, the origin of nearness and distance, remains a mere assertion as long as those phenomena are thought to exist within a closed ground. What should a place be, other than a delimited *open*? The dual image of *Erklüftung* takes for granted a density and originary solidity hat is contrary to both the intuition and the semantics of space.[43] If Being were really to be opened only in *Erklüftungen*, as the rock is broken by its cracks and rifts, all openness would be the result of a rifting, of a splitting spatial dynamic, but not an originary constituent of any such dynamic.

The strongest counterimage to the idea of *Erklüftung* appears in the second passage. This image is the principal idea of the essay *Art and Space* (1969), the idea that the void is itself a "bringing forth [*Hervorbringen*]" because it is "twins with what is essential about place [*mit dem Eigentümlichen des Ortes verschwistert*]."[44] The void, the emptiness of indeterminate phenomenal space, is not created through a projection or through the sundering of ground. This openness is rather merely disclosed and formed. One can see this already in the prints by Eduardo Chillida for which Heidegger wrote his text:[45] the void and

294 | *Paths in Heidegger's Later Thought*

emptiness of the white paper are precisely *not* first opened up by the concealing black but only shaped through and delimited by it. It is also worth noting
that Heidegger here no longer speaks of Dasein as being of potentiality or of
the temporal unity of understanding that is being projected. Rather, particular things, works of modern sculpture, are concerned when he says that these
are the "searching-projecting establishing of places [*suchend-entwerfende Stiften
von Orten*]."[46] In such a way, Heidegger silently returns to the notion of projection as projection *of something upon something else*, to the meaning typically
attributed to *entwerfen* and the idea of *Entwurf* as a specific configuration of the
possible. Instead of thinking of projection as a projection into the indeterminate surface of the future, as in *Being and Time*, it is now evident that there is
something that is projected, namely places, and that there is something within
which projection takes place, namely the void. By means of an *Entwurf*, places are
sought out and shaped within space.

For the philosophical attempt to understand projecting, this reveals that projecting must relate to the openness associated with the clearing and the void (as
its conditions of possibility) and also to that which is created in projecting (places
of experience). Rather than its fusion with the ground in the idea of *Erklüftung*,
one would turn to situations localized in the open, located in the clearing, to
understand projecting. Having returned to the idiomatic meaning of *Entwerfen*, one can also turn to drawing, skiagraphy,[47] or sculpture[48] as paradigms
for understanding projection. One would return to those place-determining
things designers enable to be[49] and to the practice of architecture as paradigms
for understanding *Entwerfen*. Although it was never a matter of a simple choice
between alternatives, it is for good reason that Heidegger rejected all three images
of projection, of ground, and of *Erklüftung* and that he eventually opted for the
clearing as the absolute metaphor for thinking the site of truth and the condition
of possibility of manifest presence.[50]

Notes

1. Blumenberg, *Paradigms for a Metaphorology*, 3.
2. Blumenberg, *Paradigms for a Metaphorology*, 3.
3. See Blumenberg, "Licht als Metapher der Wahrheit"; Derrida, "White Mythology."
4. In their recent translation of *Contributions to Philosophy (Of the Event)*, Daniela-
Vallega Neu and Richard Rojcewicz render *Erklüftung* as "sundering." Though this
translation—in distinction to "fissure," which they use for *Zerklüftung*—justly emphasizes
the dynamic character of this process, it breaks the link between *Erklüftung* and *Zerklüftung*
and related verbs. I will thus leave both words untranslated in occurrences where I wish to
emphasize this connection.

5. Grimm and Grimm, *Deutsches Wörterbuch. E–Forsche*, 878.
6. Grimm and Grimm, *Deutsches Wörterbuch. Z–Zmasche*, 704.
7. Stifter, *Werke Und Briefe*, 80.
8. Grimm and Grimm, *Deutsches Wörterbuch. Biermörder–D*, 1633: "DURCHKLÜFTEN, *durch und durch spalten*. der kieselschiefer ist so vielfach durchzogen und durchklüftet." The reference to Goethe can be found in Goethe, "Gebirgs-Gestaltung im Ganzen und Einzelnen," 632.
9. Goethe, "Gebirgs-Gestaltung im Ganzen und Einzelnen," 631.
10. Goethe, "Gebirgs-Gestaltung im Ganzen und Einzelnen," 628.
11. Goethe, "Gebirgs-Gestaltung im Ganzen und Einzelnen," 628.
12. Goethe, "Gebirgs-Gestaltung im Ganzen und Einzelnen," 630.
13. Goethe, "Gebirgs-Gestaltung im Ganzen und Einzelnen," 633.
14. Heidegger here obviously varies Kant's claim that "reason only understands what it produces in accordance with its own projection [*die Vernunft nur das einsieht, was sie selbst nach ihrem Entwurfe hervorbringt*] (Kant, *Kant's Gesammelte Schriften*, B XIII). All translations are my own.
15. Heidegger, *Sein und Zeit*, 197; Heidegger, *Being and Time*, 144.
16. Heidegger, *Sein und Zeit*, 193; Heidegger, *Being and Time*, 141.
17. See, for instance, the contribution by Alexander Schwarz to the volume *Suchen, Entwerfen, Stiften* as a professional statement from an architect. Florian Arnold's recent proposal for a philosophy of design is titled *Logik des Entwerfens*.
18. This is because for Heidegger, understanding is essentially understanding oneself (*sich verstehen*), namely understanding oneself in one's possibilities and understanding one's own there as potential being.
19. Heidegger, *Sein und Zeit*, 433; Heidegger, *Being and Time*, 313.
20. Heidegger, *Sein und Zeit*, 447; Heidegger, *Being and Time*, 322.
21. Heidegger, *Sein und Zeit*, 197; Heidegger, *Being and Time*, 144.
22. Heidegger, *Sein und Zeit*, 378 and passim; Heidegger, *Being and Time*, 273 and passim.
23. Heidegger, *Sein und Zeit*, 193; Heidegger, *Being and Time*, 141.
24. Heidegger, *Sein und Zeit*, 377; Heidegger, *Being and Time*, 273–74.
25. For a discussion of how the inherent tension of Heidegger's magnum opus defines his later works, see Keiling, *Seinsgeschichte*; Keiling, "Heidegger's *Black Notebooks*"; and Keiling, "Phenomenology and Ontology."
26. Heidegger, *Holzwege*, 63; Heidegger, *Off the Beaten Track*, 47.
27. See Keiling, "Of the Earth."
28. See Heidegger, *Holzwege*, 63; Heidegger, *Off the Beaten Track*, 47.
29. Heidegger, *Beiträge zur Philosophie*, 310; Heidegger, *Contributions to Philosophy*, 245–46.
30. Heidegger, *Beiträge zur Philosophie*, 310; Heidegger, *Contributions to Philosophy*, 245–46.
31. Heidegger, *Beiträge zur Philosophie*, 311; Heidegger, *Contributions to Philosophy*, 246.
32. Heidegger, *Beiträge zur Philosophie*, 312; Heidegger, *Contributions to Philosophy*, 247.
33. Heidegger, *Beiträge zur Philosophie*, 312; Heidegger, *Contributions to Philosophy*, 247.
34. Heidegger, *Beiträge zur Philosophie*, 312; Heidegger, *Contributions to Philosophy*, 247.
35. Heidegger, *Beiträge zur Philosophie*, 312; Heidegger, *Contributions to Philosophy*, 247.
36. Heidegger, *Beiträge zur Philosophie*, 312; Heidegger, *Contributions to Philosophy*, 247.

37. On the notion of the fourfold, see Mitchell, *Fourfold.*
38. On the logic of imagining contradictions, see Sallis, *Logic of Imagination,* chap. 1 and 3.
39. Heidegger, GA 14:82.
40. Heidegger, *Beiträge zur Philosophie,* 312; Heidegger, *Contributions to Philosophy,* 247.
41. See Caillois, "Natura pictrix."
42. Heidegger, *Holzwege,* 61; Heidegger, *Off the Beaten Track,* 46.
43. See Figal, *Unscheinbarkeit,* 22–37
44. Heidegger, "Die Kunst und der Raum," 209.
45. Reproduced in Mitchell, *Heidegger among the Sculptors,* 79–80.
46. Heidegger, "Die Kunst und der Raum," 209.
47. See Derrida, *Mémoires D'aveugle.*
48. See Mitchell, *Heidegger among the Sculptors,* esp. 66–91.
49. See Keiling, "Letting Things Be for Themselves."
50. A first version of this chapter was part of my dissertation *Opened Grounds: Studies on Foundation and Truth in Phenomenology* (2013), a second version was published in German in the volume *Suchen. Entwerfen. Stiften* (ed. David Espinet and Toni Hildebrandt) in 2014. I thank all those who helped me think (or see) through Heidegger's metaphors with (I hope) increasing clarity.

Bibliography

Arnold, Florian. *Logik des Entwerfens. Eine designphilosophische Grundlegung.* München: Wilhelm Fink, 2018.

Blumenberg, Hans. "Licht als Metapher der Wahrheit. Im Vorfeld der philosophischen Begriffsbildung (1957)." In *Ästhetische und metaphorologische Schriften,* 139–71. Frankfurt am Main: Suhrkamp, 2001.

———. *Paradigms for a Metaphorology.* Translated by Robert Savage. Ithaca, NY: Cornell University Press, 2010.

Caillois, Roger. "Natura pictrix." *Cahiers du musée de poche* 1 (1959).

Derrida, Jacques. *Mémoires D'aveugle. L'autoportrait et Autres Ruines.* Parti Pris. Paris: Réunion des Musées Nationaux, 1990.

———. "White Mythology: Metaphor in the Text of Philosophy." In *Margins of Philosophy,* 207–72. Translated by Alan Bass. Chicago: University of Chicago Press, 1982.

Espinet, David, and Toni Hildbrand, eds. *Suchen, Entwerfen, Stiften. Randgänge Zum Entwurfsdenken Martin Heideggers.* Paderborn: Fink, 2014.

Figal, Günter. "Seinkönnen in der Welt. Zur Phänomenologie des Entwerfens." In *Freiräume. Phänomenologie und Hermeneutik,* 118–29. Tübingen: Mohr Siebeck, 2017. doi:10.1628/978-3-16-155399-8.

———. *Unscheinbarkeit. Der Raum der Phänomenologie.* Tübingen: Mohr Siebeck, 2015.

Goethe, Johann Wolfgang von. "Gebirgs-Gestaltung im Ganzen und Einzelnen." In *Sämtliche Werke, Briefe, Tagebücher und Gespräche. Schriften zur allgemeinen Naturlehre, Geologie und Mineralogie,* 628–35. Sämtliche Werke, Briefe, Tagebücher und Gespräche / Johann Wolfgang Goethe. Hrsg. von Dieter Borchmeyer. Frankfurt am Main: Deutscher Klassiker, 1989.

Grimm, Jacob, and Wilhelm Grimm. *Deutsches Wörterbuch. Biermörder–D.* Vol. 2. Deutsches Wörterbuch. Leipzig: Hirzel, 1860.

———. *Deutsches Wörterbuch. E–Forsche.* Vol. 3. Deutsches Wörterbuch. Leipzig: Hirzel, 1862.

———. *Deutsches Wörterbuch. Z–Zmasche.* Fotomechan. Nachdr. d. Erstausg. 1956. Vol. 31 (=Bd. 15). Deutsches Wörterbuch. München: Dt. Taschenbuch, 1999.

Heidegger, Martin. *Being and Time.* Translated by Joan Stambaugh. Revision and with a foreword by Dennis J. Schmidt. Albany, NY: State University of New York Press, 2010.

———. *Beiträge Zur Philosophie (Vom Ereignis).* GA 65. Edited by Friedrich-Wilhelm von Herrmann. Frankfurt am Main: Klostermann, 1989.

———. *Contributions to Philosophy (Of the Event).* Translated by Richard Rojcewicz and Daniela Vallega-Neu. Bloomington: Indiana University Press, 2012.

———. *Holzwege.* GA 5. Edited by Friedrich-Wilhelm von Herrmann. Frankfurt am Main: Klostermann, 1977.

———. "Die Kunst und der Raum." In *Aus der Erfahrung des Denkens,* GA 13, edited by Herrmann Heidegger. Frankfurt am Main: Klostermann, 203–10.

———. *Off the Beaten Track.* Translated by Julian Young and Kenneth Haynes. Cambridge: Cambridge University Press, 2002.

———. *Sein und Zeit.* GA 2. Edited by Friedrich-Wilhelm von Herrmann. Frankfurt am Main: Klostermann, 1977.

———. *Zur Sache des Denkens.* GA 14. Edited by Friedrich-Wilhelm von Herrmann. Frankfurt am Main: Klostermann, 2007.

Kant, Immanuel. *Kant's gesammelte Schriften. Kritik der reinen Vernunft (1787).* 2nd ed. Kant's Gesammelte Schriften. Berlin: Reimer, 1904.

Keiling, Tobias. "Heidegger's Black Notebooks and the Logic of a History of Being." *Research in Phenomenology* 47, no. 3 (2017): 406–28. doi:10.1163/15691640-12341377.

———. "Letting Things Be for Themselves: *Gelassenheit* as Enabling Thinking." In *Heidegger on Technology,* edited by Aaron Wendland, Christos Hadjioannou, and Christopher Merwin, 96–114. London: Routledge, 2018.

———. "Of the Earth: Heidegger's Philosophy and the Art of Andy Goldsworthy." *Journal of Aesthetics and Phenomenology* (2017): 125–38. doi:10.1080/20539320.2017.1396699.

———. "Phenomenology and Ontology in the Later Heidegger." In *The Oxford Handbook of the History of Phenomenology,* edited by Dan Zahavi, 251–67. Oxford: Oxford University Press, 2018. doi:10.1093/oxfordhb/9780198755340.013.17.

———. *Seinsgeschichte und phänomenologischer Realismus. Eine Interpreation und Kritik der Spätphilosophie Heideggers.* Tübingen: Mohr Siebeck, 2015. doi:10.1628/978-3-16-153565-9.

Mitchell, Andrew J. *The Fourfold: Reading the Late Heidegger.* Evanston, IL: Northwestern University Press, 2015.

———. *Heidegger among the Sculptors: Body, Space, and the Art of Dwelling.* Stanford: Stanford University Press, 2010.

Sallis, John. *Logic of Imagination: The Expanse of the Elemental.* Studies in Continental Thought. Bloomington: Indiana University Press, 2012.

Schwarz, Alexander. "Finden, Erfinden, Entwerfen. Gedanken zum Entwurf des Neuen Museums, Berlin." In *Suchen, Entwerfen, Stiften. Randgänge Zum Entwurfsdenken*

Martin Heideggers, edited by David Espinet and Toni Hildebrandt, 13–20. Paderborn: Fink, 2014.

Stifter, Adalbert. *Werke und Briefe*. Edited by Johannes John. Vol. 8 of Schriften zur bildenden Kunst. Im Auftrag der Kommission für neuere deutsche Literatur der Bayerischen Akademie der Wissenschaften hrsg. von Alfred Doppler. Stuttgart: Kohlhammer, 2011.

TOBIAS KEILING completed a PhD in philosophy at the University of Freiburg, Germany, and at Boston College. He is currently a Feodor-Lynen fellow of the Alexander von Humboldt-Stiftung at Somerville College, Oxford. In addition to his book *Seinsgeschichte und phänomenologischer Realismus*, he has published numerous articles, including the chapter on the later Heidegger in the *Oxford Handbook of the History of Phenomenology*.

Contributors

Jussi Backman, University of Jyväskylä

Claudia Baracchi, University of Milano-Bicocca

Damir Barbarić, Institute of Philosophy in Zagreb

Thomas Buchheim, University of Munich

Diego D'Angelo, University of Würzburg

Günter Figal, University of Freiburg

Sylvaine Gourdain, Université Saint-Louis in Brussels

Tobias Keiling, Somerville College, University of Oxford

Jeff Malpas, University of Tasmania

Nikola Mirković, University of Koblenz-Landau

Andrew J. Mitchell, Emory University

Tristan Moyle, Anglia Ruskin University, Cambridge

Hans Ruin, Södertörn University

Markus Wild, University of Basel

Guang Yang, Tongji University Shanghai

Index of Names

Index of Concepts

Index of Ancient Greek Concepts

CPSIA information can be obtained
at www.ICGtesting.com
Printed in the USA
BVHW030446040320
573973BV00003B/1